America in the Kitchen

from

Hearth to Cookstove

An American Domestic History
of
Gadgets and Utensils
Made or Used in America from 1700 to 1930

A Guide for Collectors

by

Linda Campbell Franklin

Photographs by Paul Persoff

SECOND EDITION

HOUSE OF COLLECTIBLES, ORLANDO, FLORIDA 32811

To
M.M.F., R.D.F., P.H.P.,
and
To the memory of
James A. Keillor
and
Dorothy Sara

International Standard Book Number: 0-87637-339-2
Library of Congress Card Number: 78-54417
Printed in the United States of America
Copyright © 1978 by House of Collectibles, Inc.
Helton Drive at Rasch Road
Florence, Alabama 35630
All Rights Reserved

ACKNOWLEDGMENTS

I am deeply indebted to my friends and family for their enthusiastic and never-flagging help with this book.

I am especially grateful to my friend Paul Persoff who did the photography; to my mother, Mary Mac Franklin, who helped me with the encyclopedic section; to my father, Robert Dumont Franklin, who sent me pages of information and packages of homemade muffins.

I could not have found any more helpful collectors than Mr. and Mrs. James A. Keillor, Sr., of Wading River, New York. They opened their home, their barn, their collection, and their minds to me. Part of The Keillor Collection has remained as a private, family collection, but with Mr. Keillor's death, a public auction was held and now many of the pieces shown in this book are in new, and we hope just-as-loving hands.

Special thanks go to Brenda Woodward, who sat in a rocking chair in my crowded study with a dictionary on one knee, and the typescript on the other, helping me with elusive commas and stubborn phrases; and to Carmile S. Zaino, who gave me many practical suggestions; and to Melvin Adelglass for assistance with the photographs and the loan of pieces from his collection.

Almost everywhere I applied for help, I received it: from Ray Townsend, who gave me my first tour of Williamsburg and who lent me many valuable catalogs; from Dorothy Sara who, after writing a lot of books herself, felt it was time I wrote one; from Mickey Donaldson, who has spurred me on for eleven years; from Margaret Minich, who made a delicious batch of beaten biscuits just to show me how it's done; from my brother Robbie, who always comes up with a pertinent question; and from all the people, libraries, and organizations who have helped me gather information.

Extract from *The Haunted Bookshop* by Christopher Morley, reprinted by permission of J. B. Lippincott Company.

PICTURE SOURCES & CREDITS

Paul Persoff photographed the pieces from the private collections of the James A. Keillors, Rita Keillor, Paul Persoff, Ruth Persoff, Mary Mac & Robert Dumont Franklin, Carmile S. Zaino, Melvin Adelglass, Mickey Lee Donaldson, Peter & Madeline Persoff, Jane Pope, Margaret Minich, Gerald Kornblau, Elizabeth C. Reed, Nancy VandenBerg, Marvin Tanner, Norman Mintz & Melanie Cohen, Emma Landau, Harry Kislevitz, the author, and the Michie Tavern Museum. The pictures from old trade catalogs and books, and a piece from the collection of William Hodges were photographed by the author. Other photographs courtesy New Bedford Whaling Museum, and the Bucks County Historical Society. Second edition cover photographed by David Arky.

Preface

"Nothing's so hard but search will find it out."

Seek and Find, Robert Herrick, 1591-1674

Ten years ago I began collecting old kitchen gadgets and utensils. I was attracted to the weight and the feel of them: the gleam of tin and nickel-plated iron; the smoothness of wooden knobs and handles; the neatly-fitted gears; the whirring blades of egg beaters; the devouring maws of cherry pitters and food grinders; the ingenuity of apple parers; the simple collaboration of mincing knives and chopping trays. I despised Space Age molded shapes, chromium armor, plastic brass. I was intrigued by the ingenious and sometimes inapt devices invented by hundreds and thousands of men and women during the Industrial Revolution. Ten years ago the kitchen gadgets from the 1880s and 1890s were easy to find and inexpensive. Wrought and cast iron implements from the 18th and early 19th centuries had already become valuable antiques. They were priced too high for me, and were much too heavy in aggregation for a fifth floor walk-up with a year to go on the lease! The time came, three years ago, to start collecting on paper what would eventually become this book.

I didn't realize, until I had sat in the North Hall Reading Room of the great New York Public Library for over two years, that no one could possibly write an absolutely foolproof definitive all-inclusive beats-all book on kitchen gadgets and implements *used* or *made in* America between 1700 and 1930. I knew I wanted a book which was social history, facts, and graphic beauty; I wanted a book which would help the collector and interest the non-collector. I wanted to make it obvious that art was to be found in old kitchens, so that my friends who collect weathervanes and crewel embroideries and painted blanket chests would learn to see the kindred appeal of egg beaters, trammels, wafer irons, graters, springerle molds and patent apple parers.

In my closest-thing-to a definitive book I have tried to include in the encyclopedic main body at least a mention of every kitchen thing I found a reference to. I did not exclude things which were not of American manufacture—not if they were probably brought here by immigrants from England, Germany, Ireland, Holland, Norway, Italy, Poland, or any of the other countries which gave us our multinational heritage. I have tried to describe each thing so that you will be able to recognize it and know how it was used. I made an early decision to use the gleanings from the primary sources *verbatim*. These excerpts, given with the original spellings, are identified by author and date. The sources are more fully identified in the *Bibliography*. It would have been easy to go on and on, lyricising fondly about each utensil, but the selective bibliography will serve as your guide to further reading.

Because I want to include over six hundred and fifty implements and utensils, I have had to be brief with each. At least a short book could be devoted to each thing. If I cover some entries more, or less, thoroughly than others, I have reasons. It may be that some utensils are more likely to be found in varied styles or materials; and that others will be so limited by their function to a certain shape or mechanical type that a few lines and a single picture will suffice. It is also possible, alas, that in some cases I have just not been able to unearth more information.

I have not included the very extensive fields of army and navy cooking, the combination of Mexican-Spanish food in the Southwest, the important influence of the Chinese in the East and the Northwest, or that of the Africans in the South. I could have extended my encyclopedia with several score entries. These are, perhaps, areas worth exploring by others closer to sources of information.

The pictures are as important as the descriptions. If you don't have access to the real thing, the pictures will help you understand. I have used photographs of real objects and linecuts from old catalogs. Many of the things pictured in old catalogs can safely be dated as many as twenty years before the catalog itself. 19th century catalogs and cookbooks were illustrated with line-cuts, made from drawings of photographs or actual objects. The cuts, in which the shading and outline is indicated by lines (rather than dots as in half-tone illustration), were done as wood engravings, metal (copper, zinc, steel) engravings, or as photo-engravings. You will often find exactly the same cuts in a number of catalogs, cookbooks and periodical advertisements. The cuts were obtained from the manufacturer of the object or from stock line-cut houses.

There are almost countless examples of many types of gadgets and utensils—for two reasons. Before the 1840s a large percentage of household tools were made by hand and not in a factory—either by a local blacksmith, a tinsmith, a cooper, a cabinetmaker, a turner, an itinerant craftsman, or by the householder himself or his family. Not everyone had his own ideas, and there isn't that much latitude in the design of a skillet or skewer, but the hand and the individual vision of the maker created things unique and as perfectly functional as possible.

When mass production was in full gallop, and foundry chimneys were smoking all over the country, and canned goods by the millions had to be opened, and kitchens became more efficient, hundreds of American men and women invented and patented every imaginable device for the refinement and scientific-ation of the culinary art. Man is said to be always searching for a better mousetrap: from 1860 to 1900 men and women searched diligently and imaginatively for the better can opener, egg beater, flour sifter, tea kettle, strainer, parer, . . .

The entries in the encyclopedic section are arranged alphabetically. Variant and older spellings are given in the headings in small italics. A partial list of manufacturers is given following some of the entries and cross references are given last. Recipes and directions accompany some entries in indented blocks.

Notes on the Recipes

All the gadgets and utensils in this book would be meaningless without some sense of the food which they were used to prepare. I have not made a selection of recipes to exhibit the usefulness of any and *all* combinations of implements [as the sentence *the quick brown fox jumps over the lazy dog* exercises each letter on a new typewriter]. The seventy-five recipes given here are fairly representative of types: there might, however, be more sauces, jellies and preserves, more breads, and more meats.

During the several years I spent researching this book, I studied hundreds of books and magazines, and turned through thousands of microfilm pages. My mind was tuned to *kitchen gadgets*, but towards the middle of the day my stomach would rumble and my attention was easily distracted by recipes. Recipes written by men and women to assist frugal housewives in setting noble tables on $150 a year. Some of the recipes are so interesting that I couldn't pass them by.

None of the recipes I have included have been adapted or modernized, or changed in any way. The original Fannie Farmer cookbook, published in 1896, was hailed as a real step forward because it standardized measurements and instructions. Teaspoons were always level, and nothing so inexact as a *walnut-size piece of butter* ever appeared. As you will discover, measurements are given—most of them as exact as any in Fannie Farmer—in pounds and wineglassesful. It is the recipe of oral tradition, handed from neighbor to neighbor over the wash-line, which is given in "dashes" and "dollops". In the written recipes, from the *Everlasting Syllabubs* of Elizabeth Smith in 1753 to Lizzie Strohm's *Fish Jelly* in 1888, measurements are as exact as they need be. [See the *Table of Equivalent Measures* in the Appendix.] If you feel you must approach the recipes in this book with a spirit of challenge and daring, go ahead. It should only serve to whet your appetite.

A study of the recipes and the utensils and gadgets of each age and country will give a view of the homes and the societies they were used in—indirectly, but as surely as a study of the furniture, the clothing, or the politics. Try to imagine yourself, right now, a woman standing in front of a large brick fireplace. You are dressed in long, full, heavy skirts, and an apron which is buttoned up the back and which holds your skirts as close to your legs, and as far from the fire, as possible. Your sleeves are rolled up past the elbow. Your feet hurt—you are wearing snug-fitting highbutton shoes and you've been wearing them all day and all week too. The fire is snapping and very hot. You are stirring soup in a large iron kettle hanging from a pot crane. There's a steel trivet to the left of your feet, and a coffee boiler is sitting on it keeping hot. An iron gridiron is directly in front of you, ready for the meat you will broil on it. In the ashes along the sides of the grate are roasting potatoes. You are distracted by the cat, who has just flipped the steak onto the floor. You cover your eyes in dismay. . . .When you open them, there is a large black cast iron range in the fireplace. The stove pipe runs up the chimney. There's a cupboard full of pots and pans and serving platters, and a shelf of cookbooks next to the clock. Water is boiling in the range kettle, and you open the oven to take out a pan of cornbread. Meat is cooking in a patent broiler. The cat is licking her paws: you have gone from the 18th to the 19th century, and now. . .

L.C.F.
New York City,
March 9, 1975

America in the Kitchen

from

Hearth to Cookstove

TABLE OF CONTENTS

Introduction

PATENTED PROGRESS

"Progress is the law of life."

Paracelsus, Robert Browning, 1812-1890

The hearth is simply that place where a fire is laid. A fire on a hearth was the first requirement for cooking food. The leeward side of a boulder or bush—long before a room or a cave—was the primitive kitchen. This was the Stone Age: almost 15,000 years B.C. A large flat stone was probably the first cooking utensil. It was bakestone, griddle, broiler, toaster and grill combined. A sharpened stick would have been needed to hold birds or other small game over the fire. An improvement on that simple spit was a pole supported by two sturdy, forked sticks driven into the ground. When man finally settled in communities and learned to farm, he could afford more time for cooking. Stone, and then earthenware pots allowed him to boil food in water. He used simple stone mills to grind his grains and seeds, and a closed oven was developed for baking bread.

Man became an accomplished toolmaker during the Bronze Age [3500-1000 B.C.]. He was enabled to make the bronze and copper utensils and implements he needed to cook the combined fruits of harvest and hunt. Iron was probably worked during the whole Bronze Age, but the Iron Age is usually given a starting date of about 1000 B.C. Early blacksmiths beat the slag from the impure, softened (but not liquid) iron after heating it in wood-fire forges. They made tools and vessels of wrought and then welded iron. Cast iron wasn't *deliberately* made until almost the 14th century.

Three or four thousand years ago, cooks were equipped with a rudimentary complement of implements which has remained virtually unchanged. A pot by any other name is still a pot. There is a difference between that day and the 17th and 18th centuries. A wide choice of sizes, and subtle refinements which made each utensil more suitable for a particular job expanded the simple assortment of iron or bronze knives, cauldrons, spits, ladles, and forks, and earthenware pots and vessels. With the increasing sophistication of dwellings and tastes, necessity was naturally fertile, invention multiplied, and the family of utensils grew.

Tools and machines, formerly powered by men or animals, were powered by hydraulics and by steam. This was the Industrial Revolution (or better, *evolution*) when man, woman and child worked sixteen or more hours a day in dangerous manufactories. The principles of the ingenious machinery which made this possible had long been known to scientific theorists and to some men of the Church. But it was not until power sources were efficiently harnessed for manufacturing domestic and industrial goods that the true Industrial Age was born. This developed in the middle of the 16th Century in England, and in the first part of the 19th Century in America.

Britain had iron and coal and a social system of feudal landowners and dissatisfied small farmers which encouraged the rapid growth of cities. This in turn stimulated manufacturing by affording both a demand for goods and a cheap labor market. America had iron and coal too, but until she won the War of Independence and until people began to spread out across the country, industrialization was impossible and most iron was imported. All tin came from England; and almost all sheet iron and tin plate was imported even until the 20th Century, because there were no good-sized rolling mills in the United States until then. There was too much free land to be settled and farmed, and not enough people to fill the cities to turn America into an industrial nation until quite late.

The population of America in 1790 was approximately 4,000,000. By 1820 the population was over 9,500,000; and just ten years later it had climbed to nearly 13,000,000. All those hungry mouths and busy hands! The Industrial Revolution, making up for its late start, literally steamed ahead until the end of the 19th century. Thousands of people invented tens of thousands of inventions—not all for the hearth or house. In 1833 the head of the Patent Office, John D. Craig, wanted to resign because he believed that everything "seems to have been done". Within two years, he was succeeded by Henry Ellsworth. Between 1790 and 1836 there were approximately 5,500 patents issued, although inaccurate records made that uncertain. Between 1836, when the first *numbered* patent was issued, and 1900, there were 640,166 patents granted to men and women from all over the country. Every sort of kitchen gadget formed ranks with puzzles, clothespins, type-writing machines, bicycle saddles, lawnmowers, caskets, hat fasteners, hen's nests, combination clod-crushers and land-rollers, plows, and solar generators.

> 2,400 women have secured patents but very few have made much money from them with the exception of the lady who was so fortunate as to hit upon the fluting iron, and thereby secured a small-sized bonanza.
>
> The women who have secured patents have been mostly thrifty housewives, and their inventions have been generally in the nature of kitchen utensils and domestic articles.
> [*New York Times*, December 14, 1890].

In this book are the kitchen gadgets and utensils used in America between 1700 and 1930. The effect of progress is quite visible among typical objects: while the shape of the kettle has changed very little, for example, the material from which the kettle is made has supposedly been improved. About 1930, when the new-born profession of *industrial design* sat down at its drawing boards, things began to change quite radically. Now it was no longer the limited aim to improve the workability of something, or to simplify its production: now it was that and beautification too. And that was the beginning of the end of personal integrity and individual taste in design.

As Lewis Mumford states in *The Myth of the Machine* (New York: Harcourt Brace, 1966): "The degraded or silly fantasies in furniture, pottery, and cutlery that now seek to command contemporary attention by their hideous novelty furnish ample proof, by contrast, of [the] earlier success. . ." of the forms of certain objects designed for domestic use hundreds of years before.

Things are re-designed to conform more closely to trendy profiles: this year's car, next year's rocket. A growing phenomenon is the magnetism effected by the "erstwhile quaint"* products of seven, twenty or forty years ago. It attracts many designers who are ill-equipped to be original and who are instructed, anyway, to design what surveys have indicated is wanted. This is nothing but destructive inbreeding.

Don Wallance writes, "the crusade against gingerbread, corn and schmaltz was under way. A whole world of ugliness was waiting to be transformed by pencil and airbrush." (*Shaping America's Products*. New York: Reinhold, 1956.) This book tells a history of industrial designing, and presents an acceptable case for some of it, while allowing that ". . .the designers of the twenties, many of whom came from the fields of stage design and commercial art, were stylists who set out to beautify old things with new forms— the pseudo-functionalism of sleek surfaces and streamlined contours. . . ." (*Ibid.*)

We must all admit, however reluctantly, that talk of design is relative and subjective. Many of the kitchen gadgets pictured in this book have found a place here because I liked their design, their look, or their personality. Don't dismiss all "gingerbread and schmaltz". Some of the elaborate or fanciful designs appearing in cast iron are there because a pattern for cast iron must have a number of negative spaces as well as positive forms. This insures the evenness of the casting, and its lightness and strength. According to John Stoudt (*Early Pennsylvania Arts and Crafts*. New York: A. S. Barnes, 1964), "cast iron was mainly the work of the carver who made the patterns of wood which were used in making the molds in sand. It was thus a woodcarver's craft." In a sense, the woodcarver who made casting patterns was an industrial designer seeking to beautify—sometimes with flowers and scrolls; but his basic forms were dictated by the metal to be cast.

*Coined by *House Beautiful*, March 1974. p. 101.

Half the truth behind the aesthetics of these old kitchen gadgets and utentils concern their functionality. Helen Atwater (*Selection of Household Equipment.* Washington, D. C.: U.S. Printing Office, 1915) wrote: "The well-furnished house is not one which is cluttered up with things which may be useful or attractive in themselves but which no one uses or enjoys, but one which contains those things which are necessary for convenience in working and for comfort and satisfaction in living, and no more.. . .If it were well-planned, perfectly convenient, and perfectly comfortable, it would also be beautiful, because beauty does not lie so much in the ornaments which are put on a thing as in the perfect adaptation of that thing to the use for which it is intended." You know: *form follows function.*

The other half of the aesthetic truth is in the whimsy, the embellishment, and, blush, the earnest folly of so many of the old utensils and especially the gadgets. The colonial craftsmen and artificers had difficulties. By English law, artificers who left the kingdom were liable to imprisonment, heavy fines, and the loss of inheritance rights. Some of the first artificers to come to America were apprentices and journeymen with nothing to lose, and perhaps not much skill to bring to their work. But they were required to make for the housewife only the simplest variety of frying pans, broilers, spits and pots. It would have been an extremely maladroit blacksmith who could not make an unadorned frying pan which worked.

America's winning of the War of Independence undid the hindrances to industrialization which had held back the natural inclination for invention during the hundred and fifty years of the colonial period. In 1791 Alexander Hamilton, then Secretary of the Treasury, reported to Congress the importance of encouraging basic industries by offering bounties and subsidies, and by awarding patents. These important industries included the manufacture of iron stoves, pots and other household utensils, copper and brass wares, and tin wares.

Only a small percentage of the thousands of patented inventions were assigned to a manufacturer or were ever produced. The more specialized a field of invention, the more pitfalls and dangers lie about in the paths of inventors scrambling to find a new twist. Reading the *Official Gazette* of the Patent Office is more instructive of the dreams and desires of the 19th century than it is of mechanical perfection or motive laws. Many of the inventions simply were not practical, much less workable. That did not always deter the patentees from manufacturing their inventions. The Law of Natural Selection insured that the things which failed commercially, did so because they couldn't perform and not because they were or were not delightful· and intriguing to look at. Such is not always the case now, nor has it been since the 1920s. A philosophy was developed which decreed that even that which worked well wouldn't keep on selling unless it looked new and different. Many of the objects pictured in this book remained exactly the same for decades. If it worked, it stayed in production and it stayed in the catalog.

An Encyclopedia of Essays, Definitions, Gleanings & Recipes

ADAPTER RINGS — Flat, iron rings with long handles used to adapt the holes of a range top so that handleless untensils of different circumferences can be supported.

Fig. 1. ADAPTER RING. From Willich's 1804 *The Domestic Encyclopedia*, Vol. III.

Fig. 2. SAUCEPAN resting in adapter ring. From cut in Willich's 1804 *The Domestic Encyclopedia*, Vol. III.

AETNA *[etna]* — An inverted, cone-shaped vessel placed in a saucer of burning spirits. It was used for heating or mulling small amounts of liquids quickly.

Fig. 3. AETNA. F. A. Walker, c. 1870s.

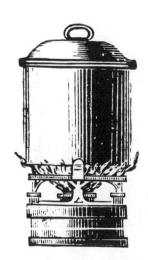

Fig. 4. AETNA. F. A. Walker, c. 1870s.

Fig. 5. AETNA. Planished tin. F. A. Walker, c. 1870s.

ALE BOOT,——SHOE—An iron or copper vessel, shaped like a boot—the long toe of which was thrust into the hot ashes or coals of the fireplace in order to warm the ale.

Fig. 6. ALE WARMERS. Left: ale boot.

ALUMINUM — A bluish, silvery metal — the most abundant on earth — always found in combination (chiefly with bauxite). It was first obtained, or freed, by Hans Oersted in 1824, or by a German chemist, Frederick Wohler, in 1827, *after* the Englishman Sir Humphrey Davy predicted in 1809 that it would eventually be freed from what was widely known as *alum.* It was not until about 1850 that a French chemist, Henri Sainte-Claire, devised a way to extract the metal from its chloride. Then, in 1886, Charles Martin Hall, of Oberlin, Ohio, succeeded in separating the metal with an electric current — an inexpensive method which virtually started the aluminum kitchenware industry.

In her column in *Ladies Home Journal,* January 1900, Maria Parloa wrote: "It is about twelve years since household articles made from aluminum were put on the market. For a time it seemed as if its high price were the only obstacle [to] the universal adoption of this metal for kitchen utensils; its lightness, smoothness, high melting point, and the fact that it is not easily broken, are all most desirable qualities. Time has not fulfilled the early promise.... First, too much was claimed...and people did not, nor do they now, know its value and its limitation, nor how properly to select and care for utensils made from it. Then the market was flooded with thin and poorly made articles which had not body enough to hold the shape. Aluminum is a soft and pliable metal and should not be made in very thin sheets when intended for cooking utensils. When cast or spun substantially these utensils are most satisfactory. All aluminum utensils are made in one piece, hence no joints nor grooves that require special cleaning care."

By 1915, "Aluminum heats quickly and so economizes fuel, comes in very good shapes, is light to handle, and very durable; it is affected by alkalies, discolors easily and is rather hard to clean. Nevertheless since it does not rust, it is especially desirable for *tea kettles, double boilers, kettle covers,* etc.... "(Helen Atwater, *Selection of Household Equipment,* 1915, [*italics mine*].) *"Illinois Pure Aluminum Co.;" "Aluminum Cooking Utensil Co. (Alcoa);" "Wagner;" etc.*

Fig. 8. ALUMINUM WARE. Goldberg, Bowen & Lebenbaum's catalog, June, 1895.

ANDIRON, FIRE-DOG, COBIRON — An *andiron* is one of two, footed, supporting frames — usually of wrought iron — placed in the fireplace for logs. The front piece is vertical and usually somewhat decorative. The horizontal member supports the burning wood. It was known as the *billet bar.* Some pairs are notched or have angled brackets on which a spit can be rested at any of several heights.

A *cobiron* is an andiron, so-named for the knob or *cob* on top of the vertical member.

A *fire-dog* is an andiron fitted with the spit supports, and is also called a *spit- dog.*

Fig. 7. ALUMINUM WARE. Viko, Aluminum Goods Mfg.; United Cigar Stores premium catalog, 1927.

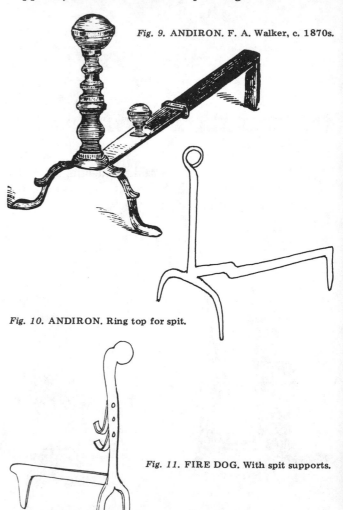

Fig. 9. ANDIRON. F. A. Walker, c. 1870s.

Fig. 10. ANDIRON. Ring top for spit.

Fig. 11. FIRE DOG. With spit supports.

APPLE BUTTER STICK — "A stick of hickory wood, somewhat like a common hoe, with holes in it." (Elizabeth Lea, *Domestic Cookery*, 1859.) It was used for stirring a kettle of slowly thickening apple butter as it cooked down.

APPLE CORER — *see* **CORER**

APPLE PARER — A cranked, but not necessarily geared, device of wood or iron for mechanically paring apples.

There are five dates offered for the birth of the mechanical apple parer. According to Siegfried Giedion, in *Mechanization Takes Command*, 1948, Eli Whitney began his career by devising an apple parer at the age of thirteen, in 1778. In 1781, Joseph Sterling of South Woodstock, Vermont, is supposed to have made the first apple parer — credited with that achievement by local legend. An apple parer, of the bench type, in the Bennington Museum in Vermont is labeled, "...made in West Woodstock, Vermont, in 1785 by Daniel Cox and his sons." Another story credits thirteen-year-old Thomas Blanchard of Worcester County, Massachusetts, with the 1801 invention of an unsuccessful apple parer. Finally, Anthony Willich in his *Domestic Encyclopedia* (1804), and James Cutbush in his *American Artists Manual* (1814), document the apple parer of Moses Coates, a mechanic of Chester County, Pennsylvania. There is no doubt that Mr. Coates did receive the first United States patent for an apple parer — this one granted February 14, 1803. Dr. Willich wrote, "A machine for paring apples has lately been invented by Mr. Moses Coates...which, on account of its simplicity, and the expedition with which it works, will no doubt come into general use.... The Editor has tried the experiment with the machine, and found it to pare apples with great rapidity."

From the beginning, whenever that was, wooden apple parers were devised to help with the job of paring hundreds of apples so that they could be sliced and strung for drying. The first ones had no gears to increase the revolutions of the apple per revolution of the hand crank, and the first apple parers may have been less efficient than attractive, and not so much ingenious as fun. They all worked on the general principle of a paring blade (similar to a safety razor or spoke shave) held to the turning apple. Practically all the home-made wooden apple parers which you may find today were made before 1850. Cast-iron parers, first appearing in the 1840s, utilized either the simple cranked movement, or the more complicated and efficient geared-up movements of the later wooden machines. Both used the same sort of cutting blade. This blade, hand-held in early parers, was spring-activated in the cast-iron devices. It followed

the apple's contour neatly. By 1874, when Edward Knight's *A Practical Dictionary of Mechanics* mentioned the [iron] apple parer as a novelty in the 1840s, over eighty patents had been issued for them.

After a few more years, some apple parers were made which did the extra jobs of coring and slicing.
"Winesap;" "1878;" "Lightning;" "Goodell White Mountain;" "Landers, Frary & Clark;" etc.

Preserved Apples

Apples, in small quantities, may be preserved by the following. First; completely dry a glazed jar, then put a few pebbles at the bottom, fill it with apples, and cover it with a piece of wood exactly fitted, and fill up the interstices with a little fresh mortar. The pebbles attract the moisture of the apples, while the mortar excludes the air from the jar and excludes the fruit from pressure. [*Willich, 1821*]

Fig. 12. BENCH APPLE PARER. Made in 1785 by Daniel Cox, West Woodstock, Vermont. L: 30"; H: 24"; 11" diameter wheel. Photograph courtesy The Bennington Museum Inc., Bennington, Vermont.

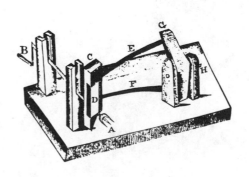

Fig. 13. APPLE PARER. Pat'd Feb. 14, 1803. Moses Coates, Chester County, Pennsylvania. Domestic Encyclopedia, 1804.

Fig. 14. STRADDLE APPLE PARER. Dated 1836. Turned wood, painted wood, iron. Three small and one large eagle stenciled with "C" and "H." L: 24"; W: 7½"; H: 9". Christian Hostetter. American. Courtesy Keillor Collection.

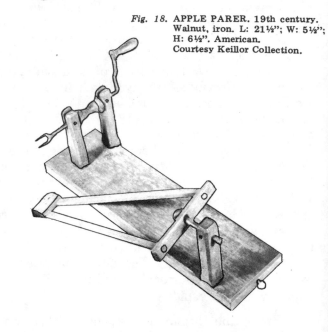

Fig. 15. STRADDLE APPLE PARER. Mid-19th century oak, pine, cherry wood, brass, iron, leather. L: 24"; W: 8½"; H: 17". American. Courtesy Keillor Collection.

Fig. 16. APPLE PARER. Mid-19th century Tiger maple, iron. L: 9½"; W: 5¼"; H: 9¾". American. Courtesy Keillor Collection.

Fig. 19. STRADDLE APPLE PARER. Mid-19 century. Wood, iron. L: 23¾"; W: 11"; H: 13¾". American. Courtesy Keillor Collection.

Fig. 20. APPLE PARER. Early 19th century. Wood with wooden gears, iron, leather strap. L: 14½"; W: 9½"; H: 10". American. Courtesy Keillor Collection.

Fig. 23. STRADDLE APPLE PARER. Early-19th century. Iron, wood painted with yellow buttermilk paint. L: 25½"; W: 5"; H: 16". Pennsylvania German. Courtesy Keillor Collection.

Fig. 21. APPLE PARER. Early-19th century. Wood, cast iron, steel. Clamped to bench or table. L: 13"; W: 6¾"; H: 7". American. Author's Collection.

Fig. 24. APPLE PARER., straps to leg. c. 1820s, 1830s. Wood, iron, leather. L: 7½"; W: 4"; H: 7". American. Courtesy Keillor Collection.

Fig. 22. APPLE PARING BENCH. Early-19th century. Wood, leather, iron. L: 27"; W: 11"; H: 31½". American. Courtesy Keillor Collection.

Fig. 25. APPLE PARER, straps on leg. c. 1820s, 1830s. Wood, iron, leather, brass. L: 6½"; W: 2½"; H: 4½". American. Courtesy Keillor Collection.

Fig. 26. APPLE PARER. Early-19th century. Wood, leather belt. L: 22"; W: 12"; H: 11¼". American. Courtesy Keillor Collection.

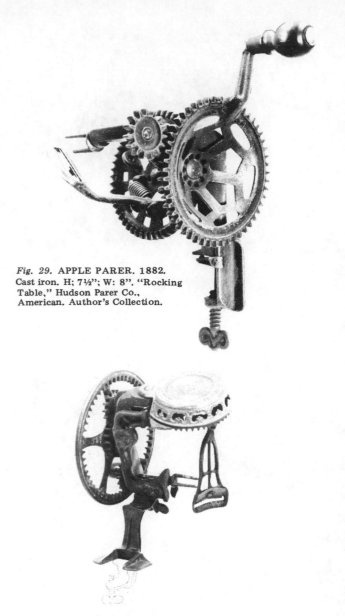

Fig. 29. APPLE PARER. 1882. Cast iron. H; 7½"; W: 8". "Rocking Table," Hudson Parer Co., American. Author's Collection.

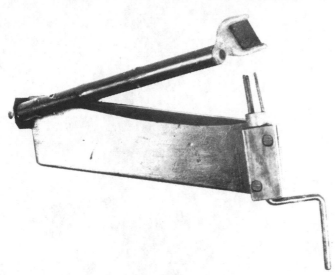

Fig. 27. APPLE PARER. Early-19th century. Wood, iron. L: 10"; W: 2½". American. Courtesy Keillor Collection.

Fig. 30. APPLE PARER. Pat'd 1878, but made for many years after. Cast iron. L;11"; W: 6". '78, Reading Hardware Co., Reading, Pa. Author's Collection.

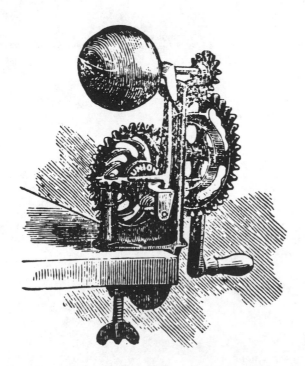

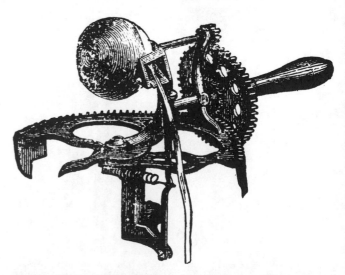

Fig. 28. APPLE PARER. Iron. F. A. Walker, c. 1870s.

Fig. 31. APPLE PARER. Cast iron, F. A. Walker, c. 1870s.

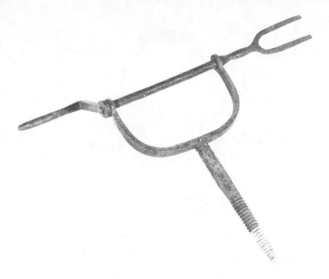

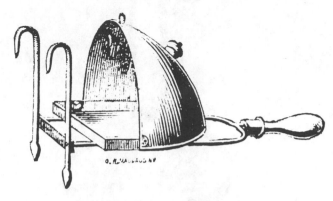

APPLE ROASTER — A tin reflecting oven with two, or more, racks or shelves for baking or roasting rows of apples in front of the fire.

Fig. 32. APPLE PARER. 19th century. Iron. H; 5½", L: 8". Screwed into wall or table top. American Courtesy Keillor Collection.

Fig. 35. CHEESE, BIRD, or APPLE ROASTER. Tin, wood, iron. F. A. Walker, c. 1870s.

Fig. 36. APPLE ROASTER. Tin.

Fig. 33. APPLE PARER & CORER. F. A. Walker, c. 1870s.

APPLE SEGMENTER — A mechanical device to quarter of further segment an apple. Most work on the lever principle. Some simple segmenters were hand-held.

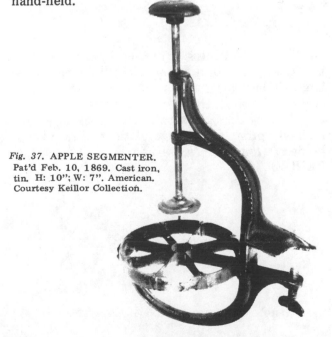

Fig. 37. APPLE SEGMENTER. Pat'd Feb. 10, 1869. Cast iron, tin. H: 10"; W: 7". American. Courtesy Keillor Collection.

Fig. 34. APPLE PARER, CORER & SPIRAL SLICER. c. 1880. Cast iron. L: 11"; H: 6½". "White Mountain," Goodell Co., Antrim, New Hampshire. Courtesy Robert D. Franklin.

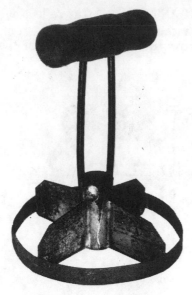

Fig. 38. APPLE QUARTERER. 1870s, 1880s. Tin, wood. L: 5½"; 4" dia. American. Courtesy Keillor Collection.

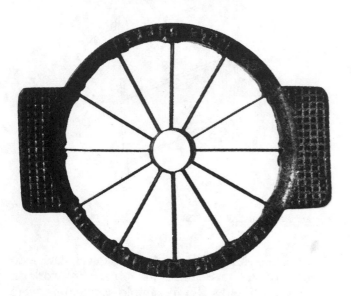

Fig. 39. APPLE CUTTER. c. 1880s. Cast iron.' 5½" dia. Rollman Mfg. Co., Mt. Joy, Pa. Courtesy Keillor Collection.

APRON — "A necessity in the kitchen, because it is a great protection against clothes taking fire, is a large kitchen apron made full length with bib, and sleeves if wished, the skirt to button close around the dress-skirt.... Have two large pockets in your kitchen apron, and in one of them always keep a holder." (*Practical Housekeeping*, 1884.) *See also* **FENDER**

Fig. 40. APRON. Butler Brothers, Chicago, Illinois, 1899.

Fig. 41. APRON.

ARSENIC — Arsenic poisoning was believed to be a danger arising from the use of some copper and brass cooking vessels, and as arsenic does occur in copper and lead this was quite possible. Arsenic, lead and verdigris poisoning were greatly feared results of cooking in poorly cared-for, or improperly cleaned or tin-lined utensils.

ASBESTOS — A fibrous mineral which is incombustible and nonconducting. It was pressed into sheets, a quarter or three-eights of an inch thick, bound with iron, and used to protect pans and crockery from direct fire in the oven or on top of the range. Asbestos mats could be cleaned by holding directly in the flame for a few minutes. *See also* **STOVE MAT**

Fig. 42. ASBESTOS STOVE LINING being applied. Montgomery Ward 1895.

Fig. 43. ASBESTOS STOVE MAT (L) & TOASTER (R). c. 1900. Asbestos, wire screen. (L) 8" square, 5" handle; (R) 8½" dia., 3½" handle. The combination stove mat and toaster on the right was made by Crown. Author's Collection.

ASPARAGUS [*sperage, sparrow-grass*] **BOILER** — A specially designed vessel for cooking asparagus in an upright position; or a kettle with a lift-out, perforated tray for supporting the fragile asparagus as it cooked, and for lifting it out unbroken.

Fig. 44. ASPARAGUS BOILER. Pieced tin. 8¾" x 6½" x 6¼". Matthai-Ingram Company, c. 1890.

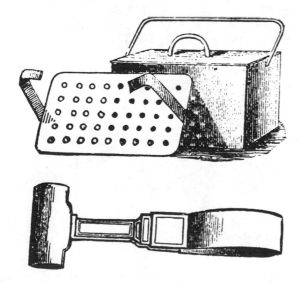

Fig. 45. ASPARAGUS BOILER & TONGS. Treasure House, 1891.

ASPARAGUS TONGS — Tongs with side, curved hands for removing bunched asparagus from its cooker without damage.

BABBITT METAL— A white metal alloy of copper, antimony and tin. Invented by Isaac Babbitt of Taunton, Massachusetts, about 1825. It was almost identical with the britannia metal of England, which was considered a nice substitute for both silver and pewter. *See also* **BRITANNIA, WHITE METAL**

BAIL HANDLE — A heavy wire handle, as for a bucket. It is also referred to as a *falling handle* by some 19th century writers. A *bail* itself was originally a bucket used on shipboard for bailing out water.

Fig. 46. PAIL. Tin. F. A. Walker, c. 1870s.

BAIN MARIE — An open vessel, of iron or copper, and either rectangular or round; filled with boiling water and large enough to hold a number of stew pans or sauce pans containing ingredients which have to be kept hot, or cooked slowly and indirectly. A *bain marie* would not be recognizable unless in use, for it would be very like any other boiler. Special sauce pans were sold as *bain marie* pans: they are deep and look very much like the inner part of a double boiler.

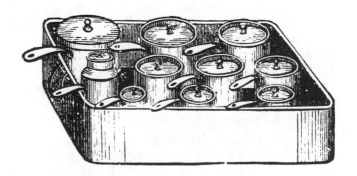

Fig. 47. BAIN MARIE. Tin. F. A. Walker, c. 1870s.

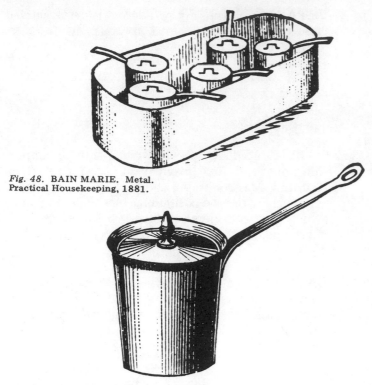

Fig. 48. BAIN MARIE. Metal.
Practical Housekeeping, 1881.

Fig. 49. BAIN MARIE PAN. Tin. F. A. Walker, c. 1870s.

BAKE BOARD — A board on which dough is kneaded and rolled.

BAKE KETTLE — *see* **DUTCH OVEN**

"BAKELITE" — A trademark name for any of a number of thermosetting plastics and resins. It was invented by the Belgian, Leo Baekeland, in 1909. It was used extensively for the handles of cooking utensils because it remained cool. It was usually black or dark brown.

BAKE OVEN — *see* **DUTCH OVEN, BAKING PAN** *or* **BAKER SHEET** —

BAKING PAN *or* **BAKER SHEET** — A shallow tin pan for baking bread or cakes in the oven. *See also* **BREAD PAN, COOKIE SHEET**

BANNOCK BOARD — A thick wood plank, sometimes with its own short, one-legged support, on which bannock cakes were baked before the fire. The word *bannock* comes from Scotland and the North of England. George Francis Dow, in a 1925 address, *"Domestic Life in New England in the 17th Century,"* said that Indian Bannock was made by mixing corn meal with water and spreading it an inch thick on a small board placed at an incline before the fire to bake. There are better recipes.

Bannock
Into one pint of Indian meal stir a pint of buttermilk; ½ teaspoon of salt; one teaspoon of molasses; one of butter; and add two well-beaten eggs; one pint of wheat flour; thin with milk to a thin batter; last, stir in two large teaspoons of soda dissolved in hot water; pour into buttered shallow pans; bake one hour in quick oven which bakes top and bottom brown. [*Treasure House of Useful Knowledge,* 1891]

Bannock
To one quart sour milk, put a teaspoon of salaeratus, dissolved in water; warm the milk slightly, beat up an egg, and put in corn meal enough to make it thick as pudding batter, and some salt; grease a pan and bake it, or you may put it in six or eight saucers. [*Lea,* 1851]

Bannocks (Irish Bread)
4 cupfuls flour
½ cupful butter
1½ cupfuls milk
½ teaspoonful salt
3 teaspoonfuls Calumet baking powder

Mix the ingredients to a soft dough; roll an inch thick, shape into cakes, six inches across, with a large cooky cutter, and bake on a hot griddle. Before taking from the fire, be sure they are baked to the heart. Split in two, butter and serve hot. [Sidney Morse, *Household Discoveries,* ca. 1909]

I used this last recipe for making bannocks to be baked on a board before an open fire. I adapted it by substituting two cups of corn meal for two cups of flour, and by adding two tablespoons of bacon fat to the butter. I also rolled the dough out to about a half inch, and think this will keep the baking time down to about twenty minutes before a hot, glowing fire.

Bannocks can be baked in a buttered spider with a buttered tin cover or pie plate. Bake over a gentle fire, shaking if the bannock sticks. [*Ladies Home Journal,* October, 1893]

Fig. 50. BANNOCK BOARD.

BANNOCK STICK — A wooden pin for rolling out bannocks.

BANNOCK STONE — A bakestone.

BASKET, CRADLE SPIT — A wrought iron spit with a basket in the center which is formed of thin strips of iron. Half of the basket was hinged or separate; the two halves were screwed together and held small cuts of meat, fowl or game without the necessity of piercing them with skewers. *See also* **SKEWER, SPIT**

Fig. 51. BASKET SPIT.

BASTER or BASTING SPOON — A spoon with a deep bowl for basting meat and fowl while it was being roasted.

Fig. 52. BASTING SPOON. Tinned iron, L: 11", 13", 15", 17", 19". Lalance & Grosjean, 1890.

BEAN POT — A heavy, fireproof pottery utensil, with a close-fitting lid, for baking beans. *See also* **DUTCH OVEN**

Fig. 53. BEAN POTS. Right: cast iron. Others: earthenware.

BEATEN BISCUIT MACHINE or DOUGH KNEADER — This is a special kind of dough kneader; a cast-iron machine resembling a clothes wringer, with its own marble-top table. The two adjustable rollers are nickel-plated, and the dough is fed through them by turning the crank. It is quite a trick to feed the heavy dough through with one hand while cranking with the other, and then trying to catch it as it comes out the other side.

The machine is best worked by two people. Beaten biscuit dough must be put through the machine enough times [about thirty] for the dough to blister and pop. "There is a little machine available that is said to make a product equally as crisp and velvety as those made by the old method; the dough will come out of the machine as smooth as buckskin and as slick as satin...." *Mary Wall,* unidentified newspaper clipping, n.d.

Beaten biscuits were originally beaten with a cook's axe, a wooden mallet, or a rolling pin on a clean stump or heavy kitchen table. They were cut out with a biscuit cutter or with a special cutter, similar to a cracker stamp, with a number of needles soldered inside which pierce a design on top of the two inch biscuit.

Beaten biscuits are a Southern treat, quite dense and chewy but not hard or crusty. Typical frozen or commercially packaged beaten biscuits barely resemble the real thing and they are practically impossible to bite into. Here are two recipes from *Mrs. Wilson's Cook Book* of 1914:

Miss Fort's Beaten Biscuit
1½ lb. flour
5 oz. lard
1½ tsp. salt
2 tsp. sugar (dissolve in water)
1 cup water
Blend with flour, lard and salt. Mix into a stiff dough with water in which sugar has been dissolved. Work well. Beat or roll until dough blisters. Bake in moderate oven until light brown.

Beaten Biscuit No. 2
1 qt. flout
½ tsp. baking powder
1 level tsp. salt
Lard size of goose egg
2/3 cup of milk and water, half of each with 1 tsp. of sugar dissolved in milk; have dough very stiff. Beat or roll until it blisters.

Most cracknels are another sort of biscuit entirely, and some were made with crackling or crisp animal fat, but perhaps this next recipe is an early beaten biscuit.

To Make Little Cracknels
Take three pounds of flour finely dried, three ounces of lemon and orange-peel dried, and beaten to a powder, and ounce of coriander-seeds beaten and searced, and three pounds of double refined sugar beaten fine and searced; mix these together with fifteen eggs, half of the whites taken out, a quarter of a pint of rose-water, as much orange-flower water; beat the eggs and water well together, then put in your

orange peel and coriander-seeds, and beat it again very well with two spoons, one in each hand; then beat your sugar in by little and little, then your flour by a little at a time, *so beat with both spoons an hour longer;* then strew sugar on papers, and drop them the bigness of a walnut, and set them in the oven; the oven must be hotter than when pies are drawn; do not touch them with your finger before they are bak'd; let the oven be ready for them against they are done be careful the oven does not colour them." (Elizabeth Smith, *The Compleat Housewife*, 1753, [*italics mine*]).

Fig. 56. BEATEN BISCUIT MACHINE closeup.

Fig. 54. BEATEN BISCUIT or DOUGH KNEADER. c. 1890. Cast iron base, marble table, nickeled iron rollers. (Table) ': 36"; W: 16"; H: 30½". (Rollers) L: 14"; 2¼" dia. Rollers adjusted closer and closer together as dough gets harder and harder to roll through. Cast iron medallion in base reads: "The DeMuth Improved Dough Kneader & Beaten Biscuit Machine, Manf'd. by J. A. DeMuth, St. Joseph, Mo." Courtesy Margaret Minich, Charlottesville, Virginia.

BEETLE — A sort of pestle, made of wood, having a heavy, flat-ended head and a handle, which itself is sometimes finished with a small, rounded head. The beetle is used for pounding and thus tenderizing meat, for crushing vegetables such as potatoes, etc. *Also called Meat Fret, Meat Tenderer, Steak Maul, Steak Pounder, etc.*

Fig. 55. BISCUIT CUTTER used for beaten biscuits. c. 1890s. Tin. H: 1½"; 2" dia. Fries. Courtesy Margaret Minich.

Fig. 57. BEETLES. c. 1900-1930. Turned wood; one- and two-piece construction. H: 11 to 12½". American. Courtesy Ruth Harkavy Persoff.

BELL METAL — An alloy of tin and copper, as is brass. But the former is three or four parts of copper to one of tin, and brass is two parts copper to one of tin. Bell metal was used for kettles, skillets, mortars and pestles, and bells. Often the culinary vessels bear the name of a bell-maker.

BEZEL SCOOP — A fruit or vegetable *baller:* a melon scoop with a corrugated bowl.

Fig. 59. BIGGIN. Greystone enameled ware, tin tip & cover. ½, ¾, 1, 1½, 2, 3, 4, 5, qts. Matthai-Ingram Company, c. 1890.

Fig. 60. BIGGIN. Planished tin. F. A. Walker, c. 1870s.

BIRD ROASTER, SPIT — (1) a tin reflecting oven with hooks for holding small fowl (or game), and a drip pan below. It was used in front of an open fire, as was (2) a stand, or rack whose height was adjustable. The cross-bar had hooks for the birds. A separate drip pan was placed beneath it on the hearth. *See also* **REFLECTING OVEN**

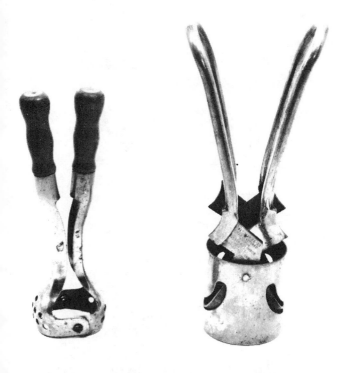

Fig. 61. BIRD ROASTER. Tin. F. A. Walker, c. 1870s.

Fig. 58. BALLERS. (Left) Pat'd Mar. 29, 192-? Nickel-plate, wood. L: 5¼"; 1½" dia. (Right) May 28, 1923. Chrome-plated steel. L: 7"; 1¾" dia. Turner & Seymour Mfg. Co., Torrington, Conn. Author's Collection.

BIGGIN — An early drip-method coffee pot invented by Mr. Biggin about 1800, and intended primarily for use at table.

"Two cylindrical tin vessels, one fitting into the other; the bottom of the upper one is a fine strainer, another coarser strainer is placed on this with a rod running upwards from its center; the finely ground coffee is put in, and then another strainer is slipped on the rod, over the coffee, the boiling water is poured on the upper sieve and falls in a shower upon the coffee, filtering through it to the coarse strainer at the bottom, which prevents the coffee from filling up the holes of the finer strainer below it." (*Practical Housekeeping*, 1884.)

Fig. 62. BIRD ROASTER. Early-19th century. Stamped, soldered tin. L: 12"; W: 8½"; H: 9". English. Pivoting back. Courtesy Keillor Collection.

Fig. 63. BIRD or SMALL GAME ROASTER. 18th century. Wrought iron. Base W: 12½"; H: 29½". American. Courtesy Keillor Collection.

Fig. 65. ROLLING COOKIE or BISCUIT CUTTER. c. 1915. Aluminum, iron. L: 6½.; W: 2-7/8". Advertises "Louella — The Finest Butter in America," and "Gold Seal Flour — For Best Results." Author's Collection.

Fig. 66. COMBINATION TOOL. F. W. Seastrand c.1912.

BISCUIT CUTTER — A tin or, later, aluminum circular cutting device used to cut biscuits from rolled-out dough. The earliest have a flat sheet of tin to which the cutting circle was soldered in spots, and to which a handle was usually also soldered. These old biscuit cutters varied in height from about ¾" to 2". The thicker dough was for rolls.

Later tin biscuit cutters are almost the same, except that the soldering is likely to be even, and the whole thing perhaps more neatly made. Several patent biscuit cutters had a revolving cutting wheel with two or three circles. This was rolled across a sheet of dough. (This same principle was used for doughnut cutters, with a smaller circle soldered or clipped inside each larger circle.)

A number of advertising cutters can be found, with the mottoes or trade names of any number of flours, baking powders or grocers. *See also* **BEATEN BISCUIT MACHINE, CAKE CUTTER, DOUGHNUT CUTTER**

Cheese Biscuit

2 oz. of butter; 2 of flour; 2 of grated cheese; a little cayenne pepper, and salt; make into paste, and roll out very thin; cut into shape desired; bake a very light brown, and serve as hot as possible. [*Treasure House*, 1891]

Fig. 64. BISCUIT CUTTER. Stamped tin. 2", 2½", 3" dia. (Biscuit cutter just like doughnut cutter. 3" dia.) Matthai-Ingram Company, c. 1890.

Fig. 67. BISCUIT or COOKIE CUTTER. c. 1910. Tin. L: 2¾". "White Lily Flour Has No Equal," Metal Specialty Mfg. Co., Chicago. Author's Collection.

BISCUIT OVEN — A tin reflecting oven, in which biscuits are baked — usually on a double tier of shelves. These biscuits included johnny cakes, bannocks, and what we think of as crackers today.

BISCUIT PAN — "Hitherto consisted only of a single vessel.... Used for beating up or whisking batters. The improved pan is formed either of metal or earthenware, inclosed within an exterior vessel, furnished with a plugged aperture, for the introduction of hot water." (Thomas Masters, *A Short Treatise*, 1850.).

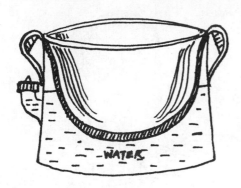

Fig. 68. MASTER'S BISCUIT PAN.

consistency, it will turn out after 15 or 20 minutes in good shape. Eat with sugar and milk or cream. For this and all similar milk preparations, peach leaves are better than any spice. Boil in the milk ½ dozen fresh leaves from the tree. Remember to take them out before you stir in the rice. [Mary Hooker Cornelius, *The Young Housekeepers Friend*, 1846]

Some flummery recipes use gelatin, but their distinguishing ingredient was always the meal or flour used in them.

BLANCMANGE MOLD — A decorative metal mold for blancmange [a cold, flavored gelatin dessert; or, as originally, a fowl—or other meat-flavored gelatin dish], or other molded desserts." Blancmange molds are found in a number of designs, among them piles of flowers, and stepped, geometric forms.

"If the molds are made to imitate roses or fruit, the fruit may be green (colored with spinach juice), and roses pink (colored with strawberry juice); if corn, yellow; and various ways of combining colors and forms will suggest themselves to the ingenious housewife." (*Practical Housekeeping*, 1884.) *See also* MOLDS, TIN

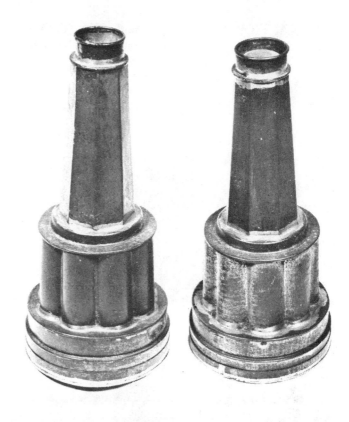

Fig. 70. BLANCMANGE MOLDS. c. 1870. Tin. H: 11½"; 5" dia. American. Courtesy Keillor Collection.

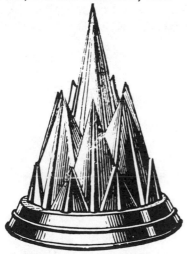

Fig. 69. BLANCMANGE MOLD. Tin. F. A. Walker, c. 1870s.

Ground Rice Flummery

Boil 1 quart milk, except that portion which you have reserved to wet a heaping teacup of rice. Stir this in when the milk boils up; put in 1 teaspoon of salt. When it has thickened, stir in a table spoonful or two of dry ground rice, let it boil up again all around, and take it off the fire as soon as you think the dry rice has become scalded. Have ready a bowl or *blancmange mould*, wet with a spoonful of milk or cold water, into which pour it. If it is of the right

BLICKIES [*blickys*] — Variously described as *any* small tin vessel, and as small, covered, cylindrical pails or other vessels. The word comes perhaps from either the Dutch *blik;* or the German *blick:* tin; or pail, or shining.

BLOCK TIN — As used in old kitchen furnishing lists, thin sheets of tin-coated iron. But actually it refers to the block of partially refined tin.

Block refers to the ingot of nearly pure tin. *Stream* or *grain tin* was finer still. Quite often the authors of early cookery books specified *block tin utensils* as the best for the money. "The best tin plate is dipped twice; this is called 'block tin,' or 'retinned ware.'" (*Hutchinson*, 1918.) *See also* LATTEN, TIN

BONING KNIFE — A short knife with a narrow blade and a sharp point for removing bones from uncooked fish, fowl and certain kinds of meat.

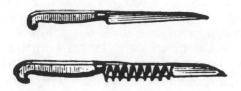

Fig. 71. KNIVES. Boning knife and garnishing knife. Carbon Steel, cast iron, wood. F. A. Walker, c. 1870s.

BORDER MOLD — A ring-shaped metal mold for forming mashed potatoes or other vegetables, force meat, or other foods into rings to garnish the serving platter. They were round or oval.

BOTTLE — A small-necked vessel made of glass, leather or stoneware.

Fig. 72. STONEWARE BOTTLE. Probably for ginger beer or sauce. H: 8¼". Author's Collection.

Fig. 73. TYPICAL BOTTLES.

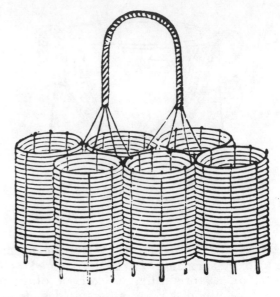

Fig. 74. BOTTLE CARRIER. Wire. F. A. Walker, c. 1870s.

BOTTLE JACK, CRANE — Similar to the dangle-spit [*which see*], except that the rotary movement is provided by a clockwork spring-wound movement which is concealed within a bottle-shaped drum above the hook. It was wound up, like a clock, with a key inserted into the side of the drum. This jack hung from a clamp, called a *jack-rack*, which was screwed or clamped above the fireplace. *See also* **CLOCKWORK JACK, PORTABLE SPRING JACK, SMOKE JACK, SPIT**

Fig. 75. BOTTLE JACK. Keyhole in side.

BOUCHE, [*bouchee*] IRON — A small iron form — corrugated, fluted or plain — with a screwed-on, long handle. It was used for forming small custard cups of pastry. Bouches were bite-sized: *bouche*

16

means *mouth* in French.

The recipe accompanying the cut of the bouche iron in a circa 1875 *F. A. Walker Catalog* is as follows:

Take two TBS of flour, drop 2 eggs into it, and mix with enough milk to make a batter, similar to fritter batter. Heat Iron in boiling lard; then dip Iron into batter, take out and leave on Iron till batter drops off.

See also DARIOLEMOLD, PATTY IRON, TIMBALE IRON

Fig. 76. BOUCHE IRON. Cast iron, wood. F. A. Walker, 1886.

BOULTEL or BOULTER — A cloth bag for sifting flour. The flour was tied into a bag of closely woven cloth and shaken.

BOX GRATER — A cabbage grater, consisting of a wooden board, fitted with a sharp cutting blade, usually set at an angle across the board. A sliding, open box held the cabbage head in place and protected the fingers.

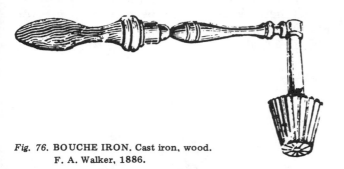

Fig. 77. KROUT CUTTER. Wood, cast steel knives. L: 26"; W: 8". Adjustable knives. Montgomery Ward, 1893.

BRAISING PAN, POT — A deep, round graniteware, earthenware, or iron pot with a close-fitting lid for slowly cooking meat, after it has been seared.

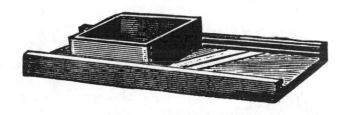

Fig. 78. BRAISING PAN. Aluminum. Montgomery Ward, 1895.

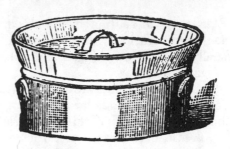

Fig. 79. BRAISING POT. Cast iron. Treasure House, 1891.

BRAKE — A dough-kneading machine, or a machine for pressing and extracting the juices from vegetables and fruits.

BRANDELETTE, BRANDISE, BRANDRETH — (1) An iron trivet, tripod, or stand, or, (2) in the case of *brandreth*, also a three or four-legged wooden frame used as a stand for a cask or a cauldron, or as a hay rick. *See also* TRIVET

BRANDER, BRANDIRON — (1) A gridiron for broiling meat down hearth, or (2) a *brander* can also refer to a utensil similar to a girdle plate: an iron utensil, the bed of which resembles a grate, for baking brander bannocks over hot coals.

BRASS — A yellow alloy of copper and tin (now zinc), sometimes with other metals in varying lesser amounts. Brass has been a popular metal for kitchen utensils and gadgets for hundreds of years — it is easily worked, and attractive. It has been used for everything from skillets, pastry jaggers, and graters to ladles, footmen, mixing bowls for eggs, and measures. *See also* BELL METAL, COPPER, LATTEN

BRAZIER — A large flat pan of heavy iron which held hot coals and over which a gridiron or grate could be placed for cooking. The brazier, like today's patio barbecue, could be moved anywhere.

BREAD BOARD — Same as PASTE BOARD, but also a board for cutting bread or for cooling it. "An oaken board, covered with heavy white flannel, is the best; over this spread a fresh linen *breadcloth*, and lay the bread on it right side up." (*Practical Housekeeping*, 1884, [*italics mine*].) *See also* PASTE BOARD

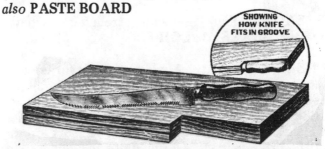

SHOWING HOW KNIFE FITS IN GROOVE

Fig. 80. BURN'S BREAD BOARD & KNIFE. The Berdan Company, 1931.

BREAD BOX — A tin ventilated box or container for storing bread, crackers, cake or other baked goods. Usually the lid was hinged and opened up the entire front of the box.

Bread was also kept in a stone jar: "When the bread is cold, place in a stone jar or tin box, which must be thoroughly washed, scalded and dried each baking day. A still better receptacle for bread is a washboiler with a close cover, kept for this purpose alone." (*ibid*.)

Fig. 81. BREAD BOX. Japanned tin, oak grained. Nests of three. L: 13¼", 15¼", 16½"; W: 9½", 10½", 11½": D: 10", 11", 12". Matthai-Ingram Company, c. 1890.

Fig. 82. BREAD & CAKE BOX. Roll top with drawer. Ivory, white, blue, green, gray, red or yellow painted tin. L: 16"; W: 11½"; H: 14½". C. B. Porter Company, c. 1915.

BREAD-BRAKE — A kneading trough or machine. *See also* **BRAKE, DOUGH-BOX**

BREAD COOLER — A wireware rack for cooling just-baked bread or cakes, and allowing air to circulate freely around the loaves. Pictured in the 1884 *Practical Housekeeping* is a bread cooler which also "answers admirably to support a roast in the dripping pan, insuring uniform cooking, and keeping the roast well up out of the drippings."

Fig. 83. BREAD COOLER & ROAST DRIPPER. Wire. Practical Housekeeping, 1881.

BREAD GRATER — A large tin grater for making bread crumbs of dry bread. It is usually a cylinder with a handle at the top. These bread crumbs were used as thickeners in puddings, in thick sauces for various meat dishes, and in the modern way — for breading foods which were to be fried. *See also* **BREAD RASP**

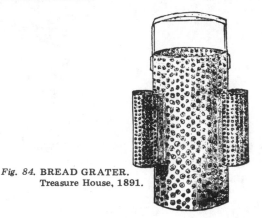

Fig. 84. BREAD GRATER. Treasure House, 1891.

BREAD KNIFE — A knife with a scalloped or fluted cutting edge. It is broader than the quite similar cake knife, and the scallops are closer together. The point of the bread knife is blunt, or truncated.

The best known patented bread knife is the Christy knife, which is part of a set of various kinds of knives. Russ J. Christy of Sandusky, Ohio, patented several models in 1889, 1891, 1893, etc. "*Lightning;*" "*Keen Kutter;*" "*Universal;*" "*Illinois Cutlery;*" "*American;*" "*Clauss;*" "*Climax;*" "*Victor;*" "*Victora;*" "*Aetna;*" "*Always Sharp;*" "*Tip Top Boy;*" etc. See also **CAKE KNIFE**

Fig. 85. BREAD & CAKE KNIVES. c. 1890s. (From top to bottom.) (1) Carbon steel. L: 13¼". Climax. (2) Carbon steel. L: 15". Tip-Top, trademark boy's head: "Tip-Top Boy." (3) Carbon steel. L: 14¾". Victora, American Cutlery Co. (4) Carbon steel. L: 14¼". Aetna, Universal, Landers, Frary & Clark, New Britain, Conn. Courtesy Paul Persoff.

ANGEL

Fig. 86. FLOUR & BAKING POWDER TRADEMARK. Pearces Mills. 1900.

BREAD MIXER or MAKER — A tin pail, which has a cranked paddle, and which could be clamped to the table. It came in different sizes. *"Eclipse;" "Universal;"* etc.

Bread: What Ought it to Be?

It should be light, sweet, tender. This matter of lightness is the distinctive line between civilized and savage bread. The savage mixes simple flour and water into balls of paste, which he throws into boiling water, and which come out, solid, glutinous masses, of which his common saying is, "Man eat dis, he no die," which a facetious traveller interpreted to mean, "Dis no kill you, nothing will." [Catherine Beecher and Harriet Beecher Stowe, *American Woman's Home*, 1869]

Fig. 87. BREAD MAKER. Universal No. 4. Landers, Frary, Clark. *Universal Household Helps,* c. 1920.

BREAD PAN — A tin pan for baking bread, with a round or flat bottom. Some were oblong, some square, some had corrugated sides. Some bread pans had close-fitting lids, like pudding molds, for steaming such breads as Boston brown bread.

"The best pan for bread is made of Russia iron (which is but little more costly than tin and will last many times as long), about four by ten

inches on the bottom, flaring to the top, and about 4½" deep." (*Practical Housekeeping,* 1884.)

Apple Bread

Boil a dozen good-sized apples that have been peeled and cored, until they are perfectly tender. While still warm, mash them in double the amount of flour, and add the proper proportion of yeast. The mass should then be thoroughly kneaded without water, as the apple juice will make it sufficiently soft. It should be left to rise 12 hours, then formed into loaves, and baked when quite light. Apple Bread was the invention of a scientific Frenchmen commended for its healthfulness. [*Ladies Home Journal,* September, 1896]

Fig. 88. BREAD PANS. Black sheet iron. From 5½" x 9½" x 2¾" to 12" x 18" x 4". Matthai-Ingram Company, c. 1890.

Fig. 89, 90. IDEAL BREAD PAN. Black tin. Double-& single-loaf pans. "Makes a crisp, moist and wholesome loaf a certainty. ...The bread is more nutritious, more tasty, and more digestible. Professor Morse, of Westfield, N.J. says bread baked in the Ideal Bread Pan is a remedy for dyspepsia and of the highest nutritive value." Matthai-Ingram Company, c. 1890.

Fig. 91. BREAD PAN. Pat'd August 3, 1897. Blackened tin. (Certain tin ware for baking, and broiling was deliberately blackened as part of the manufacturing process.) L: 12½"; W: 5"; H: 3½". Ideal. Courtesy Robert D. Franklin.

Fig. 92. BROWN BREAD PAN. Tin. F. A. Walker, c. 1870s.

Fig. 93. CORN BREAD PAN. Pat'd July 6, 1920. Cast iron. L: 12½"; W: 5½". Krusty Korn Kobs, Junior, Wagner Ware, Sidney, Ohio. Courtesy Gerald Kornblau.

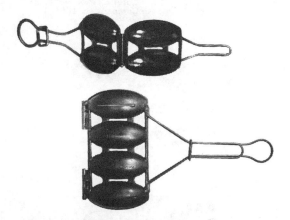

Fig. 94. CORN BREAD MOLDS. c. 1880. Cast iron. Wagner Ware. Left, open: L: 15"; W: 6". Makes two. Right, closed: L: 20"; W: 12". Makes four. Finished breads approximately 1¾" x 5½". Courtesy Keillor Collection.

BREAD RAISER — A large tin, bowled vessel with a ventilated lid. It was used to protect and cover bread while the dough rose.

Fig. 95. BREAD RAISER, ventilated cover. Stamped tin. From 14-7/8" x 5½" to 19-7/8" x 6¾". From 8 to 21 qts. Matthai-Ingram Company, c. 1890.

BREAD RASP — A piece of tin, curved in an arch, and pierced with many rough holes. It was mounted to a board. The bread rasp was used to rasp sugar, nutmegs, breadcrust, and especially to remove burnt crusts. Bread was baked in a brick oven, often placed directly on the bricks, and the bottoms were sometimes unavoidably burned.

Another sort of bread rasp is a toothed piece of wrought iron which resembles a woodworker's rasp. It has a curved wooden handle which doubles back parallel to the rasp.

Fig. 96. BREAD RASP. Early-19th century. Wrought iron, wood. L: 6½". American (?). Courtesy Keillor Collection.

BREAD TESTER — A slender metal tube or rod stuck into baking bread to test its baking progress. *See also* CAKE TESTER

BREAK — A flat wooden implement for cutting dough into pieces or lumps to form into loaves. You can still see these in operation in a pizza parlor. *Break* is also a variant spelling of *brake* [which see]. *See also* SLICE

BRICK BAT — A fragment, properly less than half, of a brick. A brick bat was recommended to be put into the middle of a hot fire to "slacken the heat." (Mrs. Glasse, *The Art of Cookery Made Plain and Easy*, 1747.)

BRIDGET — Used throughout the 19th century as the generic name for all white housemaids and serving maids. *Biddy* is another form of the name.

BRITANNIA [*brittania*] — A special variety of pewter which contains no lead, but is a compound of tin, antimony and copper. According to the *Oxford English Dictionary*, britannia was an alloy of tin and regulus of antimony and was known, before ca. 1820, as *white metal*.

"Frequently manufactured with so large a portion of copper as to render use of the article extremely unwholesome. Tea and coffee pots of this metal have been known to give the liquid contained in them so strong a taste and smell of copper..." as to make it almost equal to poison. (*Leslie*, 1840.) *See also* **BABBITT METAL, WHITE METAL**

Fig. 97. BRITANNIA WARE. The Great Industries of the United States. Hartford, Chicago, Cincinnati: J. B. Burr & Hyde, 1873.

BROILER — (1) A footed steel or iron grate for broiling meat, fish or game. Some old ones revolved for evener broiling. These were all used down hearth. (2) A four part utensil, of iron, which was reversible and self-basting. Meat or fish was placed between the slotted center parts, and the fat dripped from the ridges of whichever end was up. (3) An iron, griddle-like base with cast ridges and a ventilated tin cover. (4) A completely different type, consisting of two wire racks, hinged together with a long handle. This was used for toasting, or for broiling fish, steaks or oysters, and is exactly like the one now used to broil hotdogs over a camp fire.

The first mentioned above is the oldest type and was used from Colonial times far into the 19th century. The second was patented around 1890 and was known as the *Morgan Broiler*. The third was advertised in the magazines and catalogs of the late 19th century as the *Reliable Ventilated Broiler*. "*Crown*;" "*Reliable*;" "*America*;" "*Morgan*;" etc.

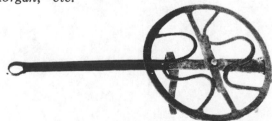

Fig. 98. ROTARY GRILL, or BROILER. 18th century. Wrought iron. L: 18"; W: 9". American. Courtesy Keillor Collection.

Fig. 99. BROILER. Tin, wire. 12½" dia. Unidentified catalog flyer, c. 1880s.

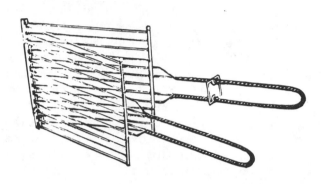

Fig. 100. BROILER. Heavy wire. 6" x 9"; 8" x 9"; 9" x 10"; 9" x 12"; 9" x 14". Matthai-Ingram Company, c. 1890.

Fig. 101. AMERICAN BROILER. Iron, wire, tin. "This popular broiler has been before the public for many years, and has done more to banish the health-destroying frying pan from the kitchen than any of its later rivals. It will always be a favorite." Practical Housekeeping, 1881.

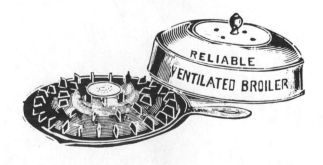

Fig. 102. BROILER, for gasoline or gas stove. Cast iron, tin cover. 10" dia. Reliable Ventilated Broiler. Montgomery Ward, 1893.

BRUSHES — A number of brushes were recommended by domestic economists for specialized use in the kitchen. Most old brushes are identical or similar in design to modern ones, except that the natural fibers and bristles have been largely replaced by plastics.

"When you buy a brush, if you don't know a fiber from a bristle, ask the dealer.... Of all the brush fibers [Bass, Kitool, Palmyra, Palmetto, Rice Root, Tampico] *Tampico*, the product of a species of cactus, is the best." (Ethel Peyser, "Brushing Up on Brushes, "*House and Garden*, April, 1921.)

Blacking brush — A stubby brush with a handle for applying stove-blacking to the kitchen range.

Pastry brush — A long, soft-bristled brush used for putting butter or egg-white glazes on pastry. They were often made of goose feathers.

Bottle brush — A long-handled brush, with the bristles or fibers forming a small cylinder which fit into the neck of the bottle. A special type, patented in the 1870s, had a crooked handle which was rotated, and which was supposed to get the bristles into every cranny of the bottle. Bottles were also cleaned with shot: a small handful is put in the bottle with some water and the bottle is shaken vigorously.

Glazing brush — A small but relatively long-bristled brush for applying gelatinous glazes to roasts, fowl and other baked dishes, and white of egg glaze to breads. *See also* **GLAZING POT**

Sink brush — A fan-shaped brush of stiff fiber or steel wire. It was used for scrubbing the sink and dirty pots and pans, and was especially good for cleaning waffle irons. A whisk broom was recommended to double as a sink brush.

Scouring brush — A fiber brush with a bristled hoop and a wooden handle. Used for scouring vegetables, and is like the vegetable brush.

Vegetable brush — "The Protean Vegetable Brush,... one of the most useful brushes on the market,... can be used for washing vegetables, scraping silk from corn, scrubbing poultry, scouring pots and pans, sprinkling clothes (for they hold enough water), and scrubbing dishes." (*Peyser*, 1921.)

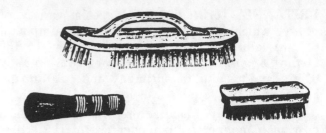

Fig. 104. BRUSHES. Butler Brothers, 1899.

Fig. 105. PASTRY BRUSH.

Fig. 106. PASTRY BRUSH. Tin, natural bristle. F. A. Walker, c. 1870s.

Fig. 107. BOTTLE WASHER. c. 1920s. Wood, fibre bristle, nickeled brass. L: 10¾". American. Author's Collection.

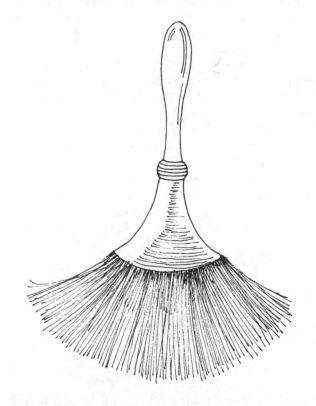

Fig. 108. SINK BRUSH.

Fig. 103. STOVE BRUSH.

Fig. 109. SINK BRUSH & DISH WASHER. Feb. 27, 1900. Steel wire, wood. 9¼" x 4". Y-R. American. Courtesy The Disshuls.

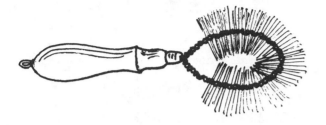

Fig. 110. SCOURING BRUSH.

BURL — *see* WOODENWARE

BUTCHER KNIFE — A knife with a fairly broad, slightly upturned, and pointed blade. The handle is usually exactly as wide as the blade where the two meet.

Fig. 111. BUTCHER KNIFE. c. 1930. Carbon steel, red brass, wood. Homemade handle. L: 12". Author's Collection.

BUTTER CHURN — *see* CHURN

BUTTER FORK — A maple, or other wood, fork, about 12" long by 5" wide, with several broad tines. It was used for removing butter from the churn.

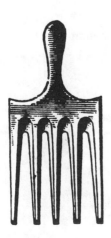

Fig. 112. BUTTER FORK. Maple. 12" x 5". Mrs. Bragg's Butter Fork. Montgomery Ward, 1895.

BUTTER HANDS — A pair of creased or corrugated wooden paddles, about 8" long, for making butter balls or other fancy shapes. The fine grooves were better than the coarse. They were sometimes called *Scotch hands*, or *butter rollers*.

Butter Hands

Let stand in boiling water for 5 minutes. Next put in cold water for 5 minutes or longer. Must be cold when used. Have large bowl half full of cold water. Cut some firm butter into pieces about the size of a hickory nut. Roll these pieces between the butter hands into any shape you please — grooved balls, little pineapples, scrolls, etc. Dip the hands frequently in ice water. [*Parloa*, 1887]

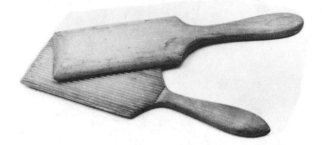

Fig. 113. BUTTER HANDS. 1890 to 1920. Wood. L: 9¼"; W: 2½". American. Author's Collection.

BUTTER MOLD, PRINT — (1) A wooden stamp, of one or two parts, which cut the butter into round or square or oblong shapes and impress the individual pat, or the half-to two-pound piece, with a design. This design is most frequently that of a plant such as wheat. Less common are animals, and most rare are eagles and other patriotic motifs. (2) A tin press which was used in a similar way to impress a design and cut a piece of butter . These were also used as cookie or jumble presses. (3) A glass mold of the same type.

A number of butter molds were hand made, and the rest were manufactured and sold by the hundreds of thousands. *"Reid;" "Blanchard;"* etc. *See also* **COOKIE PRESS**

Fig. 114. BUTTER PRINTS. c. 1870s. Wood. L: 4½". Left: two part; right: one part. American. Courtesy Keillor Collection.

Fig. 115. BUTTER PRINT. 19th century. Wood. 4¼" dia. American. Courtesy Keillor Collection.

Fig. 116. BUTTER PRINT. Wood. 19th century. Courtesy Michie Tavern Museum, Charlottesville, Virginia.

Fig. 117. BUTTER MOLD. c. 1880s. Glass, wood. L: 8¼"; 4¼"dia. American. Courtesy Keillor Collection.

BUTTER SPADE, LADLE — A wooden round, or spade-shaped implement for working butter in the tub. "For working butter, keep a wooden bowl and ladle. This last article is seldom found in New England, but always in the state of New York." (*Cornelius*, 1859.)

Fig. 118. BUTTER SPADES and LADLES. Wood. Montgomery Ward, 1895.

BUTTER TRIER — A nickel-plated, cast-steel "needle," from four to twentyfour inches long, inserted into tubs or barrels of butter for testing. In the larger tubs, all the butter was not put in at the same time, and the butter under the first few layers might not have been fresh enough to buy [or sell].

"Butter: a smooth, unctious feeling in rubbing a little between the finger and thumb expresses its rich quality; a nutty smell and rich aroma indicate a similar taste; and a bright, golden, glittering, cream-colored surface shows its high state of cleanliness. It may be necessary to use the *trier* until you become an expert in testing by taste, smell and rubbing." (*Treasure House*, 1891.)

Fig. 119. CHEESE or BUTTER TRIER. Nickeled cast steel. L: 4" to 24". Montgomery Ward, 1893.

BUTTER TROWEL — A tinned, iron trowel with a wooden handle for handling lard or butter. It was 6" to 8" long.

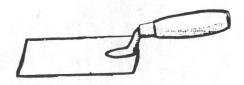

Fig. 120. BUTTER or LARD TROWEL. Tinned iron, wood. L: 6" or 8". Montgomery Ward, 1893.

BUTTER TUB — A wooden tub for the storage of butter in the creamery or dairy house. The capacity varied from ten to fifty pounds.

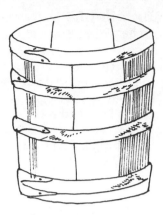

Fig. 121. BUTTER TUB. Wood.

BUTTER WORKER — A triangular wooden tray with either a corrugated pin or a wooden arm with a metal blade. The tray sat on the table or had its own stand. After the butter was well-churned, it was washed, and then worked to remove any remaining buttermilk, to salt it if desired, and to compact it.

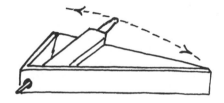

Fig. 122. BUTTER WORKER. Wood.

Fig. 123. BUTTER WORKER. Treasure House, 1891.

CABBAGE CUTTER, PLANE — A large wooden board fitted with a cutting blade, usually adjustable in depth. It was used for cutting cabbage for slaw or sauer-kraut. *Same as* **KRAUT CUTTER.** *See also* **BOX GRATER, CUCUMBER SLICER.**

Bubble and Squeak
Take from a round of beef, which has been well boiled and cold, two or three slices, amounting to about one pound to one and a half in weight, two carrots which have been boiled with the joint, in a cold state, as also the hearts of two

boiled greens that are cold. Cut the meat into small, dice-formed pieces, and chop up the vegetables together; pepper and salt the latter, and fry them with the meat in a pan in a quarter-pound of sweet butter; when fully done, add to the pan in which the ingredients are fried, half a gill of fresh catsup, and serve your dish up to the dinnertable with mashed potatoes. [*Godey's Lady's Book,* as reprinted in Gertrude Strohm, *Universal Cookery,* 1888]

Bubble and Squeak
Slice of cold boiled beef; chopped potatoes; chopped up cabbage; both previously boiled; pepper, salt and a little butter; set it aside to keep hot; lightly fry some slices of cold boiled beef; put them in a hot dish with alternate layers of the vegetables, piling high in the middle. [*Treasure House,* 1891]

Fig. 124. SLAW CUTTER. Wood, steel. F. A. Walker, c. 1870s.

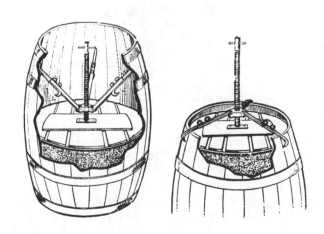

Fig. 125. SAUER KRAUT PRESS. Kuheim. Tolerton & Warfield Co., Sioux City, Iowa, c. 1900.

CABOOSE [*cabouse*] — (1) The cook-room or kitchen of merchantmen [a ship used in trading or carrying passengers] on deck — a diminutive substitute for the galley, and furnished with a set of cast iron utensils. (2) A cooking oven or fireplace used in the open air. *See also* **CONJURER**

CADDY — A container for storing dry staples such as tea. From *kati*, a Malay word, the Chinese or Southeastern Asian unit of measure which is about 600 grams or one and a third pound.

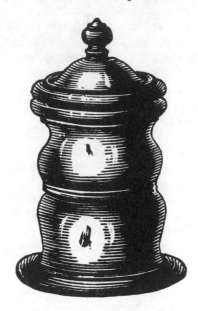

Fig. 126. CADDY. F. A. Walker, c. 1870s.

Fig. 127. CADDY. Japanned tin. F. A. Walker, c. 1870s.

CAKE BEATER — A vessel with a perforated disc turned by a crank. The whole thing came apart for cleaning, like the bread mixer did. "No dishes and spoons. No weary back and arms. Converts the drudgery of cake making into a delightful pleasure." (advertisement in *Woman's Home Companion*, March, 1897.) *See also* **BREAD MIXER, CAKE MIXER, CAKE SPOON**

General Directions for Making Cake
When cake or pastry is to be made, take care not to make trouble for others by scattering materials, and soiling the table or floor, or by needless use of many dishes. Put on a large and clean apron, roll your sleeves above the elbows, tie something over your head lest hair may fall, take care that your hands are clean, and have a basin of water and a clean towel on hand. Place everything you will need on the table, butter your pans, grate your nutmegs and squeeze your lemons. Then break your eggs, each in a cup by itself, lest adding a bad one should spoil the whole. Make your cake in wood or earthen, and not in tin. [*Cornelius*, 1846.]

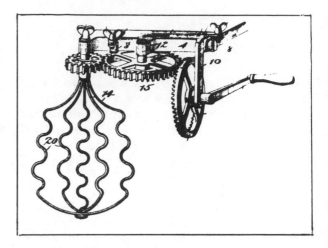

Fig. 128. CAKE-BEATER. Pat'd 1901, no.677,421. Kate H. McRae, Cripplecreek, Colorado. Official Gazette, July 2, 1901.

Fig. 129. BATTER BEATER. Wire, wood. Androck, 1936.

CAKE BOARD — *see* **PASTE BOARD**

CAKE BOX —— **CABINET** — A tin box or cabinet with shelves for storing cakes (or bread). It usually had one or two carrying handles, and was often equipped with a padlock and key.

Fig. 130. CAKE BOX. Brown japanned tin. From 10½" to 12½" dia.; from 8-3/8 to 11¼" high. Matthai-Ingram Company, c. 1890.

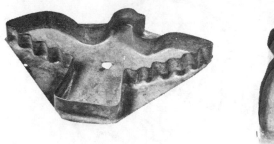

Fig. 133. CAKE CUTTERS. c. 1880s. Tin & wood. 6" x 3½"; 4½" x 2½". Amish. Courtesy Keillor Collection.

CAKE, COOKIE CUTTERS

CAKE, COOKIE CUTTERS — Tin, or other metal cutters traditionally called *hearts*, *rounds*, and *diamonds*. They were also made in the form of eagles, animals, people, stars, spades and clubs, feathers, fish, flowers, scrolls, *ad infinitum*. Some cutters have handles and some don't. The early ones were made by the householder, or by itinerant tinkers from their tin scraps. A long strip of inch-wide tin was bent and curved to form the design, and then spot-soldered to a roughly cut disc of tin. As with the biscuit cutters, spotty soldering is one sign of age. Factory made cutters are more uniform in design and construction. Sets of intricate cutters were offered by jobbers and retailers such as F. A. Walker: these sets seem too intricate, in fact, to form even-baking cookies. Surely the edges burned quite often!

Evidently some cutters were used as individual baking pans:

Whigs
½ pound of butter, the same of sugar. 6 eggs, 2 pounds flour, a pint of milk, a gill of yeast, and a little salt. Melt the butter in the milk, and pour into the flour; beat the sugar and eggs together and stir in. Add the yeast last, and be careful to mix the whole very thoroughly. Bake in tin hearts and rounds in the stove, or baker, or in muffin rings. [*Cornelius*, 1859]
See also CAKE PAN

Fig. 134. COOKIE CUTTER. c. 1910-1930. Fluted tin. 2" dia. American. Author's Collection.

Fig. 135. CAKE CUTTER. Tin. F. A. Walker, c. 1870s.

Fig. 132. CAKE CUTTERS. Round, diamond. Tin. F. A. Walker, c. 1870s.

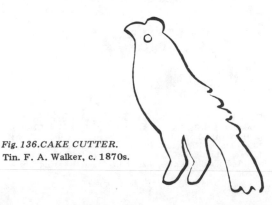

Fig. 136. CAKE CUTTER. Tin. F. A. Walker, c. 1870s.

Fig. 137. BOX OF CAKE CUTTERS. Tin. F. A. Walker, c. 1870s.

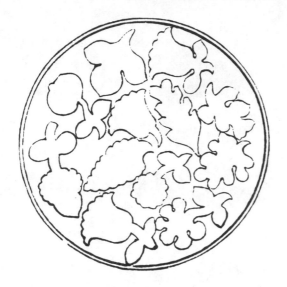

Fig. 138. BOX OF CAKE CUTTERS. Tin. F. A. Walker, c. 1870s.

CAKE GRIDDLE — *see* **GRIDDLE**

CAKE HIVE — A domed tin cover, with a base, used for protecting cakes from the ravages of flies and circulating room air. *See also* **CAKE BOX**

CAKE KNIFE — A long-bladed knife, similar to the bread knife [which see], except that the scallops or serrations are further apart.

Fig. 139. CAKE or BREAD KNIVES. The scallops are closer together for bread than cake. c. 1890s. Carbon steel. (Top) L: 14¼". Christy, Fremont, Ohio. (Bottom) L: 14¼". Clauss, Fremont, Ohio. Christy also made a line called "Comet," the only difference being iron handles which were corrugated. A complete set of any of these would have included a cake knife, bread knife, and paring knife. Author's Collection.

CAKE MIXER, MAKER — A vessel with a beating blade, similar to the bread mixer but s h a l l o w e r. *See also* **BREAD MIXER, CAKE BEATER, CAKE SPOON**

Fig. 140. CAKE MIXER. Pat'd July 15, 1873. American Machine Co., Philadelphia, 1880s.

CAKE MOLD — (1) The same as *cake pan*, or (2) a closed metal or earthenware mold for baking certain types of cakes in various geometric or animal forms. One of the most well-known cake molds is the lamb, or the chicken, both of which were probably used for baking Easter cakes.

Fig. 141. QUEEN CAKE PANS. Tin. Imported. F. A. Walker, c. 1870s.

CAKE PAN — A tin pan: round, oblong, oval, s q u a r e, d o d e c a h e d r a l [12 sided], octagonal, hexagonal, scalloped, turk's head, plain or tubed. Some cake pans had removable bottoms, and hinged sides, so that the cake could easily be removed. These were called *spring molds*, or *pans*.

Small cake pans are what we would call cupcake pans, and were joined together with metal strips or in a frame. These also were plain or fluted.

Some cake pans were shaped in such a way that when put together, like a puzzle, they formed a large heart, a diamond, a cross or a circle. "Delmonico;" "Perfection;" "Misses Lisk's;" etc. See also **HOOP, MOLDS, TIN**

Lightning Cake

Yolks of 4 eggs; 3 tablespoons of sugar; the same of flour; about 2 tablespoons of milk; the juice of half a small lemon; the whites of three eggs, beaten to a stiff froth; mix with the yolks, flour, etc.; put in a buttered pan and quick oven.[*Treasure House*, 1891]]

Fig. 143. CAKE or PIE TINS. Tin. 7½" to 10" dia. 1" deep. Square is 8" x 8", 1½" or 2½" deep. Montgomery Ward, 1895.

Fig. 142. CHICKEN CAKE MOLD. c. 1890 to 1910. Tin. 7-5/8 x 2¾" x 5¾"... G.M.T. Co., Germany. Courtesy Melvin Adelglass.

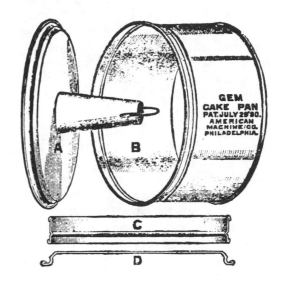

Fig. 144. CAKE PAN. Perfection Recipes & Catalog, c. 1890s.

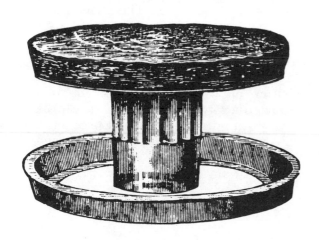
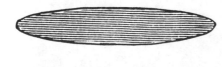
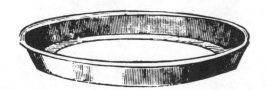

Fig. 145. CORN CAKE PAN. Stamped tin, solid frame. 6, 8, 9 or 12 cups. Matthai-Ingram Company, c. 1890.

Fig. 146. CAKE MOLD. 12 parts. Tin. F. A. Walker, c. 1870s.

Fig. 147. SCALLOPED CAKE PAN. Stamped tin. 8" x 2½"; 9¾" x 2¾". Matthai-Ingram Company, c. 1890.

CAKE SPOON — A slotted or perforated metal or wooden spoon for stirring cake batter. As the batter went through the slots it was supposed to "double the amount of work done by" the spoon. (*Practical Housekeeping*, 1884.) In 1889, the *Ladies Home Journal* recommended a wooden cake spoon to be used with a stoneware or china mixing bowl. "*Ideal;*" "*Favorite;*" "*Rumford;*" "*Androck;*" "*A & J;*" "*Ekco;*" etc.

> **Adjuncts to cake making. —**
> Get every article ready previously to its being wanted, and place before the fire, that it may become gently heated. Have a good sized bowl, a strong wooden spoon, a good egg beater, the sweetest of butter, powdered sugar, and flavoring. A wooden spoon is useless without an untiring arm to wield it. [*Treasure House*, 1891]

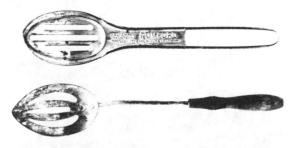

Fig. 148. CAKE SPOONS. (Bottom) c. 1915. Tin, wood. L: 12¼". (Top) Pat'd Oct. 6, 1908. Tin, wire. L: 12". Saltsmans Improved Royal Rumford Cake Mixer & Cream Whip. American. Author's Collection.

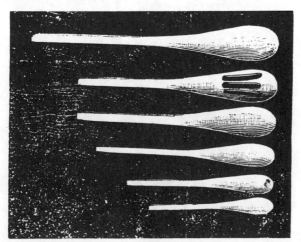

Fig. 149. CAKE SPOON & MIXING SPOONS. Wood. F. A. Walker flyer, c. 1880.

Fig. 150. CAKE SPOON. c. 1910. Tin, wood. L: 11". American. Courtesy Paul Persoff.

CAKE TESTER — A splint or straw off a broom, or a knitting needle, stuck into the cake to see if it is done. "The broom splint has occupied a prominent position among aids to cooking for an indefinite time, and housekeepers who are immaculate in other matters... often take a splint from a broom with which they have, perhaps, swept the kitchen. ... A much better way is to buy a cheap little brush-broom, and keep it for this and no other purpose; one will last a lifetime." (Emma Babcock, *Household Hints*, 1881.) *See also* **BREAD TESTER**

Fig. 151. WHISK BROOM. Butler Brothers, 1899.

CAKE TIN, — PAN, SPOUTED or TUBED — A tin, enameled ware, or earthenware cake pan with a *tube* or *spout* in the center. This enables the cake to cook more evenly, by distributing the heat to the center of the cake. *See also* **CAKE PAN**

> **Poor Man's Pudding**
> 1 cup molasses; 1 of sour milk; ½ cup butter or beef drippings; 1 teaspoon soda; flour to make as stiff as can be easily stirred; use raisins as taste or purse dictate; put in a *spouted cake tin* and steam three hours; eat with sweetened cream or any sauce preferred. [*Treasure House*, 1891]

Fig. 152. TURK'S HEAD CAKE MOULD. Stamped tin. 7¼" x 3¼"; 8" x 3¾"; 9" x 3¾"; 9½" x 4"; 11¼" x 4". Matthai-Ingram Company, c. 1890.

Fig. 153. OCTAGON CAKE MOULD with tube. Stamped tin. 8½" x 3"; 9½" x 3"; 10" x 3½"; 10½" x 3½"; 11" x 3-5/8". Matthai-Ingram Company, c. 1890.

Fig. 154. TUBED & SCALLOPED CAKE PAN. c. 1895. Tin. 8" dia.; H: 2". American. Author's Collection.

Fig. 155. CAKE PAN. Tin. F. A. Walker, c. 1870s.

Fig. 156. BUNDT CAKE MOLD. Aluminum. First copied by Northland Aluminum Products of Minneapolis, Minnesota in 1949 from the original cast iron mold made in Europe in the 19th century.

CAKE TURNER — A plain, or perforated, or pierced, or slotted flat metal implement with a long handle used for flipping pancakes, turning fried eggs, etc. They are usually, and incorrectly, called *spatulas* today.

The older cake turners are wrought iron, and were highly polished. They are quite heavy when compared with the light and flexible cake turners with wooden handles of the late 19th and early 20th centuries.

Cake turners will make one of the most interesting specialized collections, because although they are basically the same shape and size, they are found with hundreds of different perforated and slotted designs. Look for hearts and flowers in early turners, and rows or patterns of round holes in later ones. "A & J;" "Ekco;" "Androck;" "Matthai Ingram;" etc.

Fig. 157. CAKE TURNER. c. 1920s to 1930s. Cast aluminum. L: 12½"; W: 3¾". Royal Brand, Made in Germany. Author's Collection.

Fig. 158. CAKE TURNER. c. 1915. Steel, wood. 12½" x 3-1/8". WB/W. Courtesy Melvin Adelglass.

Fig. 159. CAKE TURNER. c. 1935. "Rustless" ("Stainless" has been X-ed out), wood. 13¼" x 3½". A & J. Courtesy Melvin Adelglass.

Fig. 160. CAKE TURNER. c. 1910. Tin, wood. L: 14¼"; W: 4". American. Author's Collection.

Fig. 161. CAKE TURNER. c. 1890-1910. Tin. L: 10¾"; W: 2¾". Perhaps Pilgrim Novelty Co., which made this turner as an advertising piece for Rumford Baking Powder. American. Author's Collection.

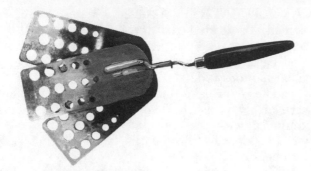

Fig. 162. CAKE TURNER. Pat'd 1936. Stainless steel, wood. L: 12½"; apreads from 2-5/8" to 8½". Coradon, N.Y.C. Courtesy Mickey Lee Donaldson.

Fig. 163. CAKE TURNER. c. 1920. Tinned steel, wood. L: 12"; W: 3". American. Author's Collection.

Fig. 164. CAKE TURNER. c. 1910. Tinned steel, wire. L: 14¾". American. Author's Collection.

Fig. 165. CAKE TURNER. c. 1910. Tinned steel, wood. L: 15". American. Author's Collection.

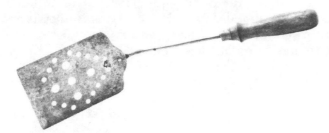

Fig. 166. CAKE TURNER. c.1920. Tinned steel, wood. L: 11-1/8". A & J. Author's Collection.

Fig. 167. CAKE TURNER. c. 1920. Tinned steel, wood. L: 12-5/8". A & J. Author's Collection.

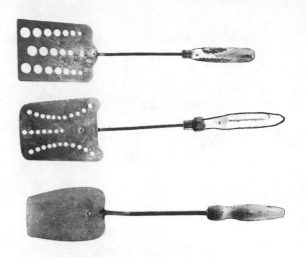

Fig. 168. CAKE TURNERS. c. 1910-1930. Steel, wood. Top to bottom. (1) L: 13½". A & J. (2) L: 14¼". A & J. (3) L: 14¼". WB/W. American. Courtesy Paul Persoff.

Fig. 169. CAKE TURNER. c. 1900. Sheet metal with iron. L: 13". American. Author's Collection.

CAN — (1) A metal vessel for holding liquids — usually cylindrical in shape. (2) A vessel of tinned iron, in which food is sealed for preservation, and which may be cylindrical, or flat and rectangular in form.

Nicolas Appert, a French chef, pickler and brewer discovered in 1809 (after years of research) that food could be sterilized with heat while in their containers. It was many years before these containers were made of tin: they were made of glass for many decades, and are often called *fruit jars.*

Home canning was either putting food up in jars or later in cans. Even the housewife could literally *can* her food. The cans were boiled, the hot food put in, and the top soldered on. A hole was punched in the lid and the can boiled again — the steam escaped through the hole. The hole was then immediately soldered closed, using a tipping copper and solder. If a can was found with two holes, both soldered up, it indicated that someone had taken a spoiled batch of food, re-heated and re-sealed the cans. It was best to leave such cans alone! Even today, with modern processes, botulism is an ever-present, if rarely active, spectre.

Commercial canning was in widespread practice by the 1830s, and there are still evidences of huge dumps of tin cans from the Gold Rush of 1849. The trade in preserved provisions was so great that "there is scarcely a city or large town either in Europe or the Colonies where you cannot find oysters and peaches in canisters labelled from Baltimore." (Philip William Flower, *History of the Trade in Tin*, 1880.) Flower reported that 45,000,000 one-pound cans of food were being made in Baltimore every year by 1880!

Fig. 173. CANDLESTICK. Planished tin. F. A. Walker, c. 1870s.

Fig. 170. CANS. c. 1910. Tin. 4¾" x 2-7/8"; 5½" x 3-1/16". 12 oz. and 16 oz. cans. Royal Baking Powder. Author's Collection.

Fig. 171. CANNED FRUIT & VEGETABLES. Butler Brothers, 1899.

CANDLE BOX — A tin cylindrical container for candles, with a hinged lid, and which hung horizontally on the wall; or, any box used for that purpose.

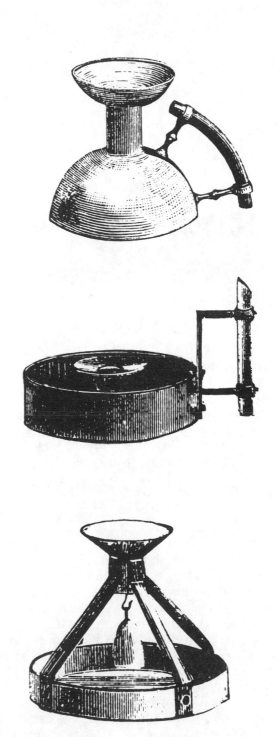

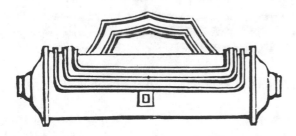

Fig. 172. CANDLE BOX. Plain or japanned tin. F. A. Walker, c. 1870s.

CANDLESTICK — Broad-based candlesticks were used in the kitchen so that they could not easily be knocked over. Kitchen candlesticks were often quite similar to chamber sticks. The so-called *hogscraper* stick, an inelegant tin stick usually of the push-up type, was commonly used in the kitchen.

Fig. 174, 175, 176. CANDLESTICKS. Painted tin. F. A. Walker, 1886.

Fig. 177. CANDY-MAKING KITCHEN. From a photograph postcard, c. 1910. Courtesy Melvin Adelglass.

CANDY-MAKING UTENSILS — Most of the utensils used in candy-making had other general uses. They are: skimmer, ladle, kettle, jelly bag, shallow basin or pan, marble slab, baking pan, funnel, sieve, sifter, tin sheet, molds, mortar and pestle, rolling pin, tea kettle steamer, double boiler, grater, enamelled ware sauce pans and kettles. Some special tools are the *hoarhound cutter* [which see] and *candy modelling tools*, see next entry.

CANDY MODELLING TOOLS — "Four tools are required — a *rose stick*, the thin, flat end being used for forming the leaves of roses out of the paste by flattening a piece on a table until it is of the required form and size; the other end for fluting and making borders, etc. A *foot tool*, used for forming the edges and borders, the circular end being used to work underneath any part or circular mouldings, and also for the paws of animals. A *cutting tool*, for which purpose the curved thin end is used, also for the formation of leaves, and the opposite end for fluting; a *gouge*, used in the formation of leaves for flowers. The curves of each t o ol are also used for different purposes in modelling, and for forming the raised and depressed parts. There are many others, but these will be sufficient, with the *dotting* or *pointing*

t o ol; a piece of round pointed stick will do for this last." (*Treasure House*, 1891, [*italics mine*].)

Fig. 178. CANDY MODELLING TOOLS. Treasure House, 1891.

CANISTER [*cannister*] — A small case or box, usually of tin or other metal, used for storing fairly small quantities of tea, coffee, flour, sugar or biscuits. "Tin cans of meal and sugar, stone jars of salt,... Tin boxes are best receptacles for food that would attract mice and weevils. They are, to be sure, more expensive than wooden buckets, but they are lasting and perfectly secure. Should have labels, and if they are made to order, have labels painted on them at the same time. Such boxes as cracker manufacturers use will answer this purpose and may be obtained through the grocer." (Maria Parloa, *Kitchen Companion*, 1887.) You will often find the japanned canisters, with a snug-fitting lid, stenciled in yellow on the common brownish maroon ground.

A number of canisters were originally tin containers for such products as plug tobacco. The colorful, attractive designs were intended to discourage the housewife from throwing out the tin, and hence the advertising.

Something which you may mistake for canisters, but which was a tobacco humidor, are the quart-sized brass or nickel-plated cans with tight-fitting lids. These lids were fitted inside with a small sponge and a wire spring clip. I am sure that more than one housewife commandeered her husband's humidor, and, after cleaning it thoroughly, used it for corn meal or crackers. *See also* **CADDY**

Fig. 181. GEM CANISTER. Embossed tin. 1 and 2 pound capacity. Matthai-Ingram Company, c. 1890.

Fig. 182. CANISTER. Late-19th century. Tin-lined copper with copper lift-out tray for sifted flour. 6¾" dia.; H: 7". American. Courtesy Mary Mac Franklin.

CANNIKIN [*canikin*] — A small can or drinking vessel. *See also* **PANNIKIN**

CAN OPENER — An instrument, usually with a puncturing point and a cutting blade, for opening cans. "Can openers are of many syles and there are few satisfactory ones." (*Hutchinson*, 1918.)

The later openers had a handle or crank which turned the cutting blade. One even had a revolving platform which held the can and moved it around a stationary blade.

Some can openers were called *sardine openers*, and were used for opening the square or oblong sardine can. *See also* **SARDINE SHEARS**. "*Delmonico;*" "*Sterling;*" "*Yankee;*" "*Hopper's;*" "*Stand-by;*" "*Perfect;*" "*Baumgarten;*" "*Ten in One;*" "*Anchor;*" "*Tilt-Top-o-Matic;*" "*Edlund Junior;*" "*Peerless;*" "*Norlund's;*" "*Vulcan Cut;*" "*Midget;*" "*Sprague;*" "*Star;*" etc.

Fig. 179. COFFEE CANISTER. c. 1890s. Japanned & stenciled tin; hinged lid. H: 5¾"; W: 4-1/8". American. Author's Collection.

Fig. 180. KITCHEN SET, nested. Ivory, white, blue, green gray, red or yellow painted tin. 4¼" x 5½"; 6" x 6½"; 6¾" x 7"; 7½" x 8"; 10" x 6½"; 14½" x 10½" x 9¾". C. B. Porter Company, c. 1915.

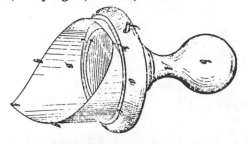

Fig. 183. CAN-OPENER. Pat'd 1880, no. 228,595. William E. Brock, New York City, N.Y. Official Gazette, June 8, 1880.

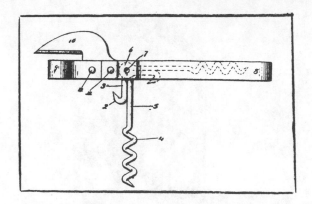

Fig. 184. COMBINATION-TOOL. Pat'd 1908, no. 902,868. Abner Fenn, Meriden, Connecticut, assignor to The Browne & Dowd Mfg. Co., Official Gazette, Nov. 3, 1908.

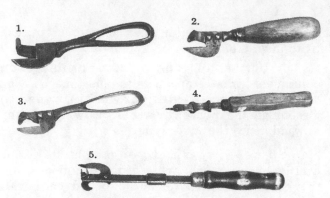

Fig. 188. CAN OPENERS. Cast steel, wood. (1) c. 1915. L: 5¼"; (2) c. 1900-1910. L: 5½"; (3) c. 1910. L: 5½"; (4) Midget. Pat'd 17/19/04. L: 6-1/8"; (5) Vulcan Cut Can & Bottle Opener. 1910. L: 8-7/8". American. Author's Collection.

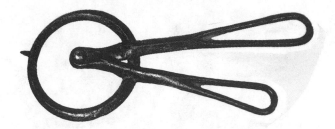

Fig. 185. CAN OPENER. Pat'd May 7, 1889. Cast iron. 8½" x 3¼". American. Author's Collection.

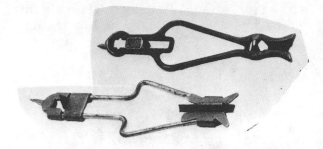

Fig. 189. CAN OPENERS. (Bottom) c. 1910. Iron, cast steel, tin. L: 6¾". Dandy Gold Medal. (Top) Pat'd Aug. 12, 1902, Mar. 31, 1903. Iron, tin. L:6½". (Knife-sharpening stone missing.) Peerless. Author's Collection.

Fig. 190. CAN OPENER. Nickeled steel, tempered steel blade, wood. L: 8½". A & J. Edward Katzinger Company, 1940.

Fig. 191. CAN OPENER. Nickeled steel, wood. L: 8½". A & J. Edward Katzinger Company, 1940.

Fig. 186. CAN OPENERS. (1) c. 1895. Wood, steel. L: 8-7/8". (2) Multiple use, with corkscrew. c. 1900. Cast steel. L: 5½". (3) Anchor Opener, bottle cap opener. c. 1900. Cast steel L: 4". (4) Ten-In-One, New Jersey Patent Novelty Co., Passaic, N.J. c. 1910. Steel. L: 7½". (5) Tilt-Top O-Matic. c. 1920. Steel. L: 3". (6) Edlund Junior, Edlund Co., Burlington, Vt. Pat'd April 21, 1925; May 12, 1925; June 18, 1929. Wood, steel. L: 6¼". (7) c. 1915. Tool steel. L: 7¾". (8) Peerless. Pat'd February 11, 1890. Cast metal, tool steel. L: 6½". (9) Multiple use. c. 1930. Steel, wood. L: 6-7/8". (10) Norlunds 3-in-1: can opener, bottle opener, knife sharpener. c. 1915. Steel. L: 4½". Author's Collection.

Fig. 187. CAN OPENER. 19th century. Iron. L: 9¾". Baumgarten. American. Courtesy Keillor Collection.

Fig. 192. TABLE-MOUNTED CAN OPENER. Pat'd Oct. 1, 1921, Aug. 8, 1922, and April 10, 1923 — seven years before the first wall-mounted opener. Nickeled iron, blue wood knob. L: 7"; H: 4". Blue Streak, Turner & Seymour Mfg. Co., Torrington, Connecticut. Author's Collection.

Fig. 193. SARDINE OPENER. Steel, wood. F. A. Walker, c. 1870s.

Fig. 194. BOTTLE OPENER. c. 1900. Steel, wood. L: 5". Havell, Irvington, N.J. Author's Collection.

CARBONIZER or PIPE INCINERATOR — A double cylinder of sheet iron, the inner pipe being perforated. A hole was cut in the smokestack of the kitchen range, the carbonizer slipped into this opening, and the refuse placed in the pipe was slowly carbonized by the heat and smoke. A very similar device was inserted into the stove pipe and used for warming plates or keeping bread dough warm.

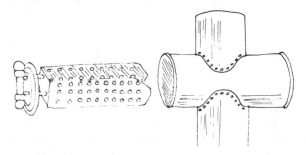

Fig. 195. CARBONIZER.

CARBON STEEL — Steel which derives its physical properties from the presence of carbon. All steel has carbon in it, but other alloys, such as stainless steel, owe their specific properties to the presence of other metals.

A carbon steel knife can be well-sharpened, again and again, and will hold its keen edge longer than a stainless steel knife. Old carbon-steel knives are often found with but a quarter or a half of their blade remaining. The over-zealous and unskillful use of a grindstone probably shortened the lives of many knives.

CAST IRON — *see* **IRON**

CAST STEEL — *see* **IRON**

CAUDLE-CUP — A cup, with or without a lid (but most frequently with), for serving caudle or other hot liquid food to invalids.

Caudle
Beat up one egg to a froth; add one wineglassful of sherry and ½ pint of gruel; flavor with lemon peel and nutmeg, and sweeten to taste. [*Treasure House*, 1891]

Gruel
Mix 2 tablespoons of corn meal with one of wheat flour, or oat meal alone; and sufficient cold water to make a thick batter; if the gruel is liked thick, stir it into 1 pint of boiling water; if liked thin, add more water or milk; season the gruel with salt, and let it boil 6 or 8 minutes; stir frequently; take it from the fire; put in a piece of butter the size of a walnut, and pepper to the taste; turn it on toasted bread, cut in small pieces , or serve in a breakfast cup. [*ibid.*]

Fig. 196. BABY CUP or INVALID CUP.

Fig. 197. CAUDLE CUP or INVALID CUP.

CAULDRON [*caldron*] — A large open kettle or boiler, used for soups, for boiling large joints of meat, for boiling laundry and, prescriptively, by witches for stewing bat wings and gall of toad.

Round about the caldron go.
In the poisoned entrails throw.
Toad, that under cold stone
Days and nights has thirty-one
Sweltered venom sleeping got,
Boil thou first i' the charmed pot.
[William Shakespear, *Macbeth*, Act IV, Sc. i]

CEREAL COOKER — *see* **DOUBLE BOILER, FARINA BOILER**

CHAFING DISH or CHAFFERN — A two or three-part metal vessel which holds burning charcoal or other fuel, and upon which another vessel containing food to be kept warm may be placed. *See also* **BRAZIER**

Fig. 198. CHAFING DISH. Agate enameled ware. Lalance & Grosjean, 1890.

CHAIN CLOTH — *see* **POT CLEANER**

CHARCOAL BROILER — A round or oblong utensil which consists of a pan for the bed of coals, the grill for the meat, and the ventilated lid. One type, advertised in the *Ladies Home Journal*, May 1899, "may be set on any stove or range." The coal bed was replaced by the stove heat. *See also* **BRAZIER, BROILER**

CHARLOTTE RUSSE MOLD, — CUP — A stamped metal mold, with a number of designs, both geometric and organic. It is very similar to blancmange molds and jelly molds, and was probably interchangeable in the kitchen. All of these molds had to be wet with cold milk or water before the food was poured in.

Charlotte Russe

Whip one quart rich cream to a stiff froth, and drain well on a nice sieve. To one scant pint of milk add six eggs beaten very lightly; make very sweet; flavor high with vanilla. Cook over hot water [in a double boiler] till it is a thick custard. Soak one full ounce Cox's gelatine in a very little water. When the custard is very cold, beat in lightly the gelatine and the whipped cream. Line the bottom of your mould with buttered paper, the sides with sponge-cake or lady-fingers fastened together with the white of an egg. Fill with the cream; put in a cold place, or in summer on ice. To turn out, dip the mould for a moment in hot water. In draining the whipped cream, all that drips through can be re-whipped. [Miss Neill's recipe, *The Every-day Cook-Book*, as it appeared in *Strohm*, 1888]

Fig. 199. CHARLOTTE RUSSE CUP. Planished tin. 3" dia. Lalance & Grosjean, 1890.

CHEESE CURD WHIPPER — *see* **CURD WHIPPER**

CHEESE CUTTER — A slicing implement whose cutting edge is a fine but strong wire — often stretched on a frame like a coping saw. The wire is drawn down through the cheese, and cuts well because there is little resistance.

Fig. 200. CHEESE SLICER. c. 1920 to 1949. Wire. L: 6-5/8". American. Author's Collection.

CHEESE HOOP, — BAIL — A broad hoop or cylinder, usually of wood, in which the curd is pressed during cheese-making. Cheese-cloth was stretched across it to hold the cheese. The *hoop and folla* [foller] were used together. *See also* **CHEESE PRESS, CHEESE VAT**

CHEESE KNIFE — A large spatula used to break up the curd for cheese-making. It is also a knife with a curved blade for cutting cheese. *See also* **CHEESE CUTTER, CURD KNIFE, CURD WHIPPER**

CHEESE MOLD — The wooden or metal container in which cheese curd is pressed, and which creates the distinctive shapes of different cheeses.

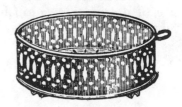

Fig. 201. CREAM CHEESE MOULD. With or without cover. Pieced tin. 6¼" x 2". Matthai-Ingram Company, c. 1890.

Fig. 202. COLANDER or CHEESE MOLD. 19th century. Pierced tin. 6" x 6"; H: 2½"; with short legs. American, Pennsylvania German. Courtesy Keillor Collection.

CHEESE PRESS — Consisted of a large wooden frame, with a platform for the hoop, and equipped with a *foller* or *folla* which pressed the curds after the whey was drained out. The press was screwed tight until the cheese became solid.

In mechanics, the definition of *follower* is the plate or block by which pressure is applied in various kinds of presses.

Because cheese-making is a mystery to anyone who has never seen it done, and particularly to anyone who has never even seen a cheese press complete with all its parts, I will transcribe the entire cheese-making chapter from the [*Treasure House of Useful Knowledge*, 1891]

CHEESE, To Make. In making cheese, put the greater portion of the milk into a large tub to which add the remainder, sufficiently heated to raise the temperature to that of new milk; whisk and cover the tub. It is allowed to stand until completely turned, when the curd is gently struck down several times with the *skimming dish*; after this it is allowed to subside. The *cheese hoop,* covered with *cheese cloth,* is next placed on a horse or ladder over the tub, and filled with curd by means of the skimmer; care being taken to allow as little as possible of the oily particles or butter to run back with the whey. The curd is pressed down with the hands and more added as it sinks. This process is repeated until the curd rises to about 2 inches above the edge. The newly-formed cheese, thus partially separated from the whey, is now placed in a clean hoop, and a quantity of salt,

to taste, added, as well as of annatto, when that coloring is used, after which a board is placed over and under it, and pressure applied for about two or three hours. The cheese is next turned out and surrounded by fresh cheese cloth, and then again replaced in the hoop, and submitted to pressure in the *cheese-press* for 8 or 10 hours, after which it is commonly removed from the press, salted all over and again pressed for 15 to 20 hours. The quality of the cheese depends on this part of the process , for, if any of the whey is left in the cheese, it rapidly becomes bad-flavored. Before placing it in the press the last time, pare the edges smooth; then wash the outside of the cheese in warm whey or water; wipe it dry, and cover the outside of it with annatto or reddle.

CHEESE PRESS. — A good cheese press may be made at a trifling cost. The uprights are 2 by 4 inch scantling, 4 or 5 feet long, with pieces of the same fastened to the bottom as braces; 30 inches from the floor stout cleats are nailed firmly to the uprights, upon which rests a 2 inch plank, which serves as a table. Upon this plank is a cheese hoop, with a cheese to be pressed. Above this is a stout strip of 2 by 2 stuff, with ends resting in mortises cut in the uprights. This strip should be 5 or 6 feet in length. Under it, in the center, is a block which rests upon a round *follower* the exact size of the cheese to be pressed. The power is furnished by the eccentrics, or arms, which are merely levers with unequal circular ends. These work on a bolt which pierces the circle near the top. To the ends of the arms fasten strings, which are tied to the side of the table to maintain the pressure. When the cheese is placed in the hoop, the follower and block adjusted, by pulling down upon the eccentrics a pressure of any required degree is applied upon the cheese; both the board and strip being elastic, the pressure is maintained as long as applied. [*italics mine*]

Fig. 203. CHEESE PRESS. Homemade of wood. See text. Treasure House. 1891.

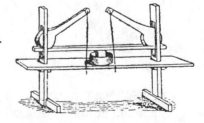

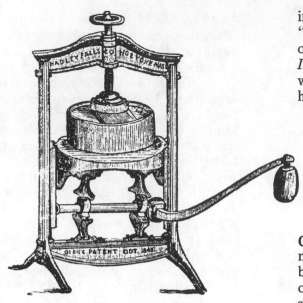

Fig. 204. CHEESE PRESS. Pat'd Oct., 1848. Dick's Patent, Hadley Falls Co., Holyoke, Mass. Catalog fragment, c. 1870s.

CHEESE SCOOP — A pointed spoonlike implement for scooping out cheese from the vat.

CHEESE TOASTER — A reflecting oven for melting cheese on toast or on top of other dishes. One pictured in an *F.A. Walker Catalog* was advertised as a cheese, bird or apple roaster.

To Roast Potatoes

Put them in a tin Dutch oven, or cheese toaster; take care not to put them too near the fire, or they will get burned on the outside before they are warmed through... [Mary Randolph, *The Virginia Housewife*, 1855]

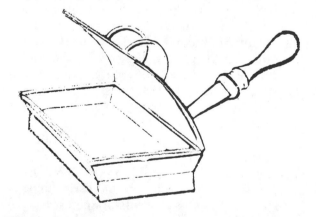

Fig. 205. CHEESE TOASTER. Planished tin, wood. F. A. Walker, c. 1870s.

CHEESE TRIER — A semicircular piece of sharp steel inserted into a vat of cheese to withdraw a sample for testing. *See also* **BUTTER TRIER**

CHEESE VAT or TUB — The cylindrical "vessel in which the curds are pressed and the cheese shaped

in cheese-making." (*Oxford English Dictionary*.) "A round vat in which the curd is formed and cut or broken in cheese making." (*Webster's Second International Dictionary*.) From other sources, it would seem that the vat or tub is also used for heating the milk.

> My greatest objection, after all to the use of butter and cheese both, grows out of the consideration that their manufacture involves a great amount of female labor, while no substantial benefit is obtained. [William Alcott, *The Young Housekeeper*, 1842]

CHERRY STONER, — SEEDER — A device or machine for removing the stones from cherries, one by one, or two by two. There are various types, all of which had the express purpose of removing the stone without squashing the fruit. One type had a levered action which punctured the cherry and pushed the seed out the other side. This could be used for olives too. In another type, the cherries are fed into a split hopper, and a crank is turned, which rubs the cherries against a slightly ridged plate. This is the *"Enterprise,"* and works fairly well. *"Rollman;" "Enterprise;" "New Standard;" "Goodell;"* etc.

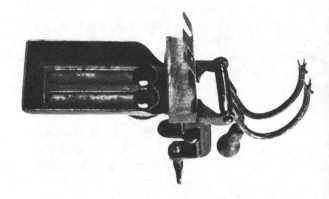

Fig. 206. CHERRY STONER. c. 1895. Cast iron, wood, leather gasket. W: 6¼"; H: 8". "The Family Cherry Stoner," Goodell Co., Antrim, New Hampshire. Courtesy Robert D. Franklin.

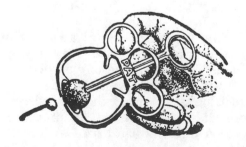

Fig. 207. PERFECTION CHERRY SEEDER. "It fits the hand. Seeds and stems at the same time — no other seeder will do this. ...For the housewife who has long desired an article to take the place of the hand, at the same time permitting the same degree of care in selecting the fruit." F. W. Seastrand, c. 1912.

Fig. 208. CHERRY STONER. c. 1900. Tinned cast iron, wood. W: 5½"; H: 10". New Standard No. 50, Mt. Joy, Pa. Courtesy Robert D. Franklin.

Fig. 209. CHERRY STONER. Pat'd March 31, 1903. Tinned cast iron. 9" x 12". Enterprise No. 2, Enterprise Mfg. Co., Philadelphia. The No.s 1 & 2, unlike the No.s 17 & 18, do not have a regulating device which made it possible to adjust for different size cherries. Courtesy Robert D. Franklin.

CHINESE STRAINER — A conical, wire-mesh strainer with a rim and a handle for straining soup stock. Also called a *tapering strainer.* *See also* **SOUP STRAINER**

CHITTERLING SCOOP — Most probably a small wooden scoop used for stuffing chitterlings — the large or small intestines, usually of pork — for sausages. I could find but one reference, undefined, to a chitterling scoop and that was in the December 25, 1973 *Collector's Weekly,* in an article about collecting primitives.

CHOCOLATE MILL, — POT — A spouted vessel of tin, pottery or silver with a handle, and a lid which permitted the handle of the wooden muller to stick up through it and be dashed up and down

to froth the hot chocolate.

Chocolate is composed of cocoa and sugar. Its nutritive power is great, and its use is recommended to men of letters, consumptive people, and ladies, whose charms a cup of chocolate every morning for breakfast, is said to preserve surprisingly. [*Treasure House,* 1891]

Fig. 210. CHOCOLATE POT with MUDDLER. Planished tin. F. A. Walker, c. 1870s.

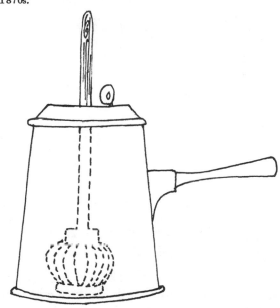

Fig. 211. CHOCOLATE MILL.

CHOCOLATE MOLDS — Tin or pewter molds, usually in the form of animals, eggs, chickens, or lambs, for forming large chocolates; and in a number of geometric shapes for forming small candies.

CHOP FRILLS or CUTLET FRILLS — A strip of white paper, cut and/or curled, and circled around the bone of a chop or cutlet, the end of a roast turkey leg, leg of lamb, etc. Some are quite simple, and others are formed of layer upon layer of fancy cut paper.

Fig. 212, 213. CHOP FRILLS. *Mrs. Beeton's Household Management*, c. 1940.

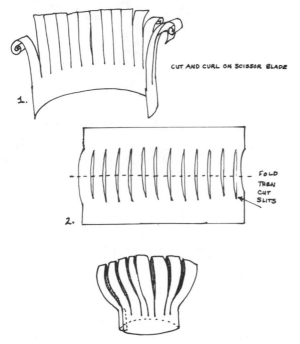

CUT AND CURL ON SCISSOR BLADE

1.

FOLD THEN CUT SLITS

2.

Fig. 215. CHOPPING KNIFE. 18th century. Wrought iron, wood. 6¾" x 7". American. Courtesy Keillor Collection.

Fig. 214. CHOP FRILLS. (1) Simplest type; (2) Double frills. This type can be used to create the three or four-tier frills as in picture above.

CHOPPING, — MINCING KNIFE — One, two or even three broad steel or wrought-iron blades connected to an iron or wood handle.

There is an enormous variety of shapes and styles, as everybody had his own idea what the ideal chopping knife should be. In colonial days, and before mass-production of relatively few types, this essential kitchen tool was hand-made and each one was unique. Sometimes the blades of other household or farm tools were fashioned into chopping knives.

The handles attach to the blades with double tangs, a single tang, a brace shank, or an offset single shank. Some late-19th century patent knives had two or three crossed blades with a knob handle. Chopping knives were used for hashing meat, chopping vegetables, and were used with a wooden bowl or tray.

Fig. 216. CHOPPING KNIFE. 18th century. Wrought iron, wood. 7" x 7¾". American. Courtesy Keillor Collection.

Fig. 217. CHOPPING KNIFE. 18th century. Wrought iron, wood. 8" x 9". American. Courtesy Keillor Collection.

Fig. 218. CHOPPING KNIFE. 18th century. Wrought iron, wood. American. Courtesy Keillor Collection.

Fig. 221. CHOPPING KNIFE. Mid-19th century. Wrought iron, wood. American. Courtesy Keillor Collection.

Fig. 222. CHOPPING KNIFE. Handle at right angle to blade. 19th century. Wrought iron, wood. 5½" x 6". American. Courtesy Keillor Collection.

Fig. 219, 220. CHOPPING KNIFE, pivoting blade. Two views. 19th century. Steel, wood. 6½" x 6¼". American. Courtesy Keillor Collection.

Fig. 223. CHOPPING KNIFE. c. 1870s. Iron. Courtesy Keillor Collection.

Fig. 224. CHOPPING KNIFE. 19th century. Iron, wood. 10" x 3". American. Courtesy Keillor Collection.

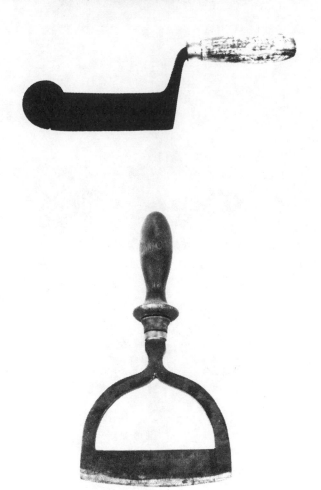

Fig. 227. CHOPPING KNIVES. c. 1890. Cast steel, wood. (Top) H: 6-3/8"; W: 7½". (Bottom) H: 5-5/8"; W: 8". American. Author's Collection.

Fig. 228. CHOPPING KNIFE. c. 1910. Nickeled steel, tube handle. H: 4-5/8"; W: 5¼". American. Author's Collection.

Fig. 225. CHOPPING. 19th century. Iron, wood. 5" x 9". American. Courtesy Keillor Collection.

Fig. 226. CHOPPING KNIFE. Pat'd 1892. No. 468,893 by Frank M. Palmiter, Milton, Wisconsin. Official Gazette, February 16, 1892.

Fig. 229. CHOPPING KNIVES. c. 1900. Cast steel, iron, wood. (Left) H: 5¼"; W: 5¼". (Right) H: 6"; W: 5¾". American. Author's Collection.

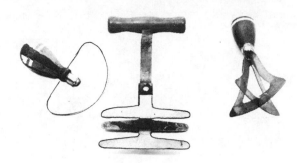

Fig. 233. CHOPPING KNIVES. (Left to right) (1) c. 1930s. Stainless steel, wood. 4¼" X 3-7/8". (2) Pat'd 1938. Stainless steel, wood, spring. 7½" x 3¾". Foley Chopper. (3) c. 1925. Stainless, wood. 6" x 3". A & J. Author's Collection.

Fig. 230. CHOPPING KNIFE. c. 1885. Carbon steel, wood. L: 6¾"; W: 5¼". Hachinette, France. Author's Collection.

Fig. 231. MINCING KNIFE. Double steel blades, iron, wood. Matthai-Ingram Company, c. 1890.

Fig. 234. CHOPPING KNIVES. (Top) Oct. 20, 1892. Cast steel blade, cast iron, H: 5"; W: 6-1/8", Double Action. (Bottom) 1920s. Stainless steel blade, cast iron. H: 5"; W: 6-1/8. Voos. American. Author's Collection.

Fig. 232. CHOPPING KNIFE. C. 1890s. Cast iron, steel. H: 5½"; W: 5¾". American. Author's Collection.

Fig. 235. CHOPPING KNIFE. Cast steel. May be taken apart. J. B. Foote Foundry Company, 1906.

Fig. 236. MINCING KNIVES. (Top) nickeled steel, wood. (Bottom) stainless steel, wood. Androck, 1936.

CHOPPING TRAY, — BOWL — A long, two or three inch deep wooden tray in which food is chopped; and a round wooden bowl serving the same purpose. The bowls are still made. "The tray will last almost a lifetime. The round wooden bowls, though not as durable, are yet very useful , and there should be at least one in the pantry." (*Parloa*, 1887.)

Fig. 237. CHOPPING TRAY. Hardwood. 11" x 22"; 10" x 20"; 9" x 18". Montgomery Ward, 1895.

Fig. 238. CHOPPING BOWL. Hardwood. 13", 15", 17", 19" dia. Montgomery Ward, 1895.

CHURN — A machine for making butter by means of an up and down or a turbine dasher. "The churn dasher will very likely gather the butter. But a good method is, when the butter is made, to throw into the churn a small piece of butter which will form a nucleus around which the franules will collect." (*Scientific Artisan*, 1859.) Some churns are small, with a capacity of from three to nine pints. Some of them were made of glass, and had screw-on lids and cast-iron gears, and wooden blades. Some churns are much larger, and hold from two to sixty gallons. One type was the *rocker churn*, which looks rather like a baby rocker with a lid. The body of the churn, traditionally pictured as a upright keg, was square, rectangular, round, or keg-shaped — the keg being upright or held at an angle in a frame. *See also* DOGS, SYLABUB CHURN, WHIP CHURN

Butter Without a Churn

Take a wooden bowl, or any suitable vessel, and having first scalded and then rinsed it with cold spring water, place cream in it. Now let the operator hold his hand in water as hot as can be borne for a few seconds, then plunge it in cold water for about a minute, and at once commence to agitate the cream by a gentle circular motion. In five minutes, or less, the butter will have come, when, of course, it must be washed and salted according to taste, and in the summer season it will usually be found necessary to bring the cream out of the cellar a quarter hour before churning, to take the excessive chill off. In winter place the vessel containing the cream over another containing water to warm it; then continue to agitate the cream intil the chill has departed. [*Scientific Artisan*, 1859]

Fig. 239, 240. CHURN. c. 1870-1900. Blue buttermilk-painted wood. L: 20"; W: 18½"; H: 29". American. Courtesy Keillor Collection.

Fig. 244. CHURNS. Tolerton & Warfield Co., Sious City, Iowa, c. 1900.

Fig. 241. CHURN. Pat'd. May 28, 1889, Oct. 27, 1891, Nov. 17, 1891. Tenneessee white wood, iron hoops. 1 to 60 gallons. Diamond Balance Churn Co., c. 1891.

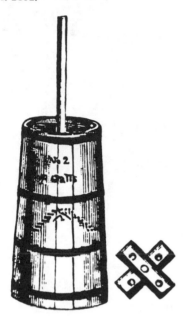

Fig. 245. CYLINDER CHURN. Cedar, galvanized iron hoops. Will churn 2, 3, 4 and 5 gallons. Montgomery Ward, 1895.

Fig. 242. DASH CHURN. Stripped cedar, brass hoops. 3, 4, 5 and 6 gallon. Montgomery Ward, 1893.

CLAM BAKER — A baking pan of tin or earthenware, or individual patty pans, for baking clams in the oven.

CLEAVER — A sharp, broad-bladed knife for cutting large pieces of meat into joints or roasts.

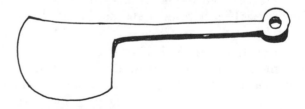

Fig. 246. CLEAVER. 18th century. Wrought iron.

Fig. 243. BUTTER CHURN. c. 1910. Glass, cast iron, tin, wood. H: 13"; W: 4¾". The "Premier" Two Minute Butter Machine, Culinary Mfg. Co., Orange, N.J. Author's Collection.

Fig. 247. CLEAVER. c. 1890s. Tool steel, wood. L: 12¼"; W: 3¾". American. Courtesy Marvin Tanner.

Fig. 248. CLEAVER. Pat'd May 1886. Tool steel, wood. L: 13"; W: 4". Samuel Lee, L.F. & C. American. Courtesy Marvin Tanner.

Fig. 249. CLEAVER. c. 1890. Tool steel, wood. L: 12"; W: 3-7/8". Magnetic Steel, I.F.W. & S. Co. Courtesy Marvin Tanner.

Fig. 250. CLEAVER. Late-19th century. Steel, lead handle replacing original wood handle. 13½" x 4-1/8". Russian or Polish. This cleaver, one of a pair used in preparing kosher food, was brought to this country in 1903. The handle was repaired about that time. Courtesy Marvin Tanner.

"For sale, Willard's much esteemed patent Clock Jacks, they are valuable above the other roast meat jacks, being moveable, and may be used in any room. They require less fire and will roast meat in a shorter time than any other." (Advertisement in the *Daily Advertiser*, New York City, August 1785.) Both Simon and Aaron Willard, brothers, were clockmakers; this was probably Simon. They were geniuses with clocks, but I don't see how a jack could disarrange the orderly and law-bound march of time! *See also* BOTTLE JACK, DOGS, PORTABLE SPRING JACK, SMOKE JACK, SPIT

Fig. 251. CLOCK JACK. 18th century. Cast, wrought & machined iron. From the kitchen behind Wetherburn's Tavern, Colonial Williamsburg, Virginia.

CLOCK — A clock was considered indispensable in the kitchen for timing cooking. They were very expensive in the 18th century because they were entirely handmade. An early itinerant clock-maker could almost depend on selling a clock to a housewife if he left it with her, "just to try," on his way through town. On his trip back she would buy it gladly if it worked and kept good time.

Most kitchen clocks were simple and round and hung on the wall. A shelf or mantle clock was also common, after 1800 when Eli Terry made them, but shelf space in the kitchen was and is valuable.

CLOCK JACK — A geared, clockwork mechanism, usually run by weights, which turned a spit by means of a pulley and belt. It was also called a *watchwork engine.*

The clock jack was fixed to the mantle above the fireplace, off to one side. It had to be hung high enough to allow the full travel of the weights. Most clock jacks are made of brass and iron. Fine ones may be seen at various restorations. Some clock jacks were fitted with adjustable governors or fly wheels, by which means the speed of the turning could be somewhat regulated.

Fig. 252. CLOCK JACK, weight driven. c. 1800. L: 9"; W: 7". Brass, iron, rope, stone. The governor on top has adjustable "wings" or vanes to regulate the speed. English. Courtesy Keillor Collection.

COAL HOD or SCUTTLE — A pail-like vessel for coal, with one scoop-like lip. It was sometimes called a *coal vase* in refined Victorian catalogs.

Fig. 253. COAL HOD. Japanned tin. F. A. Walker, c. 1870s.

Fig. 254. COAL HOD. F. A. Walker, c. 1870s.

Fig. 255. COAL VASE. Japanned tin. F. A. Walker, c. 1870s.

COB-IRON — *see* **ANDIRON**

COCKROACH TRAP — Like an apron and a clock, a necessity in the kitchen. "Every home should be provided with cockroach traps. They are made of brown earthenware, and are to be bought for a trifle at the pottery shops. Bait them with molasses mixed with a little water, and set them about at night, when the lights are removed. The hellebore plant, laid about in large quantities in places they frequent, will sometimes expel them. Another: boil roots of pokeberry plant until dissolved in water, mix with molasses, and put in traps or old saucers." (*Leslie*, 1840.) F.A. Walker advertised several styles — all designed to lure a curious or hungry roach up the side of the vessel, into which he would fall and be unable to escape.

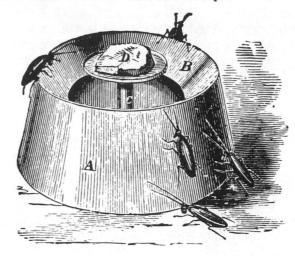

Fig. 256. ROACH TRAP. F. A. Walker, c. 1870s.

Fig. 257. ROACH BELLOWS. Tin, wood, cloth. F. A. Walker, c. 1870s.

COCOA-DIPPER — A distinctive dipper with a very rounded bowl, and usually a nicely-turned wooden handle. The bowl had a small pouring lip.

Fig. 258. COCOA-SHAPE DIPPERS. (Top) Stamped tin, steel shank, enameled wood. Bowl: 4-1/8" x 2¾"; 5" x 3½". (Bottom) Stamped tin. same measurements. Matthai-Ingram Company, c. 1890.

COCO-BOLO [*cocoabolo*] — A tropical American tree, having hard, dark purple-brown wood, banded with lighter streaks. It was used for the handles of some kitchen utensils, such as knives, forks and serving pots or kettles. There is also an East Indian tree, the *cocowood* or *cocoa-wood*, which might possibly have been meant.

COFFEE BOILER — *see* **COFFEE POT**

COFFEE MILL or GRINDER — There are several types of coffee mills: the *side mill*, which is sort of a half-hopper attached to a board which, in turn, is attached to the wall; the *box mill*, which is simply a wooden box with a drawer to catch the ground coffee, and a crank and hopper on top; and the rather spectacular cast-iron mill with a large hopper on top and a pair of fly wheels, one of which has a handle for turning. This type came in a variety of sizes, the smallest of which were suitable for home use. The larger sizes were used on the counters of thousands of grocery stores across the country. Some of the box mills — the so-called *French style* — are made of lovely wood, and have brass and cast iron parts. Most of these were not made in America, but they were certainly used here.

Fig. 261. COFFEE MILL. Hardwood, cast iron. Holds 1 pound. Parkers Columbia Coffee Mill, No. 260. Montgomery Ward, 1895.

Fig. 259. COFFEE MILL. Iron hopper. No. 2, 4 oz. capacity. "Highly ornamented and handsome in appearance. All our Family Mills are 'Pulverizers' and are especially adapted for making 'French' Coffee." Enterprise. The Enterprising Housekeeper, 1898.

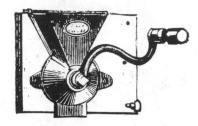

Fig. 262. EAGLE SIDE COFFEE MILL. Pat'd 1860s. F. A. Walker, c. 1870s.

Fig. 263. COFFEE GRINDER. c. 1900. Wood, cast iron, tin. 6-5/8 x 6-5/8" x 10"; one pound capacity. "Challenge Fast Grinder," Sun Mfg. Co., Columbus, Ohio. Author's Collection.

Fig. 260. COFFEE MILL. F. A. Walker, c. 1870s.

COFFEE PADDLE, — STICK or SPOON — A wooden utensil for stirring coffee beans in the oven or on top of the stove while they roasted. It could, obviously, be confused with any wooden paddle or spoon.

> Coffee sometimes produces great excitement, and a sensation of restlessness and heat ensues. For throwing off this condition, fresh air is the best antidote. [*Treasure House*, 1891]

COFFEE POT — A lidded pot of tin or graniteware (or pottery or silver), with a spout, or a lip, and a handle. The type you would expect to see in a Remington painting of cowpokes in the old West was large, with a lip and a bail handle. They were sometimes called *coffee boilers*. The very old pots, made from patterns by tinsmiths, and often painted or decorated with punch marks, have long graceful spouts arching up like swan necks from near the bottom of the pot. Do not confuse this with the similar pot which had a crooked spout: it was used for filling kerosene lamps.

One coffee pot, which I have seen two pictures of, has two spouts: one directly opposite the handle, and one only a quarter of the way round the pot. It is likely that this was a sample. A book review of *The Furniture of Our Forefathers*, by Esther Singleton and Russell Sturgis, [*New York City*, 1900] which was printed in *House and Garden*, September 1901, stated "Mr. Sturgis calls our attention to '...the coffee pot with a choice of spouts, so that the mistress of the house can pour in the English or the French way at pleasure."

Special *strainers* with spring clips were made for the spouts of both coffee and tea pots, and as a lot of early coffee was made by boiling the grounds in water, perhaps with a crushed eggshell to clear it, this strainer was a welcome nicety. *See also* **BIGGIN**

Fig. 265. COFFEE BOILER. Tin. F. A. Walker, c. 1870s.

Fig. 266. CROOKED-SPOUT COFFEE POT. 19th century. Typically painted.

Fig. 264. COFFEE BOILER. Pieced tin, body & lip of one piece. 2, 3, 4, 6 qts. Matthai-Ingram Company, c. 1890.

Fig. 267. COFFEE POT. c. 1830. Earthenware. 6"w, 10½" h. Thomas Haig, 456 N. 4th St., Philadelphia. Courtesy Keillor Collection.

Fig. 268. COFFEE POT. Spout on side. Pieced tin, copper bottom. 2, 3, 4, 6 qts. Matthai-Ingram Company, c. 1890.

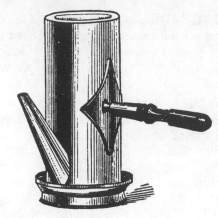

Fig. 271. COFFEE POT. F. A. Walker, c. 1870.

Fig. 269. COFFEE POT, spout on side. Pieced tin, some have copper bottoms. From ½ to 6 qts. Loose or hinged covers. Matthai-Ingram Company, c. 1890.

Fig. 272. COFFEE POT. United Profit-sharing Corporation, 1914.

Fig. 273. COFFEE & TEA MAKERS. The People's Home Journal, Dec. 1910.

Fig. 270. COFFEE BOILER. Pieced tin, copper bottom. 2, 3, 4, 6 qts. Matthai—Ingram Company, c. 1890.

Fig. 274. SPOUT STRAINER. Wire. 1¾" dia. Androck, 1936.

Fig. 275. SPOUT STRAINER. Wire. 1¾" dia. Matthai-Ingram Company, c. 1890.

COFFEE ROASTER — A usually spherical iron vessel which revolves on a pivot, for roasting coffee beans; or, a tin cylindrical perforated box which turned on a spit in front of the fire. Later roasters were made to be used on the range. *"Griswold;" "Burpee's Imperial;" etc.*

Fig. 276. COFFEE ROASTER. c. 1870s. Iron wood. L: 16"; W: 7½"; H: 2½". American. Courtesy Keillor Collection.

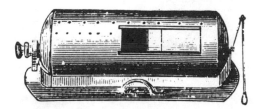

Fig. 277. COFFEE ROASTER. Sheet iron. F. A. Walker, c. 1870s.

Fig. 278. COFFEE ROASTER, for range. c. 1880s. Cast iron, iron, tin. 9" dia. Griswold Mfg. Co., Erie, Pa. Courtesy Keillor Collection.

Fig. 279. COFFEE ROASTER. Sheet iron. F. A. Walker, c. 1870s.

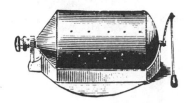

Fig. 280. COFFEE ROASTER. Tin. F. A. Walker, c. 1870s.

COFFIN — A pastry shell or mold for baked food.

COGGLING WHEEL — *see* JAGGER

COLANDER [*cullender*] — A bowled utensil of tin, graniteware, aluminum or earthenware, with ear handles, and closely perforated on the bottom (and sometimes the sides.) It is used as a sieve or strainer to separate the liquid part of substances from the solid. Some colanders have a little ring base, and some have three or four feet. If the ring is soldered or attached, it is called *foot fast;* if it is unattached, it is *foot loose.*

Fig. 281. COLANDER. F. A. Walker, c. 1870s.

Fig. 282. COLANDER. Pieced tin, tinned iron handles. 9¾", 11" dia. Matthai-Ingram Company, c. 1890.

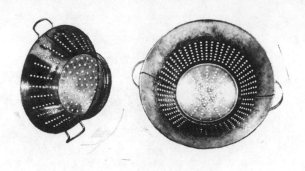

Fig. 283. COLANDERS. c. 1890s. Tin. 9¾" dia. x H: 3¾"; 12" dia. x H: 4¼". American. Courtesy Mary Mac Franklin.

Fig. 287. COLANDER, foot loose. Stamped tin. From 9-7/8" to 13" dia. Matthai-Ingram Company, c. 1890.

COMBINATION DIPPER — Essentially a funnel with a lot of screwed-on, or set-in attachments. It was used for sprinkling clothes, straining tea or coffee, as a pint measure, for baking small cakes with a tube or spout formed by the funnel, as a colander or coarse strainer, and for poaching eggs. In the Pennsylvania Dutch country it was and is used for making *drechterkuche* or funnel cakes. A batter is made of approximately 4 eggs, 4 cups of milk, 4 cups of flour, 2 tablespoons of sugar and a bit of salt and baking soda. The batter should run through the funnel rather slowly as it is moved in twists and turns over a kettle of boiling lard. The funnel cakes are brown almost immediately and are taken out, drained on paper, and sprinkled with powdered sugar.

Fig. 284. COLANDER. Stamped tin. F. A. Walker, c. 1870s.

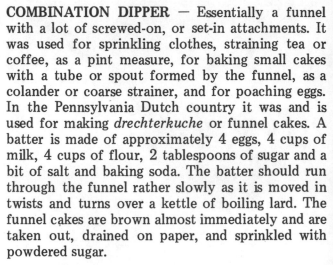

Fig. 288. COMBINATION FUNNEL-DIPPER. c. 1890s. Tin. 6 parts. L: 8½"; W: 4-3/8"; H: 5¼". American. Author's Collection.

Fig. 285. COLANDER STRAINER. Androck, 1936.

Fig. 286. COLANDER, foot fast. Stamped tin. From 9-7/8" to 13" dia. Matthai-Ingram Company, c. 1890.

Fig. 289. COMBINATION DIPPER. F. W. Seastrand, c. 1912.

COMFIT PAN — A large shallow pan of tin or enameled ware with a flat bottom, and sometimes fitted with a mesh rack or tray. It is also called a *crystallizing pan*.

Comfits

These are small seeds preserved in sugar. Sift the seeds in a hair sieve; put them in the comfit pan, and rub well about the bottom until warm; boil clarified loaf sugar; pour over the seeds about 2 tablespoons; rub and shake about the pan, until dry; give another charge and repeat the above process; give 4 or 5 charges, increasing the amount of syrup each time, dusting flour over them before the last charge; sift them in a hair sieve; put them again in the pan and proceed as before until the required size. [*Treasure House*, 1891]

CONJURER or PATENT CONJURER — "A very useful and valuable machine is recommended to the public as a cheaper and more expeditious way of cooking and boiling water.... A kettle of water may be boiled in six minutes, with a sheet of paper, a few shavings, or any combustible.... It will cook a steak very nicely in three minutes, also veal cutlets, mutton chops, hash meats, etc...." (*Advertisement* from a 1797 newspaper.)

The conjurer, and other little stoves which required a small amount of fuel, were especially adaptable for use on shipboard, in camp, or even in travelling carriages. They were often referred to as "ships' hearths."

"The real and first inventor" (*ibid.*) was claimed to be a man named Lloyd in London. Whether it was Lloyd or James Tate, William Whittington, Stephen Beck or another prolific English inventor of the late 18th century, we do not know. Tate, Whittington and Beck all received a number of patents for ship's hearths or stoves.

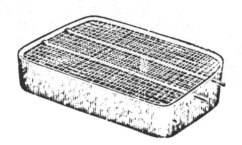

Fig. 290. CONFECTIONER'S CRYSTALIZING PAN. Steel, wire. 11" x 16" x 2½". Matthai-Ingram Company, c. 1890.

Fig. 291. BAKING a cake. Shows a coal hod, tea kettle, & range. Glenwood & Elmwood Ranges & Parlor Stoves advertising trade card. 3½" x 5¼". 1883. Author's Collection.

Fig. 292. COOKING IN CAMP. From a photograph postcard, c. 1910. Author's Collection.

Fig. 293. COOKING in a pot or cauldron suspended from a crane. To the left is a coffee urn. "Friday" Dillworth Coffee Advertising trade card. 2-7/16" x 3-5/16". 1880s. Author's Collection.

COOK — To prepare food for eating by one or more of a number of processes including baking, broiling, roasting, grilling, boiling, braising, frying, steaming, simmering, scalding, parboiling, stewing, poaching or toasting. All these processes obviously involve subjecting the food to heat: cooked food does not, however, have to be eaten hot. *Cookery* involves many more food-preparation methods than cooking with heat. Subjecting food to cold temperatures (admittedly this is often after cooking) is one method. Freezing preserves some foods and makes new dishes out of others — as with ice cream. Marinating and pickling subject the food to some degree of chemical or physical change aimed at preserving it. Smoking might be considered a method of cooking, but it is almost as indirect as drying buffalo jerky in the prairie sun. I believe a distinction can be made between cooking and preserving methods: to cook food is to prepare it for eating shortly after cooking. To preserve food is to prepare it so that it may be eaten when needed. Baked sea biscuits and hearth cakes were baked for preserving.

The word *cook* is related etymologically to a number of English words including *apricot*, *biscuit*, *concoction*, *kiln*, and *kitchen*, but not directly related to either *cake* or *cookie*.

COOKBOOKS — Not every housewife had a cookbook, or needed one, or would have been able to read it if she had. But by the end of the 18th century there were a number of cookbooks available in America. Probably the first two cookbooks of American authorship were *The Frugal Housewife; or, Complete Woman Cook* by Susanna Carter, Philadelphia, 1796; and *American Cookery, or the Art of Dressing Viands, Fish, Poultry and Vegetables, and the Best Modes of Making Puff-pastes, Pies, Tarts, Puddings, Custards and Preserves, and all Kinds of Cakes, from the Imperial Plumb to Plain Cake – Adapted to This Country, and All Grades of Life* by Amelia Simmons, Hartford, Connecticut, 1796. Amelia described herself as an "American orphan," but her book was probably less an original American work than an edited transcription from an English cookery book.

A large number of English cookbooks were available to, and probably owned by, American housewives in the 18th century. These included *The British Housewife...* by Mrs. Martha Bradley, 176-?; and *The Compleat Housewife; or, Accomplished Gentlewoman's Companion* by Elizabeth Smith, 1727, which was published in Williamsburg, Virginia in 1742, and as such was probably the first cookbook actually printed in the British American colonies. Three other cookbooks were favorites: *The Art of Cookery Made Plain and Easy* by Hannah Glasse, 1747; *The House-keeper's Pocket-book, and Compleat Family Cook* by Mrs. Sarah Harrison, 1733; and *The Experienced English Housekeeper* by Elizabeth Raffald, 1769.

Certainly not many servant-cooks of the 18th century in America could read, and it was the lady of the house or her housekeeper who took the treasured cookbook, or the copybook of transcribed favorites, out or down to the kitchen to instruct the cook in some new dish.

Later cookbooks, from the middle to the end of the 19th century, were widely distributed, and studied for their expert advice on domestic economy, marketing, and preparing food. The most well-known of the authors are Catherine Beecher and Harriet Beecher Stowe; Maria Parloa, who founded the Boston Original Cooking School; Isabella Beeton; Marion Harland; and Sarah Tyson Rorer of the *Ladies Home Journal*. Perhaps the most famous of all the first ladies of food is and was Fannie Farmer, who went to the Boston Cooking School to learn to be a cooking teacher, and graduated at the age of thirty-two. Her book, *Boston Cooking School Cook Book*, was a celebrated attempt to give the world a scientific cookbook with exact, and therefore always duplicatible, measurements. Fannie wrote six other cookbooks in the early 20th century, and a regular column for *Woman's Home Companion*.

COOKIE CUTTER — *see* **CAKE, COOKIE CUTTER**

COOKIE PRESS — A small tin and wood hand press, similar to a sausage stuffer or a frosting tube, used for making decorative drop cookies or butter pats. Another sort is similar to a butter print and forms the cookie and impresses it with a design.

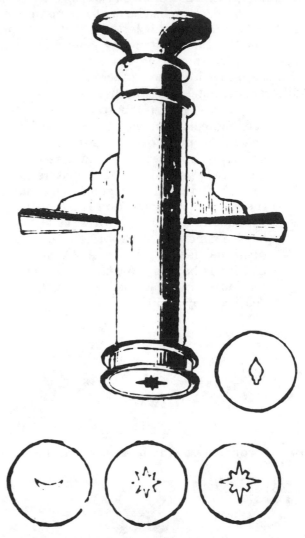

Fig. 294. JUMBLE MOLD, BUTTER PRESS. Tin. F. A. Walker, c. 1870s.

COOKIE SHEET — A flat sheet of tin or iron, usually with a very low raised edge, for baking cookies in the oven.

COPPER — A very malleable, ductile reddish or pinkish metal found in various ores. Compounded with other metals it forms babitt metal, bell metal, brass, britannia, nickel silver, German silver; that is, both yellow and white metals.

> The Chinese are known to possess the secret of manufacturing copper utensils perfectly white.... the discovery of this secret would be important for the arts in the United States as copper abounds in

them, and ought to be attempted by the medical gentlemen on board the Canton Ships. [*Willich*, 1821]
See also **VERDIGRIS**

CORER — A tin or steel instrument, with a cylinder of fairly small diameter having a sharp, truncated cutting end. It is used for coring apples, tomatoes, etc. The corers had either a T-handle, a wooden knob, or no handle at all. Some were made with a long, sharpened slot, and that made parers of them. Another type, nearly identical, was a tin tube, slightly smaller at one end than the other, and sharp-edged on the smaller end. These came in different diameters and lengths.

Tomatoe Butter

Peel and cut 25 pounds of tomatoes into halves and press out the seeds. Allow 8 pounds of apples, peeled and cored, and quartered. Weigh the whole mixture and to each pound allow ½ pound sugar and the juice of ½ lemon. Boil the tomatoes and apples together, stirring until you have a smooth, thick paste. Add the sugar and lemon juice, boil 20 minutes and it will be ready to can. Bake some of the butter in a pie shell. [*Ladies Home Journal*, May 1900]

Fig. 297. CORER. c. 1890s. Tin, wood. L: 6¼". American. Author's Collection.

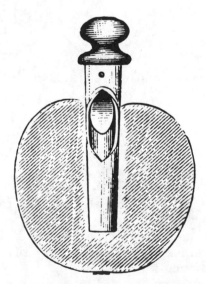

Fig. 295. CORER. 1880 to 1900. Tin. L: 6". American. Author's Collection.

Fig. 298. APPLE CORERS. Tin tubes. Different sizes for different apples. Practical Housekeeping, 1881.

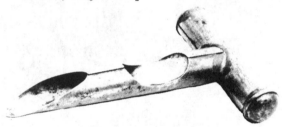

Fig. 296. GEM APPLE CORER. Tin, wood. "The Gem Apple Corer has a patent wood handle and a blade inside of tube which enables the core to be taken out, leaving a bottom in the apple like a cup. It will take out the entire core if desired." Matthai-Ingram Company, c. 1890.

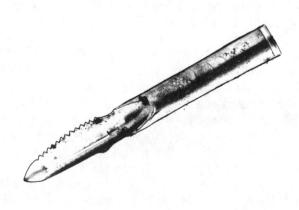

Fig. 299. PEELER & CORER. Pat'd 1937. Heavy tin. L: 5". Real-A-Peel, Tarrson Co., Chicago. Author's Collection.

Fig. 300. COMBINATION PARER & CORER. Two parts. Pat'd 12/30/1913. Tin, wood. L: 9½". Dandy. American. Author's Collection.

Fig. 301. APPLE CORER & PARER. Stainless steel, wood. L: 6½". A & J. Edward Katzinger Company, 1940.

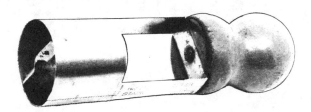

Fig. 302. CORER. c. 1935. Stainless steel, wood. 4¾" x 1¼". The Perfect Corer, Kitchen Novelty Co., Atlantic City, N.J. Author's Collection.

CORK — The bark of the cork-oak, which was used for stoppers and plugs. *Monbin, nyssa, licorice* roots were all used for the same things. "When corks are too large to go into a bottle, throw them into hot water for a few moments, and they will soften." (*Practical Housekeeping*, 1884.) *See also* **CORK PRESS**

CORK EXTRACTOR — A machine or device, usually worked by a lever, for removing corks from bottles. It was *not* a corkscrew.

CORK PRESS — (1) A levered mechanical device for putting corks securely in bottle mouths. (2) A cast iron, levered device for sizing soaked corks. This press can make six to eight different sizes. (3) A wooden cylinder which fits over the neck of the bottle, and a follower which pushes a cork into the bottle. This is also called a *cork driver*.

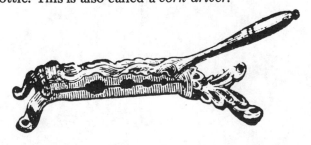

Fig. 303. CORK PRESS. Painted cast iron, wood. F. A. Walker, c. 1870s.

Fig. 304. CORK DRIVER. Pat'd Aug. 25, 1885. Wood. L: 11¾" (unextended); 2¼" dia. John Sommers, "Best Star of Bottling," Newark, N.J. Courtesy Keillor Collection.

CORK PULLER — A device to grab and hold a cork securely while it is withdrawn from the bottle. It could be either a levered mechanical device, or something simple — a grapple — which was held in the hand and which used elbow grease for motive power. *See also* **DISH CLOTH HOLDER**

Fig. 305. CORK PULL, DISH-CLOTH HOLDER, LAMP CHIMNEY CLOTH HOLDER. Wood, wire. Practical Housekeeping, 1881.

CORKSCREW — An instrument for drawing corks from bottles, which consists of a steel, spiral screw with a sharp point, and some sort of handle. The handle is usually transverse — T-shaped — although other types were common, such as a ring or hoop.

Folding pocket corkscrews were hinged at the meeting of the screw and handle, and the screw folded into the embrace of the hooped handle. Many advertising corkscrews of the late 19th century had a protective wooden tube, threaded on the inside, into which the corkscrew could be screwed. Some corkscrews had a loose ring which fit over the bottle's neck, and had as part of that ring a wire cutter. A brush for cleaning cellar dust from the bottle and its cork was often incorporated in one end of the T-handle.

M. L. Byrn of New York City was granted the first U.S. corkscrew patent, No. 27,615, in 1860. But corkscrews date from at least the beginning of the 15th century, and probably the Romans had them. "*Davis Pocket;*" "*Seely's Flavoring Extracts;*" "*Walker's Self-Pulling;*" "*Williamson's;*" *etc.*

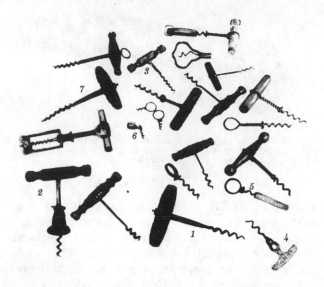

Fig. 306. CORKSCREWS. 1870s - 1920s. (1) Turned wood, steel. 6" L. 4" W. Belonged to my grandfather, Charles McRee Wilson. (2) Wood, steel. Pat'd Aug. 10, 1887. 5¾" L. 4½" W. Williamson Co., Newark N.J. (3) Wood, steel. 3-7/8", L. 3-1/8" W. Williamson's. (4) Nickel-plated steel. 3½" L. 2" W. LUND. London. (5) Pat'd 1890. "Solid steel advertising corkscrews. Printed to order by the thousand. L. H. Wentworth & Co., Novelty Dealers, Farmington, N. H." 4" L. as shown. (6) Tin, steel wire. Opens to 1½" L. Listerine. Both (1) and (7) were originally fitted with brushes to dust off corks before opening. The bristles were stuck in one end of the wooden handle. (2) has a wire cutter half way down the shaft. All author's collection.

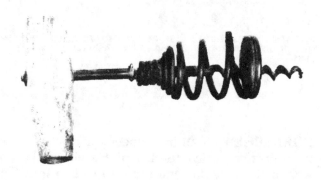

Fig. 307. CORKSCREW. c. 1920. Iron, wire, wood. L: 6". American. Author's Collection.

Fig. 308. LUND'S CORKSCREW. F. A. Walker, c. 1870s.

Fig. 309. CORKSCREWS. F. A. Walker, c. 1870s.

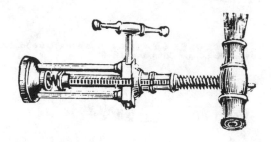

Fig. 310. CORKSCREW. Iron. F. A. Walker, c. 1870s.

Fig. 311. WIRE CUTTER. F. A. Walker, c. 1870s.

CORN DRYER — A wire or iron rack with about ten hooks or pins to stick with drying ears of corn. These could be hung up on the rafters, on the back porch, in the kitchen.

Fig. 312. CORN DRYER. Late-18th, early-19th century. Wrought iron. L: 19". American. Courtesy Keillor Collection.

Fig. 313. SEED-CORN TREE. Pat'd 1908, No. 878,271. James C. Blackford, Chicago Ill. Official Gazette, Feb. 4, 1908.

CORN GRATER — A coarse grater for removing the kernals from dried or fresh corn cobs.

CORN POPPER — "As reported in the Concord, New Hampshire *People and Patriot:*

'The First Cornpopper Laughed At'

In the winter of 1837, Mr. Francis P. Knowlton of Hopkinton, N.H., purchased of Mr. Amos Kelley a sheet of wire netting from his manufactory on the main road, and constructed the first cornpopper ever made. The various parts were cut the required shape and sewed together with wire. Mr. Knowlton then made some for Judge Harvey and Judge Chase, which they sent to various parts of the United States as curiosities. Thinking he could see a field of usefulness for the newly-conceived article, Mr. Knowlton made several and took them to Concord to a hardware store, hoping to introduce before the public a useful utensil and to receive a reasonable remuneration. His production was scorned and ridiculed by the proprietors and they refused to have anything to do with it.

He gave up and Mr. Amos Kelley began pressing them into shape out of wire and they slowly grew in favor. [*New York Times,* August 3, 1890]

Although it was reported in that article that the first cornpopper was presented to the Antiquarian Society, the Society reported in 1973 that they have never heard of Mr. Knowlton's cornpopper, and I fear that it has been lost forever. Anyway, cornpoppers have certainly increased in favor over the years, and for many years were the same basic design: a perforated tin, or wire-screen box with a long handle.

Popcorn Pudding

Pop some corn nicely, then roll it as fine as you can. One pint of corn to one quart of sweet milk; add a small piece of butter, 1 teaspoon salt, beat 2 eggs with enough sugar to sweeten the milk; mix

all together. Bake 20 minutes. [*The Housewife,* August 1904]

Fig. 314. CORN POPPER. c. 1910-1940. Wire mesh, steel wire, wood. L: 25"; W. 5-3/8"; H: 1-7/8". American. Author's Collection.

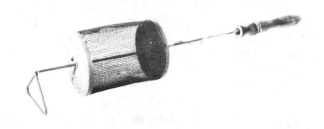

Fig. 315. CORN POPPER. c. 1870s, 1880s. Wire screen, tin, wood. L: 26½"; 4½" dia. American. Courtesy Keillor Collection.

CORRUGATED SPOON — A wire-rimmed spoon, the bowl of which is a corrugated piece of metal. It was used for egg-beating.

Fig. 316. CORRUGATED SPOON. Metal. "While not equal to the improved egg-beaters, they are several steps in advance of the old method." Practical Housekeeping, 1881.

COTTER POLE — *see* **TRAMMEL**

CRACKER STAMP, —— **TAMP** — An iron stamp for pressing punctured designs or initials on crackers before baking. *See also* **BEATEN BISCUIT MACHINE**

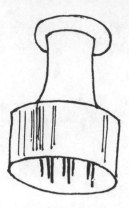

Fig. 317. CRACKER STAMP.

Fig. 319. CREAM WHIP. c. 1890s. Tin, cast iron, wood. L: 6"; W: 4½"; H: 8". Fries. Courtesy Keillor Collection.

CRANE — A wrought-iron bar, well supported at the pivot end with a strong bracket, and which could be swung in and out of the open fireplace: the support of pots, kettles, griddles, etc., hung from it. The crane was an advance from the *lug pole*, which was placed in a fixed position in the chimney. The pots were hung from the crane at any level by means of adjustable trammels, trammel chains or pot hooks. *See also* **LUG POLE**

Fig. 320. CREAM WHIPPER & EGG BEATER. c. 1935. Glass, stainless steel, wood. H: 5½"; W: 3½". Androck. Courtesy Paul Persoff.

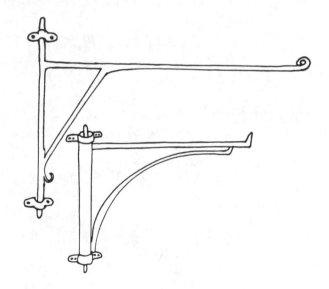

Fig. 318. CRANES.

CRASH — A coarse, very absorbent linen or cotton cloth used for kitchen towels. It was also used for straining fruits for jellies. It was sometimes called *glass towelling* because it was used for drying dishes.

CREAM WHIP or SYLABUB CHURN — A small cylinder with a perforated dasher which served as an egg beater or a cream whipper. Nothing could whip up a high froth like a cream whip. *Same as* whip churn. *See also* **SYLABUB CHURN**

Fig. 321. TURBINE CREAM WHIP. Androck, 1936.

CRIBBLE — A sieve, colander or strainer for flour or meal. Also, that which is left in the sieve after the fine flour is sifted out: that is, the bran or coarse meal, also called *shorts*. Cribble bread is therefore whole wheat bread. *See also* MIDDLINGS

CROQUETTE MOLD — A tin mold used for shaping croquettes of chicken, ham or veal. *See also* CUTLET MOLD

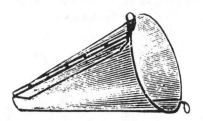

Fig. 322. CROQUETTE MOLD. F. A. Walker flyer, c. 1880.

CROUT CUTTER — *see* CABBAGE CUTTER

CRULLER FRYER — *see* POTATO FRYER

CRUMB KNIFE — *see* TELLAR KNIFE

CUCUMBER SLICER — A wooden board, fitted with a diagonal, removable sharp blade, and an opening under the blade. The cucumber is passed over the blade and the slices fall through. It is identical, except in size, to the cabbage cutter.

CUP-SWAB — "In washing tea things, it is a great saving of the hands to use a little cup-swab or mop, such as are made by the society of Shakers, with woolen or thrum on the end." (*Leslie*, 1840.) A cup-swab is a little dish mop of twisted wire, into which was twisted wool or cotton yarn. Thrum is the waste yarn left on the loom, or the fringe of warp threads. *See also* SWAB

CURD KNIFE — A long, rectangular frame with many cutting blades going either crosswise or lengthwise. Used for cutting the curds into fine pieces during cheesemaking.

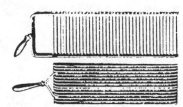

Fig. 323. CURD KNIVES. Wood handles, steel blades. Horizontal blades: W: 4, 6, 8, 10, 12"; L: 20". Perpendicular blades: 6, 8, 10, 12, 14, 15, 20"; L: 20". Montgomery Ward, 1895.

CURD WHIPPER — A long implement with four or five, inch-wide, spring steel blades fastened to a wooden handle. Used for breaking the curds into small pieces.

Fig. 324. CHEESE CURD WHIPPER. c. 1880s. Spring steel, wood. L: 24½". American. Courtesy Keillor Collection.

CURFEW — From the French *couvre-feu*, or fire-cover. A large, semi-circular or quarter-sphere, domed cover of sheet brass, copper or iron, with a handle. It was used to cover the glowing embers of a wood fire at night, and was pushed to the back of the fireplace thereby cutting off the supply of air. In the morning the curfew was removed and the fire could be quickly restarted with a few puffs of the bellows.

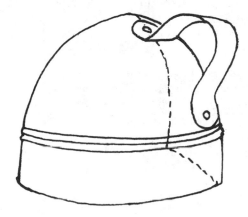

Fig. 325. CURFEW.

CUSTARD KETTLE — A double boiler, "made of iron with another kettle inside, the latter lined with tin." (*Practical Housekeeping* 1884.)

Fig. 326. CUSTARD KETTLE. Outer kettle is iron, inner kettle is block tin. Practical Housekeeping, 1881.

CUTLET BAT — A wooden mallet for beating on a "tough cutlet." (*Goodholme*, 1877.) *See also* **BEETLE**

CUTLET MOLD — A small, shallow tin mold, shaped like a lamb chop or a drumstick, for forming cutlets of chicken, veal, or ham. Croquettes were formed in cylinders, cones, balls or cutlets. A real cutlet has a bone, and a cutlet bat is for real, and tough, cutlets. But the molded cutlet is composed of minced meat, spices, onion and egg, and is tasty and nicely decorated with a chop frill.

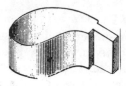

Fig. 327. CUTLET CUTTERS. Tin. F. A. Walker, 1886.

Fig. 328. LEG OF MUTTON MOLD. Tin. F. A. Walker, 1886.

CUTTING BOARD — A hardwood board for cutting meat or bread. The board for meat may have a shallow trough, or several grooves to catch the gravy. The bread board, if round, was sometimes used as a lid for stoneware crocks. It often had a carved border of flowers or a motto such as "Give us this day our daily bread."

DANGLE SPIT — A group of hooks suspended by a cord, the winding and unwinding of which provided some rotary movement for the meat on the hooks. Some of these had a pair of wings or governors which assisted the winding and unwinding. *See also* **BOTTLE JACK**

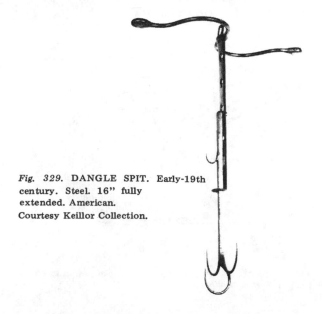

Fig. 329. DANGLE SPIT. Early-19th century. Steel. 16" fully extended. American. Courtesy Keillor Collection.

DARIEL [*daryel*] MOLD — A small tin mold for making a sort of egg custard called *dariels*. The molds are called *tin dariels* or *individual jelly cups* in the ca. 1870 *F. A. Walker Catalog*. A 14th century recipe for dariel called for milk, eggs, saffron, sugar and salt. (*The Forme of Cury*.)

There is a lot of confusion about whether a *dariel* and a *dariole* are the same thing. In the eminently satisfying *Oxford English Dictionary*, *dariel* is given as a variant for *dariole*. I would like to make a distinction, or at least to record one. Read the next entry and make up your own mind.

Fig. 330. DARIEL CUP. F. A. Walker flyer, c. 1880.

DARIOLE MOLD — A plain or fluted, stamped or pressed, metal mold for "baking cakes and corn muffins as well as timbales, etc.. Two qualities. Several sizes, smallest about $1.25 a dozen. Some come from France." (*Parloa*, 1887.) The *Oxford English Dictionary* defines a dariole as a small pasty filled with meat, herbs and spices in the 14th century, and then a light cream tart or custard-filled pasty in later centuries. *Webster's Second International Dictionary* defines a madeline cake as a dariole. Mrs. Beeton, in 1872, gave several dariole recipes, one of which called for coating the mold with a thin aspic, and another for coating the mold with butter and sprinkling with crumbs. *See also* **MOLDS**

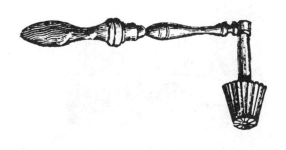

Fig. 331. DARIEL or DARIOLE MOLD. Cast iron, wood. F. A. Walker, c. 1870s.

DEEP FAT BASKET, — FRY BASKET — A woven wire basket, round, square or oblong, for suspending food to be deep-fried in a kettle of hot or boiling fat. With either one long handle or two smaller handles, which served to support it on the rim of the kettle of fat.

One type, called a *bird's nest basket*, had two wire baskets, one slightly smaller than the other, both with long handles. "Shredded potatoes were arranged in the larger basket. The smaller basket fit into that and was filled with potato balls. The baskets were immersed in hot fat, and when the potatoes were cooked, the smaller basket was lifted from the larger, the nest carefully taken from the basket and the balls turned into it." (*Ladies Home Journal*, January, 1900.) *See also* FRYING KETTLE; POTATO, CRULLER FRYER

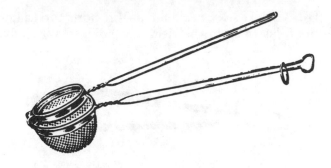

Fig. 334. BIRD NEST FRYER. Tinned wire. Outside bowl, 3¼" or 4" dia. Androck, 1936.

Fig. 332. FRY BASKET. Tinned ware. 7" to 10" dia.; 3-3/8" to 4¾" deep. Androck, 1936.

BERRY WASHER

KETTLE BOTTOM

Fig. 333. FRY BASKET, BERRY WASHER, KETTLE BOTTOM, BROILER. Coarse or fine mesh. 7", 8" dia. F. W. Seastrand, c. 1912.

DEMIJOHN — From the French *dame-jeanne*. A large bottle, of glass or earthenware, with a bulging body and narrow neck, most often encased in wicker or rushwork, and with one or two ear handles. Miss Eliza Leslie in 1840 declared them useful for vinegar and molasses.

DIGESTER — A vessel (first made of cast brass) into which is put meat and water. A lid is closely screwed or fastened on. Over a moderate fire, the meat is reduced to a pulp in six to eight minutes. Some digesters had a safety valve, but were nevertheless exceedingly dangerous. "A strong close vessel in which bones or other substances may be subjected to the action of water or other liquid at a temperature and pressure above those of the boiling point, so as to be dissolved. Originally called from its inventor: *Papin's Digestor*, and dates from 1681." (*Oxford English Dictionary*.)

Denys Papin, a Fellow of the Royal Society in England, said of his invention: "the oldest and hardest cow-beef may be made as tender and as savoury as young and choice meat." (*Abridgments*, 1873.)

Fig. 335. SOUP DIGESTER. Planished tin. F. A. Walker, c. 1870s.

DINNER HORN — A simple tin horn for calling the folks in from the field when dinner was ready.

Fig. 336. DINNER HORN with double call. Pieced tinware. L: 14". Matthai-Ingram Company, c. 1890.

DIPPER — Essentially a cup or bowl with a long handle. The handle usually sticks up straight (or nearly so) from the rim. The dipper was for dipping water or milk, and is like a ladle, although you will never hear of a "punch dipper." *Ladle* and *dipper* are both Old English words, but *ladle* was used 800 years before *dipper*.

Dippers are made of iron, tin, enamelled ware, wood, gourd, aluminum, brass, etc. *See also* **COCOA-DIPPER, LADLE**

Fig. 337. DIPPER. 19th century. Iron, wood. L: 18"; W: 7". American. Courtesy Rita Keillor Collection.

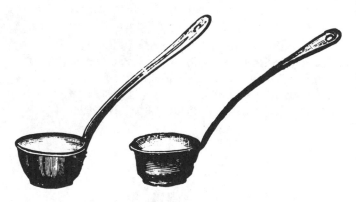

Fig. 338. CUP DIPPERS. Stamped tin. (Right) forged handle. (left) threaded handles. From 4" to 5-1/8" dia. Matthai-Ingram Company, c. 1890.

Fig. 339. DIPPER. Tin. 2 qts. (Probably Matthai-Ingram.) Butler Brothers, 1899.

Fig. 340. DIPPERS. Agate enameled ware, wood. Bowls: 4½" x 3" to 6¾" x 3¾". Lalance & Grosjean, 1890.

DISH CLOTH HOLDER — A wire implement with three or four "fingers" which pinch and hold a dishcloth when a ring is slipped down around the wires. The holder has a long handle, and was also sold as a lamp-chimney-cloth holder and a cork puller, but surprisingly not as a pickle grapple. Some were shorter and sturdier than others and were probably better for dishes and corks, while the longer, more flexible ones would have been better for cleaning kerosene lamps.

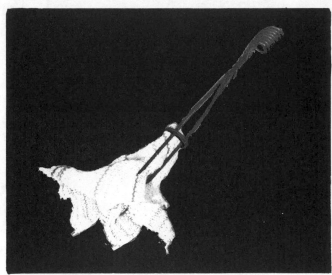

Fig. 341. DISH RAG HOLDER. c. 1890. Iron wire. L: 10¾". American. Courtesy Keillor Collection.

DISH CLOTH (WIRE MESH) — *see* **POT CLEANER**

DISHCOVERS — (1) Wire mesh covers which are domed; also called *fly screens*. They were available in a number of graded sizes, round or oval, and the metal rims were japanned in red, green or blue. They were set over dishes of food on the table. (2) Flat, block-tin covers used for saucepans or kettles. (3) Domed tin (or other metal) covers used to keep food hot on serving platters or dishes.

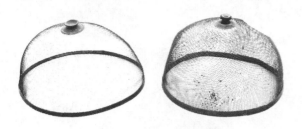

Fig. 342. DISH COVERS or FLY SCREENS. 1870s to 1910. Iron wire, japanned tin rims. H: 5", 7½"; 7¼" dia. American. Author's Collection.

DISH DRAINER — A wirework, or wooden-dowel, or perforated-metal rack for holding dishes and flatware during rinsing, after washing, and before (or instead of) wiping. Most had specially spaced wires or pins for supporting plates in an on-edge position. Some had flat bottoms and could be used as bread coolers. "The Ford Dish Drainer consists of two separate articles — a neat, strong wire basket, with a smaller basket inside, and a drip pan. The smaller dishes are set on edge in the small basket, and the longer ones between the two, there being space enough below the basket in the drip-pan to hold the water which drains off.... This drain was the invention of a woman, and its convenience shows that she knew what she wanted." (*Practical Housekeeping*, 1884.)

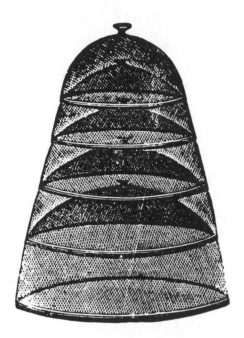

Fig. 343. WIRE DISH COVERS. Blue-japanned tin, wire. Oval or round. Oval: 8" to 18"; Round: 6" to 14". Matthai-Ingram Company, c. 1890.

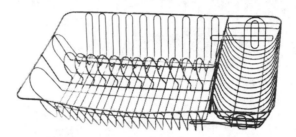

Fig. 345. DISH DRAINER. c. 1910. Wire. L: 18¾"; W: 12"; H: 3-7/8". Probably Marlboro Wire Goods Co. (See Toy Dish Drainer.) American. Author's Collection.

Fig. 346. DISH DRAINER. c. 1890. Wooden dowels, wood, rubber feet. L: 17¾"; W. 11½"; H: 2¾". American. Author's Collection.

Fig. 344. DISH COVERS. Planished tin. F. A. Walker, c. 1870s.

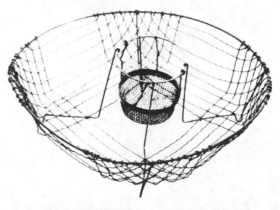

Fig. 347. DISH DRAINER. 1890 to 1920. Wire. 15" dia.; H: 5¼". American. Author's Collection.

Fig. 348. DISH DRAINER. Wire. Practical Housekeeping, 1881.

Fig. 349. DISH DRAINER. Androck, 1936.

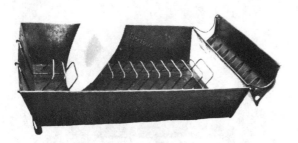

Fig. 350. DISH DRYER. c. 1930. Tin, wire. L: 19½"; W: 12"; H: 3-7/8". No. 199, Androck. Author's Collection.

Fig. 351. DISH DRYER. Charcoal (blackened) tin, wire. 18" x 11½". Androck, 1936.

DISH PAN — A large, deep pan with ear handles, made of tin or earthenware.

Fig. 352. DISH PAN. From IX (heavy) to IXXXX (ex-extra heavy) stamped tin. From 8 to 30 gallon. Matthai-Ingram Company, c. 1890.

DISH WARMER, PLATE WARMER — (1) A wireware rack for plates, to be set on top of the stove or range. It could also be used as a dish-drainer or cake cooler. (2) A sheet iron, open-fronted box with legs, in which plates were stacked, and set in front of the fire. This was the older type, and some may still be found that date from the early 18th century. *See also* **CARBONIZER, HOB**

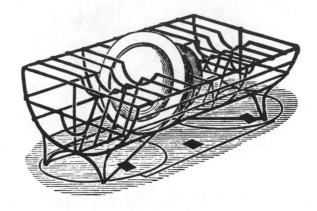

Fig. 353. DISH WARMER. Wire. For heating dishes on the top of a stove. Practical Housekeeping, 1881.

Fig. 354. PLATE WARMER. Early-19th century. Tin, cast iron. Courtesy William Hodges, Ridgefield Antiques, Charlottesville, Va.

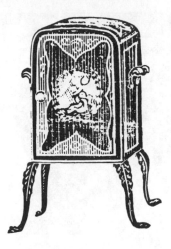

Fig. 355. PLATE WARMER. Heavy metal, cast iron legs, japanned "artistic finish." Matthai-Ingram Company, c. 1890.

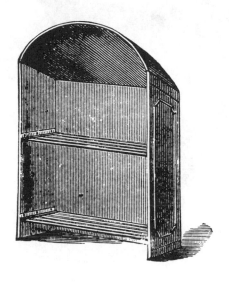

Fig. 356. PLATE WARMER. Tin. F. A. Walker, c. 1870s.

DISH-WASHER — The old ones, and they were available in the latter part of the 19th century, were four-legged, free-standing, large metal bins or tubs. They had lids, and racks inside for the dishes, and a cranked paddle-wheel, a drain and a hose hook-up. The Stevens Dish-Washer was advertised in 1891 as " the only dish-washing machine ever invented for the household and the only one in use in hundreds of homes.... Stevens Dish-Washing Machine Company, Cleveland." (*Ladies Home Journal*, August 1891.)

Personally I think the only way to wash dishes in the home is by hand, so I'm not convinced that those hundreds of households were happy with their Stevens. Christopher Morley presents a whole dishwashing philosophy in *The Haunted Bookshop.*

"But I am forgetting my duties as host," said Mifflin. "Our dessert consists of apple sauce, gingerbread, and coffee." He rapidly cleared the empty dishes from the table and brought on the second course.

"I have been noticing the warning over the sideboard," said Gilbert. "I hope you will let me help you this evening." He pointed to a card hanging near the kitchen door. It read:

ALWAYS WASH DISHES
IMMEDIATELY AFTER MEALS
IT SAVES TROUBLE

"I'm afraid I don't always obey that precept," said the bookseller as he poured the coffee. "Mrs. Mifflin hangs it there whenever she goes away, to remind me. But, as our friend Samuel Butler says, he that is stupid in little will also be stupid in much. I have a different theory about dish-washing, and I please myself by indulging it.

"I used to regard dish-washing merely as an ignoble chore, a kind of hateful discipline which had to be undergone with knitted brow and brazen fortitude. When my wife went away the first time, I erected a reading stand and an electric light over the sink, and used to read while my hands went automatically through base gestures of purification. I made the great spirits of literature partners of my sorrow, and learned by heart a good deal of *Paradise Lost* and of Walt Mason, while I soused and wallowed among pots and pans. I used to comfort myself with two lines of Keats:

'The moving waters at their
priest-like task
Of pure ablution round earth's
human shores----'

Then a new conception of the matter struck me. It is intolerable for a human being to go on doing any task as a penance, under duress. No matter what the work is, one must spiritualize it in some way, shatter the old idea of it into bits and rebuild it nearer to the heart's desire. How was I to do this with dish-washing?

"I broke a good many plates while I was pondering over the matter. Then it occured to me that here was just the relaxation I needed. I had been worrying over the mental strain of being surrounded all day long by vociferous books, crying out at me their conflicting views as to the glories and agonies of life. Why not make dish-washing my balm and poultice?

"When one views a stubborn fact from a new angle, it is amazing how all its contours and edges change shape! Immediately my dishpan began to glow with a kind of philosophic halo! The warm, soapy water became a sovereign medicine to retract hot blood from the head; the homely act of washing and drying cups and saucers became a symbol of the order and cleanliness that man imposes on the unruly world about him. I tore down my book rack and reading lamp from over

Fig. 357. DISH WASHING OUTSIDE! From a photograph postcard, c. 1910. Author's Collection.

the sink.

"Mr. Gilbert," he went on, "do not laugh at me when I tell you that I have evolved a whole kitchen philosophy of my own. I find the kitchen the shrine of our civilization, the focus of all that is comely in life. The ruddy shine of the stove is as beautiful as any sunset. A well-polished jug or spoon is as fair, as complete and beautiful, as any sonnet. The dish mop, properly rinsed and wrung and hung outside the back door to dry, is a whole sermon in itself. The stars never look so bright as they do from the kitchen door after the ice-box pan is emptied and the whole place is 'redd up,' as the Scotch say." [Christopher Morley, *The Haunted Bookshop*, 1923. By permission of J.B. Lippincott Company]

Fig. 359. PAN. Tin. F. A. Walker, c. 1870s.

Fig. 360. PLATE SCRAPERS. (Top) c. 1932. White rubber, painted handle. 5¾" x 2½". Daisy, Schacht Rubber Mfg. Co., Huntington, Ind. (Bottom) c. 1925. White rubber, tin, wood. 5¾" x 2½". WB/W. Author's Collection.

Fig. 358. WASHING DISHES. Unidentified periodical illustration, c. 1880s.

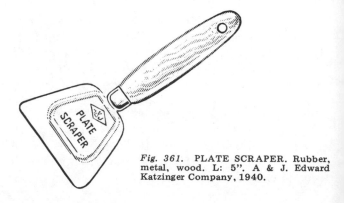

Fig. 361. PLATE SCRAPER. Rubber, metal, wood. L: 5". A & J. Edward Katzinger Company, 1940.

Fig. 362. KITCHEN CLEANER & POLISH DREDGER. 1928. Cardboard, tin. H: 5". Silver-Seal, Century Metalcraft Corp., Chicago, Ill. Author's Collection.

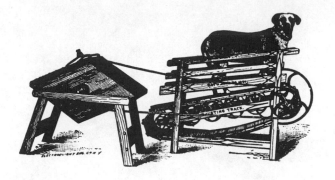

Fig. 364. DOG POWERED CHURN, Pat'd May 28, 1889, Oct. 27, 1891, Nov. 17, 1891. Diamond Balance Churn Co., c. 1891.

DISPATCH — "Joseph Rose has purchased a quantity of Tin Ware, amongst which are a large parcel of Dispatches, they are worthy of the name as they will cook a beef steak in about four minutes sufficiently to put on the table." (An *advertisement* in a 1779 New York newspaper.)

DIVIDED SAUCEPAN — *see* **SAUCEPAN**

DOGS — Not only did dogs lie about on the warm hearth, getting underfoot and chasing the cat, but the less fortunate ones were put to work in some kitchens. It is probable that few *dog spits* were used in America. The dog was put into a cage above the fireplace and made to run on a treadmill which turned the spit. Muscular short-legged dogs were the best for this purpose. Much more common was the dog-power *churn*, also operated by a treadmill. As the dog walked, the dasher was moved up and down. Lucky house dogs today don't do much beyond licking the supper plates.

DOUBLE BOILER — Two kettles, one inside the other, with room for boiling water in the larger, outer kettle. It was used to cook foods which would scorch or burn if cooked over direct heat. A *cereal cooker*, *farina boiler*, and a *milk boiler* are all double boilers.

"Double block tin kettle for stewing with all the water outside: an inner kettle, about 3 or 4" each way smaller than outer one, inside of which it is suspended by means of 2 small iron rings just below rim of smallest kettle and tied with twine to 2 corresponding rings placed in inside of large kettle — about 2 or 3" below top. Both have close lids and falling handles. Excellent for boiled custard; stewing apples. They are the same principle as the French *Bain Marie*." (*Leslie,* 1840.) "If you don't have all the modern conveniences for boiling custard, ie., one pail to set within the other — use a common iron kettle, put a stick across it, and hang a tin pail on the stick." (*Babcock,* 1881.) The later double boilers were typically of tin, and then aluminum, and the inner pan fit snugly inside the larger outer pan, and rested on its rim. This inner pan stood one or more inches above the other and required only one lid. *See also* **BAIN MARIE, FARINA BOILER**

Fig. 363. TWO-DOG CHURN. Montgomery Ward, 1895.

Fig. 365. CEREAL COOKER or FRUIT STEAMER. Montgomery Ward, 1895.

Fig. 366. DOUBLE BOILER. Mid-19th century. Iron, copper. 13½"
dia.; H: 16½". American. Courtesy Keillor Collection.

Fig. 367. DOUBLE BOILER. Aluminum. 2 qt. size. The Berdan Company, 1931.

Fig. 369. DOUGH MIXER & KNEADER. Tin, cast iron. Universal. Practical Housekeeping, 1881.

DOUGH-BOX — TRAY — A wooden box, or trough, which sometimes stood on its own frame, or sat on a table. Bread dough was mixed and kneaded in it, and left to rise. The box had a lid, which served to make the dough-box useful as a table or work surface.

DOUGHNUT CUTTER — A tin cutter with an inner and outer ring, and a handle. Another type (mentioned in *BISCUIT CUTTER*) was rolled across the dough leaving a trail of cut out doughnuts. Originally the doughnut was a fried dough ball.

Fig. 370. DOUGHNUT CUTTER. Tin. F. A. Walker, c. 1870s.

Fig. 368. KNEADING TROUGH in a bakery. Cyclopedia of Useful Arts & Manufacturers. Edited by Charles Tomlinson. New York, London: George Virtue, 1852, 1854. 2 Vol.

Fig. 371. FRENCH DOUGHNUT CUTTER. Stamped tin. 3", 4" dia. Matthai-Ingram Company, c. 1890.

DOUGH-BRAKE — A machine for kneading and mixing dough without using the hands. It consists of a metal pan and a cranked pair of large kneading blades. *See also* **BRAKE, BREAD MIXER**

DOUGH-KNEADER, -MAKER, -MIXER— "A pair of rollers, one corrugated lengthwise and the other transversely, working in a frame with two inclined boards." (*Knight*, 1874.) Also: the same as a bread-mixer: a pail with kneading paddles. *See also* **BEATEN BISCUIT MACHINE**

Fig. 372. DOUGHNUT CUTTER. c. 1915. Tin. L: 2½". American. Author's Collection.

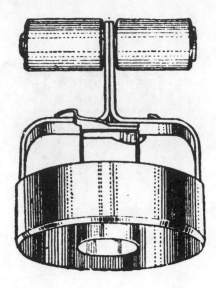

Fig. 375. SATURN FOOD & DOUGHNUT CUTTER. The Berdan Co., 1931.

Fig. 373. DOUGHNUT & PASTRY CUTTER. c. 1890. Tin, wire. L: 6½"; 3" dia. American. Author's Collection.

DOUGH-RIB — An iron or wooden implement for scraping and cleaning out the dough-box. See next entry.

DOUGH SCRAPER, — SCRAPE, — GRATER — A small iron hoe for scraping dough from the dough board, or the dough-box.

Fig. 376. DOUGH SCRAPER. 19th century. Wrought iron. L: 3¾"; W: 3". American. Courtesy Mary Mac Franklin.

DOUGH SPUR — *see* **JAGGER**

DOUGH-TROUGH — *see* **DOUGH-BOX**

DOWN HEARTH — The slab of stone or iron, or the bricks which form the floor of the fireplace, both inside and in front of. To prepare a meal "down hearth" is simply to cook it in front of, or over, a wood fire or embers in the fireplace.

Fig. 374. COMBINATION DOUGHNUT CUTTER & CORER. Two parts. c. 1905. Tin. 3-7/8" x 3". American. Author's Collection.

Journey Cake

Pour boiling water on a quart of meal, put in a little lard and salt, and mix it well; have an oak board with a rim of iron at the bottom, and an iron handle fastened to it that will prop it up to the fire; put some of the dough on it, dip your hand in cold water and smooth it over; score it with a knife, and set it before the coals to bake." [Elizabeth Lea, *Domestic Cookery*, 1859]

Johnny-Cake

Sift one quart of Indian meal into a pan; make a hole in the middle, and pour in a pint of warm water, adding one teaspoon of salt; with a spoon mix the meal and water gradually into a soft dough; stir it very briskly for a quarter of an hour or more, till it becomes light and spongy; then spread the dough smooth and evenly on a straight, flat board (a piece of the head of a flour-barrel will serve for this purpose); place the board nearly upright before an open fire, and put an iron against the back to support it; bake it well; when done, cut it in squares; send it hot to table, split and buttered. [Mary Stuart Smith, *Virginia Cookery-Book*, as it appeared in *Strohm*, 1888] *See also* **BANNOCK, HEARTH CAKE**

Fig. 377. FLOUR DREDGER. Tin. F. A. Walker, c. 1870s.

Fig. 378-A. PEPPER BOX. Planished or japanned tin. F. A. Walker, c. 1870s.

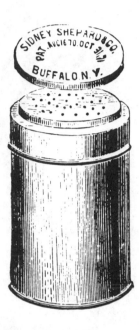

Fig. 378-B. DREDGER SPICE CAN. Pat'd Aug. 16, 1870, Oct. 31, 1871. Tin. 1-5/8" x 2½" to 2½" x 2½" x 4". Sidney Shepard & Co., Buffalo Stamping Works, c. 1872.

DREDGER, DREDGE, DREDGING BOX, or DRUDGER — A metal container with a close lid perforated with a number of fine or coarse holes for salt, pepper, flour and sugar. "Two kinds — English have concave covers and come in the best of tin. Flat dredgers, of common tin, usually are badly finished. They are often Japanned. Serve well for pepper. Always have a rather small salt dredger, and have the pepper dredger of the smallest size in Japanned ware. This will reduce the chances of choosing the wrong one." (*Parloa*, 1887.) "A box with holes in top, used to sift or scatter flour on meat when roasting." (*Beecher and Stowe*, 1869.)

It was believed that floured meats lasted longer, and it did make a nice gravy. After a roast was turned and done on the spit, it was dredged with flour and turned a few times more to make a bubbly gravy or froth just before serving up. Make your mouth water?

Fig. 379. DREDGER. c. 1890s. Pale green glass, tin. H: 6"; W: 3¼". Flat on one side to push against wall or stove back. "2107-3" molded in bottom. American. Author's Collection.

Fig. 380. DREDGE BOX. Tin or japanned tin. F. A. Walker, c. 1870s.

Fig. 381. FLOUR DREDGE. Planished tin. 5" x 2½", 6" x 3". Lalance & Grosjean, 1890.

DRESSER — Originally a table on which meat was dressed or prepared for the table. Later, shelves were added above and cupboards below — for the storage of plates and serving pieces, and linens. "Strips of leather, nailed around the edge of dresser shelves are very convenient receptacles for spoons or similar utensils in constant use." (*Leslie*, 1840.)

Fig. 382. "WELSH" DRESSER.

Fig. 383. SPOON HOLDER. Leather strip tacked to shelf edge.

Fig. 384. KITCHEN-DRESSER. Pat'd July 26, 1887, by John Roth, Chicago, Illinois.

DRINK MIXER, LIQUID MIXER — An egg beater, or something quite similar, but either larger or smaller. *See also* EGG BEATER

Fig. 385. SILVER EGG BEATER, United Profit Sharing, 1914.

Fig. 386. LIQUID MIXER. Pat'd 3/30/15. Glass, iron, tin, wood. Archimedean screw action. H: 16"; 3½" dia. 30 oz. capacity. Trademark shown near lid. American. Author's Collection.

Fig. 388. EGG BEATER or MIXER. Pat'd June 11, 1907. Green glass, cast iron, tin. 3-7/8" dia.; H: 12". Standard Specialty Co., Milwaukee, Wisconsin. Root Mason jar. Author's Collection.

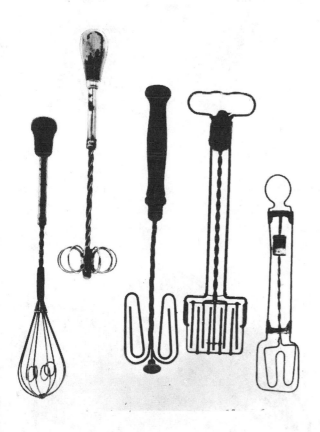

Fig. 389. EGG BEATER or LIQUID MIXER. c. 1929. Glass, nickeled iron. H: 11¼"; 3¾" x 3¾". One quart capacity. Even Full, New Keystone Beater, Culinary Utilities Co., NY. Author's Collection.

Fig. 387. EGG BEATERS & LIQUID MIXERS. All Archimedean screw movement. Left to right: (1) Tin, wood, wire. L: 12¼". Made in Germany. (2) Tin, wood, wire. L: 11". Made in England. (3) October, 1907. Wire, wood. L: 12½". A & J. (4) April 10, 190-? Wire. L: 11¾". The Up To Date Egg & Cream Whip. (5) Wire. L: 9¼". Horlick's. Author's Collection.

DRIPPING PAN — A rectangular, shallow tin or iron pan for catching fat drippings under roasting meat. Used under the spit, in the oven, in a reflecting oven roaster. Old recipes often say to bake bread and biscuits in the dripping pan, *after* it has been cleaned. Nothing was more necessary than a pan to keep the fats and precious juices from dripping on the hearth and being lost. Fat that was not used for basting with a spoon or ladle was made into gravy, or poured into a save-all to be clarified and made into tapers or soap.

Fig. 390. DRIPPING PANS. 35 different sizes from 6" x 9" and 18" x 19". Matthai-Ingram Company, c. 1890.

DUTCH CROWN — A band of wrought iron, fitted with hooks, and with arched stretchers. It was used for suspending game or birds in the larder. It was also called a *pot crown* and used for hanging utensils and implements in the kitchen.

Fig. 391. DUTCH CROWN. 18th century. Wrought iron. H: 8"; W: 8½". American. Courtesy Keillor Collection.

DUTCH OVEN, BAKE KETTLE, BAKE OVEN — An "iron kettle with a heavy, tight-fitting lid. This is often used for outdoor cooking, and during the war the soldiers were delighted to get possession of one of these ovens to bake their pork and beans in, or their corn bread or pone. The oven was lowered into the ground, level with the top, and the lid covered with live coals. There is no oven which bakes pork and beans and imparts the same delicious flavor, especially when the appetite has been sharpened by outdoor work or sport and a moderate degree of fasting." (*Practical Housekeeping*, 1884.)

The distinguishing feature of the dutch oven is the lid, the edge of which is turned up as much as an inch, in order to retain the hot coals piled on it when the pot is standing in the embers. It also had a bail handle and the older ones had three legs which were long enough to hold it above the embers. It really served as an oven, as it baked evenly from below and above.

A reasonable explanation for the name is given by Louise Peet and Lenore Sater in *Household Equipment*, 1940. "Dutch ovens were brought to America by the Pilgrims. As is well known, the Pilgrims spent some years in Holland before coming to America. The *Mayflower* was a tiny vessel and baggage limited. The dutch oven could be used for such a variety of cookery that it took the place of several other pots and pans and was, therefore, a favorite utensil of the early settlers."

Fig. 392. DUTCH OVEN. Cast iron. Practical Housekeeping, 1881.

Fig. 393. BAKE or DUTCH OVEN. Cast iron. 10", 11", 12", or 14" dia. "Designed for camp use; can be set in center of wood fire without injury to contents." Montgomery Ward, 1895.

EARTHENWARE — Utensils and vessels made of a low-fired clay, and finished with a soft and porous glaze. Such earthenware was used for baking dishes and casseroles (or other utensils used for low-temperature cooking), and for plates, bowls and crocks. These utensils were fashioned after 17th and 18th century pottery of the Dutch, English and German ancestors of the potters.

During the 18th century, *earthenware* often referred to the cream-colored *Queensware* (first made by Wedgwood) which was imported from Nottingham, Stafford and Kent in England and used on thousands of American tables. An advertisement in the late 18th century listed these "Earthenwares. Egyptian, Etruscan, embossed red China, agate, green, black, colliflower, white, and blue and white stone, enamelled, striped, fluted, pierced, and plain." (Alfred Coxe Prime, *The Arts and Crafts in Philadelphia, Maryland, and South Carolina 1721-1785*, 1929.)

Households, particularly farm houses, were supplied with earthenware by potters and potteries all over the country from the earliest colonial times to the Civil War, at which time china, glass and tinware displaced it. *See also* **QUEENSWARE, SALT GLAZE**

EGG BAKER — A two-handled earthenware or enameled ware dish for baked or shirred eggs. The capacity varied from one to twelve eggs.

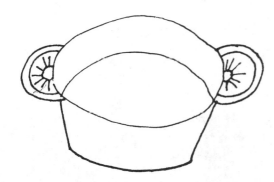

Fig. 394. EGG BAKER. Earthenware.

EGG BEATER — One of many implements for beating eggs. There are three basic types: (1) the fixed beater which receives its motion solely by the motion of the arm of its user. This type includes the many different *whisks* — of wire (spoon, balloon or spiral); of wood, such as the hickory stick with curly shavings and the pine-twig swizzle stick; the fork; the dried bones of a turkey wing; and even the spread fingers of one's own hand. (2) The *rotary movement, multiple-bladed* beater operated by geared wheels, and (3) the *single-blade*, perforated disk, or wire beater operated by pushing up and down on the principle of the Archimedean Screw.

Some oddities include a bow-drill wooden beater, a spiral dasher, and a cord-driven slotted bar.

When the first Dover rotary egg beater was patented on May 31, 1870, one hundred and forty egg beater patents had been granted. Many of these came to be manufactured, but just as many never were. "The Dover is generally regarded as the best in the market,... by an ingenious contrivance, the inner circle revolves in a contrary direction to the outer circle." (*Practical Housekeeping*, 1884.) The Dover is the keystone of any collection of egg beaters. It has a cast-iron handle and two gears, plus a small "pinion gear," and tinned blades. It came in a great number of sizes for use in the home and in hotels and institutions. The Dover Stamping Company manufactured two styles before the famous one: the *Earle's Patent* and the *Monroe's Patent*. Timothy Earle was a prolific inventor from Smithfield, Rhode Island. In his "Specifications for an egg-beater," with which he was granted patent number 39,134 on July 7, 1863, Earle wrote: "Various devices have been employed for the purpose of beating eggs more expeditiously than by the familiar hand-process. One of these devices consists of two wire-frames, one within the other, and made to revolve in opposite directions; another consists of a propeller blade inside of a wire frame, the frame and blades being made to revolve in opposite directions, and still another consists of a propeller blade which is made to rotate while a pair of beaters have at the same time a reciprocating motion. All these machines, and all others with which I am acquainted, possess the common fault that the beaters, whether of wire or of the form of propeller-blades, do not cut the yolks and whites of the egg, but literally beat them. Now, as the albumen of an egg consists of a peculiar thick, glazy substance, it can be worked more effectually with a cutting instrument than with one which has a blunt edge. In fact, so well is this understood that housewives universally make use of the blade of a knife for the purpose." The egg beater Earle patented had a rack-and-pinion movement, but the one sold so successfully by Dover featured the same cutting blades operated instead by a geared wheel. It was advertised then as "the most effective Egg Beater made. Held in the hand with an immovable rest, it stands firmly wherever placed and will beat eggs with greater rapidity than any other."

A Dover assignor, Thomas Holt of Tarrytown, New York, was a busy inventor. His egg beater, the *Cyclone*, had perforated blades, and was patented in 1901.

Beating the Whites of Eggs
On breaking eggs, take care that none of the yolk becomes mingled with the

whites. A single particle will sometimes prevent their foaming well. Put the whites into a large flat dish, and beat them with an egg-beater made of doubled wire, with a tin handle; or with a cork stuck crosswise upon the prongs of a fork. Strike a quick, sharp stroke through the whole length of the dish. Beat them in the cellar, or some other cool place, till they look like snow and you can turn the dish over without their slipping off. [*Cornelius, 1846*]
"Taplin;" "Holt Dover;" "Earle Dover; " "Household Jewel;" "Wonder;" "Munroe;" "Cyclone;" "Aluminum Beauty;" "A & J;" "Up to Date;" "Easy;" "Ladd;" etc.

Fig. 398. EGG WHIP. Tinned wire. "Diamond" pattern. Androck, 1936.

Fig. 399. EGG WHIPS. Wire, wood. Androck, 1936.

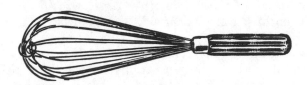

Fig. 395. BAKERS' EGG WHIP. Tinned wire, wood. L: 12", 14", 16". 8 bows. Androck, 1936.

Fig. 400. EGG WHIP. Tin, wood. Androck, 1936.

Fig. 396. EGG WHIPS & WHISKS. 1880s to 1940s, several manufactured exactly the same throughout the period. (1) c. 1930. Wire, wood. L: 12". Possibly A & J. (2) c. 1890. Wire. L: 13". This doubles as a chimney-cloth holder. (3) c. 1920 - 1940. Wire. L: 12¼". (4) c. 1890. Wire. L: 11¾". "Surprise Egg Beater." (5) c. 1900 to 1930s. Wire. L: 12". "Diamond," Androck. (6) c. 1880s - 1900. Heavy wire. L: 11½". "The Sensible." (7) c. 1890. Wire. L: 12¼". This is also a cloth-holder and an egg lifter. (8) c. 1940, but this type goes back to the 1870s, usually with a wooden handle. Wire. L: 8¾". Author's Collection.

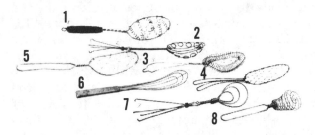

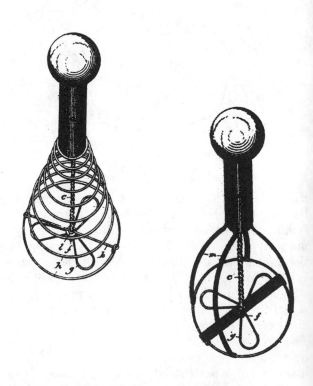

Fig. 397. EGG WHIP. Tinned wire. Androck, 1936.

Fig. 401. EGG BEATER. Pat'd 1899, No. 618,029. Gilbert M. Fitch, Beverly, N.J. Official Gazette, Jan. 17, 1899.

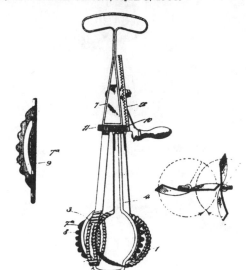

Fig. 402. EGG BEATER. Pat'd 1900, No. 646,736. Thomas Holt, Tarrytown, N.Y. Official Gazette, April 3, 1900.

Fig. 405. EGG BEATER. Pat'd Feb. 4, 1902. J. B. Foote Foundry Company, 1906.

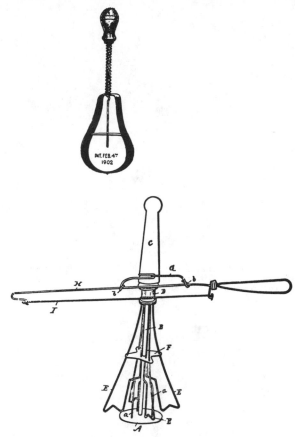

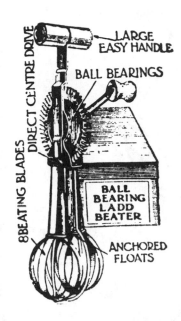

Fig. 406. EGG BEATER. Pat'd 1892, No. 472, 803. Howard M. Brittain, Martin's Creek, Pa. "The object I have in view is to apply the well-known bow-drill movement to a peculiarly- constructed beater, whereby the work can be more easily done and in less time than heretofore." Official Gazette, April 12, 1892.

Fig. 407. EGG BEATER. Pat'd 1891, No. 454,194. David A. Wilkinson, St. Louis, Missouri. "It is well known and amply illustrated and proved in the culinary arts that the best motion for the agitating and beating of eggs is the natural motion or movement imparted by the hand of the cook. In pursuance of the fact I desire to achieve as the object of my invention a motion or movement as nearly resembling that motion as mechanical ingenuity and skill can approach." Official Gazette, June 16, 1891.

Fig. 403. LADD BALL BEARING EGG BEATER. The Berdan Company, 1931.

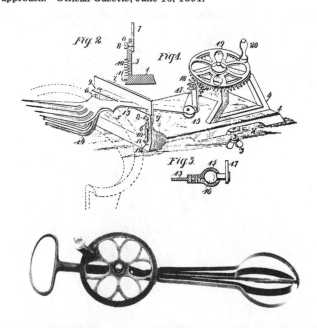

Fig. 404. EGG BEATER. Pat'd April 14, 1903. Cast iron, tin. L: 12¼". Taplin's Dover Pattern Improved. Courtesy Harry Kislevitz.

Fig. 408. EGG BEATER. 1880 to 1920s. Cast iron, tin. L: 10¼"; W: 2-7/8". Dover. Author's Collection.

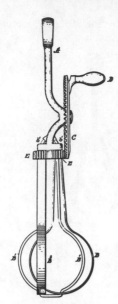

Fig. 409. EGG BEATER. Pat'd 1891, No. 463,818. Edward H. Whitney & John L. Kirby, Cambridge, Massachusetts, assignors to The Dover Stamping Company, Boston. Official Gazette, Nov. 24, 1891.

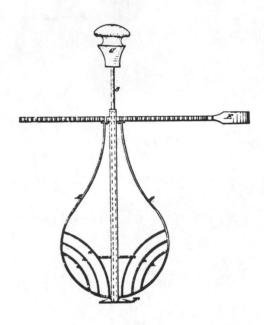

Fig. 413. EGG BEATER. Pat'd 1863, No. 39,134. Timothy Earle, Smithfield, Rhode Island. Official Gazette, July 7, 1863.

Fig. 410. EGG BEATER. c. 1890. Cast iron, tin, wood. L: 17". Dover No. 14, hotel size. American. Courtesy Keillor Collection.

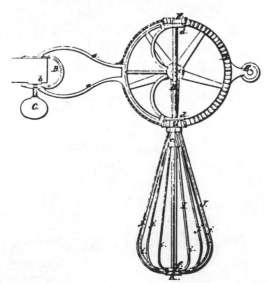

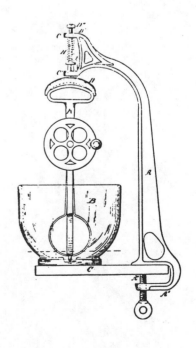

Fig. 411. EGG BEATER. Pat'd 1859, No. 23,694. James F. Monroe, Fitchburg, Massachusetts, and Edwin P. Monroe, New York. Official Gazette, April 19, 1859.

Fig. 414. EGG BEATER. Pat'd 1880, No. 225,003. Timothy Earle, Valley Falls, Rhode Island. Official Gazette, Mar. 2, 1880.

Fig. 415. PEERLESS EGG BEATER. F. A. Walker, c. 1870s.

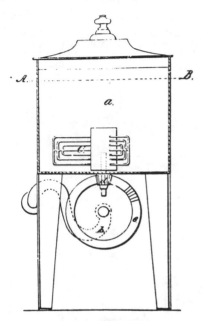

Fig. 416. EGG BEATER. Pat'd 1856, No. 16,267. Ralph Collier, Baltimore, Maryland. Official Gazette, Dec. 23, 1856.

Fig. 417. EGG BEATER. Pat'd 1901, No. 678,456. William G. Browne, Kingston, N.Y. Official Gazette, July 16, 1901.

Fig. 418. EGG BEATER. Pat'd 6/25/1901, 7/16/1901. Cast iron (some are nickel-plated), perforated tin blades. L: 11¾" (some are 11½"). Cyclone. Author's Collection.

Fig. 419. EGG BEATER. Cast iron, wire. "It consists of a spirally coiled wire, which in use opens and closes with exceeding rapidity, and instead of cutting the egg, as most beaters do, thoroughly aerates it...." Montgomery Ward, 1895.

Fig. 420. 3-MINUTE EGG BEATER. F. A. Walker, c. 1870s.

Fig. 421. EGG BEATER. Pat'd Nov. 24, 1908. Cast iron, tin, wood. L: 12¼.; W: 4". "Light Running," Taplin Mfg. Co., New Britain, Conn. Author's Collection.

Fig. 424. EGG BEATER., Pat'd Mar. 23, 1920, May 2, 1921. Nickeled steel, tin, wire, wood. L: 11". Whipwell. American. Author's Collection.

Fig. 422. EXPRESS EGG BEATER. A. E. Rayment Supply Co., Rockford, Illinois, c. 1910.

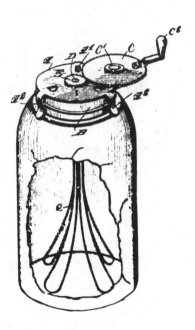

Fig. 425. EGG BEATER & CREAM WHIP. Pat'd 1908, No. 903,515. George Snyder, Kensington, Maryland. Official Gazette, Nov. 10, 1908.

Fig. 423. EGG BEATER. Pat'd July 7, 1908, No. 892,856, by Earnest W. Ladd, Washington, D.C. L: 11½". Ladd No. 1 United Royalties Corp., N.Y.C. Courtesy Melvin Adelglass.

Fig. 426. SPIRAL EGG BEATER. Wood, wire. "Cheaper though not so good as the 'Dover.'" Practical Housekeeping, 1881.

Fig. 427. EGG BEATER. Pat'd Nov. 28, 1916. Stainless, tin, wood. L: 10¾". Merry Whirl. American. Author's Collection.

Fig. 430. EGG BEATER & PITCHER. Nickeled iron, tin, wood, glass. Quart size pitchers. (Left) 4 wing, vertical handle beater. (Right) 8 wing, spade handle beater. A & J. Edward Katzinger Company, 1940.

Fig. 428. EGG BEATER with MEASURING CUP. Oct. 9, 1923. Nickeled-steel, glass, wood. H: 12"; W: 5". A & J. Courtesy Melvin Adelglass.

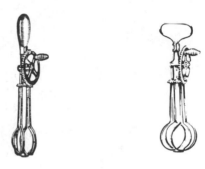

Fig. 431. EGG BEATERS. Nickeled & tinned steel; nickeled steel, wood. L: 10". 11". All 4 wing. A & J. Edward Katzinger Company, 1940.

Fig. 429. EGG BEATER with CUP. Pat'd Oct. 9, 1923. Glass, nickeled steel, wood. H: 11¼"; W: 4½". A & J. Author's Collection.

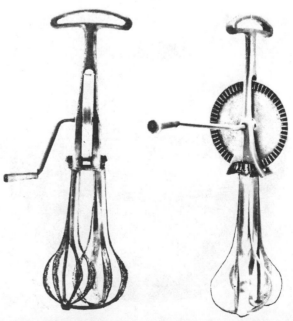

Fig. 432, 433. EGG BEATER. Two views. Pat'd April 20, 1920. Cast & sheet aluminum. L: 10-3/8". Marked either Aluminum Beauty, or Aluminum Beauty Beater VIKO Instant Whip. Ullman Aluminum, Division, N.Y. Courtesy Elizabeth C. Reed.

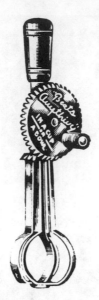

Fig. 437. EGG BASKET. 1890 to 1940. Wire. 7-7/8" x 7-7/8" x 3¼". American. Courtesy Mary Mac Franklin.

Fig. 434. EGG BEATER. Nickeled steel, wood. L: 7¼". "Beats anything in a cup or bowl." A & J. Edward Katzinger Company, 1940.

Fig. 435. TURBINE EGG BEATER or CREAM WHIP. c. 1930. Stamped metal, wire. L: 10¼". Cassady- Fairbanks Mfg. Co., Chicago. Courtesy Jane Pope, Charlottesville, Va.

Fig. 438. EGG HOLDERS. c. 1930. Wire & wood; wire. L: 7¾"; 9½". American. Author's Collection.

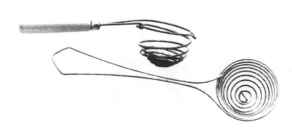

EGG BOILER — An implement of some sort to hold one or more eggs in boiling water. One type is a wire spoon. *See also* **EGG STAND**

Fig. 439. EGG BOILER.
F. A. Walker, c. 1870s.

Fig. 436. BEATING BOWL. Heavy tin. 17" x 7", 18" x 7½", 20" x 8". Lalance & Grosjean, 1890.

EGG CANDLER — A device, like a lantern with an egg-sized window, for looking at eggs against a light to determine freshness. There is an air bubble in the egg, and the smaller the bubble the fresher the egg. A black spot in the egg meant trouble: this egg was disposed of very carefully!

Fig. 440. EGG CANDLER with kerosene lamp. c. 1860. Glass, tin, brass. H: 13½". American. Courtesy Keillor Collection.

EGG CODDLER — A tin, straight-sided vessel with ear handles and a lift-out egg holder. The two parts were heated with hot water. The water was poured out, the eggs arranged in the holder, and the vessel again filled with boiling water and kept in a warm place for ten minutes. This type of coddler was used as a serving piece. Another, simpler type is the perforated tin dish for one or two eggs which could be placed in boiling water and lifted out by its own long handle. *See also* **EGG POACHER**

Fig. 441. EGG CODDLER. F. A. Walker, c. 1870s.

Fig. 442. INTERNATIONAL EGG CODDLER. Pat'd 1897. Manning, Bowman & Co. flyer, c. 1900.

EGG FRYER — A flat, cast-iron pan with a short handle, resembling a spider except for the egg-sized depressions in it. The depressions were round or oval usually, but one unusual one created hearts sunny-side up. *See also* **MUFFIN PAN**

Fig. 443. EGG FRYER. Stamped tin. F. A. Walker, c. 1870s.

Fig. 444. EGG FRY PAN. Tin 4 eyes: 9¾" dia.; 5 eyes: 12" dia.; 6 eyes: 12¼" dia.; 8 eyes: 14¼" dia. Lalance & Grosjean, 1890.

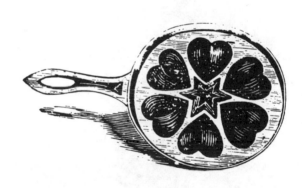

Fig. 445. EGG FRYER. Cast iron. F. A. Walker, c. 1870s.

EGG GLASS — *see* **HOUR GLASS**

EGG OPENER — A small-toothed scissor for opening "raw or soft-boiled eggs," according to an advertisement for The Champion Egg Opener, which appeared in *Ladies Home Journal*, January 1889. An egg is so easy to open when raw that I would suppose this opener to be more useful for boiled eggs. Another type was "a small circular knife with a saw edge. Placed over top of boiled egg and pressed firmly, the knife cuts the top and afterward lifts it off." (*Ladies Home Journal*, September 1899.) *Same as* **EGG SCISSOR**

EGG POACHER — One type is a flat pan with shallow rings and a single upright handle. It was lowered into the water, and the eggs were formed in circles. "Silver and Co.'s new egg poacher has a lever by which the joined rings can be lifted and the eggs slid off. Place it in a pan of boiling water, with a teaspoon of salt to pint of water. Let water boil 2 minutes; draw back pan where water will hardly bubble, and break an egg into each ring. Let the eggs stand for almost 3 minutes and they will be done. Always be sure to have the poacher hot and in the water before the eggs are put in." (*Parloa*, 1887.)

Another, much-advertised type consisted of a stand with a long vertical handle and little legs. It held a number of removable perforated cups for the eggs.

Perforated strainer spoons were used for poaching eggs too.

Fig. 449. EGG POACHER. Tin. 5 eggs. Buffalo Steam Egg Poacher. Montgomery Ward, 1893.

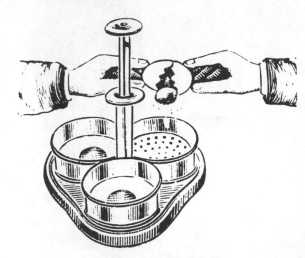

Fig. 450. MARYLAND EGG POACHER. Pieced tin. "The Maryland Egg Poacher is far simpler and more easily cleaned than the higher-priced contrivances, and does the poaching evenly, better and with less trouble. It can be used in an ordinary stew pan as well as a skillet. A little automatic catch at the top of the standard holds the rings while the cooked eggs are removed with a knife." Matthai-Ingram Company, c. 1890.

Fig. 446. EGG POACHER. Metal. Practical Housekeeping, 1881.

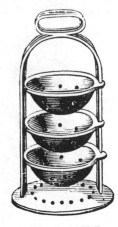

Fig. 447. EGG POACHER. Tin. F. A. Walker, c. 1870s.

Fig. 451. EGG POACHER. Tin. F. A. Walker, c. 1870s.

EGG SCALE — A small scale for determining weight and therefore market size of eggs, usually one by one. *"Acme;" "Jiffy Way;" etc.*

Fig. 448. EGG POACHER, 2 eggs. c. 1880. Tin & wire. 9¼" x 6". Kreamer Mfg. Co. Courtesy Rita Keillor Collection.

Fig. 452. EGG SCALE. Pat'd June 24, 1924. Cast & sheet aluminum. L: 10½"; W: 3½"; H: 4½". "Acme Egg Grading Scale," Specialty Mfg. Co., St. Paul, Minn. Author's Collection.

Fig. 453. EGG SCALE. 1940. Painted sheet metal. L: 7-1/8"; W: 2¾"; H: 5¾". "Jiffy Way," Owatonna, Minn. Author's Collection.

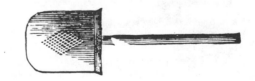

EGG SEPARATOR — "An inventor has taken pity on the women who find it difficult to separate the white of an egg from the yolk. His device is in the form of a cup with a slit in one side of the bottom. The egg is broken into the cup and the white passes through the slit, leaving the yolk in the cup." (*Ladies Home Journal*, September, 1899.) This type is found with single or double slits; in tin, aluminum, enameled ware, and pottery. Many egg separators were advertising give-aways.

Another type, the *Dollie Egg Separator*, was advertised in the 1890s by Miss Dollie Washburne of New York City. It was supposed to separate ten eggs in one minute and a child could use it. This separator was a simple, small, tilted trough, with long narrow slits. The egg was broken at the high end, and as it slid down the trough, the white fell through the slits into one bowl placed underneath, and with a splash, the yolk fell off the low end into another bowl.

Fig. 455, 456. EGG SEPARATOR. "Housewives appreciate this article on sight, and you will have no trouble in disposing of a large quantity in every community. Agents can carry 2 dozen or more in their pockets." F. W. Seastrand, c. 1912.

EGG SLICE — A utensil for removing omelets or fried eggs from the pan. It is like a cake-turner. "Fry them brown in fresh butter; then take them out with an egg slice." (*Glasse*, 1796.) *See also* **CAKE TURNER, FISH SLICE**

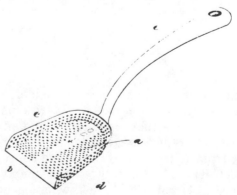

Fig. 457. EGG SLICE. Tin. F. A. Walker, c. 1870s.

Fig. 454. EGG SEPARATOR. c. 1900 to 1920. Aluminum. With glass setting-eggs. L: 6-3/8"; W: 3¾". American. Author's Collection.

Fig. 458. EGG LIFTER. Pat'd 1890, No. 433,546. Ann E. Smith, Springfield, Ohio. Official Gazette, Aug. 5, 1890.

EGG SLICER — A device with cutting wires for slicing hard-boiled eggs. If the sliced egg was turned a quarter of the way around, some slicers could then dice the egg.

Fig. 461. EGG HOLDER. Wire. (Dover Stamping Co.) F. A. Walker, c. 1870s.

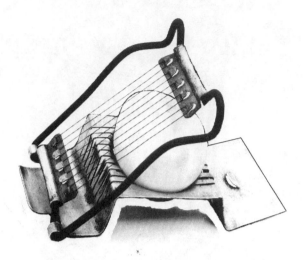

Fig. 459. EGG SLICER. 1930 to 1950. Sheet aluminum, wire. L: 5"; W: 2¾". American. Author's Collection.

Fig. 462. EGG STAND. Wire. Dover Stamping Co. F. A. Walker, c. 1870s.

Fig. 460. EGG SLICER & DICER c. 1935. Cast aluminum, wire. 4" x 4". Bloomfield Industries Inc., Chicago. Courtesy Paul Persoff.

EGG STAND — A wire rack or holder with an upright handle in the center. It was used for holding eggs while they were boiled, and afterward for the table. Stands were made in various sizes, holding from four to twelve eggs, and are very lacy and Victorian. Another type was simply some ingeniously twisted wires which, when opened out, held six eggs, and which could be folded up and put away.

Fig. 463. EGG STAND. c. 1870s to 1890s. Wire. W: 6¾"; H: 6¾". Author's Collection.

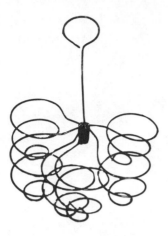

Fig. 464. EGG BOILER or STAND. c. 1900. Folding wire. W: 6";
H: 7". American. Author's Collection.

ELECTRICITY — "...The cook's domain, the
kitchen, bewilders us by the number and variety of
things electrical.... The electric range...; a little
motor attached to either the metal polisher and
knife-sharpener, the coffee-grinder, or
meat-chopper as required. Eggbeaters, dish washer,
potato-peeler, waffle-iron, cereal-cooker, egg
boiler, toaster, percolator, and tea pot; all electric.
It is but a short time since electricity has become a
recognized factor in luxurious and comfortable
living and has found its way into many households
where it is deemed a necessity and not a luxury."
(*House and Garden*, September, 1907.)

The first American electric motor was
patented by Michael Faraday in 1837, but it was
not until 1889 that a Serbian-born American
inventor named Nikola Tesla marketed a small, 1/6
horsepower electric fan. Having literally ushered in
the Electric Age, Tesla died in poverty in 1943 at
the age of 86.

There was an entire electric kitchen at the
Columbian Exhibition in Chicago in 1893. Each
saucepan, water heater, broiler or boiler was
connected to its own electrical outlet. But even as
late as 1920 people were disillusioned with
electrical cooking utensils because they burned out
easily and repairmen were few and far between.
The most commonly found old appliances are
electric toasters, waffle irons and coffee makers.
"Prometheus;" *"Electrix-United Drug Co.;"*
"General Electric;" *"Dominion:"* *"Universal;"*
"Westinghouse;" etc.

Fig. 466. ELECTRIC PERCOLATOR. 2 qt. size. The Berdan
Company, 1931.

Fig. 467. ELECTRIC TOASTER. Pat'd 1920, 1927. Nickel-plated
copper, wood. L: 8"; W: 4¼"; H: 7". "Electrex," United Drug Co.,
Boston. Author's Collection.

Fig. 465. ELECTRIC PERCOLATOR & TOASTER. Slack Mfg. Co.,
Chicago, Illinois, c. 1925.

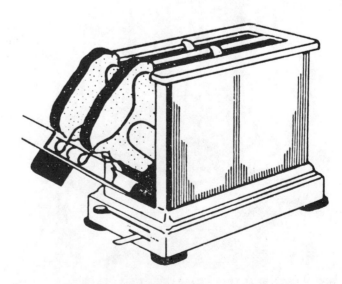

Fig. 468. ELECTRIC TOASTER. 1930s. Nickel or chromium
plated. Household Equipment, 1940.

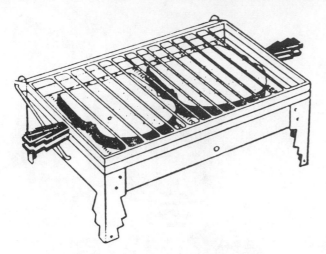

Fig. 469. ELECTRIC TOASTER. c. 1930s. Nickel or chromium plated, probably bakelite handles. Household Equipment, 1940.

Fig. 469-B. ELECTRIC TOASTER. 1905. Model X2. General Electric Company's first electric toaster. Photograph courtesy General Electric Company.

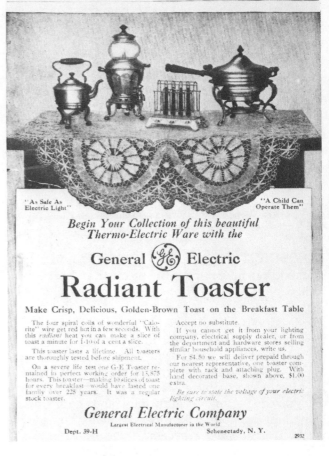

"As Safe As Electric Light"   "A Child Can Operate Them"

Begin Your Collection of this beautiful
Thermo-Electric Ware with the

General Electric

Radiant Toaster

Make Crisp, Delicious, Golden-Brown Toast on the Breakfast Table

The four spiral coils of wonderful "Calorite" wire get red hot in a few seconds. With this radiant heat you can make a slice of toast a minute for 1-10 of a cent a slice.

This toaster lasts a lifetime. All toasters are thoroughly tested before shipment.

On a severe life test one G-E Toaster remained in perfect working order for 13,875 hours. This toaster—making 10 slices of toast for every breakfast—would have lasted one family over 225 years. It was a regular stock toaster.

Accept no substitute.

If you cannot get it from your lighting company, electrical supply dealer, or from the department and hardware stores selling similar household appliances, write us.

For $4.50 we will deliver prepaid through our nearest representative, one toaster complete with rack and attaching plug. With hand decorated base, shown above, $1.00 extra.

Be sure to state the voltage of your electric lighting circuit.

General Electric Company
Largest Electrical Manufacturer in the World
Dept. 39-H   Schenectady, N. Y.

Fig. 469-D. ELECTRIC APPLIANCES. c. 1910. Advertisement appearing in Good Housekeeping Magazine. Photograph courtesy General Electric Company.

Fig. 469-C. ELECTRIC TOASTER. 1908. Floral-painted porcelain base. Model D12. General Electric Company. Photograph Courtesy General Electric Company.

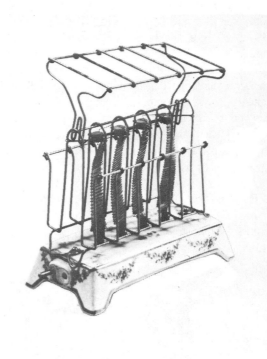

Fig. 469-E. ELECTRIC TOASTER. 1908. Floral-painted porcelain base and warming rack above. General Electric. Photograph courtesy General Electric Company.

ENAMELED WARE, PORCELAIN ENAMEL —

Iron ware, coated with a high-fired, vitreous (glasslike) composition. It was first invented, and applied to sauce pans by Dr. Hinkling in 1799, and refined and extended to use on all kitchenware by a man named Clarke in 1839. It was used, with special appreciation for its qualities, for preserving kettles, soup and stew pots, and saucepans. "There is no chance of appendicitis in using enamel ware for never has any intestinal disturbance been found to have originated from chipping enamel, as has been said by enamel's enemies." (*Peyser,* 1922.) There were enemies for nearly all materials used for kitchen utensils, and it has to be supposed that some of the enmity was generated by the manufacturers who were in competition. Most of the writers and domestic economists, however, had the interests of the housewife at heart and were trying to create order from bewildering chaos.

"Light in weight, easy to clean, and little affected by fruit or vegetable acids. Excellent for mixing and for keeping dishes in, but cheaper grades do not stand up to heat or wear. Enamel should be free of bubbles and have smooth finished edges." (Helen Atwater, *Selection of Household Equipment,* 1915.)

"Domestic enameled ironware is not very durable, the base being of iron.... Imported Bohemian ware, nearly all foreign ware is in blue and white, and is more attractive than the mottled graniteware of the American producers, was imported about three years ago.... Steel is the base of imported ware and it will last three times as long." (*New York Times,* March 1890.)

Full lines of enameled, *agateware, glazed-ware,* or *graniteware* were offered by all the wholesale houses and the retail mail-order catalogs. Look for Syenite, pink, gray, blue, white, brown, and turquoise; and for "Old Ivory," triple-coated with green outside, ivory inside; "Purity," gray; "Polar," white and white; "Dresden," triple-coated, mottled white-lined ware with white on blue outside; "Titan," gray mottled. *"Lalance & Grosjean;" "Iron Clad Mfg. Co.;" "Matthai-Ingram Greystone;" "Republic Stamping Old English;" "Biddle Hardware Co.;" etc.*

Fig. 471. "WINDSOR" SAUCEPAN. Agate enameled ware, tin. ¾ to 3½ qts. Lalance & Grosjean, 1890.

"POLLY PUT THE KETTLE ON"

Fig. 472. ENAMELED WARE. Patent Granite Iron Ware advertising trade card. 3¼" x 5¼". 1884. Author's Collection.

Fig. 470. IMPROVED BERLIN SAUCE PAN. Greystone enameled ware, tin. 1½, 2½, 4, 4½, 5½, 7½, 10 qts. Matthai-Ingram Company, c. 1890.

ENGLISH HAMMERED PAN — *see* FRY PAN, RUSSIAN IRON

ETNA — *see* AETNA

FARINA BOILER — A double boiler, or cereal cooker, usually with straight sides and a long fluted lip or pouring spout, in the outside vessel. This lip was for pouring off, or adding, boiling water. *Farina* is the flour or meal of any corn, nut, or starchy root. *See also* **DOUBLE BOILER**

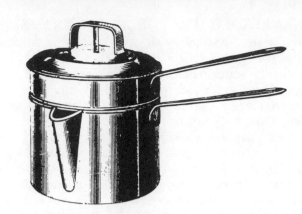

Fig. 475. FARINA SAUCE PAN. Pieced tin. Inside boiler: 2, 3, 4, 6 qts. Matthai-Ingram Company, c. 1890.

Fig. 476. FARINA BOILER. Tin. F. A. Walker, c. 1870s.

Fig. 473. FARINA BOILER. Greystone Enameled ware. 2, 3, 4, 6 qts. Matthai-Ingram Company, c. 1890.

FENDER or FEND-IRON — A metal frame about ten to fifteen inches high, with a usually decorative panel; or, a heavy wire-mesh folding screen, placed in front of the open fire to keep hot coals from rolling out of the raised grate into the room. [The wire-mesh panel which had its own little feet, and which did not fold, was called a *fire screen.*] Some fenders are quite handsomely made of brass and steel, and some are equipped with padded seats, although these would not have been for the kitchen. One fender or fire screen, called a *skirt protector,* resembles a wire-mesh apron.

Some specific utensils were made to hang from, or be supported by the fender frame, for cooking or warming food such as little cakes and tea. *See also* **FIRE-BAR TRIVET, PLATE REST**

Fig. 474. FARINA HAMMERED BOILER. Tin. 1, 1½, 2½, 3 quart capacity inside boiler. Lalance & Grosjean, 1890.

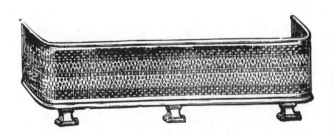

Fig. 477. FENDER. F. A. Walker, c. 1870s.

Fig. 478. SKIRT PROTECTOR. F. A. Walker, c. 1870s.

FIBRE WARE or WOOD-PULP WARE — Utensils and containers molded of wood-pulp and chemically treated to make them impervious to liquids. They held liquids and solids, hot or cold. Very light-weight, they were unfortunately easily crushed. This discouraged the originally enthusiastic market of the late 19th century, and curtails the success of today's collector. In old catalogs it was also referred to as *Indurated Fibre Ware*. The Standard Fiber-ware Company of Mankato, Minnesota, advertised a line of pails, basins, etc., of flax fiber in 1891.

Fig. 479. INDURATED FIBRE WARE PAIL. Cordley & Hayes Indurated Fibre Ware, 1889.

Fig. 480. SCOOP. Cordley & Hayes, Indurated Fibre Ware, 1889.

Fig. 481. SLOP JAR. Indurated fibre ware, Cordley & Hayes, 1889.

FIREBACK, FIRE- or BACK-PLATE — A heavy, cast-iron plate, usually nearly square with a rounded or vaulted top, which stands in the rear of the fireplace and serves to protect the back wall and to reflect the heat of the fire back towards the room. Firebacks were used for the same purpose as the large boulders which some early builders incorporated in the back of a brick or stone fireplace.

Many of them were quite beautifully cast, with rugged or elegant designs. In Henry Mercer's *The Bible in Iron*, Starkie Gardner's article in *Archaeologia* (Volume 56, Part I) is quoted as noting several styles. "(1) Moulded from Loose Stamps until about 1640; (2) Coats of arms, royal and private, cast from single moulds; (3) Allegories, badges, illustrations of current events, satires, etc.; (4) Bible scenes...; (5) Flemish firebacks higher than wide, with rich borders, dolphins, cupids,...."

The firebacks were cast in damp caster's sand (sometimes mixed with powdered charcoal) which was enclosed in a wooden frame. The designs had been pressed into the sand with either several carved wooden stamps, several household objects, or a single carved mold pattern. The molten iron was ladled into the impressions in the sand and allowed to cool and harden.

Firebacks are related to cast-iron stove plates (which date back hundreds of years in Germany, Scandinavia, Holland, and then America) only in their appearance and the method of manufacture. Their purpose was entirely different. The usually rectangular stove plate was actually part of a heating stove, either a "five-plate," a "six-plate," or a "ten-plate."

The subject matter of the stove plate casting is usually religious; and there are wide margins which were covered by the angle-iron corner rims which, when bolted, held the stove together.

Fig. 482. STOVE SIDE PLATE. Anywhere between 1750 and 1820. Cast iron. H: 20¾"; W: 22½". Reversable for right or left. The design of three rabbits "is probably traditional and is the solution of a puzzle [published long after the plate was made] in 'The American Boys Book' (New York, c. 1864.) 'Draw three rabbits, so that each shall appear to have two ears, while, in fact, they have only three ears between them.'' The Bible in Iron, 1961. Photograph courtesy of the Mercer Museum of The Bucks County Historical Society, Doylestown, Pennsylvania.

Iron furnaces in Massachusetts and southern New England (although there were furnaces in New York, New Jersey, Pennsylvania, Delaware, Maryland, Virginia, North Carolina, South Carolina, Georgia, Alabama, Kentucky and Tennessee) were probably the source for most of America's firebacks.

They were not made for more than a few years after the beginning of the 19th century. Joseph Sandford, who wrote the chapter on firebacks in the Mercer book, speculates that "the influence of Benjamin, Count Rumford's theories of fireplace construction, published in 1796, was felt on both sides of the Atlantic and may have been a factor in making the fireback obsolete in America." (*The Bible in Iron*, 1961.) Count Rumford stressed the importance of reflective surfaces, but said that iron was among the worst materials, along with other metals.

Some firebacks, much later than the plates set in the back of the fireplace, were an attached part of the grate. Most of these also had the typical arched or vaulted top, but were usually longer than high.

FIRE-BAR TRIVET — A fender or a grate accessory. *See also* **PLATE REST**

Fig. 483. FIREBACK. 1588. Cast iron. L: 42"; H: 27". 35". Called "The Armada" or "Spanish Armada" Fireback this was cast as an "allusion to the Spanish Armada which took place in 1588. The fleur de lys and Tudor roses refer to Queen Elizabeth. The I.F.C. may have been the craftsman responsible for the design and manufacture of the fireback." Records of the Sussex (England) Archaeological Society. A very similar fireback fragment is pictured in *The Bible in Iron*. English. Courtesy Keillor Collection.

FIRE-DOG — *see* **ANDIRON**

FIRE—IRON — An iron or steel implement for striking a light, making a spark, used in the 14th, 15th and 16th centuries.

FIRE-IRONS — Iron steel implements for tending domestic fires (as opposed to foundry fires); including the *shovel*, *tongs*, *poker*, and the older *slice bar* which had a long handle and a broad flat end, and was used for clearing out ashes.

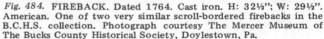
Fig. 484. FIREBACK. Dated 1764. Cast iron. H: 32½"; W: 29½". American. One of two very similar scroll-bordered firebacks in the B.C.H.S. collection. Photograph courtesy The Mercer Museum of The Bucks County Historical Society, Doylestown, Pa.

Fig. 485. FIRE-IRONS. F. A. Walker, c. 1870s.

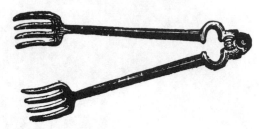

Fig. 486. COAL TONGS. Iron, wire spring. Matthai-Ingram Company, c. 1890.

FIRE KINDLER — A device with a flammable oil, or kerosene-absorbing head of a composition material, and a long handle. The head was lit with a match, or in another fire, and used like a torch to light a fire.

The *Yankee Kindler* had an asbestos-filled bulbous head and advertised "100 fires with 3 cents of oil" in 1899. The *Oval Kindler* advertised "over Half Million in Use" in 1897. The *Smith's Fire Kindler* was patented in 1871. It had its own tin container. The label read, in part, "Put in tin two inches of Kerosene Oil. In one hour it will thoroughly soak; then it is always ready for use. When the fire is well started, put it out by a quick puff, endways then place in Tin." The *New England Fire Kindler* consisted of a little pot of kerosene and a torch-like kindler.

A homemade kindler could be made like this:"Melt together 3 pounds resin and a quart of tar, and stir in as much sawdust and pulverized charcoal as possible, spread the mass on a board to cool, and break into lumps the size of a walnut. Light one with a match, and it burns for some time with a strong blaze." (*Practical Housekeeping,* 1884.)

Fig. 488. FIRE KINDLER. Pat'd Oct. 10, 1871. Composition, wire, wood, tin, paper label. L: 8¾". Smith's No. 1, Dubuque, Iowa. "Directions for using. Put in Tin, 2 inches of Kerosene Oil. In one hour it will thoroughly soak, then it is always ready for use. When the fire is well started, put it out by a quick puff, endways, then place in Tin." Courtesy Keillor Collection.

Fig. 489. FIRE LIGHTER. Brass. The American Eagle, American Hardware Stores, 1918.

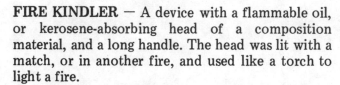

Fig. 487. FIRE KINDLER. 1890-1900. Composition, wire. L: 8". Author's Collection.

Fig. 490. FIRE LIGHTER. "Wright" iron. Cape Cod Fire Lighter. The American Eagle, American Hardware Stores, 1918.

FIRELESS,— FUELLESS COOKER — A zinc or wooden box, tin-lined, with from one to four wells for the utensils to be set in. Soapstone disks were preheated and placed at the bottom of the wells; they retained sufficient heat to cook food. "Boils, stews, roasts, steams, bakes and fries," according to early – 20th century advertisements. The fireless cooker was portable, and was often carried out to the fields in the morning so that the farmers could have a hot meal. As it required no fuel, it could safely be left to cook dinner or supper while the housewife and the family were out. *"Rapid Fireless Cooker;" "Ideal Toledo Cooker;" "The Peerless;" "Caloric;" etc.*

Fig. 493. FISH BOILER. Pieced tin. 17" x 9½" x 6¾"; 20" x 11" x 8¼". Matthai-Ingram Company, c. 1890.

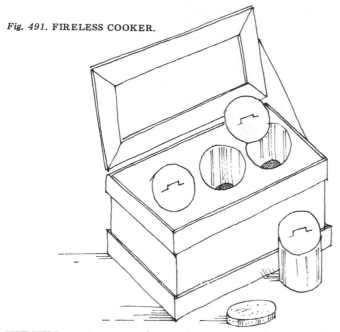

Fig. 491. FIRELESS COOKER.

FIRKIN — A cooper's product, a wooden-staved container. "An English measure for liquids, fish, butter which is the fourth part of a barrel; it contains eight gallons of beer. Two firkins make a kilderkin." (*Beecher and Stowe,* 1869.)

FISH KETTLE, or BOILER — "A long, light, straight-sided vessel with a loose and perforated tray with handles which sits off the bottom. The fish rests on the tray and is lifted out, and drains on this tray." *(Parloa,* 1887.) The fish kettle is usually tin-lined copper or steel and looks like other boilers. It always has a lid.

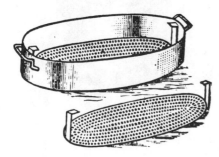

Fig. 492. FISH KETTLE. Perforated tin. Practical Housekeeping, 1881.

FISH MOLD — A fish-shaped tin or tin-lined copper mold for fish aspics, etc.

Fish Jelly

Take a two-pound haddock, one onion, and half rind lemon; just cover with water, and boil; remove all the bones and skin; flake the fish, or pound it in a mortar, with a tablespoonful of butter, pepper and salt to taste. Put back the bones, reduce the liquor to one pint, add a quarter of a packet of gelatine (previously dissolved in a quarter of a tumbler of cold water). Make some veal forcemeat, without suet, roll in small balls, and drop into boiling water; they will cook in seven minutes. Decorate a mould with the balls and rings of lemon, mix the strained liquid with the pounded fish, and, when nearly cold, pour into the mould. Hard-boiled eggs may be made over in this way. [*Strohm,* 1888]

FISH ROASTER — A utensil for roasting whole, small fish in front of the fire. Some can hold several fish and are similar to the bird roaster. Others are small and low and only one fish can be roasted.

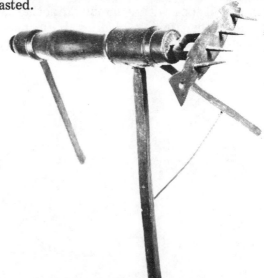

Fig. 494. FISH ROASTER. 18th century. Wood, wrought iron. L: 19"; 7½" fish; H: 16". English. Courtesy Keillor Collection.

FISH SCALER — A kind of knife, the blade set at an angle from the handle, for scraping off fish scales.

Fig. 495. FISH SCALER. Japanned iron. L: 9". Montgomery Ward, 1893.

FISH SLICE — A perforated, long-handled implement, like a cake turner, for turning frying fish, or for sliding it off the fish kettle tray.

FISH STRAINER — A flat, perforated tray with handles for taking fish from a boiler; or an earthenware slab with holes, placed at the bottom of a dish to drain liquid from a boiled fish after it has been served. *See also* **FISH KETTLE**

FLANNEL and COARSE NAPKIN STRAINERS — These are squares of coarsely woven and unbleached cotton or linen material, suspended over a bowl from a frame, and used to strain jellies or soups. The flannel was also fashioned into bags for the same purpose. *See also* **JELLY STRAINER**

FLAN RING — A ring mold for cooking the custard flan; also, a ring or hoop set flat on a cookie sheet and used for baking flan or pastry.

FLEETING [*flitting*] DISH or FLIT — A shallow dish with a ring handle used for skimming cream from milk. *See also* **SKIMMER**

FLEXIBLE POT SCRAPER — One type, advertised in January 1897 in *Woman's Home Companion*, was a pair of parallel, flexible and curved metal blades with a handle. Another type was a single, wider flexible blade with a handle. A spatula was also used as a pot scraper. *See also* **POT CLEANER**

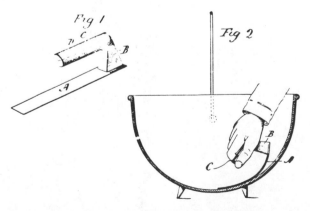

Fig. 496. KETTLE SCRAPER. Pat'd 1894, No. 522,794. Hermann F. W. Lemke, Clinton, Connecticut. Official Gazette, July 10, 1894.

FLOUR BIN and SIFTER — Various types, but basically a large (usually japanned) tin container with a tight-fitting lid, two wire handles, a built-in sifter ¾ of the way down, and a drawer or pan at the bottom which catches the sifted flour. These combination bins came in 25 to 100 pound sizes. "Does away with barrels, sacks, pans, scoops and sieves. It is ornamental and indespensable." Advertisement in an 1890 *Ladies Home Journal* for the Perfection bin. *"Perfection;" "Columbia;" "Cream City;" "Tyler's;" "Clipper;"* etc.

Fig. 497. FLOUR BIN & SIFTER. c. 1900. Tin, screen. H: 14"; 11¼" dia. American, possibly Cream City, Geuder, Paeschke & Frey Co., Milwaukee, Wis. Author's Collection.

Fig. 498. FLOUR BIN & SIFTER. Japanned tin. 25 & 50 pound capacities. Cream City, Geuder, Paeschke & Frey Co., 1925.

FLOUR-BOLT -₄[*bolter*] —A flour sieve, or a flour or meal sifter. *Bolting cloth* is fine wire-mesh, silk, or other cloth used for bolting. *See also* **BOULTER**

FLOUR BOX — A tall, tin canister holding 25, 50 or 100 pounds of flour for storage. The flour box was usually japanned or painted, and had a hinged cover. In the 18th century a *flour box* referred to a dredger.

Fig. 499. FLOUR CAN. Japanned tin. 30, 60, 100 pound capacity. Matthai-Ingram Company c. 1890.

FLOUR BUCKET — A wooden or tin bucket with a tight lid for storing fairly small amounts of bolted or sifted flour or Indian meal. *See also* **CANISTER**

FLOUR SCOOP — A small tin, wood, or aluminum short-handled shovel. It was for scooping about a cup of flour at a time from bin or barrel. Some scoops were much larger, and were used by grocers. The *covered scoop* had a partial cover which kept the flour from falling out the back of the scoop.

Fig. 501. FLOUR SCOOP. Stamped tin. F. A. Walker, c. 1870s.

FLOUR SIEVE — *see* **SIEVE**

FLOUR SIFTER — A sieve with a mechanical action for forcing the flour through the screen or mesh. One type is a tin cylinder with a convex mesh bottom and wire or metal blades which were moved in a rotary fashion by a crank which stuck out the side of the handle itself, as in the *Hunter*. Another type had a spring in the two-part handle, and by squeezing the two parts together and releasing them, over and over, the blades swept the bottom of the sifter — back and forth. Another type had a flat mesh bottom and a sort of propeller action with a crank on top. The Sidney Shepard Shaker Sifter — "Sift with One Hand" — was another flat-bottomed sifter. It was held in one hand and shaken sideways. A freely moving, but attached plate in the bottom rubbed the flour through the sieve.

The Hunter Sifter was manufactured by the Fred J. Meyer Mfg. Co., of Covington, Kentucky, and was widely advertised for use as a sifter, mixer, scoop, measure and weigher. It could be used for sifting flour, straining soup, making tomato jam, washing rice, straining starch, wine and fruit. In many Hunter ads in the late 1880s and early 1890s they offered a toy sifter which would "afford amusement to any little girl" (and show her mother how well the Hunter Sifter worked), for as little as a 2 cent stamp in 1889, and as much as a 6 cent stamp just six or seven years later. *"Pastry;" "World;" "Banner;" "New Standard;" "Bristol;" "Magic;" "Success;" "Shepard;" "Hunter;" "Favorite;" "Victor;"* etc.

Fig. 500. FLOUR SCOOP. F. A. Walker, c. 1870s.

Fig. 502. FLOUR SIFTER. 1889. Tin, wire, wood. L: 11¼"; 4¾" dia; H: 6½". Hunter's Sifter. "Standard of the World." The Fred J. Meyers Mfg. Co., Hamilton, Ohio, New York. "It's the most useful Kitchen utensil made." Author's Collection.

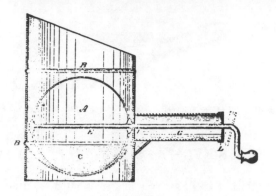

Fig. 506. FLUE STOPPER.

Fig. 503. FLOUR-SIFTER. Pat'd 1879, No. 218,121. Jacob M. Hunter, Cincinnati, Ohio. Official Gazette, Aug. 5, 1879.

Fig. 504. EARNSHAW'S FLOUR SIFTER. F. A. Walker, c. 1870s.

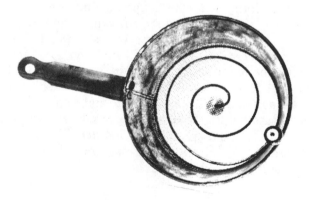

Fig. 507. FLUE STOPPER. Lithographed picture, gold lacquered tin. 8", 10¼" dia. C. B. Porter Company, c. 1915.

Fig. 505. FLOUR SIFTER. c. 1910. Tin, wire, screen. L: 9¼"; W: 5¾"; H: 2¼". American. Author's Collection.

FLUE STOPPER — A round metal plate, 6" to 9" in diameter, with spring clips to hold it in the stove flue. They were also used to cover, in a decorative manner, the gaping hole left when the heating stove was taken down for the summer, and the stove pipe removed.

Some flue stoppers were plain; others were stamped and finished in "brass," or had a painted or lithographed center representing a rural scene, flowers, Delft designs, etc.

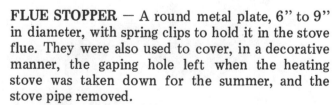

Fig. 508. FLUE STOPPER. Stamped tin, wire spring. 7-5/8" dia. Matthai-Ingram Company, c. 1890.

FLY FAN — Early kitchens, and early houses for that matter, often did not have window screens although even in the 17th century brass or copper screening was available and was used in windows. A fly fan, or at least someone to shoo flies, was necessary. One mechanical fly fan, with scrim wings, was the *Fowler Improved Fly Fan*. It ran for 75 minutes on one winding of the cross piece at the top of the cast-iron base. This was a keyless clockwork action, and a lost key was no problem. The Fowler was manufactured by the National Enameling and Stamping Company of Baltimore, also called Matthai-Ingram.

Fig. 512. ILLUSTRATION from "Fight the Fly," booklet put out in 1915 to tell people about the dangers of flies and how to combat them. International Harvester Co., Chicago.

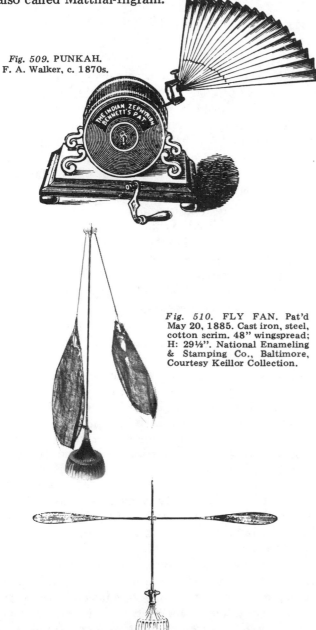

Fig. 509. PUNKAH. F. A. Walker, c. 1870s.

Fig. 510. FLY FAN. Pat'd May 20, 1885. Cast iron, steel, cotton scrim. 48" wingspread; H: 29½". National Enameling & Stamping Co., Baltimore, Courtesy Keillor Collection.

Fig. 511. THE IMPROVED KEYLESS FLY FAN. Pat'd June 20, 1885, March 1, March 8, 1887. "It drives all flies away by the shadow and movement of the wings while revolving, will run one hour and a quarter at each winding, and can be rewound at any time by simply turning cross-piece at the top of base.... The improvements of our Keyless Fans over all others consist of patent adjustable wing-holder (which admits of wings revolving at any angle — an important advantage where space is limited). The patent automatic stop-catch prevents unwinding when wings are taken off. Interior machinery, strengthened and simplified, and specially adapted for easy motion and long wear.... We are the patentees and sole manufacturers." Matthai-Ingram Company, c. 1890.

FLY KILLER — What we call a "fly swatter." The *King Fly Killer*, patented January 9, 1900, claimed "... made of a specially prepared light steel wire netting; it kills without crushing, and you can clean your entire house of all flies in a few minutes."

Swat the Fly

Oh every fly that skips our swatters,
Will have five million sons and daughters,
And countless first and second cousins;
Of aunts and uncles, scores and dozens,
And fifty-seven million nieces;
So knock the blamed thing all to pieces.
[*Walt Mason*, in *"Fight the Fly,"* International Harvester, 1915]

FLY TRAP or CATCHER — A device for luring flies into a baited cage or trap where they could be easily killed. It was made of wire mesh or glass, and the flies were supposed to fly in and be unable to fly out.

Fig. 513. CLOCK WORK FLY TRAP. F. A. Walker, c. 1870s. In 1869 a similar device was patented by Charles Kallmann of Newburg, N.Y. He stated: "The nature of my invention consists in combining two useful instruments into one, the clock and the fly trap.... The power to revolve a small cylinder which is covered with cloth, which is saturated with a solution of sugar or molasses in water, to invite flies and mosquitoes to sit down on the drum, is so very small that, if it is attached to a clock, its effect would hardly be felt by the spring of the clock." Official Gazette, April 6, 1869.

Fig. 514. FLY CATCHER. F. A. Walker, c. 1870s.

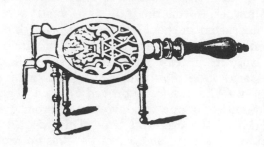

Fig. 517. FOOTMAN. F. A. Walker, c. 1870s.

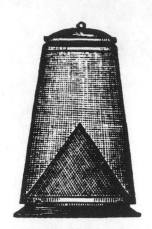

Fig. 515. FLY TRAP. Wire. "The trap here is the invention of a lady, and is a perfect success.... The flies are attracted inside the cage by bait and can't get out, and are easily killed and trap set for more." (Dover Stamping Co.). Practical Housekeeping, 1881.

FOLLER [*folla*] — *see* **CHEESE PRESS**

FOOD CHOPPER — *see* **MEAT CHOPPER**

FOOD PRESS — *see* **RICER**

FOOTMAN — An iron, steel or brass (or any combination) trivet with four legs from 8" to 15" high. It was for use in front of a parlor or keeping-room fire. It was more decorative than the plain trivet which was used in the kitchen. A tea kettle, placed on a footman, would keep nice and hot all through tea-time.

 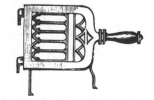

Fig. 516. FOOTMEN. Brass, ebony. F. A. Walker, c. 1870s.

FORK — An implement with a handle and two or more tines [*prongs, tangs*] and useful for stabbing into food to hold it steady while carving; firmly while toasting; or securely while eating. A fork is more suitable for sticking into food than sliding under it, but any book on table manners will insist that a fork should be slid under a pile of beans or buttered carrots and not stabbed into it.

> I eat syrup with my peas.
> I have did it all my life.
> Not because I like it,
> But it keeps 'em on my knife!
> [*as recited all her life by my grandmother, Grace Campbell Franklin, Memphis, Tennessee*]

The fork was not generally used at table until the reign of James I, ca. 1611, in England. Forks were known in Europe long before that. The first fork mentioned in history belonged to a Byzantine lady who took a golden *prong* to Venice as a bride in the 11th century. This fork caused a great sensation, and Peter Damian, later a Bishop, preached against it and scolded the lady for using a golden prong to convey food to her mouth, when God had given her fingers for that same purpose.

Governor John Winthrop brought a fork to America in 1630, carefully cased in a leather box with a bodkin and a knife. It is supposed to have been the only table fork in the Colonies during the early days.

Originally forks were made for two purposes: toasting and handling food, especially meat. These forks, nothing but a long handle and two sharp tines, were much larger than table forks, and were known as *flesh forks* or *toasting forks*. Some were made of one piece of wrought iron or steel; or a heavy wire, bent in half, twisted to form a handle, and sharpened. Anyone who has been to a wienie roast has held a similar fork in his hand. Other forks, more sophisticated, and for use on the table for carving, had a knife-guard which kept the sharp knife from slipping up the shaft of the fork.

104

Fig. 518. FORKS. 1890s. Wood (Cocobolo, rosewood), bone, steel. L: 7½". Just seven varieties of probably over a hundred handle designs. American. Author's Collection.

Fig. 519. SERVING FORK. F. W. Seastrand, c. 1912.

Fig. 520. FLESH FORK, two-pronged. Tinned wrought iron. L: 20", 24". Lalance & Grosjean, 1890.

Fig. 521. FLESH FORKS. Tinned wrought iron. L: 13", 15", 18", 20", 22", 24". Lalance & Grosjean, 1890.

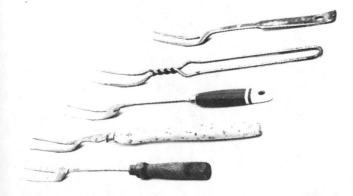

Fig, 522. FLESH FORKS. 1900 to 1940; earliest on far right. Three on bottom are stainless steel; others tinned iron. L: 11" to 14½". American. Courtesy Paul Persoff.

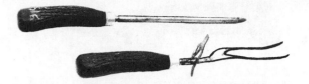

Fig. 523. CARVING FORK & STEEL. c. 1915. Thermoplastic cast to look like stag horn, steel. L: 10½", 13". American. Author's Collection.

FORK CLEANER — An implement composed of close rows of wire or fiber brushes which clean between the tines of a fork. Also, "keep a box or small keg, filled with chopped hay or straw and fine sand, in alternate layers, pressed down very hard, and having sand mixed with the brick dust on top. The contents must be kept closely packed and damp. Plunge the steel parts of the fork a few times into this; then wipe them afterwards." (*Leslie,* 1840.) *See also* "fork stick" *under* **KNIFE BOARD**

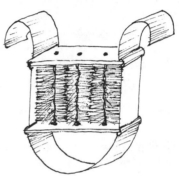

Fig. 524. FORK CLEANER. Pat'd Oct. 25, 1892, by Fritz Lehman.

FOUR DE CAMPAGNE — A utensil for cooking with fire over and under, like a dutch oven. Many of the recipes in Alexandre Dumas' classic *Le Grand Dictionnaire de Cuisine* call for such a utensil, in which the braising pot is set in hot coals and the special lid, with raised edges, was piled with coals. Sometimes the *Four de campagne* [literally, *country oven*] referred to what was called a *tin kitchen* in New England. *See also* **BRAISING PAN, DUTCH OVEN**

FRACTURES — The glass or earthenware utensils which had broken parts (such as the handle or footed-base) replaced by a tinsmith with tin.

FRENCH COOK'S KNIFE — A large, fairly broad-bladed knife with a pointed end. The handle is smaller in width than the blade.

Fig. 525. FRENCH COOK'S KNIFE. c. 1920s. Carbon steel, wood. L: 12". Guelon, France. Trademark boy with ladder. Author's Collection.

Fig. 526. FRENCH COOK'S KNIFE. 19th century. Carbon steel, wood. L: 11". French. Author's Collection.

FRENCH FRY-PAN — An omelet pan. *See* **FRY PAN**

FRENCH WARE — Seamless tinned ware, when first manufactured in America, was called *French ware* because it originated in France. *See also* **TIN**

FRICTION, — LUCIFER MATCH — Simply, a match ignited by friction. Invented by the English chemist, John Walker, in 1827. In America, friction matches were first made in Springfield, Massachusetts, in 1834, and were known by the makers' names: [Daniel] *Chapin and* [Alonzo] *Phillips.* The business was sold to a firm in Boston and the matches were then known as *Boston matches.* Phillips' patent gave the ingredients of his match head as chalk, phosphorous, brimstone and glue. Before the Chapin and Phillips matches, slender, sulpher-coated splints were ignited by tinder.

Friction matches were quite commonly called *lucifers,* or *lucifer matches.* They were not by any means safety matches, although it was written: "a new lucifer match has been invented, by the application to their opposite extremities of inflammable substances, which thus isolated are unaffected by friction, and *can only be ignited by contact with each other.*" (*Scientific Artisan,* November 1858, [*italics mine*].) This might be interpreted to mean that two matches were needed for each light, but it sounds dangerous and most friction or lucifer matches were. *See also* **MATCHES, MATCH SAFE**

FRILLS — *see* **CHOP FRILLS**

FRITTER BAKER — An iron, to be dipped in batter and then into boiling lard, cast in some small decorative shape. *See also* **BOUCHE IRON, PATTY IRON, VIENNA CAKE MOLD**

Fig. 527. FRENCH FRITTER BAKER. Iron. F. A. Walker, c. 1870s.

Fig. 528. FRITTER BAKERS. Iron tin. F. A. Walker, c. 1870s.

FROSTING and ECLAIR TUBE — A cloth, paper, or rubber tube, attached to a small cone-shaped metal tip. This tip came in a number of sizes and opening styles. These tubes were used for filling eclairs, and for working magic with frosted cakes. Similar ornamenting was done with savory jellies, butter or lard on tongue, roast chicken, hams, etc., and the same tubes were used.

Fig. 529. FROSTING & ECLAIR TUBES in case. c. 1870s. Tin. Case L: 6¼". American. Courtesy Keillor Collection.

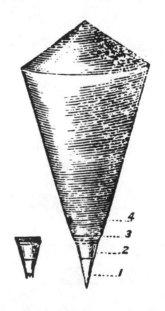

Fig. 530. ORNAMENTER for icing. Rubber or paper bag, metal tube in many available patterns. Prof. C. H. King's Eclipse Ornamenter, Orange, N.J. Practical Housekeeping, 1881.

Fig. 531. ORNAMENTING DESIGNS. "This appears a good deal on paper, but is really nothing when you come to do it." Prof. C. H. King, Practical Housekeeping, 1881.

Fig. 534. FRUIT JAR FUNNEL. c. 1890 - 1910. Tin. 5" dia.: H: 3-7/8". American. Author's Collection.

Fig. 532. CHAUDFROID DISHES showing ornamentation. Mrs. Beeton's Household Management, c. 1940.

FRUIT JAR FILLER — A tin or enameled ware funnel with a wide mouth and a wide neck. It usually has a little ring handle. It is the wide and fairly short neck which distinguishes the fruit jar funnel from the regular funnel. A similar utensil is the small sausage-stuffer which has a neck bigger than a funnel, but smaller than a fruit jar filler. The fruit jar filler was used by grocers for filling bags of dry meal or other food, and was called by them a *bag filler*.

FRUIT JAR HOLDER, —— LIFTER — A metal or wooden device to remove a fruit jar from boiling water, or to hold it securely while unfastening the lid.

Fig. 535. JAR HOLDER. "Clasps and holds the jar without danger of breaking it." Practical Housekeeping, 1881.

FRUIT JAR WRENCH — A tool for tightening or loosening a metal, screw-type canning jar lid. Quite a number of these were patented over a long period of time. Continuous-thread seals or caps were made throughout the 19th century, although they became common only in the second half.

Fig. 533. FRUIT JAR FILLER. Aluminum. 5" x 4¼". Montgomery Ward, 1895.

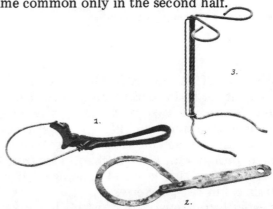

Fig. 536. JAR WRENCHES & JAR HOLDER. (1) May 18, 1917. Iron, wire. L: 7¾". Best S. Co., Lancaster, Pa. (2) c. 1910. Iron. L: 8". A. C. Williams, Ravenna, O. (3) Wire. L: 6". American. Author's Collection.

Fig. 537, 538. MASON JAR SEALER & OPENER. White metal, leather strap. F. W. Seastrand, c. 1912.

Fig. 539. JAR WRENCH. C. 1910. Iron, wood. L: 8½"; Inside dia. 2-3/8" to 2¾". American. Author's Collection.

FRUIT LIFTER or SUGAR AUGER — An implement for lifting dried fruit packed tightly in a barrel. There are two types: one is exactly the same as a *sugar auger* and like any auger it consists of a transverse handle (for leverage) and three twisted prongs with a single shaft. This fruit lifter is very pretty and graceful looking — like two ballerinas in a pirouette. Another type is a truncated broad-tined "fork" with a long shaft and a T-handle. Both types were used by inserting into the barrel of stuck-together fruit and twisting.

Fig. 540. SUGAR AUGER or FRUIT LIFTER. c. 1860s, 1870s. Wrought iron, wood. L: 16½". American. Courtesy Keillor Collection.

FRUIT PARER — "Owning a rotary fruit parer saves energy and caters to your sense of form, as the fruit can be served unangular and with little waste." (*Peyser*, 1922.) An apple parer could be used for peaches or pears or for other thin-skinned, firm-fleshed, fairly round fruit, but it worked best with an apple. *See also* **APPLE PARER, PEACH PARER**

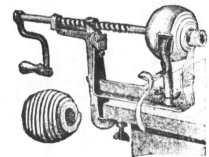

Fig. 541. APPLE PARER, CORER & SLICER. Treasure House, 1891.

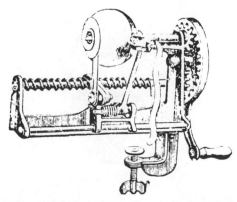

Fig. 542. APPLE PARER & CORER. F. A. Walker, c. 1870s.

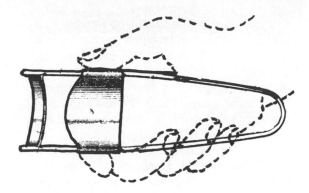

Fig. 543. FRUIT or VEGETABLE PEELER. Pat'd 1904, No. 757,551. Theodore M. Guest, Moravia, N.Y. assignor to Grant P. Sommerville. Official Gazette, April 19, 1904.

FRUIT PRICKER — "Made with a piece of cork and some needles, is a great saver of time and patience when one is preserving plums and other fruits with their skins. Cut a slice about ½" from a large cork and press through it a dozen or more coarse needles. Tack the cork to a board, needle side up, of course. Just strike the fruit on this bed of needles and you have a dozen holes at once. When you have finished your work, remove cork from board, wash and dry; dip needles in oil, wrap up and put away." (*Ladies Home Journal*, May 1899.)

FRUIT, WINE, VEGETABLE or JELLY PRESS — An implement for pressing fruits or vegetables through small apertures. One type has a perforated basket which holds the fruit or vegetable (particularly potatoes) and a levered plate which presses the food through the perforations. This is also called a *ricer*. Another has a geared crank action, either rack and pinion or screw, and the follower presses the food down against the perforated bottom of a basket insert, and from there out a straight spout into a bowl. This type was a combined sausage-stuffer, fruit and lard press. A third type had a hand wheel on top which forced a follower against the fruit. *"Yale;" "Sensible;" "Enterprise;" "Kreamer;" "Rollman;"* etc. See also **MEAT PRESS**

Fig. 544. FRUIT, WINE & JELLY PRESS. Pat'd June 8, 1888. Tinned iron. Enterprise. The Enterprising Housekeeper, 1898.

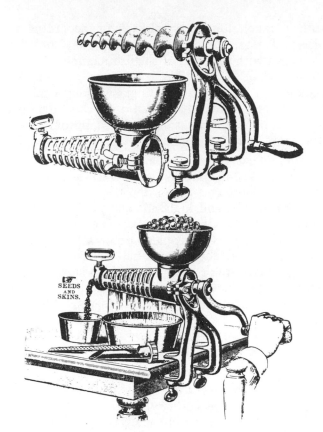

Fig. 545, 546. FRUIT PRESS. Pat'd Sept. 30, 1879. Enterprise Manufacturing Co. of Pa., 1881. (Also, Treasure House, 1891.)

FRYING BASKET — *see* **DEEP FAT BASKET**

FRYING KETTLE — A kettle used for deep-fat frying. Usually straight-sided and made of iron or tin. Some were especially made with a basket which hung from the kettle handle.

Celery Fritters
Boil some thick but tender stalks of celery in salted water; when done dry them in a cloth; cut them in equal lengths about 1½"; dip them in a batter; fry to a golden color; sprinkle fine salt well over and serve. [*Treasure House,* 1891]

Carrot Fritters
Beat 2 small boiled carrots to a pulp with a spoon; add 3 or 4 eggs and ½ handful of flour; moisten with cream, milk or a little white wine; sweeten to taste; beat all well together; fry them in boiling lard; when of a good color, take them off and serve; squeeze over them the juice of an orange; and strew them over with a finely sifted sugar. [*ibid*]

FRY, FRYING PAN — A shallow pan in a number of types including: short-handled cast-iron pans (also called *spiders*) which could fit in the oven and were therefore useful for hash, spider corn-cake and baked omelets. Another, the most common, was the so-called *French polished fry-pan* with a much longer handle. Then, according to Maria Parloa, "for an omelet pan, nothing compares with the pans of English hammered ware. Heavier than, but similar in shape to French pan. Handles are longer." The English frying pan had straight sides, a rolled edge, and two short handles, but a saute pan had straight sides approximately 3½" high, and a long handle.

The first American patent for a fry pan was granted in 1864. It was almost identical to a frying pan with ridges cast across the bottom which was patented in England in 1839. The ridges made the pan, in effect, a sort of gridiron. The 18th century fry pan was heavy wrought iron, with a handle often as long as three and a half or four feet. Tin frying pans weren't heavy enough to serve as well as the cast iron, but finally cast-aluminum was used to make a light and very durable pan. *"Acme;" "Dover;" "Lalance & Grosjean;" "Enterprise;" "Matthai-Ingram;" etc.*

Marion Harland had some things to say about

The Vagaries of the Kitchen

"Twenty-seven religions have I found in this country!" writes a French tourist, "and but one gravy!"

Had the satirist been familiar with the machinery of the average American kitchen, he might have added — "and that is made in the frying pan."

Our housewife may be unversed in the matter of steamers, braising and fish-kettles. The chances are as ten to one that she never owned a gridiron, and would laugh a patent "poacher" to shrillest scorn. Were any, or all of these given to her, and their uses enlarged upon intelligently and enthusiastically, she would shake an unconvinced head and brandish her frying-pan in the face of anxious innovators and disgusted reformers. A convenient implement? Hear her testimony and behold her practice.

For breakfast, her family is nourished, be it winter or summer, upon fried bacon, or salt pork, fried mush and fried potatoes. The bacon is cooked first; done to a slow crisp, and set aside to "sizzle" out any remaining flavor of individuality, while she gets the mush ready. The meat comes out, and the slices of stiffened dough go in, first to absorb, then to be (still slowly) cooked by the hot fat. All the fat is soaked up before the cold, boiled potatoes, cut into clammy "chunks" are put in. In fact, the last relay of mush is scorched to the bottom of the pan, and the bits of pork, clinging to the sides, are unsavory

cinders. A great spoonful of lard sets all that to rights, and is just melted when the potatoes are immersed in it. Browning, under this process, is an impossibility, but a few outside pieces burn satisfactorily, and the rest smoke as the contents of the invaluable utensil are dished. Breakfast is ready...

The colander — the most efficient check upon that Lord of Misrule, the frying-pan — inasmuch, as by its use, some of the reek and drip may be got rid of before the food is served — is seldom in our housewife's hands, except when squash or pumpkin pies are to be made. Least of all does she think of employing it in serving vegetables....

I was more hopeful, ten years ago, than I am now, of possible reformation among the reigning autocrats of the culinary department. "Mother," is joined to her sooty idol, the *FRYING PAN;* to her family pie crust, to boiled tea, to undrained beets, and drained (instead of wiped) china....

The one ray of light comes from the fact that some of our young girls are beginning to look upon cookery as a practical science. [*Harland,* 1889]

Fig. 547. POTATO or CRULLER FRYER. Pat'd July 8, 1879. Bright iron. From 9 to 14" dia. A deeper version was patented July 8, 1880. Lalance & Grosjean, 1890.

Fig. 548. FRY PAN. English hammered iron. From 6½" to 12" bottom dia. Lalance & Grosjean, 1890.

FUNNEL—A tin, enameled ware, or pottery inverted cone, with a long narrow neck through which liquid or powder coming out a large opening can be made to go into a small. Some have brass wire-mesh strainers built in midway. *See also* COMBINATION DIPPER, FRUIT JAR FILLER

Fig. 549. FRYING PAN. 18th century or early-19th. Wrought iron. L: 50"; 14¼" dia. American. Courtesy Keillor Collection.

Fig. 550. "CENTRAL" FRY PAN. Pat'd Nov. 27, 1877 and Jan. 1875. Iron. From 8" to 12" dia. Lalance & Grosjean, 1890.

Fig. 553. FUNNEL. Aluminum. Goldberg, Bowen & Lebenbaum's Monthly Price Current (catalog), June 1895.

Fig. 554. FUNNEL. F. A. Walker, c. 1870s.

Fig. 551. STANDARD FRY PAN. Black tin. From 8" to 13" diameter. Matthai-Ingram Company, c. 1890.

Fig. 552. FRYING PANS. Katzinger Co., 1940.

Fig. 555. FUNNEL. Aluminum. ½ pint or 1 pint size. This funnel cost 48 cents in the ½ pint size, whereas the agate funnel of the same size cost 17 cents, and the tin one was 3 cents. Montgomery Ward, 1895.

Fig. 556. FUNNEL. c. 1940. Spun aluminum. H: 2¾"; 2¾" dia. American. Author's Collection.

GARLIC RIDDLE — A wirework coarse sieve for mincing or pressing garlic.

GARNISHING KNIFE — *see* **VEGETABLE CUTTER**

GARTH — A wooden cake pan in the form of a hoop. *See also* **CAKE PAN, FLAN RING**

GAS TOASTER — A wire-mesh, hand-held implement with wire "fingers" to hold slices of bread for toasting over a gas or oil stove. The Fairgrieve patent gas toaster, patented in 1897, was guaranteed to toast without taste or odor. *See also* **TOASTER**

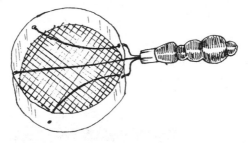

Fig. 557. FAIRGRIEVE GAS TOASTER. Pat'd 1897. Detroit, Michigan.

GEM PAN — A heavy, cast-iron pan with a number of shallow, or deep, cups for baking the little muffin breads called *gems*. They were often used interchangeably with *popover pans*.

A gem pan is supposed to be quite different from a muffin pan, but no doubt many gems were made in muffin pans and popover pans. "Bake in gem pans, or if you have not these you may use patty pans; but I would get the gem pans; you will save so much time whenever you bake, and run less risk of burning your hand and wrist. It pays in the end to get all these little improvements."

(*Babcock*, 1881.) *See also* **MUFFIN PAN, POPOVER PAN, ROLL PAN**

Gems
These are the simplest form of bread, and if properly made are certain to be light and sweet. A hot oven and hot pans are prime essentials, and there must be no delay between making and baking. The coldest water, ice-water preferred, should be used. Use either whole-wheat or Graham flour, three parts of flour to one of water.... For a dozen gems allow one large cup — a half pint — of ice water, one even teaspoon of salt, and three cups of flour. Stir in the flour slowly, beating hard and steadily, not less than ten minutes. The pans should have been set on top of the stove, and oiled or buttered. Fill them 2/3 full, and bake about ½ hour. [Mrs. Helen Campbell, in *Good Housekeeping Discovery Book, No. 1*, 1905]

Graham Gems
To 1 quart of Graham flour add ½ pint fine white flour; enough milk or water, a little warm, to make a thick batter; no salt or baking powder; have the oven hotter than for biscuits; let gem-pans stand in the oven till you get ready; beat batter thoroughly; grease your pans; drop in while the irons are smoking hot; bake quickly a nice brown. [*Treasure House*, 1891]

Graham flour was named after the Reverend Sylvester Graham (1794-1851), an American who was the first to recognize the value of eating whole-wheat flour, bran and all. He spent a lot of his life trying to get the word to the cooks and housewives of America, and was ridiculed and considered nothing but a mad faddist by some. He had a large and enthusiastic following however, and many recipes throughout the 19th century called for *Graham flour*.

GILL — A United States liquid unit equal to ¼ United States liquid pint. Also a British unit equal to ¼ Imperial pint; but in British dialect, a half-pint. It is possible that in early-18th century American recipes that the dialectal half-pint was meant. Later recipes, however, which call for a gill, require a half-cup or four ounces.

GIRDLE PLATE — A griddle for baking small cakes and oatbread. Some had a half-hoop handle and were hung from a pot hook on a crane in the fireplace. Some were meant to stand on a trivet or brandiron on the down hearth and had a bow handle, a hoop, or a small handle on the side. *See also* **GRIDDLE**

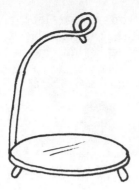

Fig. 558. GIRDLE PLATE.

GLAZING BRUSH — see BRUSHES

GLAZING POT,— KETTLE — A double boiler utensil for boiling gravies, soups or glazes. The meat glaze is gravy or clarified soup boiled until it becomes a paste and gelatinizes on cooling. It was used as a species of varnish, usually for braised dishes, and it could be flavored and spiced to taste.

Fig. 559. GLAZING POT & BRUSH. Treasure House, 1891.

GRANITEWARE — Ironware coated with a gray ceramic enamel suggesting the appearance of granite. More rarely it refers also to an earthenware with a speckled gray glaze. See also ENAMELED WARE

Fig. 560. GRANITEWARE. Pottery. Butler Brothers, 1899.

Fig. 561. GRANITEWARE advertising trade card. c. 1880s.

GRAPE SCISSORS — Small scissors with curved, pointed blades, for separating grape stems from the bunch. They were used primarily at the table.

GRATE or GRATE-IRON — A framework of horizontal iron bars, raised a bit above the hearth floor, in which the coals rest in the fireplace, or upon which food can be roasted by laying a grid across the grate. See also GRIDIRON

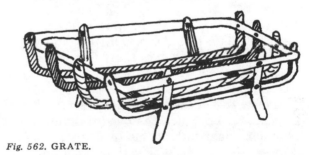

Fig. 562. GRATE.

GRATER — A metal implement, usually of tin, with a rough surface. Certain foods, including raw vegetables, bread and cheese, are rubbed over the surface to reduce them to shreds or crumbs. Most graters have a punched, jagged pattern of holes.

The smallest graters were for lemon peel, nutmegs, and burned toast, and came in a variety of styles. The *nutmeg graters* are the most diversified, and a number of mechanical graters were patented. The basic, unadorned nutmeg grater was simply a small curved piece of finely-punctured tin, with a back, a bottom, and a little lidded compartment on top for storing nutmegs. This type is still manufactured and sometimes, unfortunately, sold as antique. *Caveat emptor.* The basic mechanical grater was a grating surface over which the nutmeg was rubbed — contained in a box with a spring which held it tight to the grater. The container tracked the edges of the grater. This type operates on the same principle as the box grater [which see]. Very fine silver nutmeg graters were used in the 17th and 18th centuries, and were carried by gentlemen for use when they were travelling, or away from home. Ceramic graters, not with punctures, but with rough "divots" of clay, served to rasp lemon peel. Other fine graters were used for the same purpose.

Brussels Sprouts

Trim neatly and wash them; put them to boil in plenty of salted water; when almost done, strain them and dry them in a cloth; put them in a saucepan with a large piece of butter, pepper, salt and grated nutmeg to taste; toss them gently on the fire until they are quite cooked. [*Treasure House*, 1891]

Larger graters were for everything from horse-radish to cheese. The basic types, in different sizes, are: (1) the arched piece of punctured tin, or other metal, with a flat back or a stiff wire frame. This type has a hooped handle. (2) A flat grating surface with several grades of coarseness and a slicer in the center. Sometimes this type had four sides, and four different grades of coarseness. (3) The revolving grater, consisting of a hopper, a punctured grating drum, and a crank. The food was usually held in the hopper — against the revolving drum — with a heavy glass or wooden follower. A number of these graters had interchangable grating drums. Most of them were screw-clamped to the table. (4) A cylinder of punctured tin with a hoop handle, and sometimes short feet which held the grater above the work surface.

Dover Stamping Company, Matthai-Ingram, and Lalance & Grosjean, among others, all sold *grater blanks* from which the local tinsmith or the householder could fashion his own graters. These blanks were tin, and came in various grades. But tin was not the only metal used. There is a lovely large grater made of brass at Williamsburg. Some graters were made of galvanized iron, such as the *Apollo*, which advertised it could "slice everything in the vegetable line," (*Ladies Home Journal*, April 1899.) Nutmeg Graters: *"Edgar;" "Monitor;" "T.L. Holt;" "Dover;" "Boye;" "Unique;"* etc. Others: *"Ekco;" "All in One;" "Kitchen Novelty Co.;"* etc.

Cucumber Catsup

1 bushel of table-sized cucumbers; pare and grate them on a large grater into a sieve; squeeze and drain the pulp until very dry; add black pepper and salt; rub in thoroughly with the hands. Fill ordinary fruit jars half full of pulp; take

white wine vinegar, let it come to a boil, and fill the jars; stir thoroughly, and seal the jars while hot. Put a tablespoon of oil on top each jar to keep it air-tight. [*Treasure House*, 1891]

Fig. 563. GRATERS. Early-19th century. Punched tin, wood. Left: 8" x 2¾"; Center: 15" x 3¼"; Right: L: 9¾"; W: 6½"; H: 3½"; Homemade. American. Courtesy Keillor Collection.

Fig. 564. GRATER. 18th century. Wrought iron. L: 15½"; W: 7". American. Courtesy Keillor Collection.

Fig. 565. NUTMEG GRATERS. 19th century. Tin, wood, cast iron. Left to right: (1) L: 7". Pat'd March 9, 1886. Cast iron crank. (2) L: 7". Common Sense Grater, 1869. (3) and (4) two views of a grater. L: 5-1/4". American. Courtesy Keillor Collection.

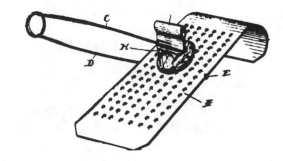

Fig. 566. GRATER. Pat'd 1904, No. 775,973. Charles B. Hibbard, Grand Rapids, Mich. Official Gazette, Nov. 29, 1904.

Fig. 567. NUTMEG GRATER. c. 1870s. Wood, brass, tin. L: 7½".
American. Courtesy Keillor Collection.

Fig. 570. NUTMEG GRATER. Pat'd Aug. 18, 1891. Tin, wire,
wood. L: 5-7/8; W: 5¼". Edgar. Author's Collection.

Fig. 568. NUTMEG GRATERS. 19th century. (1) Wood, tin. 5" 1.
(2) and (3) Tin, wood. Spring-loaded. L: 6¼"; L: 3½". (4) Wood,
tin. Springloaded. L: 6¼". American. Courtesy Keillor Collection.

Fig. 571. NUTMEG GRATERS. 19th century. Tin, wood. Left to
right: L: 5"; 5"; 6-1/2"; 7", Dated 1867. American. Courtesy
Keillor Collection.

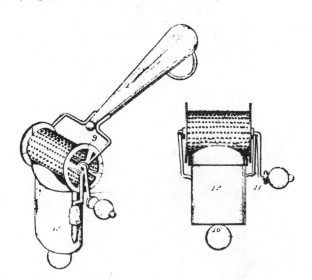

Fig. 569. NUTMEG-GRATER. Pat'd 1898, No. 604,751. John W.
Hart, Pittsburg, Kansas, assignor to William J. Kaemmerling. Official
Gazette, May 31, 1898.

Fig 572. GRATERS. 19th century. 3 homemade tin, and tin &
wood graters: L: 5"; L: 7-1/2"; and L: 6". 2 nutmeg graters: Tin,
nickeled iron, wood. L: 4"; W: 2-3/4", dated 1870. Tin, Wood. L:
4-3/4"; W: 4-1/8". All American. Courtesy Keillor Collection.

Fig. 573. GRATERS. 19th century. Tin and tin & wood. Left: Nutmeg grater. 7-1/2" x 2-1/3". Homemade. Center: Made with grater blank. 14" x 3-1/3". Right: Box grater. 8-1/2". Holt, 1887. All American. Courtesy Keillor Collection.

Fig. 577. COMBINATION GRATER & SLAW CUTTER. Galvanized iron, steel blades, tin grater. J. B. Foote Foundry Company, 1906.

Fig. 574, 575. GRATERS. c. 1890. Tin with handles. Both: L: 4¼"; W: 3". American. Author's Collection.

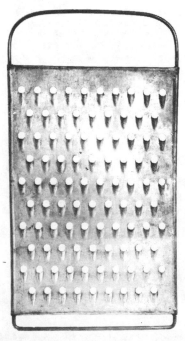

Fig. 578. GRATERS. Left: c. 1900. L: 16"; W: 6¼". Right: c. 1910. L: 9½"; W: 4¾". Punched tin. American. Author's Collection.

Fig. 576. CYLINDRICAL GRATER. c. 1910. Tin. 3¾" dia.; H: 9¼". Grates very fine, fine & medium. American. Author's Collection.

Fig. 579. GRATER. c. 1915-1930. Tin. L: 12"; W: 6¼". American. Author's Collection.

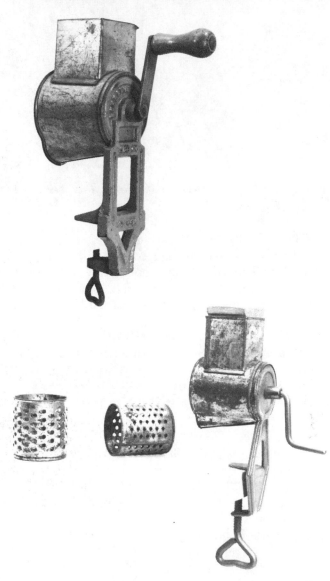

Fig. 583. REVOLVING GRATER. c. 1935. Cast iron, tin, wood. L: 8½". Lorraine Metal Mfg. Co. Author's Collection.

Fig. 580. COMBINATION GRATERS. Top: Tin. 4" x 7½". Coarse, medium, fine perforations. Bottom: Tin. Two views of grater, slicer and cutter. 4¼" x 3¼" x 7½". For grating coarse and fine, slicing potatoes and cutting slaw. Cream City Ware, Geuder, Paeschke & Frey Co., Milwaukee, Wis., 1925.

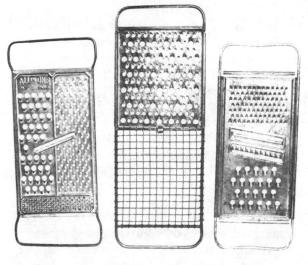

Fig. 581. GRATERS. Tin, wire. Left to right: (1) All-in-one. c. 1940. 4¼" x 10-5/8". (2) Made in Germany for Kitchen Novelty Co, Atlantic City, N.J. c. 1895. 4½" x 12½". (3) Ekco. c. 1935. 4-1/8" x 10½". American. Author's Collection.

Fig. 584. REVOLVING GRATER. c. 1935. Tin, nickel, wood. 3 grades of grater drums: coarse, fine, medium. L: 6½". Probably Lorraine. Author's Collection.

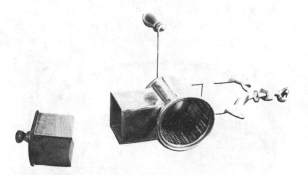

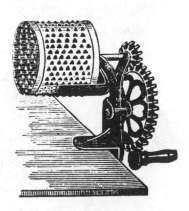

Fig. 582. REVOLVING GRATER. c. 1930s. Tin, cast iron, wood. 3¾" dia. of grater drum; L: 13". BME No. 620, Germany. Courtesy Mary Mac Franklin.

Fig. 585. REVOLVING GRATER. Metal. Practical Housekeeping, 1881.

Fig. 586. REVOLVING GRATER. Pat'd Aug. 14, 1866. Cast iron & tin, wood. 10½" x 11½". Enos Stimson. Courtesy Keillor Collection.

GRATIN DISH — A rather deep, three-piece utensil used for baking and serving fish, meat or vegetables. The three parts consist of a frame, a supporting rim, and an inner dish. The food was baked in the dish, and served at table with the frame and the rim.

Au gratin literally means "with grating". A dish so prepared is covered with a layer of bread or cracker crumbs and baked so as to form a light crust. Often a recipe for scalloped vegetables will call for a buttered crumb crust — the dish to be baked in a casserole.

Tomatoes au Gratin

This simple and delicious dish is made by cutting some ripe tomatoes in half, putting them in a buttered dish with breadcrumbs, butter, pepper, and salt, and baking till slightly browned on the top. [*Arthur's Home Magazine*, as published in *Universal Cookery Book*, 1888.]

GRAVY STRAINER — A vessel with a wire-mesh bottom, or perforations, and a handle. It was used for straining gravy or clarifying soup stock. *See also* **CHINESE STRAINER, SOUP STRAINER, TAPERING STRAINER**

Fig. 587. GRAVY STRAINERS. Tin. 3¾" to 6-7/8" dia. Lalance & Grosjean, 1890.

GRIDDLE or GIRDLE — A flat utensil with a little—or highly-polished surface for baking batter cakes. Several styles included one with a bail handle; one with a single long handle; and the Schofield Patent Cake Griddle, which was actually a hinged griddle with four to eight small griddles and one large one. The batter was first dipped onto each of the small griddles, and when they were done on one side, each small griddle was turned out on the long one. This left the little griddles free for another load of batter.

A soapstone griddle did not require greasing, but the objection to it was that cakes and muffins baked on it weren't tender. (Muffins were baked on a griddle in muffin rings, laid on it.) An artificial stone griddle was described as "a new article for the kitchen, is light and durable, and, it is claimed, does away entirely with grease and smoke in making the breakfast pancakes. Soapstone griddles are often used, but this is a much cheaper and equally as good a substitute." (*Practical Housekeeping*, 1884.) "*Sun;*" "*Schofield's;*" "*Never Break;*" "*Enterprise;*" "*Matthai-Ingram;*" etc.

New England Fire Cakes
by Mrs. F.D.J.

Make a pie crust not quite so rich as for puff paste. Cut off small pieces and roll out thin about the size of a breakfast plate, as nearly round as possible. Have a griddle over the fire, and bake a nice brown, turning it when done on one side and browning nicely on the other. When done, put on a plate and butter it well. Have ready another cake, and bake, piling one upon the other, and buttering each piece, until all you have made are cooked. Serve them quite hot, cutting down through all the layers. This is very nice if, as you butter each piece, preserved strawberries or raspberries are spread upon each layer. It is an old-fashioned New England cake, and in olden times was cooked in iron spiders, propped up before the kitchen fire; hence its name. It is a very nice short cake, to be eaten hot, for supper or breakfast. [*Home Cook Book*, 1876]

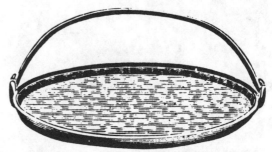

Fig. 588. CAKE GRIDDLE. Enameled iron. Bail handle. 10" to 14" dia. Montgomery Ward, 1893.

Fig. 589. GRIDDLE. c. 1870s, 1880s. Cast iron, hinged. L: 13½"; W: 10½". Stuart Peterson. Courtesy Keillor Collection.

GRIDDLE GREASER — A wire device with a grease-absorbing roller; or a cast-iron device with a cup for the grease and a snap-on cloth cap. The fat kept the cloth greasy and it was rubbed on the hot griddle. This W.H. Bixler griddle greaser was also a griddle scraper, but care had to be taken not to scratch the surface.

"Tie a strip of muslin on the end of a round stick, and use to grease bread and cake-pans, gem-irons, etc." (*Practical Housekeeping*, 1884.)

Rice Fritters

Boil 1 teaspoonful of rice until it is tender; strain upon it 1 quart of milk; let it boil ten minutes; cool it; add flour enough to make a batter as thick as will fry easily on the griddle; 2 tablespoonfuls of yeast; let it rise 3 hours; add 2 well-beaten eggs, and cook on a heated griddle. [*Treasure House* 1891]

To do away with the grease on the griddle for baking cakes, have the ordinary iron griddle ground smooth on a grindstone and rubbed off with a piece of fine sandpaper wrapped around a block of wood. If the griddle be rubbed with a turnip, the desired smoothness will be obtained and the unpleasant smoke done away with. [*ibid*]

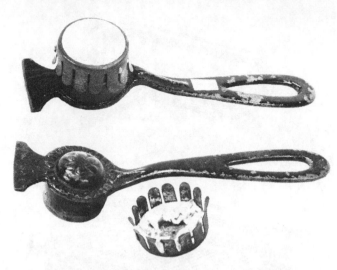

Fig. 591, 592. GRIDDLE GREASER & SCRAPER. Pat'd July 22, 1873. Cast iron, tin, cloth. L: 7¼". W. H. Bixler. "To prepare the greaser for use—Fill the bowl of No. 2 with lard, then place upon it the perforated cap No. 4, over this cap lay the circular piece of cloth, and then put on and press up tightly the spring ring No. 3, which holds both cloth and cap in place. Be sure and press up the ring far enough to prevent its scraping the griddle. After the cloth is first put on, rub a little lard on the outside before using." Courtesy Keillor Collection.

GRIDIRON — A cast-iron stand with an openwork grating. Round, square or rectangular. Many early gridirons revolved: this type was sometimes called a *whirling gridiron.*

"Place the steak on a hot, well-greased gridiron, turn often so that the outside may be seared at once; when done, which will require from five to ten minutes, dish on a hot platter, season with salt and pepper and bits of butter.... A small pair of tongs are best to turn steaks, as piercing with a fork frees the juices. If fat drips on the coals below, the blaze may be extinguished by sprinkling with salt, always withdrawing the gridiron to prevent the steak from acquiring a smoky flavor. Always have a brisk fire, whether you cook in a patent broiler directly over the fire, or on a gridiron over a bed of live coals.... A steel gridiron with slender bars is best, as the common broad, flat iron bars fry and scorch the meat, imparting a disagreeable flavor." (*Practical Housekeeping*, 1884.) *See also* **BROILER**

Fig. 590. GRIDDLE GREASER. F. W. Seastrand, c. 1912.

Fig. 593. GRIDIRON. Tin. 12" x 12". Lalance & Grosjean, 1890.

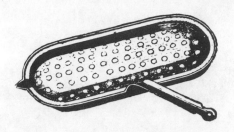

Fig. 594. OVAL GRIDIRON. Heavy tin. From 15" x 7" to 20½" x 9¾" to fit 6", 7", 8" and 9" stove holes. Lalance & Grosjean, 1890.

Fig. 595. DELUXE GRIDIRON. Cast iron, steel. 18½" x 10". Androck, 1936.

GRILL — A gridiron or grating used for broiling meat or fish over hot coals, as over a brazier.

Fig. 596. ROTARY GRILL. 18th century. Wrought iron. L: 18½"; W: 10". American. Courtesy Keillor Collection.

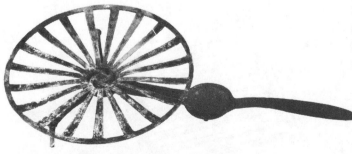

Fig. 597. ROTATING GRILL. 18th century. Wrought iron. L: 25"; 13½" dia. Has lubricating grease cup under pivot. American. Courtesy Keillor Collection.

GRINDER, GRINDSTONE — A cranked, or treadle-operated disk of natural sandstone, held by an axle in a framework, and used for sharpening edge tools: knives, scissors, axes, hoes, etc. Small grinders could be screw-clamped to a kitchen table. Some grinders had emery wheels.

Fig. 598. GRINDSTONE. Montgomery Ward, 1895.

HAIR SIEVE [*hersyfe, herseve*] — A wooden-hooped sieve with a woven hair mesh. The hair was usually horsehair, and often woven by the Society of Shakers in a plaid, using black and white horsehairs. The hair sieves were made in many sizes and were used for sifting flour, and for straining wet foods. *See also* **SIEVE**

Apple Biscuit

Boil 12 fine apples until they become pulpy; take them out and rub through a hair sieve; add 2 lbs. of powdered loaf sugar, and 2 or 3 drops of oil of lemon or cloves; mix together; roll the mixture into separate masses of the size and thickness of a bun; cut them into any shape desired; then dry in a very slow oven. [*Treasure House*, 1891]

HAM BOILER — A very large, oblong, sheet-iron or tinned-copper utensil with a perforated, lift-out tray. It was used for boiling whole hams, turkeys and fish. "An ordinary wash-boiler, *thoroughly cleaned*, may be used, with care in cleansing both before and after using." (*Practical Housekeeping*, 1884.) All the boilers were practically the same, except in size, and a lift-out tray could be improvised. *See also* **FISH KETTLE**

Fig. 599. HAM BOILER. F. A. Walker, c. 1870s.

Fig. 600. HAM or PRESERVE BOILER. c. 1870s, 1880s. Tin-lined copper, cast iron. L: 12½", W: 7½"; H: 7". American. Courtesy Mary Mac Franklin.

Fig. 601. HAM BOILER. Pieced tin. L: 17", 18½", 20"; H: 9½", 10¼", 11". Matthai-Ingram Company, c. 1890.

HAM HOOK — *see* **MEAT HOOK**

HAM SLICER — A long, very narrow-bladed knife.

HANDLES — There are a number of handle types for all the utensils and gadgets used over the centuries. Today we are accustomed to calling all handles by that single, non-descriptive word. But we are also used to a kitchen stove on which any kind of pot or pan can be placed, and our only concern with the handle is that it does not stick out beyond the front edge of the stove, and that if it is hot we have a pot holder to protect our hands.

But depending on the source of heat, and the position of the utensil, the handle was once a very important design concern. A long straight handle is found on utensils which had to be maneuvered over a very hot open fire. Some frying pans, for example, had three or four foot handles. Toasting forks and salamanders had long handles too. Kettles and pots had so-called *falling* handles — bail handles which could be hooked to the pot crane, or dropped to the side when the kettle was moved from the fire. Saucepans, pots and skillets made to fit into the holes or wells in the top of a range had to have handles which angled up and then out.

Some early writers even suggested that such pans be made with the handle riveted to the inside of the pan, so that it would sit evenly in the well. Adapter rings were used with some range kettles or pots which were handle-less. Double boilers were constructed or improvised with a mind to the proper handle for the innner kettle, and how it would fit the outer kettle.

Some kettles and boilers, as well as colanders, chafing dishes and braziers were made with two small *ear* handles of wire or ½"-wide strips of metal.

Almost all the wrought-iron handles of 18th century utensils were made with either a hole or a tight loop at the end, so that the utensil could be hung from a nail or hook. Most utensils are still made that way.

Various techniques and materials were used to make the handle cooler, or less heat conductive. They were covered with or made of wood; or twisted in a tight spiral so that the heat had to travel just that much further; or cast with holes which allowed air to circulate more freely. Some late 19th century tin and enamel skillets and sauce pans had specially designed hollow handles. Horn or ivory was sometimes inserted between the metal shaft and the wood of the handle, as both were extremely poor heat conductors. Stag handles are horn, usually left with its natural appearance. Bakelite and other synthetics were used during the first decades of the 20th century.

Fig. 602. BAIL HANDLES.

121

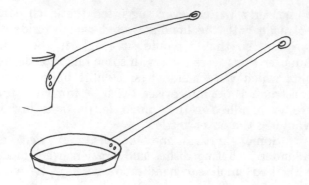

Fig. 603.

Fig. 604. BAIL HANDLE. Indurated fibre ware pail. Cordley & Hayes, Indurated Fibre Ware, 1889.

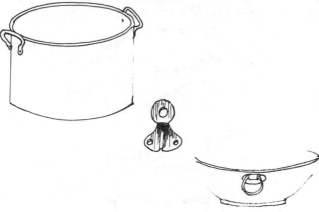

Fig. 605. EAR HANDLES.

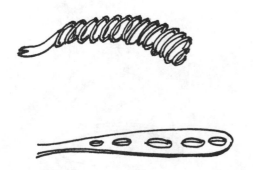

Fig. 606. HANDLES designed to reduce heat conduction.

Fig. 607. TEA POT HANDLE. Enameled wood, tin shanks. L: 5¼", 5¾". Tinners' Trimmings & Supplies, Matthai-Ingram Company, c. 1890.

HASH DISH and LAMP — A form of chafing dish with an alcohol lamp under the dish. An advertisement in a Tory newspaper, *The Royal Gazette*, published in New York City in 1781 read: "To be sold, a compleat camp kitchen, 10 guineas, made of double Block tin as wholesome as silver. A tea kettle, a coffee pot, a chocolate pot and mill, a butter saucepan, 6 saucepans with a cover, 4 soup pots with covers, 6 spoons, a hash dish and lamp, a Spice box, a bread grater, a Dutch oven, a cheese toaster, 7 stew pans with covers, 2 frying pans, a gridiron, a large boiling pot, a Carp or fish kettle, a Dripping pan and baster, a skimmer and a soup laddle, a slice and ragout spoon, a pepper and flour box, a cullender and 2 beer pots, 12 patty pans, and 2 tart pans."

Recipes for hash from various cookbooks from the 1700s through the late 1800s are more like stew than the hash a modern reader would probably expect.

To Hash Roasted Mutton

Take your mutton half roasted, and cut it in pieces as big as a half-crown; then put into your saucepan half a pint of claret, as much strong broth or gravy (or water, if you have not the other) one anchovy, and eschalot, a little whole pepper, some nutmeg sliced, salt to your taste, some oyster-liquor, a pint of oysters; let these stew a little, then put in the meat, and a few capers and samphire shred; when it is hot through, thicken it up with a piece of fresh butter roll'd in flour; toast sippets, and lay in your dish, and pour your meat on them. Garnish with lemon. [*E.Smith*, 1753.] (*Samphire is a fleshy herb which grows on or near the beach.*)

And another:

Hash

Cut some beef in nice little slices from the bone; remove all the hard parts and skin; put the gravy in a saucepan with 1 pt. of water, 3 tablespoonfuls of catsup, 1 dessert-spoonful of minced savory herbs, 1 onion chopped fine, ½ teaspoon of salt and 1/3 of cayenne; let these stew together for 15 minutes; take a cupful of flour; stir it well into the stewpan and stew for 10 minutes longer; strain it through a sieve; return it to the pan; place the slices of beef in it and keep the saucepan on the side of the range until the meat is heated through — not boiled, or it will become hard; a few minutes before serving add ½ wineglass of tarragon vinegar; arrange some toasted sippets round a very hot dish, and serve the hash immediately after it is cooked. [*Treasure House*, 1891]

Fig. 608. HASH DISH. Planished tin. F. A. Walker, c. 1870s.

Fig. 609. TENSION CHOPPING KNIFE. Pat'd 1867. Steel. "In this knife the blades are ... kept firm by the tension of the frame in which they are set. It does very rapid work, and is an excellent knife for family use. Most people consider hash a very delicious breakfast dish, in spite of all the hits newspaper paragraphers have made on it, and a good implement for making it is indispensible." *Practical Housekeeping*, 1881.

Fig. 610. MEAT CHOPPER. Wood, cast iron. *Practical Housekeeping*, 1881.

HEARTH CAKE — A cake baked on the hearth. *See also* **BANNOCK, GIRDLE PLATE, GRIDDLE, HOECAKE, JOHNNY CAKE**

HEARTH OVEN — A tin reflecting oven for roasting birds, apples, etc. There were special types for each, and refinements such as built-in drip pans and adjustable shelves. In some the spit could be turned by hand or hooked up to a clockwork machine. *See also* **APPLE ROASTER, BIRD ROASTER, PORTABLE SPRING JACK, REFLECTING OVEN, TIN KITCHEN**

Fig. 611. HEARTH OVEN. 19th century. Tin. L: 18"; W: 10": H: 15". "The Highland Hearth." Courtesy Keillor Collection.

HERB GRINDER — A utensil for grinding dried herbs and spices. One type is a cast-iron boat-shaped mortar with a rolling pestle shaped like a wheel with knob handles. *See also* **QUERNE, SPICE MILL**

Fig. 612. HERB OR SPICE MILL. Possibly 18th or early 19th century. Cast iron, wood. L: 18"; W: 4-1/2"; wheel: 7" diameter. Possibly American, although new information indicates it is typically ancient Japanese. Perhaps brought to America on a clipper ship? Courtesy Keillor Collection.

HOARHOUND [*horehound*] **CUTTER** — A multiple-bladed roller for cutting sticks of candy after the candy has been poured into a pan or onto a marble slab to cool.

Hoarhound Candy

7 lbs. sugar, white or brown; ¼ oz. cream of tartar; 1 qt. water; ½ pint strong hoarhound tea; boil to the feather; grain against the sides of the pan with spoon, 2 or 3 minutes; then pour out onto slab; form into flat sticks, rolls or drops, with a hoarhound cutter, which are made in two styles, with movable knives or with fixed divisions. [*Treasure House*, 1891]. If, when the sugar is boiled, the skimmer is dipped in and shook over the pan, and then given a sudden flirt behind, the sugar will fly off like feathers; this is called the feathered stage. [*ibid*]

Fig. 613. HOARHOUND CUTTER. Treasure House, 1891.

HOB — A level projection at the back or side of an open fireplace, upon which a pot is placed to be kept warm. The hob is also the brick, stone, or iron frame of the fireplace. The hob of a range is the level shelf at the back. It is also called the *overhead warming shelf*.

HOECAKE — Originally a cake baked on the broad, thin iron blade of the cotton field hoe. It is similar to the johnny cake and other hearth cakes.

Virginia Hoe Cake

Pour warm water on a quart of Indian meal; stir in a spoonful of lard or butter, some salt, make it stiff, and work it for 10 minutes; have a board about the size of a barrel head, (or the middle piece of the head will answer), wet the board with water, and spread on the dough with your hand; place it before the fire; prop it aslant with a flat-iron, bake it slowly; when one side is nicely brown, take it up and turn it, by running a thread between the cake and the board,

then put it back, and let the other side brown. These cakes used to be baked in Virginia on a large iron hoe, from whence they derive their name. [*Lea*, 1859] *See also* HEARTH CAKE

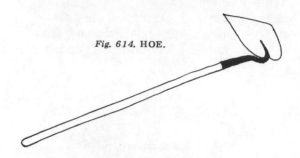

Fig. 614. HOE.

HOGSHEAD — A large cask or barrel, particularly one containing from 63 to 140 gallons. A hogshead is a unit of measure, but it will rarely be called for in a recipe.

HOOP — (1) A deep, round, cake pan, often with a removable bottom, and sometimes with a spring-clip fastener. Also called a *spring-form*. (2) A wooden hoop to hold the curds when making cheese. *See also* CAKE PAN, CHEESE PRESS

HOUR GLASS — If there weren't a clock in the kitchen, or a watch on the cook, an hour glass was necessary for timing cooking. The sand ran from one half to the other in exactly one hour. An hour glass is an obconical, thin-waisted glass, closed at both ends and filled with fine sand, mercury, or "the best hour glasses are those which are filled with egg shells, well-dried in an oven, finely pulverized or sifted; as they show the passage of time with greater exactness than common sand." (*Willich*, 1821.) One pictured hour glass is nearly 200 years old, and is typical of the old ones in that it consists of two glass cones, bound together at the waist with chamois, and protected by a sort of wooden cage.

The hour glass was called an *egg glass* when made for timing boiled eggs.

Fig. 615. EGG GLASS. F. A. Walker, c. 1870s.

Fig. 616. EGG GLASS. F. A. Walker, c. 1870s.

Fig. 617. EGG GLASS. F. A. Walker, c. 1870s.

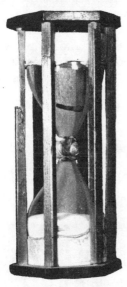

Fig. 618. HOURGLASS. 19th century. Glass, wood, paper, leather. 3½" dia. H: 8-5/8". Two separate, blown glass flasks tied together with chamois leather. Courtesy Michie Tavern, Charlottesville, Virginia.

HULLER or STRAWBERRY HULLER — A small, simple tin instrument — a pincher — which is made of springy metal. It was used for pinching out the hulls of strawberries or other small berries. "Is light, simple, small and cheap, and does away with the necessity of pressing the fingers close against the fruit." (Parloa, *Ladies Home Journal.* 1899.)

To Make Strawberry or Raspberry Fool
Take a pint of raspberries, squeeze and strain the juice with orange-flower water; put to the juice five ounces of fine sugar; then set a pint of cream over the fire, and let it boil up; then put in the juice; give it one stir round, and then put it into your bason; stir it a little in the bason, and when it is cold use it. [*E. Smith*, 1753]

Fig. 619. STRAWBERRY HULLER & PIN FEATHER PICKER. Pat'd Dec. 18, 1906. Spring steel. 1¼" x 7/8". Nip-It. Courtesy Nace VandenBerg.

ICE CHIPPER or CHISEL — A steel, pronged chisel for taking small ice chips off the block. There are several types, including one with a guard — not to protect the hand, but to ensure the uniform smallness of the chips. The Star Ice Chipper, sold in the late 1890s, was all iron, and "only a minute's time is required to reduce a 15 or 20 pound block of ice."

Fig. 620. ICE CHISEL. Polished steel blade, iron band, wood handle. Matthai-Ingram Company, c. 1890.

Fig. 621. CROWN ICE CHIPPER. Pat'd April 8, 1884. American Machine Co., Philadelphia, Perfection Recipes & Catalog, 1880s.

ICE CREAM FREEZER — A double tub; originally the outside tub was wood, the inner one tin. The space between was filled with ¼ salt and ¾ ice, and the cranked gears on top rotated the inner can so that the cream within was agitated and stirred by beaters.

The first freezer was supposed to have been invented by Nancy Johnson in 1846. Her freezer was granted a patent in 1848, but to a William Young.

The *Improved White Mountain Ice Cream Freezer* advertised in 1895 that it would make ice cream in three minutes. All of the freezers were practically identical by the turn of the century, but "when not possessed of a machine, having procured the necessary ingredients, secure a small, deep tub, not less than 8" greater in diameter than the inside can or freezer; see that the tub has a hole in the side near the bottom, with a plug, which can be drawn at pleasure, to let off surplus water which would retard freezing. Have near at hand a spatula of hard wood, with which the cream can be scraped from the sides of the freezer. Have also a smaller one with which to mix coarse salt and ice together, and deposit same between the can and the ice tub. Pound the ice fine. When the cream is flavored, place it in the freezer, which put in the tub; pile the salted ice around it; if there is a crank, turn it slowly at first, increasing in speed as the cream hardens; when the mixture is congealed, remove the lid, take out the dasher, cut away the cream from the sides, mix the cream with the spatula until it is smooth and soft; reinsert the dashers; cover the can again, and work until the cream is hard and well set. If there is no crank, use the spatula repeatedly instead. For ease and rapidity, there is, of course, nothing so good as a well-constructed, quick and reliable freezing machine, such as the *American.*" (*Treasure House,* 1891.) *"Polar Star;" "Up-to-Date Baird;" "Packer's Standard;" "Peerless Iceland;" "Blizzard;" "Lightning;" "Gem;" "Jack Frost;" "White Mountain;" "Husky;"* etc.

Fig. 624. ICE CREAM FREEZER. American Machine Co., Philadelphia. Treasure House, 1891.

ICE CREAM MOLD — One of a number of rather gothic, tin or pewter molds used for ice cream, but related in design to fancy molds used for blancmange, charlotte russe, and jellies. Other designs were animals and plants. Some of the molds from an 1886 *F.A. Walker Catalog* include: lion, eagle, Minerva, swan, elephant, boar, cornucopia, flower bouquet, stag, sheep, squirrel, canteloupe, Bacchus, and asparagus. The gothic piles of tetrahedrons and spires were one-part tin molds. The others, of pewter or lead, were two-part molds which were hooked together for freezing.

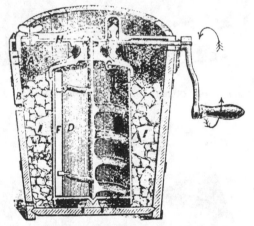

Fig. 622. ICE CREAM FREEZER. The American Machine Co., c. 1890.

Fig. 623. ICE CREAM FREEZER. Wood, iron. 2, 3, 4, 6, 8, 10 qts. Matthai-Ingram Company, c. 1890.

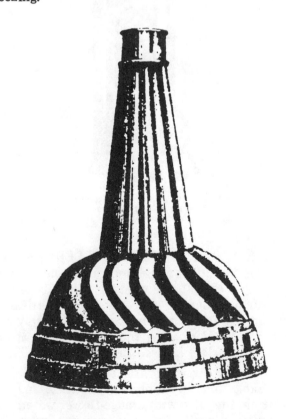

Fig. 625. ICE CREAM MOULD. Planished tin. 2, 3, 4 qts. Lalance & Grosjean, 1891.

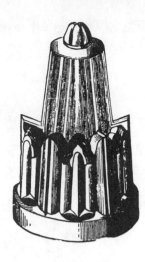

Fig. 626. ICE CREAM MOLDS. Tin. F. A. Walker, 1886.

Fig. 627. LEAD ICE CREAM MOLD. F. A. Walker flyer, c. 1880.

Fig. 628. LEAD ICE CREAM MOLD. F. A. Walker flyer, c. 1880.

ICE CREAM SCOOP, − DISHER, − DIPPER, or SERVER − A simple or complex implement for serving up portions of ice cream. Some, the early ones, made cone-shaped portions, and others made slick ice cream balls. Most have a mechanism which moves a blade around the inside of the scoop and which releases the ice cream from the sides. All ice cream scoops work better if they are first dipped into hot water. *"Benedict Indestructo;" "Myers Deluxe Chromium Disher;" "Gilchrist Pyramid;" "Gilchrist 31;" "Gilchrist 30;" "Arnold 51;" etc.*

Tea Ice-Cream

Pour over four table-spoons of Old Hyson tea, a pint of cream, scald in a custard-kettle, or by placing the dish containing it in a kettle of boiling water, remove from the fire, and let stand five minutes; strain it into a pint of cold cream, put on to scald again, and when hot mix with it four eggs and three-fourths pound sugar, well beaten together; let cool and freeze. [Miss A.C.L. In *Practical Housekeeping,* 1884]

Fig. 629. ICE CREAM CORNET DISHER. c. 1870s, 1880s. Tin. L: 8". No. 9. American. Courtesy Rita Keillor Collection.

Fig. 630. CLAD'S ICE CREAM SPOON. Tinned iron, wood. L: 12", 14", 16", 18", Lalance & Grosjean Company, 1890.

Fig. 631. ICE CREAM SERVER. c. 1930. Nickeled brass, copper. 10½" x 2½". Gilchrist 30. Courtesy Norman Mintz, Melanie Cohen.

Fig. 632. ICE CREAM SCOOP. c. 1935 to 1950. Cast aluminum. L: 7½". "...ESSUS." Italian. Author's Collection.

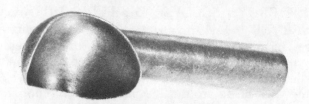

Fig. 633. ICE CREAM DIPPER. c. 1935. Cast aluminum. L: 7". Designed by Sherman Kelly and manufactured by Roll Dippers, Inc., this dipper is in the Museum of Modern Art, NYC, Design Collection. Author's Collection.

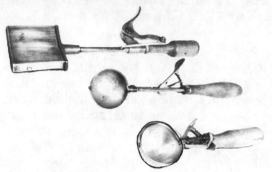

Fig. 634. ICE CREAM DISHERS. c. 1930s. Top to bottom: (1) Wood, cast & plated metals. L: 12½"; W: 3¼"; (2) Wood, plated copper. L: 10-7/8"; W: 2-1/8. Gilchrist's No. 31. (3) Wood, cast aluminum. L: 8½"; W: 2½". American. Author's Collection.

ICE PICK

ICE PICK — A very sharp metal spike, about five to seven inches long, with a wooden or metal handle. It was used to chip or cut demarcation lines in a large block of ice so that a smaller hunk could be broken off.

Fig. 635. ICE PICK. Iron, wood. F. A. Walker, c. 1870s.

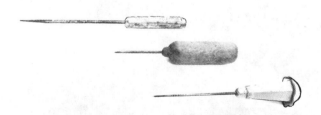

Fig. 636; ICE PICKS. (Top to bottom) (1) Pat'd 3/24/14. Nickel steel & steel. L: 8¾". The 4 sides read: "John A. Schwaz- 838-840 Broadway, Brooklyn, High Grade Furniture, Columbia Grafonolas." (2) c. 1900 to 1910. Steel, wood. L: 6¾". (3) 1930s. Steel, wood, nickel-plated ice-crusher head. L: 7-5/8". Probably Androck. Author's Collection.

ICE SCOOP

ICE SCOOP — A heavy-duty, galvanized tin or iron scoop used for crushed ice.

Fig. 637. ICE SCOOP. c. 1890. Galvanized metal, cast iron, wood. L: 7¾"; W: 3". American. Author's Collection.

ICE SHAVER — SHREDDER

ICE SHAVER, — SHREDDER — A tinned or nickel-plated steel implement with a sharp blade or cutter and a receptacle for the ice shavings. It was scraped across large ice blocks and made little shavings used for desserts, water ices, cooling liquors, or as a cooling medium in the sickroom. *"Gem;" "Brighton;" etc.*

Fig. 638. ICE SHREDDER. Tinned or nickel-plated iron. Adjustable for coarse or fine. Enterprise. The Enterprising Housekeeper, 1898.

Fig. 639. ICE SHREDDER. Enterprise Hardware Co., 1902.

ICE TONGS

ICE TONGS — An iron tool used to pick up ice blocks. The family size opened to 16 or 18", but the pair the ice man used was much larger.

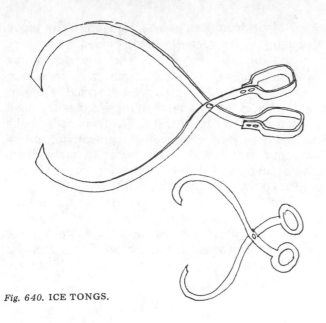

Fig. 640. ICE TONGS.

INDIVIDUAL MOLD — A single serving, small mold, usually stamped or pressed of tin. The designs included plain, fluted, scalloped, shell-shaped, and rosettes. They were used for individual servings of jelly, cake, patty, pudding, or aspics. A cutlet mold is, in a sense, an individual mold. *See also* **MOLD, TIN**

Fig. 641. INDIVIDUAL JELLY MOLD. Tin. F. A. Walker, c. 1870s.

Fig. 642. INDIVIDUAL JELLY MOLDS. Tin. F. A. Walker, c. 1870s.

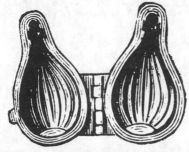

Fig. 643. INDIVIDUAL MOLD. Tin. F. A. Walker, c. 1870s.

IRON — A heavy, malleable, metallic element which is silvery white when pure, red when rusted, and usually black when cast or wrought into a utensil. "Iron accommodates itself to all our wants and desires, and even to our caprices; ... equally serviceable to the arts, the sciences, to agriculture, and war; the same ore furnishes the sword, the ploughshare, the scythe, the pruning-hook, the needle, the graver, the spring of a watch or of a carriage, the chisel, the chain, the anchor, the compass, the cannon and the bomb." (William Fairbairn, *Iron, Its History...*, 1865.) Unbelievably, Fairbairn did not mention any of the several hundred uses of iron in the kitchen.

Joseph Jenks cast the first iron about 1642 in the American colonies at the Saugus Iron Works in Massachusetts. By tradition, this first iron object was a one-quart pot, with ear handles and three little legs. Jenks lived from 1602 to 1683, and left a son who carried on his iron works in Rhode Island.

Cast and wrought-iron utensils were made and used in America from the 17th century through the 19th. Inroads on its status as patriarch were made by tin, which was lighter [a method of tinning cast iron was developed in France about 1859]; by aluminum, which didn't corrode; by enameled ware, which didn't react with the food; and finally by stainless steel, which had all the advantages of tin, aluminum and enameled ware. But some iron utensils will probably never be replaced, for they are unique in the service they give. "Cast iron is still common, but being replaced by materials lighter and less expensive. Good iron pans and skillets are excellent for some kinds of cooking, however, because they heat more evenly than others and last for generations." (*Atwater*, 1915.)

Two recipes for seasoning a cast-iron utensil are as follows:

Boil ashes or a bunch of hay or grass in a new iron pot before cooking in it; scour well with soap and sand, then fill with clean water, and boil one or two hours. *[Practical Housekeeping, 1884]*

The best way to prepare a new iron kettle for use is to fill it with clean potato-peelings, boil them an hour or more, then wash the kettle with hot water, wipe it dry and rub it with a little lard; repeat the rubbing for 6 times after using. In this way you will prevent rust, and all the little annoyances liable to occur in the use of a new kettle. *[Babcock, 1881]*

Fig. 644. POURING MOLTEN IRON INTO MOLD. The Great Industries of the United States. Hartford, Chicago, Cincinnati: J.B. Burr & Hyde, 1873.

Fig. 645. FORGING IRON. *The Great Industries of the United States,* 1873.

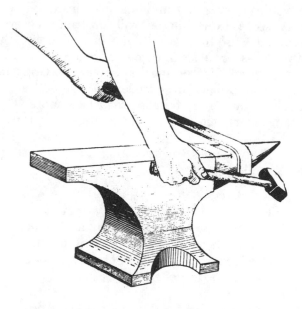

Fig. 646. BLACKSMITHING. Audels Plumbers & Steam Fitters Guide No. 4. By Frank D. Graham. New York: Theo. Audel & Co., 1926.

ISINGLASS [*icing-glass, isonglas, etc.*] — A fine gelatin or glue prepared from the swimming bladders of fishes. The air bladders are also called *sounds.* They are boiled in water, then strained; the fat is taken off, and they are boiled again to the right consistency. Isinglass was used for gelatinizing desserts and clearing coffee.

"Made from Beluga and Sturgeon. The mode of making it just recently made public — long kept a secret by the Russians. The sounds, or air bladders, are taken while fresh, slit open and washed and dried. Then they are formed into rolls the thickness of a finger and pegged with small wooden pegs and left to dry. The form called cake isinglass is formed of bits and fragments put into a flat metal pan with a little water to make them adhere; then dried. Used for brewing, for medicine, and for cookery...." (*Willich,* 1821.)

Isinglass is the name often and mistakenly given *mica,* a mineral which closely resembles some forms of processed isinglass, and which was used in the doors of stoves, in lantern windows, etc. *See also* **MICA**

JACK — *see* **BOTTLE-, CLOCKWORK-, PORTABLE SPRING-, ROASTING-, SMOKE-,**

JAGGER — A small implement with a fluted, jagged, or toothed wheel set in a handle, which is run around the edge of an unbaked pie crust to flute or ornament the edge, and/or to trim the edge, and to seal the lower and upper crusts by pressure. Some jaggers did not have a moving wheel, but were pressed on the edge, doing an inch or so of crust at a time. They were made of iron, wood, brass, ivory, scrimshaw, tin, aluminum, pottery, and various combinations. Other names for a jagger are: *jag, jagging iron, coggling wheel and dough spur, pie crimper, pie trimmer, runner, rimmer.* A jagger was also used for cutting rolled dough or pastry into scalloped figures and for cutting lattice strips for open-work pie crusts.

Fig. 647. JAGGERS. (Left) c. 1920s. Wood, galvanized tin. Homemade using machine-made handle. L: 6½". (Right) c. 1920s, 1930s. Cast aluminum. L: 4¾". (Bottom) c. 1880s. Machine-turned wood, ebony wheel. L: 4¾". American. Author's Collection.

Fig. 648. JAGGER. c. 1870. Wood. L: 8". American. Courtesy Keillor Collection.

Fig. 649. PIE CRIMPER. Treasure House, 1891.

Fig. 650. PASTE JAGGERS. Lalance & Grosjean, 1890.

Fig. 651. JAGGER. c. 1880s. Brass. L: 4½". American. Courtesy Mary Mac Franklin.

Fig. 652. JAGGER. F. A. Walker, c. 1870s.

Fig. 655. PIE CUTTER & CRIMPER. Pat'd March 10, 1908, No. 881,738, by Alexander Stillwagen, Pittsburg, Pa. F. W. Seastrand, c. 1912.

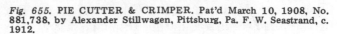

Fig. 656. TART SEALER. Pat'd 1938. Tin, wood, cast aluminum. Spring-loaded. L: 2-7/8"; W: 2-7/8". Tart Master. American. Author's Collection.

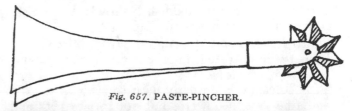

Fig. 657. PASTE-PINCHER.

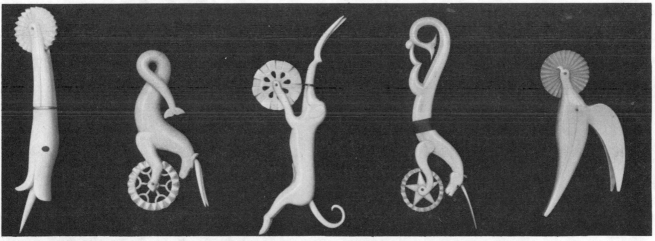

Fig. 653. JAGGERS. 19th century. Whale ivory scrimshaw. Approximately 5" to 8" long. The fanciful and real creatures represented by these pastry jaggers were carved by sailors, most particularly those on whaling vessels. Photo courtesy the New Bedford Whaling Museum, New Bedford, Massachusetts.

Fig. 654. DOUGH CUTTER., c. 1910. Iron, wood. L: 6-3/8". Especially good for cutting lattice strips. American. Author's Collection.

JAPANNED WARE — Tin or iron ware with an opaque varnish finish. "True, genuine Japan, like the Salamander / Lives in the flames, and stands unalterable." (*A Treatise of Japanning*, 1688.) Lacquered, or japanned ware became popular because of the enormous interest in the 18th century in the lacquered wooden cabinets and screens from the Orient. A lot of the japanned ware in America, and in American collections, came originally from Wales: from the works in

Pontypool, Monmouth, and Usk, Breconshire. The art flourished there in the 18th and early 19th centuries. These were often elegant pieces — not used in the kitchen — such as tea caddies, chafing dishes, cheese cradles and toast racks. All nice enough for the parlor, and as highly prized as silver. Pontypool ware was crimson, maroon, or Prussian blue, with an all-over meandering line called *stormant*. A simulated tortoise shell was also characteristic. The Usk ware had metallic silver or gold stripes, and gold stars against grounds of crimson, black, dark red, or chocolate brown.

Throughout the 18th century, ladies looking for a new and genteel art answered the newspaper advertisements of men who offered to teach japanning in the home. All the colors and varnishes, and the gold and silver leaves, were available from a number of shops in Boston. It wasn't until about 1800, however, that professional tinsmiths began offering painted or japanned ware. As the years passed, less and less of the ware was actually baked, and by the end of the 19th century, the glorious rainbow of colors [which included Vermilion, Cinnabar (both a vermilion and a green), Red Lead, Ultramarine, Prussian Blue, Naples Yellow, Smalt (like Cobalt blue), Gamboge (a reddish yellow), Verdigrise, Orange Lake, Indian Red, Brown Ochre, Umber, White Lead, Lamp Black, and Ivory Black] had been reduced to red, blue, green, and brown, and finally brown alone.

Toleware is properly used to refer to the old and fine japanned ware, but not to late 19th and early 20th century painted tin. "Among the most useful and jaunty things in tin is the so-called Japan ware which is but painted tin." (*Peyser*, 1922.) And that was true by 1900. These jaunty things included spice boxes, canisters, bread boxes and the handles of some implements.

JAR HOLDER — *see* **FRUIT JAR HOLDER**

JAR OPENER, — WRENCH — Similar to the fruit jar wrench, but used for opening commercially produced jars and wide-mouth bottles of food. The Edlund *Top Off* is one of the most efficient of these openers and can open any lid from 1-1/8" to 4-3/8" in diameter.

Fig. 658. JAR LID WRENCH, bottom view. 1933. Iron, wood. W: 1-5/8"; extends from 1-1/8" to 4-3/8". "Top Off Jar & Bottle Screw Top Opener," Edlund Co., Burlington, Vt. Courtesy Mary Mac Franklin.

JELLY BAG — A cloth bag for straining jelly.

JELLY-CLOTH — The cotton or linen coarse flannel, or cheesecloth, used for straining jellies.

JELLY MOLD — A stamped or pressed tin mold, quite decorative, in the form of stacked ears of corn, bunches of grapes, piles of roses, melons, hedgehogs, stars, hens, eggs, packs of cards, fish, etc. It was used for molding sweet or savory jellies for the table. Like other molds, it was recommended that the mold be "damp" or "lightly oiled" before pouring in the jelly. *See also* **MOLDS, TIN**

The following is a recipe for the red fruit of the hawthorne tree:

Red-Haw Jelly
Wash the haws well, and put on in a kettle with water sufficient to almost cover them (not too much water). Boil until they are soft. When cool enough, express the juice thoroughly through a thin muslin cloth. To three pints of juice add two pints of granulated sugar, and boil until it bubbles. Less boiling will answer if it is not desired to mould into "shapes" or "designs." It is a firm and handsome jelly for moulds. The taste is delicious, resembling *guava* jelly. [Lizzie Strohm in *Strohm*, 1888]

Fig. 659. JELLY MOLD. Tin. F. A. Walker, c. 1870s.

Fig. 660. JELLY MOLDS. Tin. F. A. Walker, c. 1870s.

Fig. 661. JELLY MOLD. Tin. F. A. Walker, c. 1870s.

JELLY SIEVE — A wire-mesh deep sieve for straining jelly.

JELLY STRAINER — A cone-shaped strainer of perforated tin, or long cloth bag suspended from a frame, for straining jelly.

Fig. 662. JELLY STRAINER. Tin. F. A. Walker, c. 1870s.

Fig. 663. JELLY STRAINER. Tin. F. A. Walker, c. 1870s.

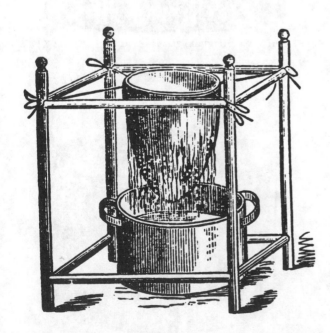

Fig. 664. JELLY STRAINER. Homemade of wood, string, cloth. About 12" high. Treasure House, 1891.

Fig. 665. JELLY BAG STRAINER. Wire, cloth. 6" dia., three 8" legs; 8" dia., four 8" legs. Androck, 1936.

JUICE EXTRACTOR — A device designed to get the juice from a lemon or orange, usually by rubbing it hard on a ribbed cone called a *reamer*. One type, the *Manny Lemon Juice Extractor*, is of clear glass, and has a reamer molded in the center. The dish has pouring lips and a seed barrier at the base of the reamer. *See also* **LEMON SQUEEZER, MEAT SQUEEZER**

Fig. 666. EASLEY'S REAMER-JUICER. Pat'd 1888. Glass.

JULIEN [*julienne***] SOUP CUTTER** — A device for mechanically making long thin strips of raw vegetables to be put in clear soups. *See also* **POTATO CUTTER, VEGETABLE SLICER**

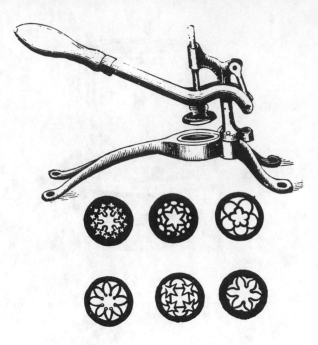

Fig. 667, 668. JULIEN SOUP CUTTER & CUTTING DISKS. F. A. Walker, c. 1870s.

KETTLE [*kittle*] — One of many types of utensils of metal: brass, copper, iron, enameled iron, tin, bell metal, and bronze. "Every kitchen needs: 2 tea kettles, one small, one large; 2 brass kettles of different sizes for soup boiling, etc.; Iron kettles lined with porcelain are better for preserves. The German are best. Too hot a fire will crack them, but with care in this respect, they will last for many years; tin covered butter kettle; tin covered berry kettle; ..." (*Beecher and Stowe*, 1869.)

Fig. 671. STRAIGHT KETTLE. Greystone enameled ware, tin cover. From 6" x 4" to 9-3/8" x 6". This same cut was used for the seamless bucket. Matthai-Ingram Company, c. 1890.

KEELER [*keiler*] or **KEELFAT** — A shallow tub or vessel for cooling liquids.

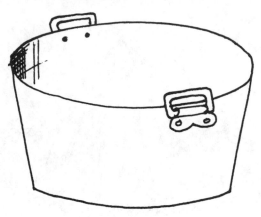

Fig. 669. KEELER. Indurated fibre ware.

Fig. 672. BUTTER KETTLE. Planished tin. 7" x 5" to 11¼" x 8½" x 5¾". Lalance & Grosjean, 1891.

Fig. 670. TUB. Pine. 27" dia. Montgomery Ward, 1895.

Fig. 673. KETTLE. Planished tin. 2, 4, 6, 8, 12, 16, pts. Lalance & Grosjean, 1890.

KETTLE LIFTER — A device which hung from the crane or a pot hook, and from which the kettle was then hung. By the easy push of a lever, the kettle, which was often heavy and unwieldy, was made to pour. It was also called a *kettle tilter* or *pourer*.

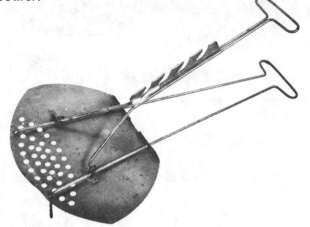

Fig. 674. KETTLE WATER POURER. Pat'd May 12, 1898. Tin. L: 16"; W: 10". American. Courtesy Keillor Collection.

Fig. 675. KETTLE TILTER. Late-18th, early-19th century. Wrought iron. L: 14"; W: 8½". Footed KETTLE. 19th century. Cast iron. English; American. Courtesy Keillor Collection.

KILDERKIN — A measure equal to 18 gallons or two firkins. Also a cask holding that amount.

KIMNEL or KYMELYN — A large tub or a very large bowl used for kneading dough or for salting meat.

KINDLER — *see* FIRE KINDLER

KITCHEN — First called "the hall," after the English fashion, or the "fire-room." It *was* the house for many people and their livestock, in early America. The family lived in the hall: cooked, ate, slept and did indoor work like weaving, spinning and candle-making there. In larger houses the kitchen was in the basement, and this was true well into the 19th century. When houses and families became more substantial, and money was spent to make them more comfortable, a kitchen entirely separate from the house was built at the back. This was usually a one room, one story structure, although a sleeping loft was often provided for servants. This early kitchen, whether in the basement or in a separate building, was basically a very large, brick "walk-in" fireplace; a brick or dirt floor; at least two windows for cross-ventilation; and was furnished with a dough box, a large work table, open shelves, cupboards and hooks, and a chair.

A major concern of pioneering women, such as Catherine Beecher and her sister Harriet Beecher Stowe, was the improvement of the kitchen; the elevation of cookery to a science; and the instruction of women in that science. Their aim was not to liberate the woman from the kitchen, but rather from the antiquated and inefficient kitchen. They attacked the poorly planned and smoky, smelly kitchen with great vigor, and came up with some innovative designs for saving labor. One design, which appeared in their book of 1869, was a forerunner of the built-in kitchen of the mid-20th century. It had adaptable counter space and good storage.

An earlier kitchen and cooking reformer was the famed Count Rumford, who wrote treatises on stoves and cooking and coffee and fireplaces. Count von Rumford's name was Sir Benjamin Thompson. He was born in 1753 and lived in Concord until the Revolutionary War — when his sympathies for the Royalists, and therefore England, made him abandon his home, his wife (whom he never saw again) and his daughter and go to England. He went to Munich in 1785 and set up a "House of Industry" to give the poor employment, lodging and a better living condition. It was there that he designed an efficient cooking range on which pots and pans could be placed over a concentrated heat source instead of hanging heavily from pot hooks and cranes over a fire. This range was a U-shaped brick structure with a row of small, individual fireplaces along the bottom, and a hole for a kettle or pot above each fireplace. The cook stood in the center and was able to reach out and tend a number of pots at one time. Sir Benjamin, who was now a Count of the Holy Roman Empire, retired to England to write his numerous essays. The American government invited him to return home but he did not go. He died in 1814.

Each domestic economist tried to introduce

efficiency into the scheme of the kitchen. A score of books were written in a few years in the middle of the 19th century — all of which had suggestions for the housewife: about coping in the increasingly servantless society with the problems of cooking for a family, and about creating a pleasant surround for her work. Tips on covering the floor with cocoa-matting, or linoleum, or oilcloth were matched by tips on the arrangement of furniture, lighting, ventilation, and storage. But it was well into the 20th century before a really efficient, built-in, easily cleaned kitchen was even possible.

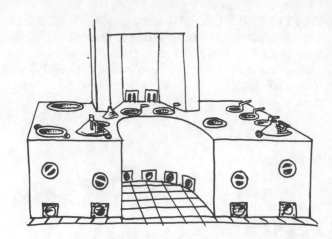

Fig. 679. U-SHAPED RANGE. Designed by Count Rumford. Each cooking hole or "eye" has its own fire and flue.

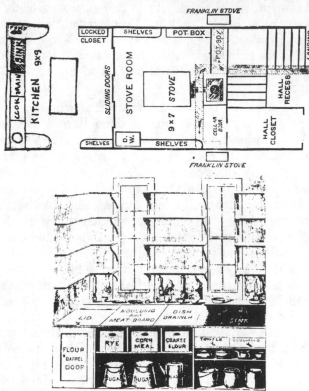

Fig. 676, 677. KITCHEN FLOORPLAN & BUILT-IN STORAGE. Two cuts. "The chimney and stove-room are contrived to ventilate the whole house. ... The sides of the stove-room must be lined with shelves; ...boxes with lids, to receive stove utensils, must be placed near the stove. ... On these shelves, and in the closet and boxes, can be placed every material used for cooking, all the table and cooking utensils, and all the articles used in house work. ...The flour barrel just fills the closet, which has a door and a lid. Beside it, is the form for cooking, with a moulding board laid on it; one side for meat and vegetables, the other for bread. Under the sink are shelf-boxes — used for scouring materials, dish-towels, also to hold bowls for bits of fats, butter, etc. Under these two shelves is room for two pails, and a jar for soap grease. Under the cook form are shelves and shelf boxes for unbolted wheat, corn meal, rye, etc. Underneath these, for white and brown sugar are wooden can pails, which are the best articles to keep these constant necessities. Beside them is the tin molasses-can with a tight, movable cover, and a cork in the spout. ..." *The American Woman's Home,* by Catherine Beecher, and Harriet Beecher Stowe, 1869.

Fig. 680. KEEPING HALL FIREPLACE. 18th century. Equipt with various broilers, trivets, skimmers, peels, skillet, cauldron, frying pan, etc. Michie Tavern, Charlottesville, Virginia.

Fig. 678. COUNT RUMFORD. The Great Industries of the United States. Hartford, Chicago, Cincinnati: J.B. Burr & Hyde, 1873.

Fig. 681. Chaotic kitchen scene, showing everything (from left to right) from a range, a gridiron, a coal hod, a rolling pin, to a saucepan. From "Love in a Cottage." Practical Housekeeping, 1881.

Fig. 682. "GETTING DINNER UNDER DIFFICULTIES" illustration. Treasure House, 1891.

KITCHEN CABINET — A space-saving piece of movable kitchen furniture. Either a table, complete with flour bins, sliding bread boards, and spice drawers; or similar tables with closed shelves above, containing various built-in amenities such as coffee grinders, flour bins and sifters, and racks for utensils and gadgets. Many of these late-19th through early-20th century cabinets are quite handsome. Some cabinets were exclusively for the storage of crockery and dishes and were hung on the wall. *See also* **DRESSER**

Fig. 683. KITCHEN CABINET TABLE. Elm with maple top, zinc-lined flour drawer. L: 4'4"; W: 2'4"; H: 2'8". Has molding board, spice & cutlery drawer, sugar & groceries drawer, flour drawer, utensil cupboard. Montgomery Ward, 1895.

Fig. 684. KITCHEN PLAQUE for ladles, skimmers, etc. Tin. L: 16½"; H: 18½". Lalance & Grosjean, 1890.

Fig. 685. KITCHEN RACK. Japanned tin. L: 23"; H: 5". With 10 utensils. F. W. Seastrand, c. 1912.

Fig. 686. KITCHEN TROUSSEAU. Tin, in iron-bound canvas trunk. 68 pieces: jelly mould, tea pot, coffee biggin, pepper box, flour dredge, 2 saucepans, preserve kettle, wash basin, cullender, turk's head mould, 3 milk pans, pudding pan, gridiron, spout strainer, gravy strainer, card of 8 biscuit pans, scoop, 2-pronged fork, Paste jagger, cake turner, flat skimmer, ladle, 2 dippers, oblong pan, fry pan, tea tray, crumb pan & brush, dust pan, coal shovel, tea kettle, dish pan, 2 basting spoons, 6 tea spoons, 6 table spoons, 6 forks, 6 animal cake cutters, 6 pie plates, flour sieve. Lalance & Grosjean, 1890.

KITCHEN FURNITURE — Several things found in the first kitchens have remained basic to kitchen furnishing: a broad table, a cabinet, a chair and shelves. And of course a sink and a stove. More picturesquely, and maybe even more accurately, add a rocking chair, another table, a stool, and maybe even a birdcage for the cook's canary.

Fig. 687. TOWEL RACK. F. A. Walker, c. 1870s.

Fig. 688. CHAIR. Hardwood, bentwood. Scooped seat. Montgomery Ward, 1893.

Fig. 689. STEP LADDERS. Wood. F. A. Walker, c. 1870s.

Fig. 690. KITCHEN SAWS. c. 1895. (Top) Carbon steel, wood. L: 13". (Bottom) Carbon steel, wood. L: 13½". Keen Kutter. Author's Collection.

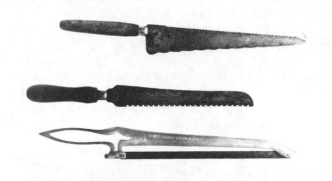

Fig. 691. KITCHEN SAWS. c. 1895. Carbon steel, wood. (Top to bottom.) (1) SAW & CAKE KNIFE. L: 14¾". Victor, American Cutlery Co. (2) L: 13½". (3) c. 1910. Carbon steel, cast aluminum. L: 15¾". "Always Sharp," Chas. Wohr, Lancaster, Pa. Author's Collection.

Fig. 692. UTILITY KNIFE & SAW. 20th century. Brass, carbon steel. Homemade. L: 9-5/8". Author's Collection.

KITCHEN GARDEN — The garden, situated ideally right outside the kitchen door, where everything from lettuce to carrots, from dill to basil, was grown.

KITCHEN SAW — Similar to the bread or cake knives, except that the blade has fine saw teeth used for cutting through bones and the joints of meat. Sometimes a bread knife has the scalloped edge on one side and the teeth of the kitchen saw on the other.

KITCHEN STEEL — A finely cross-hatched, tapered steel rod with a handle, used by running the knife blade up and down it in what, at its best, can be a graceful display of agility by the cook, and at its worst an ineffective and dangerous misadventure. If done properly it can put a very good edge on a knife. *See* **FORK, KNIFE SHARPENER.**

KITCHEN TABLE — A sturdy, broad-surfaced table, usually with one or two drawers, which might serve for chopping food, rolling out dough, or any other culinary process. "Should be of ash," instructed *Practical Housekeeping* in 1884. One type is the kitchen table and settee, which was a bench whose back was the table top, which could be folded down to rest on the bench arms and form a good-sized work surface. These date from the late 18th century through the 19th.

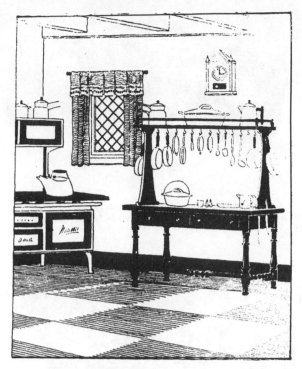

Fig. 693. "THE KITCHEN once more assumes its rightful place, eloquent in promises of food." Aunt Ellen's Booklet on Waterless Cooking. Griswold Mfg. Co., 1928.

Fig, 694. TABLE & SETTEE. Treasure House, 1891.

KNIFE — "Never put a knife in hot fat, as it destroys the temper, and the knife is useless." *(Practical Housekeeping, 1884.)* See BONING —; BREAD —, BUTCHER —, CAKE —, CARBON STEEL, CHEESE —, CHOPPING —, CLEAVER, FRENCH COOK'S —, GRINDSTONE, HAM SLICE, KITCHEN STEEL, PARING —, PALETTE —, POTATO PARER, STEEL, TELLAR —, WHETSTONE

KNIFE BOARD — A long wooden board with a box at one end for the bath brick, or common brick. A quantity of brickdust was made and sprinkled the length of the board, and the knife to be cleaned was run flat up and down the board — much as a razor is stropped. "Knife Board. — A common knife board covered with a thick buff-leather, on which are put, emery (one part), *Crocus Martis* (three parts in a very fine powder), mixed into a thick paste with a little lard or sweet-oil, and spread on the leather the thickness of ¼" — gives a far superior edge and polish to knives than the common practice of brick-dust on a board." (*Willich*, 1804.)

"Have a properly made knife-box, with board extending, on which to lay the knife to scour, wet a cloth in hot water or soft soap and water, dip in the dust which has been previously shaved off; then rub briskly and hard until all the spots are removed." (*Practical Housekeeping*, 1884.)

"Should be of soft pine, free from knots, 5 or 6 feet long, and made with feet or standers at the ends, like a bench. It will last much longer if the part most used is covered with leather. A yard is a good height for a knife board. At one end have a small box, to contain the leathers, bricks, fork-sticks, etc. What is called a Bath Brick is the proper sort for cleaning knives, it is soft and white. Rub the brick up and down on the board till you have got off a sufficiency of powder; or you may take a brick in each hand and rub together. Then, taking one knife at a time, hold the handle firmly in your hand, and with a quick motion, rub the blade (on both sides) in the brick dust.... If you have steel forks, rub their backs on the brick-dust board till very bright. Have by you a small flat stick of pine wood, shaped like a knife blade, about the length of your middle finger and covered with leather. Dip in brick dust, and rub between the prongs of the forks." (*Leslie*, 1840.)

Fig. 695. KNIFE BOARD. Mid-19th century. Painted wood, bath brick. L: 38"; W: 5½". Pennsylvania German. Courtesy Keillor Collection.

139

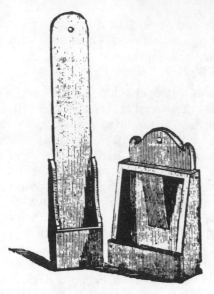

Fig. 696. KNIFE BOARDS. Wood. F. A. Walker, c. 1870s.

Fig. 699. KNIFE & FORK BOX. Japanned tin, flannel-lined, or unlined. L: 12½". An identical box, made for spoons & forks, was 9¾". (Dover Stamping Co.) F. A. Walker, c. 1870s.

KNIFE BOX — A box with slots for the storage of kitchen knives, also a *knife tray*. Nothing dulls a knife as much as tumbling about in a drawer with other knives and perhaps a jar wrench and an apple parer.

Another knife box is the fine box case for table and carving knives, which were made in pairs by cabinet-makers and which stood on the sideboard in the dining room.

KNIFE CLEANER — A device for cleaning rust or stains from knives by abrasion. *See* **POLISHER**

Fig. 700. KNIFE & FORK BOX. c. 1880s - 1900. Stenciled wood. L: 11¼"; W: 6-7/8"; H: 1-7/8". American. Author's Collection.

Fig. 697. KNIFE CLEANER. 19th century. Wood, cork. L: 18¾"; W: 5½". American. Courtesy Keillor Collection.

KNIFE, SPOON and FORK TRAY, — BOX — A wood, tin, or wicker divided tray with a handle often formed as part of the dividing panel. It was for carrying flatware and cutlery from the pantry to set the table, and from the table to the kitchen for washing.

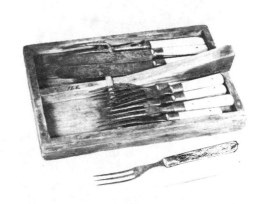

Fig. 701. KNIFE & FORK BOX. 19th century. Wood box, with steel & bone forks & knives. L: 11½"; W: 7¼"; H: 3¼". American. Courtesy Keillor Collection.

KNIFE SCOURING BOX — A box packed with hay, straw and damp sand for scouring knives and forks. *See also* **FORK CLEANER**

KNIFE SHARPENER — A small, hand-held or table-mounted tool with two little steel rollers between which the knife was run. This type still exists, often as part of a wall-mounted can opener. *See also* **GRINDSTONE, KITCHEN STEEL, WHETSTONE**

Fig. 698. KNIFE BASKET. Wicker. F. A. Walker, c. 1870s.

140

Fig. 702. KNIFE SHARPENER. Nickeled steel, wood. J.B. Foote Foundry Company, 1906.

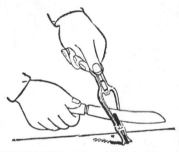

Fig. 703. KNIFE SHARPENER. c. 1915. Wood, steel. L: 6". American. Author's Collection.

Fig. 704. KNIFE SHARPENER & CAN OPENER. A. E. Rayment Supply Co., Fockford, Illinois, c. 1910.

KRAUT CUTTER — *see* CABBAGE CUTTER

KRAUT FORK —— A broad and relatively short-handled wooden fork with four or five stout tines.

Sour-Krout

Take a large, strong wooden vessel, or cask resembling a salt beef cask, and capable of holding as much as is sufficient for the winter's consumption of a family; gradually break down or chop the cabbages in very small pieces; begin with one or two cabbages at the bottom of the cask; add others at intervals; press them by means of a wooden spade against the side of the cask, until it is full; then place a heavy weight upon the top of it, and allow it to stand near a warm place for from 4 to 5 days; then place the cask in a cool situation; keep it always covered up; strew anise seeds among the layers of the cabbages during its preparation. [*Treasure House, 1891.*]

Fig. 705. KRAUT FORK. Wood.

KRAUT STAMPER — A beetle used for breaking down cabbage — the alternative to chopping or grating it very fine — for making sauerkraut. *See also* CABBAGE CUTTER

LADIES' FINGER CAKE PAN — A pan with finger-like depressions for baking six or eight ladies' finger cakes.

 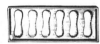

Fig. 706. CAKE PANS. Tin. F. A. Walker, c. 1870s.

LADLE — A cuplike spoon with a long straight, curved, or bent handle and usually a pouring lip. Ladles are found in wood, glass, tin, enameled ware, aluminum, silver, brass, and other materials. Ladles were used for any kind of liquid which was to be transferred, approximately cup by cup, from a large vessel to a smaller one or several smaller ones. There are soup ladles and punch ladles, and perhaps for this reason a ladle is thought of in connection with the more elegant libations. However, it is cocoa *dipper* and that lays that to rest. *See also* DIPPER

Fig. 707. PUMP LADLE. Stamped tin. F. A. Walker, c. 1870s.

Fig. 708. (Top) CREAM LADLE. Stamped tin. 1-7/8" x 1". (Bottom) OYSTER LADLE. Stamped tin. Solid or perforated. 3" x 1". Matthai-Ingram Company, c. 1890.

LADY-LOCK MOLD — (*Lady-lock* is possibly a misprint of *lady-luck*,) "A funnel-shaped mould used for ordinary cream pastry shells." (*Ladies Home Journal*, December, 1898.)

LARDING NEEDLE —, **PIN** —, **PRICK** —, **STICK** — "A piece of steel from 6 to 9 inches long, pointed at one end and having 4 slits at the other, to hold a small strip of bacon when put between them." (*Treasure House*, 1891.) Meats, such as beef roasts, which did not have much fat in or on them, were larded for cooking; that is, thin stips of bacon, best used when cold and less liable to break, were "sewed" in and out of the meat. *Barding* is a similar idea, but the strips of fat are merely laid across the surface.

Fig. 709. LARDING NEEDLES & CASE. c. 1880. Steel, painted tin. L: 9½". American. Courtesy Keillor Collection.

Fig. 710. LARDING NEEDLES & CASE. Steel, brass, tin. F. A. Walker, c. 1870s.

Fig. 711. LARDING NEEDLES. Practical Housekeeping.

LARD PAIL — A tin pail, with a close-fitting lid, for keeping lard. Lard is clarified animal fat used in cooking like any other shortening. The lard pail kept in the kitchen was often the one bought with the lard in it in the store.

Fig. 712. LARD PAIL. Matthai-Ingram, c. 1890.

LATTEN — Thin beaten brass; or iron plate covered with tin [*block tin*, or *sheet tin*].

LATTICE SLICER — A wooden-handled, tin-bladed device for cutting latticed or fluted slices of fruits, vegetables, or potatoes. Used for making Saratoga Chips, etc.

Fig. 713. FRUIT SCALLOPER. c. 1890. Wood, "special metal." "Equally good for scalloping Oranges, Grape-Fruit, Lemons, Cantaloupe, Cucumbers, Apples, etc." F. W. Seastrand, c. 1912.

Fig. 714. VEGETABLE SLICER. c. 1900. Fluted tin, wire. 4¼" x 3¼". American. Author's Collection.

LEMON SQUEEZER, LIME SQUEEZER — A hinged, two-or-three-part hand press with a reamer formed either as part of the squeezer or as an insert of glass or zinc-plated metal. These squeezers were made of wood, iron, galvanized iron, or aluminum. Another type did not use a reamer, but merely crushed the half lemon or lime between two corrugated surfaces, and the juice dripped through the perforated bowl while the seeds were trapped. "An old-time Philadelphia Housewife said yesterday: 'None of your new-fangled lemon squeezers for me. Anything, especially acid — squeezed through metal, such as many of the improved ones are, is very bad. The wooden ones do not have this fault; neither do those made of glass or porcelain. But they all have one fault that there is no getting rid of, and that is that the skin of the lemon is squeezed so that its flavor mixes with that of the juice. This is all wrong. There is but one way to squeeze a lemon, and that is the simple, old-fashioned way, between your fingers. Plenty of power can be brought to bear, particularly if the lemon is well-rolled first."

(*Ladies Home Journal*, September, 1889.) Not only should the lemon be well-rolled, but heated too: under hot water or in the oven for a few minutes. It will give twice as much juice. *"Boss;"* *"King;"* *"20th Century Power;"* *"Manny;"* *"Vaughn;"* *"Album;"* etc.

Lemon Butter

1 pound of white sugar; ¼ pound of fresh butter; 6 eggs; juice and grated rind of 3 lemons; take out all the seeds; boil all together a few minutes; till thick as honey; stir constantly; put in small jars or tumblers; cover with paper dipped in white of egg. [*Treasure House*, 1891]

Fig. 715. LEMON SQUEEZER. c. 1870s, 1880s. Maple. L: 10¾". American. Courtesy Keillor Collection.

Fig. 716. LEMON SQUEEZER. Pat'd 1868. Treasure House, 1891.

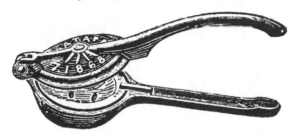

Fig. 717. LEMON SQUEEZER. Tinned malleable iron. L: 8½", 10½". Matthai-Ingram Company, c. 1890.

Fig. 718. LEMON SQUEEZER. Galvanized iron. "The one here takes a whole lemon and cuts and crushes it at the same time. It is rust-proof, easily cleaned and not liable to be broken as is the case with the wooden squeezers." Practical Housekeeping, 1881.

Fig. 719. LEMON SQUEEZER. Hardwood. Montgomery Ward, 1895.

Fig. 720. LEMON SQUEEZER. Galvanized iron. F. A. Walker, c. 1870s.

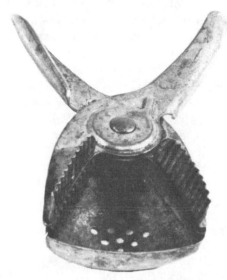

Fig. 721. LIME & LEMON SQUEEZER. c. 1930s. Zinc-plated iron. L: 6"; W: 3". Vaughn Co., Chicago. Courtesy Mary Mac Franklin.

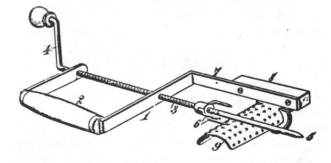

Fig. 722. LEMON GRATER. Pat'd 1891, No. 462,626. Jennie H. Cox, Winfield, Kansas. Official Gazette, Nov. 3, 1891.

LIGNUM VITAE — The very hard wood of a tropical American tree, found particularly in the West Indies. This dark, purplish-brown wood, streaked with light brown, was used for making durable beetles and mortars and pestles, and was considered practically indestructable. *Lignum vitae* is literally the *tree of life.* It is of the genus *Guaiacum.*

LOGGERHEAD — An iron implement with a bulbous or large knobbed head which was heated in the fire and used for heating liquids. *See also* **MULLER**

LUGGIE — A small wooden vessel, with a handle, or *lug*, for milk or porridge.

LUG POLE or **CHIMNEY BAR** — A pole, of wood or iron, on which a kettle or other pot was hung in the fireplace and which was set into the bricks of the chimney as it was built, at a level just above the opening. The lug pole was best made of iron, but wooden ones did exist in poor 18th century homes, and were easily charred or burned in high-reaching flames. Some fireplaces were equipped with several lug poles: one just inside the chimney, and others perhaps fastened or racked just in front of, or under the lintel. When a fireplace was built, the lug pole was built in, and when it burned or had to be replaced, the brick into which it was set on either side was removed and the new lug pole set in.

In Bennett Wood Green's *Virginia Word Book*, published in 1899, and in 1902 in Richmond, he identified "chimbly pole" and "chimbly crook" as the lug pole, and the pot hook which hangs from the pole.

Lug poles were finally replaced by the pot crane, which could be pivoted in and out of the fireplace and was more accommodating.

Lug means, among other things, a long pole or stick, and was also a measure of length equalling about 16½ feet. *See also* **CRANE**

LUG POLE EXTENSION — A wrought-iron device, the same as a *trammel*, for hanging pots or kettles from the lug pole at any adjustable height from the fire. After lug poles became extinct, the extension was no longer known by that name, but by *trammel* or *pot hook*, names which had already been used. *See also* **POT HOOK, TRAMMEL**

LUTE — "A matter to mend broken vessel." (*Cutbush*, 1814.) "Take any quantity of white of eggs, and beat them well to a froth. Add to this soft curd cheese, and quicklime, and begin beating a-new all together. This may be used in mending whatever you will, even glasses, and will stand both fire and water.... another, for the same purpose, which resists water. — Take quicklime, turpentine, and soft curd cheese. Mix these well together; and, with the point of a knife, put of this on the edges of the broken pieces of your ware, then join them together." (*ibid.*)

MACE — The outer coat of the nutmeg, used as a baking spice.

MADELINE MOLD — A tin mold, like a charlotte russe or other ornate mold, for baking madelines: a rich small cake, like poundcake, and plain or ornamented with frosting, nuts, or fruit. A madeline cake is also a dariole according to *Webster's Second International Dictionary. See also* **DARIOLE, MOLDS**

Fig. 723. MADELINE MOLD. Tin. F. A. Walker, 1886.

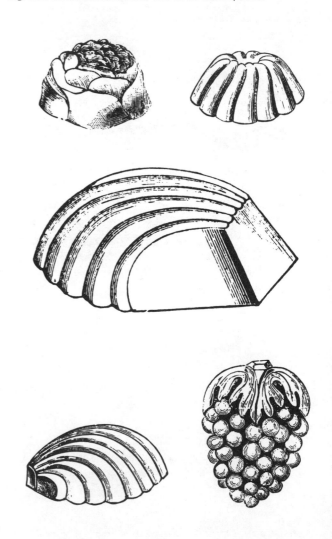

Fig. 724, 725, 726. MADELINE MOLDS. Tin. F. A. Walker, 1886.

144

MATCHES — A chronology:

1530 — *Sulphur matches* first mentioned in England. They were a wooden splint, or piece of paper, cloth, or cord, dipped in melted sulphur and ignitable by tinder.

1805 — The *chemical match* was invented. Its tip, containing sugar and potassium chlorate, ignited when it was touched to sulphuric acid.

1827 — The *friction* or *lucifer match* was invented.

1858 — A so-called *safety match* was invented.

See also **FRICTION MATCH, SPILL**

MATCH SAFE — A metal or wooden container for holding matches. Originally it had a hinged cover to keep the matches, which could be ignited by rubbing against each other, in a safe place. Sometimes the match safe was lined with a fire proof plaster-like material.

"Were I an insurance agent, remarks a writer in an exchange, I would make it an imperative rule, that every house insured by me should be provided by metal or earthen boxes, in which matches should be kept. They are often seen lying loosely upon the shelf or in the closet, where a careless servant, or an unthinking child or even a mischeivous mouse, may produce disastrous results with them. A little incident has made me very careful in this matter. One day, when about closing my room, I hastily threw a key into a drawer where were several loose papers and miscellaneous articles, and closed it; but just as it was closed, there was a glimmer of light within the drawer, which attracted my attention from its novelty. Opening it, I found that the key had struck the end of a friction match and fired it." (*Scientific Artisan*, 1858.)

Around the turn into the 20th century, stamped tin or carved wood novelty containers, most of which hung on the wall without covers or lids, were sold as "match safes." One of the most common you will see today is the little double shell, backed with a piece of brass-plated tin, which was first granted a design patent in 1859.

Fig. 727. MATCH SAFE. Metal. "The only proper place to put matches is in a metal box with a self-closing lid." Practical Housekeeping, 1881.

Fig. 728. MATCH SAFE. c. 1870s - 1890. Steel. Striker on bottom. L: 3"; W: 1-7/8"; H: 3". Large "4" with entwined branch. Author's Collection.

Fig. 729. MATCH SAFE. Assorted colored enameled tin. "Twin." Butler Brothers, 1899.

MAYONAISE BEATER — "Essentially the same as egg beaters except that they have a reservoir for holding the olive oil and regulating its flow into the beater, and also have a container for the mayonaise." (*Hutchinson*, 1918.)

Fig. 730. MAYONAISE MIXER. Universal Household Helps, Landers, Frary, Clark, c. 1920.

MEASURES — Graduated vessels with pouring lips and handles. They were originally made to measure ale or beer in public houses. They were made of pewter, brass, tin, copper, or wood, and in standard capacities for measuring liquids or grains. They generally have straight sides, or taper slightly toward the top, and have the capacity stamped into the metal. A complete set would probably comprise a quart, pint, half-pint, gill, half-gill and drop, and parts thereof. "If possible get these measures broad and low, instead of high and slender, as they are more easily kept clean." (*Practical Housekeeping,* 1884.)

Fig. 734. GRADUATED MEASURE. Pieced tin. 1 pt., 1 qt., 2 qts., 4 qts. Matthai-Ingram Company, c. 1890.

MEASURING CUP — A graduated glass or tin cup holding one or two cups of eight ounces each. "A cooking-school measuring cup — a tin cup divided by rings into quarters." (Mrs. Rorer, *Ladies Home Journal,* 1899.)

Fig. 731. MEASURES. Tin. Gill, ½, 1 pint; 1, 2, 4 Quarts. Also in copper. F. A. Walker, c. 1870s.

Fig. 732. "OLD TIME" MEASURES. Pieced tin plate. ¼ pt., ½pt., 1 pt., 1 qt., 2 qts., 4 qts. Matthai-Ingram Company, c. 1890.

Fig. 735. MEASURING CUP. c. 1890 to 1910. Tin. H: 5"; 3" dia. American. Author's Collection.

Fig. 733. THE UTILITY MEASURE. Pieced tin. ½ pt., 1 pt., 1 qt., 2 qts., 4 qts. "The Utility Measure, with Funnel Attachment, has many advantages over all others. It is a great saver of time, trouble and waste." Matthai-Ingram Company, c. 1890.

Fig. 736. MEASURING PITCHER. Butler Brothers, Chicago, Illinois. 1899.

Fig. 737. MEASURING CUPS, SPOONS, SCALE, GLASS THERMOMETER, OVEN THERMOMETER, SPATULA. "Spatula for making measurements level; a glass thermometer to give correct temperatures of boiled mixtures; kitchen scales for weighing meats and poultry to determine length of cooking time." The Art of Cooking and Serving, Sarah Field Splint, 1929.

MEASURING FAUCET — A suction faucet, which was screwed into a keg — of molasses, for example — and when the crank was turned, it would draw the amount desired. Most of these were used by grocers rather than housewives.

Fig. 738. ADVERTISING TRADE CARD. c. 1885. Red, yellow, blue, gray lithographed card. 4¾" x 2-7/8". Enterprise Mfg. Co., of Pa., Philadelphia. Pictured is a molasses faucet which "draws molasses, winter and summer, directly into a jug or bottle, without the use of a funnel...free from flies and dirt." Author's Collection.

MEASURING SPOONS — Graduated sets of metal spoons in 1/8, 1/4, 1/2 and 1 teaspoon sizes, plus 1 tablespoon. These do not date from much before the turn of the century, and only the styling of the handles, and the material, will tell you which ones are a bit older than others.

Another type of measuring spoon is the large mixing spoon, the bowl of which is marked in rings with measures for tablespoons and teaspoons.

Fig. 739. MEASURING SPOONS. (Left) c. 1940. Aluminum. L: 5½". "One Level Measure to Each Cup." Bokar Coffee. (Right) Pat'd 1900. Tin. ¼ Teaspoon or 15 drops; ½ Teaspoon or 30 drops; 1 Teaspoon or 60 drops. "Original." American. Author's Collection.

Fig. 740. MEASURING SPOON. Stainless steel, wood. L: 12-5/8". Edward Katzinger Company, 1940.

Fig. 741. MEASURING SCOOP. Nickeled steel, wood. L: 7½". ¼ cup. A & J. Edward Katzinger Company, 1940.

MEAT and FOOD CHOPPER or HASHER — (1) A machine consisting of a revolving wooden barrel and a heavy cutting blade which moves up and down while the barrel turns. This is a cranked machine first dating from the 1860s. (2) Another type screw-clamps to the table or sits spraddle-legged on the table. The meat or vegetables are fed into the hopper, the crank is turned, and the food comes out ground in small pieces. This type was made of zinc or nickel-plated cast iron.

"This little machine is indispensible in every family where sausage and mince pies are favorite dishes.... If any husband refuses to buy it, let the wife cut off his supply of hash and sausages on trial." (Practical Housekeeping, 1884.) Some meat choppers, and probably the one referred to here, came with a funnel-like attachment for stuffing sausages as the meat was ground out. "New Triumph;" "Sterling;" "Belmont;" "Dana;" "Enterprise;" "Rollman's;" "Perfection;" "Sargent's Gem;" "Saxon;" "Starrett's;" "Steinfeld;" "Wizard;" etc. See also **CHOPPING KNIFE**

Stuffed Bermuda Onion
Make a round hole in the upper end of each, dig out at least ½ of the contents; set in a dish covered with warm, slightly salted water, and bring to a simmer. Throw away the water, carefully fill the onions with minced poultry or veal, put a bit of butter in the dish to prevent burning, scatter fine crumbs thickly over the onions, and bake, covered, ½ hour. [Harland, 1889]

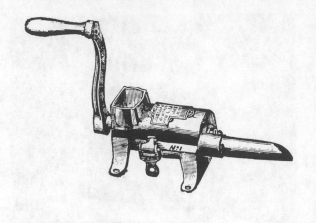

Fig. 745. MEAT CHOPPER & STUFFER. Japanned or galvanized. 6" stuffing cylinder. The Home. Montgomery Ward, 1893.

Fig. 742. MEAT CHOPPER or HASHER. Pat'd May 23, 1865. Cast iron, tin, painted wood. L: 16"; W: 7"; H: 13½". Pat'd by Leroy S. Starrett; Mfg'd by Athol Machine Co., Athol Depot, Massachusetts. Courtesy Keillor Collection.

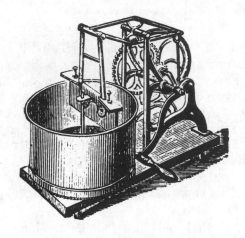

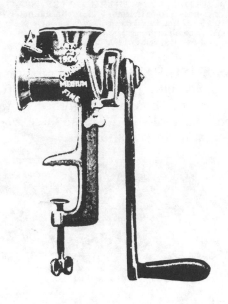

Fig. 743. MEAT CHOPPER. F. A. Walker, c. 1870s.

Fig. 746. FOOD CHOPPER. Pat'd Nov. 29, 1904. Galvanized iron. Steinfeld. United Profit-Sharing Corporation, 1914.

MEAT CRUSHER — "A pair of rollers for tendering steak." (*Knight*, 1875.)

MEAT and **FOOD CUTTER** — *see* **MEAT CHOPPER**

MEAT FRET — A wooden, metal or pottery implement with a handle and a block head, one or two sides of which have a grid of fifty or so points or small "pyramids." It was used for pounding meat and "makes Round Steak as tender as Porterhouse without mutilating or destroying its juices. Champion Meat Fret, endorsed by butchers." (*Ladies Home Journal* advertisement, 1898.) The meat fret, or *meat tenderer* as it was also called, worked by breaking down the fibers — one of the much-discussed three parts of meat: fibrine, albumin and gelatin. Other names for this implement are *steak pounder, steak maul, steak tenderer. See also* **BEETLE, CUTLET BAT**

Fig. 744. MEAT CUTTER. Nickeled iron. Adjustable height. No. 205. Montgomery Ward, 1895.

Fig. 747. MEAT FRET. c. 1890s. Blue & white pottery, wood. L: 12"; 3-1/3" dia. American. Courtesy Keillor Collection.

Fig. 748. CHAMPION MEAT FRET. 1890s.

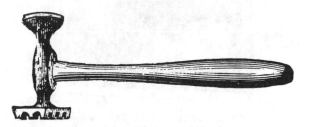

Fig. 749. STEAK TENDERER. Iron, wood. F. A. Waker, c. 1870s.

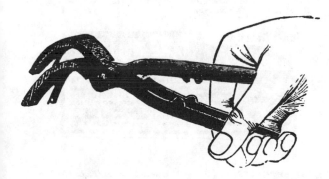

Fig. 750. UTENSIL HOLDER, Meat Tenderer, Nut Cracker. Japanned or tinned metal. J.B. Foote Foundry Company, 1906.

Fig. 751. MEAT TENDERIZER & AX. Dec. 5, 1922. Nickeled steel, wood. L: 10"; W: 4¼". Tyler Mfg. Co., Muncie, Ind. Comes apart for cleaning by means of wing nut. Author's Collection.

Fig. 752. MEAT TENDERER. Pat'd Sept. 20, 1892. Cast iron. L: 4"; W: 2¾". American. Courtesy Keillor Collection.

MEAT HOOK — An iron hook, or hooks, for suspending ham, beef, or any other joints in the smokehouse, or in the chimney, where it might smoke and therefore be preserved. Also a *ham hook*.

Fig. 753. HAM HOOK. c. 1700. Found in chimney of a house built in Plymouth, Massachusetts in 1711. Braided wrought iron. L: 7½"; W: 10". Courtesy Keillor Collection.

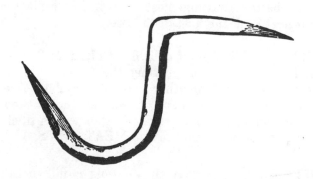

Fig. 754. MEAT HOOK to drive. Tinned iron. Lalance & Grosjean, 1890.

MEAT PAN GRATE — A rectangular metal rack which was put in the dripping pan, or other roasting pan, and on which the roast was cooked in the oven. Also called a *dripping pan grill*.

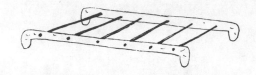

Fig. 755. MEAT PAN GRATE.

MEAT PRESS — A cranked or levered small press for getting the juice out of meat. *"Columbia;" etc.*

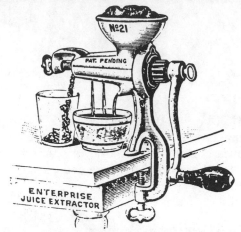

Fig. 756. MEAT JUICE EXTRACTOR. Tinned iron. Enterprise. The Enterprising Housekeeper, 1898.

MEAT ROCKER — "A mincing knife having a handle at each end, and worked by a rocking motion." (*Knight*, 1884.)

Fig. 757. MEAT ROCKER.

MEAT SAW — *see* KITCHEN SAW

MEAT SCREEN — A metal screen placed in the room before roasting meat — spitted or grilled — to reflect back the heat of the fire.

MEAT SQUEEZER or JUICE EXTRACTOR — A hand-held device for pressing the juice out of a piece of raw beef or other meat, for invalids. One type was a hinged pair of coarsely corrugated paddles which were pressed together with a thick slice of meat between. *See also* MEAT PRESS

MELON MOLD — A tin pudding mold, in the form of half a melon, with a close-fitting lid with a ring handle. It is ribbed or scalloped, and resembles a canteloupe.

MELON SCOOP — A small implement usually with two different size scoops, one at each end of a long handle. The scoops have a small hole in the bowl. *See also* BEZEL SCOOP, VEGETABLE BALLER

"MENDETS" — A plug and nut of aluminum for mending holes in pots and pans of any metal. The plug went through the hole, and the small nut was screwed on tight. A paper of *Mendets* had several different sizes. *See also* POT MENDER

Fig. 760. MENDETS CARD. c. 1940. Converse reads in part: "Fits any angle, stands extreme heat.... Remove nut and tin washer from screw of Mendet, leaving cork washer on. Then push screw of Mendet through on opposite side replace tin washer and nut. Tighten same with attachment wrench, and leak is mended." Collette Mfg. Co., Amsterdam, N.Y.

Fig. 761. MENDETS. The People's Home Journal, Dec. 1910.

MICA — A silicate crystal, built up by nature in thin, somewhat flexible leaves or sheets. It was used for translucent panels in oven doors and lanterns. *See also* ISINGLASS

MIDDLINGS — Flour, ground between coarse (*shorts*) and fine. *See also* CRIBBLE

MILK BOILER, — SAUCEPAN — *see* DOUBLE BOILER

MILK SKIMMER — *see* SKIMMER

MILL — A grinding machine, hand-powered usually, with a hopper, a sharply-grooved, iron grinding cylinder, and an adjustable pressure plate. It was used for reducing to powder or meal such things as coffee, bones, dried beans and peas, malt, barley, and whole spices — depending on size of the mill.

An early one was designed by Mr. Garnet Terry of London in 1800 or 1801. It was pictured and described in Willich's great *Domestic Encyclopedia* of 1804, and *The American Artists Manual* by James Cutbush. *See also* **MORTAR & PESTLE, MULLER**

MINCING KNIFE — *see* **CHOPPING KNIFE**

MIXING SPOON — There are any number of variations on the theme of a slotted or perforated tin or wooden spoon which allows the batter or liquid to go through the spoon while it is being mixed. A mixing spoon is not the same as a stirring spoon. A similar, and usually interchangeable spoon is the straining spoon, used for serving up vegetables out of their potlikker. *"B.M.;" "Chief;" "Kitchamajig;" "A & J;" "Androck;"* etc.

Fig. 762. PEPPER GRINDER. c. 1900. Cast iron, wood knob. L: 6"; W: 4½"; 6" handle. Wall-mounted side mill. American. Courtesy Robert D. Franklin.

Fig. 764. SLOTTED SPOONS. 1915 to 1970s. These, c. 1940. Tinned iron, wire. Left to right: (1) 10¼" x 3¾". (2) 10-7/8" x 3½". (3) 10-5/8" x 3-5/8". "Lifts, whips, mixes, mashes, crushes, strains." Chief. All American. Author's Collection.

Fig. 765. IDEAL MIXING SPOON. Pat'd 1908. F. W. Seastrand, c. 1912.

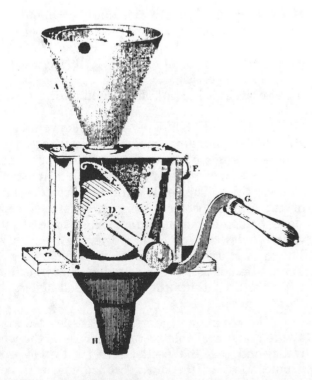

Fig. 763. MILL. Invented by Garnet Terry, London, England. Domestic Encyclopedia, 1804.

Fig. 766. MIXING SPOONS. Top to bottom: (1) Pat'd March 30, 1908. Iron, wood. L: 10"; W: 3". Ideal Mixing Spoon. Mfd. by ...ater. American. (2) c. 1915. Iron, wood. L: 10" Androck. American. (3) c. 1910. Tin, iron. L: 10¼". "Rumford Baking Powder." American. All courtesy Mary Mac Frankin.

MOLASSES CAN — A tin, tightly-covered vessel with a spout. The can was supposedly more convenient than the heavy jug. It was advised to keep a cork in the spout. "Molasses, or melasses: the gross fluid matter, which remains after refining sugar; and which cannot by simple boiling be reduced to a more solid consistence than that of common syrup, vulgarly called treacle." (*Willich*, 1821.)

Switchel

One part iced water, one part vinegar, and one part molasses. A good iced drink for the summer, and said to have been carried out to farmers as they worked in the fields.

Fig. 767. MOLASSES CAN. Japanned tin "bright colors." 10 & 20 gallon. "With drainer near the top. Drippings go back into the can — a very desirable feature." Matthai-Ingram Company, c. 1890.

MOLDS — *see* BLANCMANGE —, BORDER —, BUTTER —, CAKE —, CHARLOTTE RUSSE —, CREAM —, CROQUETTE —, CUTLET —, DARIOLE —, FISH —, ICE CREAM —, INDIVIDUAL —, LADY LOCK —, MADELINE —, MELON —, PUDDING —, TIN

MOLDING BOARD — A hardwood board for rolling out pastry.

MOLDING SHEET — A tin sheet used for rolling out pastry, and said to be superior to the wood because the dough did not stick so tenaciously to it. *See also* DOUGH SCRAPER, PASTE BOARD

Crackers

Take a large cupful of bread dough; roll out on the molding-board; spread on it a piece of butter and lard together, as large as a goose-egg; sprinkle a little flour over it; fold it up, and pound with something heavy a long time; **take a small** piece at a time; roll out very thin; stamp with a clock key, and bake very quickly. [*Treasure House*, 1891]

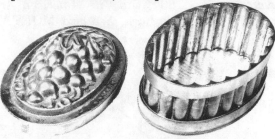

Fig. 768. MOLD. 19th century. Tinned copper. L: 5½"; W: 3¾"; H: 3½". American. Courtesy Keillor Collection.

Fig. 769. TURBAN MOULD, tubed. Tin. From 7-7/8" x 3¼" to 10" x 4". Lalance & Grosjean, 1890.

MONEL — A silvery metal alloy of about 67% nickel, 28% copper, and 5% iron and manganese. Named after Ambrose Monell, an American manufacturer who died in 1921. It was used for some appliances, sinks, stove linings, etc., but not for utensils as it is a poor heat conductor.

MORTAR and PESTLE — A bowl-like vessel and a grinding or pounding implement used together to reduce all kinds of food stuffs to paste or powder. The mortar was made of some very hard substance, and was thick. The pestle's grinding head was made of the same substance. Brass, bronze, bell metal, glass, hardwood, iron, ironstone, marble, lignum vitae, Wedgwood or other pottery were all used. The mortar usually had some type of pouring lip. The pestle consisted of a rounded, heavy head and a handle. Sometimes the handle ended in a smaller rounded head.

The commonest mortar and pestle used in the kitchen, and available to the collector, is the white Wedgwood set, the pestle having a turned wood handle. Most of the brass, bronze, and bell metal sets were used by pharmacists. *See also* LIGNUM VITAE

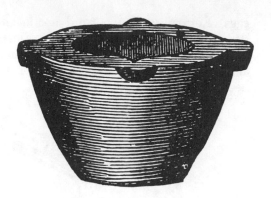

Fig. 770. MORTAR. Stoneware. F. A. Walker, c. 1880.

Fig. 773. MORTAR & PESTLE. Stoneware, wood. (Mortar) 4½" x 2¾". (Pestle) L: 6¾". Maddock's Sons, Trenton N.J. Anchor trademark. Courtesy Paul Persoff.

MUFFIN PAN — A tin frame holding from four to twelve (or even more) shallow or deep cups. These cups were either plain, or fluted in one of several styles. Muffin pans were also made in enameled ware.

In many of the older tin muffin pans, the cups can be easily lifted free from the frame. Perhaps this is only because of the method of manufacture, or possibly the cups were used as individual molds. Another muffin pan is the heavy cast iron one with eight or eleven shallow, or deep cups. They are often called *popover pans* or *gem pans*.

Muffins were also baked in pottery cups, in rings, or in individual cake pans.

Fig. 771. MORTAR & PESTLE. 19th century. Wood. 6" dia.; H: 7". Two-headed pestle, L: 7". Downturned handle attached to mortar. American. Courtesy Keillor Collection.

Fig. 774. TURK'S HEAD MUFFIN PAN. Stamped tin, solid frame. 6, 8, 9 or 12 cups. Matthai-Ingram Company, c. 1890.

MUFFIN RINGS — These are simply tin rings, about 3" in diameter and 1 or 1½" high. They were set on a griddle, or in a baking pan, and the muffin batter was poured into them and baked. The best muffins for muffin rings are probably the yeast-raised ones, rather than the quick, baking powder muffins, as the batter tends to be stiffer.

Raised Muffins

1 quart of milk; a little salt; 2 spoonfuls yeast; 2 eggs; a piece of butter the size of an egg, melted in the milk, warmed; make in the morning and raise until night, or vice versa; eggs to be put in just before cooking; flour; bake in rings in a spider over a slow fire; split and butter before sending to table. [*Treasure House*, 1891]

Fig. 772. MORTAR & PESTLE. Early-19th century. Stoneware, wood. Colonial Williamsburg, Virginia.

Fig. 775. MUFFIN RINGS. F. A. Walker, c. 1870s.

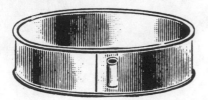

Fig. 776. MUFFIN RING. Tin. 3" dia. Montgomery Ward, 1893.

MULLER — A grinding implement used like a pestle, or beetle. Also the container in which wine or ale is heated before the fire. It is also, I believe, the instrument, such as the loggerhead, which was heated in the fire and used to heat or mull wine or ale. *Webster's Second International Dictionary* defines *mull* as *to heat, sweeten, and spice; as to mull wine.* But it says that the origin is uncertain. I would imagine that a brass or bell-metal pestle, or muller, used to heat a cup of wine, might have been said to *mull* the wine. *See also* **ALE BOOT, CHOCOLATE POT, LOGGERHEAD**

MUNTZ'S METAL — A metal alloy consisting of 40 parts zinc to 60 parts copper. Named as the "preferred" metal for making saucepans and kettles in an English patent of 1851.

MUSH STICK — A hardwood stick for stirring mush or corn meal in boiling water. "Use a hard wood paddle, two feet long, with a blade two inches wide and seven inches long to stir with ...." (*Practical Housekeeping*, 1884.)

New England Hasty Pudding,
or,
Stir-About
Boil 3 quarts water in iron pot; mix pint of Indian meal in cold water, and make it thin enough to pour easily; when the water boils, pour it in; stir well with a wooden stick kept for this purpose; it takes about an hour to boil; salt to your taste; stir in dry meal to make it thick enough, beating it all the time. Eat with milk or molasses, or butter and sugar." [*Lea*, 1859]

Hasty Pudding Sauce
1 Cup hot milk
1 Cup sugar
2 eggs
1 Tablespoon butter
Stir the butter into the boiling milk, add the sugar, and pour this on the beaten

eggs. Return to the custard kettle and stir until it begins to thicken. Flavor with vanilla, adding, if you like, nutmeg, and set in hot, not boiling, water till needed. [*Harland*, 1889]

Fig. 777. MILK SAUCE PAN. Planished tin, earthenware. F. A. Walker, c. 1870s.

NAILS — A box of nails and a ball of twine were listed by all the early cookery books as a kitchen necessity. The nails were used as hooks or pegs, and the twine was used for trussing roasts and tying parcels.

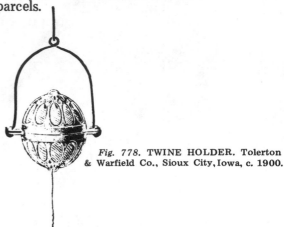

Fig. 778. TWINE HOLDER. Tolerton & Warfield Co., Sioux City, Iowa, c. 1900.

NAPKIN RINGS — "Napkins are never supposed to appear a second time before washing, hence napkin rings are domestic secrets and not for company." (*Goodholme*, 1877.) Nevertheless you would have found them in most 19th century kitchens, ready to be taken out and set with the table for the next meal.

NAPLES BISCUIT PAN — A tin baking utensil, approximately 4 x 10", divided with parallel partitions about 1½" apart. The naples biscuits were like lady fingers, and were baked six or eight to a pan: each about 4 x 1½". *See* **LADIES', FINGER CAKE PAN**

Naples Biscuit
Beat eight eggs; add to them one pound of flour, one pound of powdered sugar, one teaspoonful of essence of lemon. Bake in a quick oven. [*Strohm*, 1888]

NAPPY [*nappie*] — A round, fairly deep cooking or serving dish with a flat bottom and sloping sides.

Made of glass or earthenware; the commonest are found in yellow ware and Rockingham ware. Nappies were made in   umber of sizes between 3" and 12" in diameter. Some have a corrugated bottom.

Rice nappies are differentiated in early 20th century catalogs as having fluted sides, and a size range between 5" and 10".

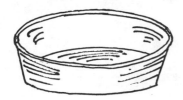

Fig. 779. NAPPY.

NICKEL — A hard, silvery-white, lustrous mineral, usually occuring in combination with arsenic or sulphur. It is both malleable and ductile. Nickel was used for plating, as with iron; or as an alloy, as with steel. "Kitchen utensils in solid nickel come from France. They are beautiful, smooth, and almost indestructible. They are cast without the slightest groove or seam, and are made very solid. They come without covers; I suppose because of the expense. The articles are costly at first,... but with proper care will last a lifetime. There is nothing to break or peel off and mingle with the food. It is to be hoped that the demand for cheaper articles may not flood the market with cheap light ware as will bring discredit on an entire class of goods ... as happened with aluminum." (Parloa, *Ladies Home Journal*, January, 1901.)

Fig. 780. NICKEL-PLATING APPARATUS. Advertisement in Scientific American, November 1, 1890.

NOODLE CUTTER — A rolling device with cutting blades. The cutter was rolled over the flattened dough and cut many rows of noodles at once. Other types screw-clamped to the table, and had just a few blades. The dough was fed through them and the handle was cranked.

NOTTINGHAM JAR — A gracefully fat-bellied earthenware vessel with a small base, a larger mouth and lid, and two ear handles. It was used for baking meat in a slow oven. The meat was placed within the jar, the lid well-pasted down, and covered with a fold of thick paper. It was also used

for jugged hare — the meat sealed in the jar, covered closely, and boiled in water.

Fig. 781. NOTTINGHAM JAR. Earthenware.

NUT CHOPPER — Usually a glass container with some sort of chopping blades either cranked or pushed up and down. *See also* **VEGETABLE CHOPPER**

Fig. 782. VEGETABLE & NUT CHOPPER. c. 1910. Glass, tin, wood. 4¼" dia.; H: 10½". The Ernestreich Co., Chicago. Author's Collection.

NUT CRACKER — A device to crack nuts, in their shells. Some are a lot more successful than others. The best device holds the nut securely while a screw or lever is forced against it. Older nut crackers have two hinged and opposing corrugated pieces, usually of iron or nickel- plated iron. Nut crackers have been made, essentially in the same fashion, for hundreds of years — in iron, steel, and wood.

Walnut Ketchup
Boil or simmer a gallon of the expressed juice of walnuts when they are tender, and skim it well; add two pounds of anchovies, 2 pounds shalots, 1 ounce cloves, 1 ounce mace, 1 ounce pepper, one clove garlic. Let all simmer until the shalots sink. Put the liquor in a pan till cold, bottle and divide the spices to each. [*Willich*, 1821]

Fig. 783. NUT CRACKER. c. 1910 to 1930. Nickeled cast iron. 3¼" x 5" as shown. Ideal (?). American. Courtesy Ruth Persoff.

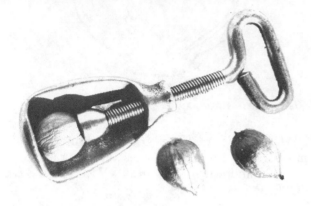

Fig. 784. NUT CRACKER. c. 1910 to 1940. Nickeled iron. L: 5" as shown. American. Courtesy Mary Mac Franklin.

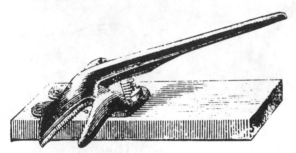

Fig. 785. NUT CRACKER. Cast iron, wood. F. A. Walker, c. 1870s.

Fig. 789. NUT CRACKER. c. 1890s. Steel. L: 5½". Adjustable. American. Author's Collection.

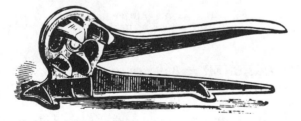

Fig. 786. NUT CRACKER. Iron. F. A. Walker, c. 1870s.

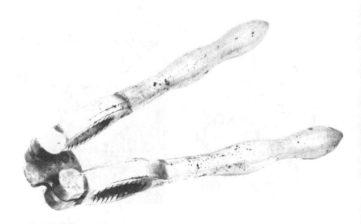

Fig. 790. NUT CRACKER. c. 1890s. Silverplated iron. L: 5¼". Adjustable for large and smaller nuts. Author's Collection.

NUT PICK — A small sharp instrument for picking the meat out of nutshells.

Fig. 787. "KNEE WARMER" NUT CRACKERS. Early-19th century. Cast iron. L: 3½" to 6". American. Courtesy Keillor Collection.

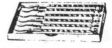

Fig. 791. NUT PICKS. Butler Brothers, 1899.

NUTMEG GRATER — *see* **GRATER**

OLIVE PITTER — An implement, working like a cherry pitter, for punching out the pit of an olive. In fact, the Rollman cherry pitter was advertised as working equally well for olives.

OMELET PAN — A shallow pan with sloping sides and a long handle, made that way so that the omelet could be slid out of the pan. *See also* **ENGLISH HAMMERED FRY PAN, FRENCH FRY PAN, FRY PAN**

Fig. 792. OMELETTE PAN. Tinned or polished iron. F. A. Walker, c. 1870s.

A Nourishing Omelet

Dissolve a saltspoon of beef-extract in half a cup of hot water, and stir into it half a cup of the crusts of whole-wheat bread rolled fine. Let them soak over the teakettle while you beat the yolks and whites of two eggs. Stir the soaked crumbs into the yolks, add a dash of salt and pepper, then stir the whites in lightly. Cook in a hot, buttered omelet-pan. Fold, and invert on a hot dish. Garnish with parsley. [*The Peerless Cook-Book:* Mrs. D. A. Lincoln. In *Strohm*, 1888]

ONION PEELER — "The earliest onion peeler I know about wore a gingham apron and sat on a chair while she peeled the onions and cried." (Henry Landis, of the Landis Valley [Pennsylvania] Museum. Response to a query to the *Chronicle*, April, 1951.)

OVEN — In the earliest homes in America, the oven was likely to be a separate structure outside the house, or kitchen. If inside, it was usually built into the back of the fireplace. This meant that the housewife had to lean over the fire to use her oven.

The first "built-in," *flue-less* ovens were heated by a fire, or by hot coals laid right in the oven, and carefully tended and regulated by adding fuel and by opening the door wider. The door had to be kept open for a draft of air to keep the fire burning. The hot coals were moved around the floor of the oven to heat the bricks evenly. When the fire was finally reduced to coals or ashes, they were raked out. If the temperature was right, the cook put the bread loaves in with a peel. Small loaves, because they required less baking time, could rest directly on the bricks. Larger loaves, cakes and pies were baked on racks or in pans. An improvement on the old oven, either at the back or the side of the fireplace, was the introduction of a separate hearth below the oven. The fire could be kept burning throughout the baking.

The trick with all the ovens was regulating the temperature in such a way that a day's baking could be accomplished with the least amount of re-firing. Bread, cakes, biscuits, puddings, and custards all required different heats and different baking times. Even in a cooling oven, a custard would set if left long enough.

Mrs. Cornelius (*The Young Housekeeper's Friend*, 1846), gave instructions for using a brick oven for five successive bakings, in this order: bread, puddings, pastry, cake and gingerbread, and last, custards. Small baking jobs could be done directly on the hearth: a space was cleared, the bread dough put on the hot bricks or stone, and a pot placed upside-down over it and then heaped with hot coals. *See also* **DUTCH OVEN, REFLECTING OVEN, TIN KITCHEN**

OVEN THERMOMETER — Thomas Masters of London invented what was probably the first oven thermometer about 1850. It was a glass ring, with mercury, and an indicator guide telling what to put in the oven when the mercury reached a particular point on the guide.

"Many test their ovens in this way: if the hand can be held in from 20-35 seconds, it is a quick oven, from 35-45 seconds is moderate, and from 45-60 seconds is slow. 60 seconds is a good oven to begin with for large fruit cakes. All systematic housekeepers will hail the day when some enterprising, practical 'Dixie' girl shall invent a stove or range with a thermometer attached to the oven so that the heat may be regulated accurately and intelligently." (*Practical Housekeeping*, 1884.)

OYSTER BROILER — A double, hinged, wire rack for holding oysters over the fire. The space between the parallel wires is 3/16". The broilers came in different sizes and were like other wire broilers or toasters except that the space between the wires was narrower.

Fig. 793. OYSTER BROILER. Wire. 6" x 9", 8" x 9", 9" x 10", 9" x 12", 9" x 14". Matthai-Ingram Company, c. 1890.

OYSTER FORK — A fork with short tines and a long handle, similar to a pickle fork.

PADLOCK — A small padlock was often used to lock up salt and sugar canisters, bread and cake boxes, and spice cabinets. Some canisters have a hasp closing through which the padlock fits.

PALETTE KNIFE — A small, flexible knife with a round-ended blade. It was used for scraping mixing bowls, etc. *See also* **SPATULA**

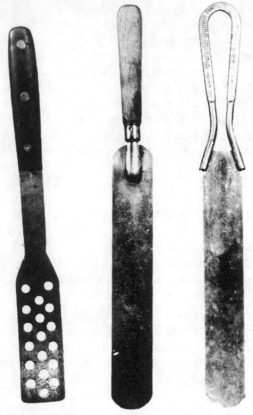

Fig. 794. PALETTE KNIVES. (Left to right) (1) Slice or egg beater. c. 1900. Steel, wood. L: 11½". (2) c. 1900. Steel, wood. L: 12¼". (3) c. 1920s, 1930s. Stainless steel. L: 12¼". "If it's varnished, we make it," Newark Varnish Works, Inc. This one obviously is also a paint stirrer. Author's Collection.

PAN — A vessel, of metal or earthenware, usually broad and shallow. Different pans were used for everything from baking or mixing bread to washing dishes.

PANNIKIN [*pannican*] — A small metal drinking vessel, usually of tinned iron.

PAPER — Paper was used by the cook for several purposes. Heavily *buttered paper* was laid over large cuts of meat before they were spit-roasted, and the cook basted over the paper. *Oiled paper* or *paraffined paper* was used for sealing stoneware jars of food. *Straw-paper* was used for draining fried foods. Cookies and little cakes were sometimes baked on *wafer paper*. Scraps of paper were threaded on a string and hung near the stove to be used like paper towels. In 1920, in a book on household arts, it was suggested that a bag be nailed on the wall near the stove for all kinds of soft paper to be used for cleaning.

Mrs. Prentice S. wrote to *Woman's Home Companion* in March 1901, that "the coarse brown paper used by most butchers is not objectionable for draining fried articles, being made of straw, which is supposed to be clean. Blotting paper is best, but it is too expensive for the purpose. If some one would put on the market a paper drainer as effective as blotting paper — and yet cheap — it would meet a long-felt want." *See also* **CHOP FRILLS**

PARING KNIFE — A small pointed knife for peeling vegetables and fruits.

Fig. 795. PARING KNIFE. Practical Housekeeping, 1881.

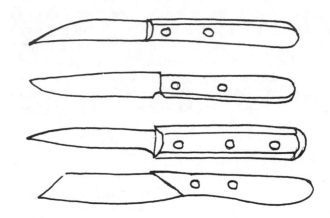

Fig. 796. PARING KNIVES. Sharp, spear & clip points.

Fig. 797. PARER. c. 1940. Wood, nickeled steel, removable razor blade. L: 7". American. Author's Collection.

Fig. 798, 799. (Top) UTILITY or SERVICE KNIFE. Early-20th century. Carbon steel, wood. L: 8¾". (Bottom) VEGETABLE KNIFE. c. 1910. Carbon steel, wood. L: 7½". Ontario Knife Co. Author's Coll.

PASTE-BOARD — A wooden board for rolling out pastry. Also called a *molding board*.

Puff Paste

1 lb. of flour, 1 lb. fresh butter, salt to taste. Divide the butter and flour in half; mix ½ of each into a pliable dough with cold water. Roll out the dough, cut off bits of the remaining ½ lb. butter (using ¼ of it at a time). Sprinkle about over the dough, sift over this ¼ of the remaining ½ lb. of flour, fold over and again roll out, but do not roll hard. When rolled, put on another ¼ of the butter and flour and roll. Continue until all the butter and flour has been used. Roll up in a towel for an hour or two when it will be ready to use. Bake with filling. Use to line gem pans, pudding pans, muffin tins, pie-pans." (*Ladies Home Journal*, October 1890.)

Fig. 800. PASTE BOARD, ROLLING PIN, CUTTER. Dr. Chase's Recipes, or Information for Everybody. Ann Arbor, Michigan: R. A. Beal, 1872.

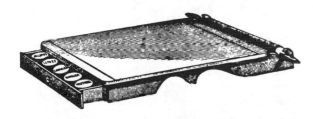

Fig. 801. CAKE BOARD & ROLLING PIN with spice drawer. "It is safe to be suspicious of any contrivance that promises too much. There is such a thing as making one implement serve too many purposes; but there seems to be no good reason why a cake board and rolling pin should not always be found together, and the spice drawer, if fastened by a spring catch so as not to slip out, would be a convenience." Practical Housekeeping, 1881.

PASTE CUTTER — An instrument for cutting pastry into fancy shapes; a cookie or cake cutter. *See also* **JAGGER**

Fig. 802. PASTE CUTTER. Tin. F. A. Walker, c. 1870s.

Fig. 803. PASTE or VEGETABLE CUTTERS. F. A. Walker, c. 1870s.

PASTE JAGGER — *see* **JAGGER**

PASTE-PIN — *see* **ROLLING PIN**

PASTE PINCHER — A small tongs with flat ends for pinching and thereby sealing, or ornamenting, the edges of pie crusts and tarts. An obsolete definiton of *pinch* is to crimp or crinkle the edge of a pie crust. *See also* **JAGGER**

PASTRY BRUSH — *see* **BRUSHES**

PASTRY FORK — A fork with broad tines and a wooden handle for working shortening into flour for pie crust or biscuits. Also used for chopping or mashing cooked fruits or vegetables.

Fig. 804. PASTRY BLENDER or MASHER. 1915 to 1940. Wood, nickeled iron. L: 9½". American. Author's Collection.

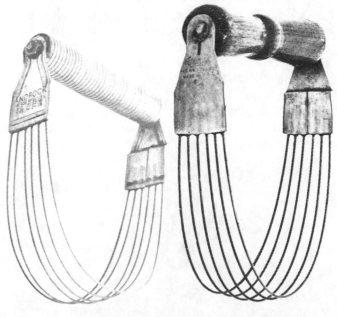

Fig. 805. PASTRY BLENDERS. Pat'd Jan. 12, 1929. Wire, wood, stainless steel. L: 5¾"; W: 4". Androck. Author's Collection.

Fig. 806. PASTRY SPOON. c. 1915. Stamped tin. L: 12". WB/W. American. Author's Collection.

Fig. 807. PASTRY SPOON. c. 1930s. Aluminum. L: 9¼". HM/Z. Trademark half-moon. German. Author's Collection.

PASTRY SHEET — A large tin sheet for rolling out dough. *See also* **MOLDING SHEET**

PATTY IRON — An iron implement, consisting of interchangeable forms for the molding of patties, and a screw-on long handle. *See also* **BOUCHE IRON, TIMBALE IRON, VIENNA CAKE IRON**

Fig. 808. PATTY IRON. c. 1915 to 1930. Cast iron, wood. L: 11"; This diamond-shaped iron screws on to the long handle. Other irons in a set would have included hearts and rounds. American. Author's Collection.

PATTY PAN [*pattipan, pateepan*] — A small tin or stoneware pan, fluted or plain, in which a patty or pasty was baked. It would have been very unusual for only one patty pan to be used, and patties were baked like muffins in quantities. An older type of patty pan was a three-legged utensil with a long straight handle and a number of cupped depressions cast into the flat surface. This is also referred to as an *egg-fryer* in some late 19th century catalogs.

Fig. 809. PATTIE PAN. Stamped tin. F. A. Walker, c. 1870s.

Fig. 810. PATTIE PANS. Tin. F. A. Walker, c. 1870s.

Fig. 811. MINCE PIE PATTY. Stamped tin. F. A. Walker, c. 1870s.

Fig. 812. SCALLOPED OYSTER PATTY. Tin 5¼" x 4¼" x 1¼". Lalance & Grosjean, 1890.

PEACH PARER — A machine, like an apple parer, for peeling peaches *and* apples. "A continuous and urgent inquiry for a machine for paring peaches, has been ringing in our ears from all Peach-growing sections, for the past five years, and in response, ... the manufacturers of the Lightning & Turn-Table Apple Parers have succeeded in obtaining and securing a device for Holding and Paring Peaches. Exhibited in 1869 at the New York, Indiana, Illinois, Wisconsin, Minnesota and St Louis Fairs and were awarded prizes by the delighted judges." (*American Agriculturist*, June 1872.)

Earlier peach parers include Ward's Peach Parer and Cutting Machine patented in 1851, and Alva Hermans' parer patented in 1859. "*Lightning;*" "*Sinclair Scott Co.;*" *etc.*

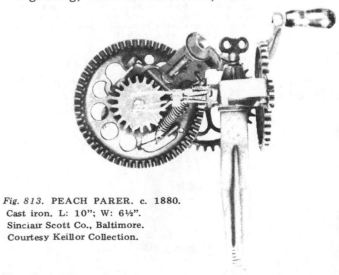

Fig. 813. PEACH PARER. c. 1880. Cast iron. L: 10"; W: 6½". Sinclair Scott Co., Baltimore. Courtesy Keillor Collection.

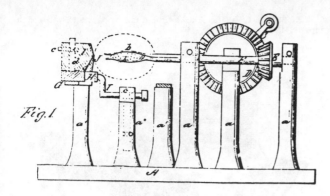

Fig. 814. PEACH PARER. Pat'd 1859, No. 26,640. Alva Hermans, Henderson, Texas. Official Gazette, Dec. 27, 1859.

PEACH STONER — A mechanical device for removing the peach pit.

Fig. 815. PEACH STONER. Cast iron. F. A. Walker, c. 1870s.

PEARL-ASH — "A fixed alkaline salt obtained by melting the ashes of burnt vegetables. The best are made from weeds." (*Willich*, 1821.) *See also* **POTASH**

PEA SHELLER — A cranked device, screw-clamped to the table, and fed with peas through the hopper. The peas were supposed to fall out the other end into a pail hung on the cast-in hook. "A boon to Housewives — Will shell a dish of peas in 5 minutes, whereas the old way took an hour. A child can operate without trouble or danger." (Advertisement for the Acme Pea Sheller in *Woman's Home Companion*, 1897.)

Pea Salad

Mix well together in a salad bowl 1 cup of shred lettuce, ½ cup tender shelled green peas, half grown, and 1 tablespoon of finely cut nasturtium stems; with a silver spoon cut up ½ cup of strawberries; mix well with ½ cup of strawberry juice; pour it over the salad in the bowl; let it stand 15 minutes and serve. [*Treasure House*, 1891]

Fig. 816. PEA SHELLER. Galvanized iron. L: 9". Acme Pea Sheller Company, c. 1900.

PEEL, SLICE, or THIBBLE — A long-handled iron or wood shovel with a flat or wedge-shaped head, which was used to place bread or pies in the oven and remove them too. *See also* **PIE LIFTER**

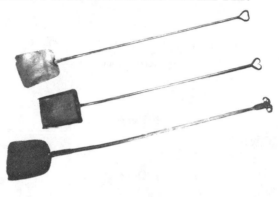

Fig. 817. BREAD PEELS. 18th century. Wrought iron. Top to bottom: L: 37½"; L: 36"; L: 43½". All about 5" wide. American. Courtesy Keillor Collection.

Fig. 818. PANCAKE TURNER or PIE LIFTER. Late-18th century. Wrought iron. L: 6½"; W: 2½". American. Courtesy Keillor Collection.

PEPPER-BOX,—— CASTOR — *see* **DREDGE**

PEPPER MILL, —— GRINDER — A hand mill, either for table use, or wall-mounted in the kitchen. *See* **MILL**

PERCOLATOR — A type of coffee maker which, because of a tube in the center, causes the hot water to filter through the ground coffee (in a basket) several times in order to extract all the essence. *See also* **BIGGIN, COFFEE POT**

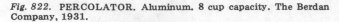

Fig. 822. PERCOLATOR. Aluminum. 8 cup capacity. The Berdan Company, 1931.

Fig. 819. COFFEE PERCOLATOR. 1915-1925. Aluminum, green glass, wood. H: 9"; 4-7/8" dia. American Aluminum Ware Co., A.A.W. Peerless Co., The Better Ware, Newark, N.J. Author's Collection.

Fig. 823. ELECTRIC PERCOLATOR. 1919. Nickeled General Electric. Photograph courtesy General Electric Company.

Fig. 820. COFFEE PERCOLATOR. 1915-1930. Aluminum, glass, wood. H: 7½"; W: 5¾". No. 69, Landers, Frary & Clark, New Britain, Conn. Author's Collection.

PEWTER [*peuter, pewtur, puter*] — An alloy of tin and lead; usually containing 1/5 its weight in lead. "Compound of tin, lead, brass or tin, antimony, bismuth & copper." (*Willich*, 1804.) *See also* **WHITE METAL**

PICKLE FORK — A long-handled, short-tined fork for getting pickles out of a barrel or deep jar, such as the cathedral pickle jar pictured. Some pickle forks had two barbed tines which "made sure of holding a pickle every time." (*Practical Housekeeping*, 1884.) Another type has two or four wire fingers which can grab the pickle. *See also* **DISH CLOTH HOLDER**

Fig. 824. PICKLE, CHERRY, OLIVE FORK. c. 1915. Nickeled iron. L: 8". No. 185-M. "Just the Tool for Small Mouth Bottles." American. Author's Collection.

Fig. 821. PERCOLATOR. Agate enameled ware. 4½" dia., 1 pt. Lalance & Grosjean, 1890.

Fig. 825, 826. CATHEDRAL PICKLE JARS. 19th century. Green glass. H: 11", 12". Courtesy Keillor Collection.

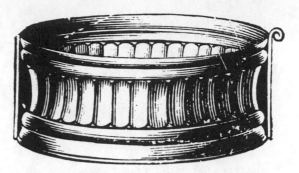

Fig. 828. FRENCH PIE MOLD, or CONFECTIONER'S MOLD. Tin. F. A. Walker, c. 1870s.

Fig. 829. PIE PLATES. Stamped tin. (Top) Scolloped. 8", 9" dia. (Bottom) Lebanon. 7", 8", 9" dia. Lalance & Grosjean, 1890.

PIE BIRD — A small, hollow, pottery (or sometimes tin) bird with a long "stem". It was placed in the center of a double-crust, deep dish meat or fruit pie as a steam vent. It kept the upper crust from collapsing.

PIE-BOARD — A wooden board on which pies are made, baked, or carried.

PIE CRIMPER — *see* JAGGER

PIE LIFTER — One type is a *peel* [which see]; another is a wire, or wire and wood device which clamps the edges of a pie, or slides under the pie pan, for removing it from the oven.

Fig. 830. PIE MOLD. Tin. F. A. Walker, c. 1870s.

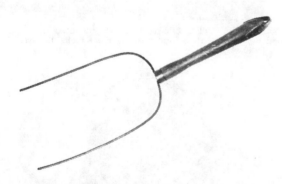

Fig. 827. PIE LIFTER. c. 1870s. Wood, iron wire, leather. L: 17½". American. Courtesy Keillor Collection.

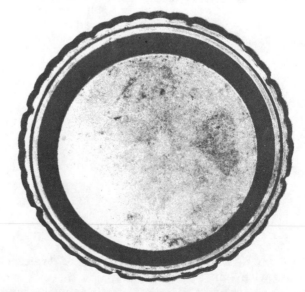

PIE PAN, — TIN,— PLATE — A relatively deep tin or earthenware dish for baking pies. Earthenware pie plates, often with a *sgraffito* (scratched in) or slip glaze motto, were made by the pie-loving Pennsylvania Germans.

Fig. 831. PIE PAN. c. 1890s. Blackened tin. 10-1/8" x 1-7/8". Author's Collection.

163

Fig. 832. KNIFE BLADE DEEP PIE PLATE. Tin. 8-13/16" x 1-1/8". Ekco. Edward Katzinger Company, 1940.

PIE PRICKER — An implement of wood or metal for piercing a pattern of holes in upper pie crusts to allow steam to escape.

Fig. 833. PIE CRIMPER, PIE PRICKER. 19th century. Wood. Crimper: L: 2½"; W: 2½". Pricker: L: 4¾". American. Courtesy Keillor Collection.

PIE RACK — A wire rack for holding a stack of pies for cooling, or for storing them in a safe.

PIE SAFE — see SAFE

PIE TRIMMER — see JAGGER

PIGGIN — An American word for a small wooden bucket with one stave longer than the others to serve as a handle. See also PIPKIN

Fig. 834. PIGGIN.

PINEAPPLE EYE SNIP — A sort of tweezer-scissors with one tip for digging out the eye and then, in action with the other, cutting tip, snipping it off.

Fig. 835. PINEAPPLE EYE SNIP. c. 1880s. Painted iron. L: 5½". American. Courtesy Keillor Collection.

PIPE INCINERATOR — see CARBONIZER

PIPKIN — A small earthenware cooking pot. Also called a *piggin*, but in this case not a wooden utensil. The word *pipkin* may come from *pipe* meaning cask, and -*kin*, a diminutive.

PITCHER — A pouring utensil with a large lip and a handle. Used for cider, water, milk, switchel, beer, and even for buckwheat batter for griddle-cakes.

Fig. 836, 837. WATER PITCHERS. Tin, "painted in bright and subdued colors; superb adjuncts to summer or city houses." F. A. Walker, 1886.

Fig. 838. BEER POT. Agate enameled ware. 3, 4 qts. Lalance & Grosjean, 1890.

164

Fig. 839. "CLOVER LEAF" PITCHER. Agate enameled ware. 4 pts. Lalance & Grosjean, 1890.

PLANISHED IRON — *see* **RUSSIAN IRON**

PLANK — A wide, thick board for roasting fish or steaks. The fish was split and tied to the board, or it was tied whole and turned over halfway through the roasting. The board was propped before the fire, or, later, used in the oven. A plank could also be used for baking biscuits or bannocks.

PLATE LIFTER — A wire device with wooden handles, which by a spring action grasped the two opposite sides of a hot plate. *See also* **PIE LIFTER**

Fig. 840. PLATE LIFTER. Wood, wire. Triumph. Montgomery Ward.

PLATE REST — A metal shelf which hooks over the fire-bar placed between andirons, or over the edge of the fender, and resting against the fire grate. Plates were kept warm on it, or serving dishes were kept hot before being put on the table. Small cakes or biscuits could even be baked on the plate rest, which was also called a fire-bar trivet.

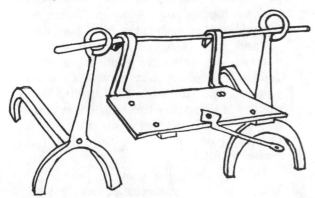

Fig. 841. PLATE REST & ANDIRONS WITH GRATE.

PLATE WARMER — *see* **CARBONIZER, DISH WARMER**

POCKET GRATER — A grater small enough to be carried in the pocket, and usually in a case of some kind. It was used for grating nutmeg or other spices into toddies and flips to suit the drinker's taste. *See also* **GRATER**

POLISHER — A wedge-shaped stone fitted with a handle, for putting a "mirror finish on knives & forks instantly." (Advertised by the Diamond Cutlery Company of New York, *Woman's Home Companion*, 1899.)

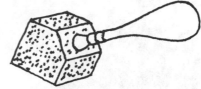

Fig. 842. POLISHER for knives.

Fig. 843. KNIFE POLISHER. c. 1915. Carborundum, wood. L: 6-7/8". American. Author's Collection.

PONTYPOOL — *see* **JAPANNED WARE**

POPCORN POPPER — *see* **CORN POPPER**

POPOVER PAN — A heavy, cast-iron muffin pan, with deep cups for baking popovers — light cakes of flour, milk, eggs, and butter which are supposed to "pop over" the edge of the cups. *See also* **GEM PAN, MUFFIN PAN**

Fig. 844. POPOVER PAN. 1890s to 19-? Cast iron. L: 11"; W: 7½"; H: 1-7/8". Wagner Ware B. American. Author's Collection.

POPOVER and PUFF CUPS — Miss Parloa, in her *Kitchen Companion*, 1887, stated unequivocally the "popovers and various kinds of puffs must always be baked in stoneware cups. They increase 4 or 5 times their original size." But some people went right on baking their popovers in popover pans, and shirring eggs in popover and puff cups.

Fig. 845. MUFFIN CUP. F. A. Walker flyer, c. 1880.

POPPYSEED GRINDER — A small hand-mill, usually of cast-iron with a brass hopper. It screw-clamps to the table edge.

Fig. 846. POPPYSEED GRINDER. c. 1890. Spun brass, turquoise-painted cast iron, wood. L: 9¼". Standard. American. Author's Collection.

PORRINGER [*porrynger, porrager*] — A small basin of metal, earthenware, or wood, with a flat, often decoratively pierced or cut-out handle. Soup, broth, children's and invalid's food is conveniently eaten from a porringer.

Fig. 847. PORRINGERS.

PORTABLE SPRING JACK — A spit jack, invented in England by Joseph Merlin in 1773, but probably used in America after the Revolution. According to Merlin, "motion is given from a spring to the spit by means of wheelwork, or by a string coiled over a fusee. The spit may be either horizontal or vertical. A reflector is used in which the spit is fixed, and this reflector may also be used when the spit is turned by a 'ventilator' [most likely a *smoke jack*]. For roasting small birds, etc., a wheel set round with a series of hooks is employed instead of the spit." (*Abridgments of Specifications Relating to Cooking, Bread-Making, and the Preparation of Confectionery, A.D. 1634-1866.* London: 1873.) The advantage of a clockwork jack driven by a mainspring was its portability. It did not have to be hung high on the wall or mantle as did a weight-driven jack. A *bottle jack* was another form of spring jack. *See also* **BIRD ROASTER, BOTTLE JACK, CLOCKWORK JACK, SMOKE JACK, SPIT**

POSNET — A small metal pot or vessel with a straight handle and three feet. Usually of iron or brass or bell-metal. It was used on the hearth as a saucepan. *See also* **SAUCEPAN, SKILLET**

POSSET CUP — A cup or bowl for holding a hot drink composed of milk curdled with ale, wine, sack or sherry, or other liquor, and often with sugar and spices added. It was used as a cold remedy, or drunk as a delicacy, and dates at least from the 16th century. Some andirons were fitted with a small cradle on the top of the upright members, called a *posset cup holder*.

Posset, flip, and egg-nog are all variations of the curdled milk recipe, and if you come across an unlabeled recipe you might not discover which of the three it is. Caudle was similar, but had the distinguishing addition of gruel.

To Make a Jelly Posset
Take twenty eggs, leave out half the whites, and beat them very well; put them into the bason you serve it in, with near a pint of sack, and a little strong ale; sweeten it to your taste, and set it over a charcoal fire, keep it stirring all the while; then have in readiness a quart of milk or cream boiled with a little nutmeg and cinnamon, and when your sack and eggs are hot enough to scald your lips, put the milk to it boiling hot; then take it off the fire, and cover it up half an hour; strew sugar on the brim of the dish, and serve it to the table. [*E. Smith*, 1753.]

Sago Posset
Macerate a tablespoonful of sago in 1 pt. of water for 2 hours on the hob of a

stove; boil for 15 minutes, assiduously stirring; add sugar with an aromatic, such as ginger or nutmeg, and a tablespoonful or more of white wine; if wine is not permitted, flavor with lemon juice. [*Treasure House*, 1891]

Hot Egg Nog

Bear the yolk of 1 egg and 1 tablespoonful of castor sugar well together, then stir in 1 tablespoonful of brandy or whisky. Bring 1 pint of milk to the boiling point, then pour over the mixed ingredients, stir well, and serve. [*Beeton*, n.d.]

Fig. 848. POSSET CUP. c. 1830. Earthenware. 5½" dia.; H: 5". Thomas Haig, Philadelphia. Courtesy Keillor Collection.

POT — An earthenware or metal (usually iron, but also bell metal, or other) vessel; cylindrical, round or pot-bellied, with a bail handle. Used for cooking a number of ways.

Fig. 849. STOVE POT, "Round Bottom. Bulged." Cast iron. 6, 7, 8, 9" (dia.?) Matthai-Ingram Company, c. 1890.

POTASH — Wood ashes from which the lye has been leached [dissolved] out. Potash-water was an aerated beverage like soda water. A whiskey and potash would have been like a whiskey and soda! The first patent granted in the United States was given on July 31, 1790 to Samuel Hopkins of Vermont for his process of making potash and pearl-ash. [A *leach* is a perforated vessel used to hold wood ashes while water is poured through them].

To remove the taste of rosin from new tin — take a hot live coal or piece of burning charcoal. Put the coal into the vessel and shake a while. Or boil in the tin some pot-ash in water. ... Season a new wood keg, bucket, etc., by scalding, and then washing with a solution of pearl-ash or pot-ash. [*Leslie*, 1840] *See also* **PEARL-ASH, SALAERATUS**

POTATO BAKING RACK — A tin rack with a number of projections to stick the potatoes on for baking in the oven.

Fig. 850. POTATO BAKING RACK. c. 1900. Tin. L: 15¼"; W: 2-1/8". American. Author's Collection.

POTATO CHIPPER and **PEELER** — A tin implement for peeling potatoes and then cutting off chips, or thin slices, for deep fat frying. Also, because it was one of those much-advertised all-in-one tools, it could be used as a "corer for apples and pears, slicer to make Saratoga chips of potatoes, apples, carrots, etc., nutmeg grater, potato chopper. The point can pick out potato eyes and the edge can scale fish." (*Montgomery Ward Catalog*, 1892.)

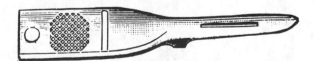

Fig. 851. POTATO CHIPPER. Steel. For peeling, slicing, coring, scaling fish, eye-ing potatoes, grating nutmegs. Saratoga Potato Chipper. Montgomery Ward, 1893.

POTATO —, CRULLER FRYER — A vessel equipped with a fry basket for deep-frying potato chips, crullers, doughnuts or other foods. *See also* **DEEP FAT BASKET, FRYING KETTLE**

POTATO CUTTER, — SLICER — A wooden implement; a board with a steel cutting blade across which the potato was rubbed to make slices or thin chips. This type was the same as the cucumber slicer, and smaller than the cabbage cutter. Another type had a metal plate with a cutting blade in the middle and a swivelling hoop which held the potato as it was passed back and forth over the blade. A third type was a hand-held implement for cutting decorative slices of potato to be used in clear soups.

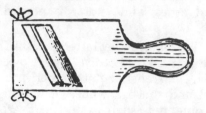

Fig. 852. POTATO SLICER. Wood, steel. Adjustable knife. Practical Housekeeping, 1881.

Fig. 853. POTATO SLICER. Universal Household Helps, Landers, Frary, Clark, c. 1920.

Fig. 854. POTATO SLICER. Iron, wood. F. A. Walker, c. 1870s.

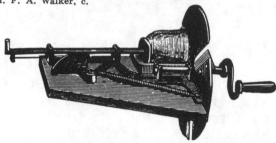

POTATO MASHER — One of several implements: (1) a beetle; (2) a ricer; (3) a perforated metal disc with a handle; (4) a heavy wire grid with a handle; or anything else which would serve the purpose.

One type, patented in 1892, combined a masher and a whip. Charles Spicer Apple, of Bellaire, Ohio, wrote in his specification: "In mashing potatoes it has been customary to first make use of a wooden masher and to then beat or lighten them with a fork or spoon. It therefore takes considerable time and a good deal of labor at present to properly prepare mashed potatoes.

"...[My] device is to be used precisely like the ordinary potato-masher.

"When in use, the lower end of the enlarged head b will mash the potatoes in the usual way and the elastic wire c will be compressed and expanded. ... This wire in thus moving through the substance will effectively beat and lighten the potatoes, which will be accomplished at the same time that [they] are being mashed." (*Official Gazette*.)

Of one of the metal disk types, Miss Parloa wrote in 1887: "In unskilled hands it gives a lighter dish of potatoes than the wooden masher, but the wooden one will be needed for other things which the wire one would not answer." *See also* **BEETLE, RICER**

Fig. 855. POTATO SLICER. Pat'd 1870, 1871. For making Saratoga chips, or cucumber garnishes. Catalog fragments, c. 1870s.

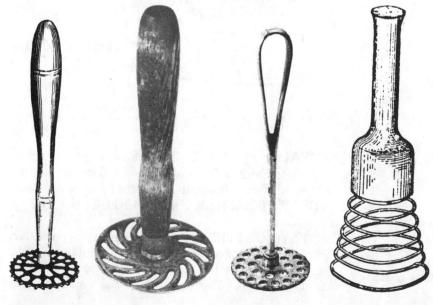

LEFT TO RIGHT:

Fig. 856. POTATO MASHER. F. A. Walker, c. 1870s.

Fig. 857. POTATO MASHER. c. 1880s - 1900. Nickeled-iron, wood. L: 7". American. Author's Collection.

Fig. 858. POTATO MASHER. c. 1890. Nickel-plated iron. L: 8¾"; E: 2¾". American. Author's Collection.

Fig. 859. POTATO MASHER. Pat'd 1892, No. 472,515. Charles Spicer Apple, Bellaire, Ohio. Official Gazette, April 12, 1892.

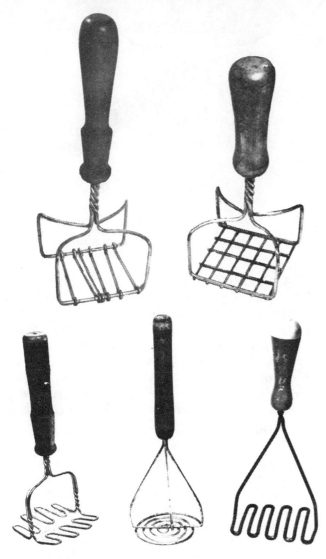

Fig. 860, 861. VEGETABLE or POTATO MASHERS. c. 1890s to 1935. Wood, wire. L: 8¼" to 10¼"; W: 3" to 4". American. Author's Collection.

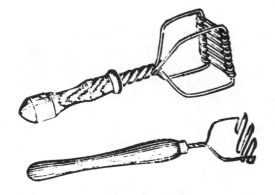

Fig. 862 POTATO MASHERS. Wire, wood. Matthai-Ingram Company, c. 1890.

Fig. 863. POTATO MASHER & FLAKER. J. B. Foote Foundry Company, 1906.

Fig. 864. POTATO or VEGETABLE MASHER. c. 1920. Wire & wood. L: 5½"; H; 4½". American. Author's Collection.

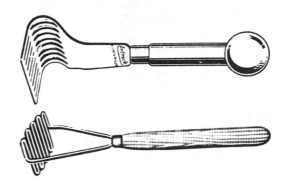

Fig. 865. POTATO RICER, MASHER. Androck, 1936.

Fig. 866. MASHER. Wood, wire. Androck, 1936.

POTATO PARER, — PEELER — Either a simple narrow-bladed sharp knife; a cylindrical corer with a blade; or a mechanical device similar to the apple parer in that the potato was fixed to a prong, a handle was cranked, a spring-action blade pressed against the turning potato, and the paring fell off.

Silver Pie
Mrs. M.L. Scott

Peel and grate one large white potato into a deep plate; add the juice and grated rind of one lemon, the beaten white of one egg, one teacup of white sugar, and one teacup of cold water. Pour this into a nice undercrust and bake. When done, have ready the whites of three eggs well beaten, half a cup of powdered sugar, a few drops of rose-water, all thoroughly beaten. Put this mixture on the top of the pie evenly and return to the oven, to stiffen a few moments. When sent to the table just cold lay a spoonful of currant jelly on the center of each piece to ornament if you wish. [*Home Cook Book*, 1876]

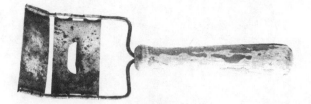

Fig. 867. PARER. c. 1900. Steel, wire, wood. 6¾" x 2¼". American. Author's Collection.

Fig. 868 PARER, CORER, ETC. 1913. Tin. L: 8-7/8". Castello's. Author's Collection.

Fig. 869. POTATO PEELER. Pat'd July 20, 1920. Tin, grit composition. L: 4½"; W: 2¼". Hamlinite. Courtesy Keillor Collection.

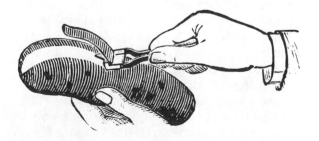

Fig. 870. POTATO PEELER. Steel. The Peerless. Montgomery Ward, 1895.

Fig. 871. UNIVERSAL PARER, CORER & SLICER. Nickeled, oil-tempered steel, wood. "For paring Potatoes, Apples, Cucumbers, Parsnips, etc., it has no equal." F. W. Seastrand, c. 1912.

POTATO PASTY PAN — A line cut in the 1872 edition of Mrs. Beeton's *Everyday Cookery & Housekeeping Book* shows this to be a deep pan with a decorative handle in the middle, and a lift-out, perforated tray. It is, in all respects, almost identical with the tray and steam vent shown in the 1804 *Domestic Encyclopedia* of Anthony Willich, which was intended to rest on a tin or earthenware pan. The following recipe is from Willich's book.

Directions for making Potatoe-pastry

Take of beef, mutton, veal, or other meat, two pounds; season it, and place it in the bottom of the steam-dish, with a bit or two of butter, (two ounces is enough for the whole pastry, including what is rubbed into the mashed potatoes), and a sufficiency of water to draw a good gravy; a few slices of carrot may be added, if the pastry is made of mutton.

Take also of mealy potatoes, one gallon; boil, peal, and mash them; rub into them a little butter; when washed, place the perforated cover over the meat, and put the potatoes smooth and even upon it, sloping them up, and pressing them very closely round the edges of the dish. The pastry may now be sent to the oven, which, if quick, will bake it in an hour.

Then the pastry is removed, the air closes the valve, the steam then rises through the perforated cover, and incorporates with the potatoes.

When served up to table, the potatoe crust may be cut off and served round; then by lifting up the perforated cover, you will find an excellent dish of beef, etc., swimming in gravy, which is to be taken out and eaten with potatoe crust; and a more palatable mixture or cheap dish, cannot be served to a family. [*Willich*, 1804]

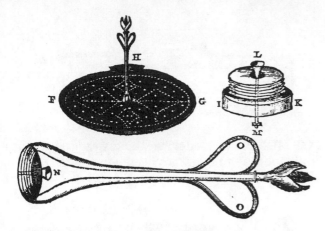

Fig. 872. PASTY STEAMER. Perforated metal, iron. *Domestic Encyclopedia, 1804.*

POTATO PRESS — A perforated narrow cylinder with a wooden press or pestle fitting inside the cylinder exactly. The cooked potatoes are put in the top, followed by the press, and the potato is expressed from the holes in the cylinder. *See also* **RICER**

Fig. 873. FRENCH POTATO PRESS. Stamped tin, wood. F. A. Walker, c. 1870s.

POTATO RAKE — A sort of peel with a curved blade, for taking potatoes out of the coals, or hot coals from the hearth. They were made of cast or wrought-iron.

Fig. 874. POTATO RAKE. c. 1800 to 1830. Iron & brass. L: 19". English. Courtesy Keillor Collection.

POTATO RIDDLE — A wirework sieve for pressing cooked potatoes through to make a mash or "sponge" of them.

Sponge for Winter Use

Peel and boil four or five medium-sized potatoes in two quarts of water (which will boil down to one quart by the time the potatoes are cooked): when done, take out and press through a colander, or mash very fine in the crock in which the sponge is to be made; make a well in the center, into which put one cup of flour, and pour over it the boiling water from the potatoes; stir thoroughly, and when cool add a pint of tepid water, flour enough to make a *thin* batter, and a cup of yeast. This sponge makes very moist bread. [*Practical Housekeeping,* 1884]

POTATO SMASHER, — POUNDER — *see* **BEETLE**

POTATO, VEGETABLE or RICE MOLD — A tin mold for forming a decorative dish of mashed potatoes or other vegetables. Also a ring or border mold.

Fig. 875. POTATO, VEGETABLE MOLDS. Tin. F. A. Walker, c. 1870s.

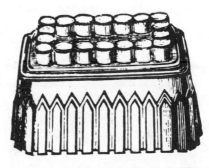

Fig. 876. VEGETABLE or RICE MOLD. Tin. F. A. Walker, c. 1870s.

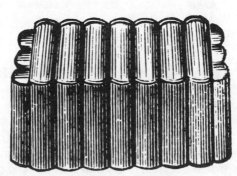

Fig. 877. VEGETABLE & RICE MOLD. Tin. F. A. Walker, c. 1870s.

POT-AU-FEU — A French term for the soup *stock pot,* left on the fire at the back of the stove.

POT CHAIN — *see* **POT CLEANER**

POT CLEANER, — SCRAPER — Any tool used specifically for cleaning pots. Includes: (1) the pot chain, a network of steel rings, "resembling an old-fashioned reticule." (*Goodholme,* 1877.) This is also called a *chain cloth.* It was used to scour out burned kettles. (2) the *flexible pot scraper* or *palette knife.* (3) "A *clam shell* is more convenient for scraping kettles and frying pans than a knife. It does the work in less time." (*Babcock,* 1881; *Treasure House,* 1891.)

Fig. 878. POT CLEANER or WIRE DISH CLOTH. c. 1880 to 1915. Treasure House, 1891.

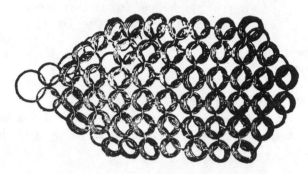

Fig. 879. POT CHAIN with handle. Wire. Matthai-Ingram Company, c. 1890.

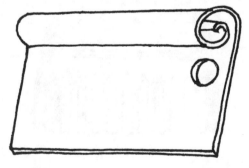

Fig. 880. SCRAPER FOR KITCHEN UTENSILS. Pat'd 1894 by Walter Leggett, Galesburg, Illinois.

POT CROWN — *see* **DUTCH CROWN**

POTHANGER, POT RACK — *see* **POT HOOK, TRAMMEL**

POT HOOK — A wrought-iron implement with a hook at one end to go over the lug pole or crane, and a hook or two at the other end on which to hang the pot or kettle by its bail handle. Originally a *pot hook, trammel, cotrall, jib-crook, hanger* and *hanging iron* were all the same thing.

Fig. 881. POT HOOK. c. 1800. Iron, brass, copper. L: 17" fully extented. Courtesy Keillor Collection.

POT MENDER — A device which was used to put a rivet in the hole of any tin, enameled ware or aluminum pot or pan. *See also* "MENDETS"

Fig. 882. POT MENDER. 1910. Wood, white metal rivets. L: 7". Arco Sanitary Mender. "For tin, enamelled & Aluminum ware. Saves money — doubles life of ware. Directions. Rivets in the handle. Ream hole to fit rivet. Hammer in place...." American. Courtesy Keillor Collection.

POT-METAL — An alloy of copper, lead, and tin made (according to the 1891 *Treasure House*) in this proportion: "Copper, 40 lbs.; lead, 16 lbs.; tin, 1½ lbs." Sometimes it is used to refer to any metal used for making pots, and particularly cast iron.

POT STAND — A small twisted-wire stand, used as a hot plate or trivet for hot tea or coffee pots, for other hot utensils, and for flower pots.

Fig. 883. TEA POT STAND. Wire. F. A. Walker, c. 1870s.

Fig. 884. TEA POT STAND. Wire. (Probably Dover Stamping Co.). F. A. Walker, c. 1870s.

PRESERVING KETTLE — A tin, brass, or enameled ware lidless kettle, with a bail handle, and usually a pouring lip. It was used for boiling fruits and their syrup for preserves. A preserving kettle was never iron or aluminum as both metals are affected by the acid of the fruits.

Tomato Jam

Remove all the seeds, pull off the skins, and boil the fruit with a pound of sugar for every pound. To every pound of tomato allow 2 lemons, rind and pulp, well boiled. [*Cornelius*, 1846]

General Directions for Preserving Fruit & Making Jellies

A kettle should be kept on purpose. Brass, if very bright, will do. If acid fruit is preserved in a brass kettle which is not bright, it becomes poisonous. Bell-metal is better than brass, and the iron ware lined with porcelain, best of all. [*ibid.*]

Fig. 885. PRESERVING KETTLE. Tin. from 1½ to 5 quarts. Lalance & Grosjean, 1890.

Fig. 886. PRESERVE SPOON. Tinned iron, wood. L: 10", 12", 14", 16", 18". Lalance & Grosjean, 1890.

PUDDING — The first sort of pudding was the stomach or entrails of a pig, sheep or other animal, stuffed with mixtures of minced meat, suet, oatmeal, and spices, and boiled. This could be kept till needed, and was very much like sausage. A later sort of pudding was a mixture of meat or vegetables enclosed in dough and boiled or steamed. By the 18th century a pudding was primarily an egg, milk and meal dish, baked in a pan, a dish or a mold — though often boiled in a bag.

PUDDING BAG — A bag of tightly-woven coarse cloth such as drilling, filled with the thick pudding mixture, tied close or loose depending on the pudding, dipped in very hot water, and heavily floured before boiling. Also called a *pudding cloth* or *dumpling cloth.*

PUDDING BOILER — A typical boiler vessel with a lift-out tray — this one used for boiling puddings in bags.

Fig. 887. PUDDING BOILER. Pieced tin. 2, 3, 4 qts. Matthai-Ingram Company, c. 1890.

PUDDING DISH — A dish of earthenware for baking or steaming puddings in the oven. These are usually tubed — and either plain, fluted, or turk's head. A cloth was laid over the dish while cooking.

PUDDING MOLD — A metal (usually tin) mold with a tight-fitting cover and sometimes with a closed-ended tube running through the center. It was used for baking or steaming puddings. The tube, as did the open tube of the spouted cake tin, insured even baking. One of the commonest shapes for the pudding mold is the melon mold. Others were fluted, plain, or turk's head.

Grandma Thomson's White Pudding

as written by Mrs. E. T. Carson of Mt. Pleasant Farm

Weigh equal quantities of best beef suet and sifted flour, shave down suet and rub into fine particles with the hands, removing all tough and stringy parts, mix well with the flour, season very highly with pepper, salt to taste, stuff loosely in beef-skins (entrails cleansed like pork-skins for sausage), half a yard or less in length, secure the ends, prick every two or three inches with a darning-needle, place to boil in a kettle of cold water hung on the crane; boil three hours, place on table until cold, after which hang up in a cool place to dry; tie up in a clean cotton bag, and put away where it will be both dry and cool. When wanted for use, cut off the quantity needed, boil in hot water until heated through, take out and place before the fire to dry off and "crisp." The above was considered an "extra" dish at all the "flax scutchings," "quilting frolics," and "log rollings" of a hundred years ago.

The same by measure is as follows: One pint best beef suet to two pints flour; mix thoroughly, season very highly with pepper and salt, sew up little sacks of cotton cloth half a yard long and three inches wide, fill nearly full, put to boil in hot water, boil from four to six hours; when done, take out, drain, let cool, hang in a dry, cool place, and when wanted for table, cut off as much as needed, put on hot water, boil until cooked through, take out, peel off cloth, put in a pie-pan, set on oven to dry and brown. [*Practical Housekeeping*, 1884]

Fig. 892. PUDDING MOLD. c. Late-19th century. Tin. L: 7"; W: 5½"; H: 4". American. Courtesy Mary Mac Franklin.

PUDDING PAN, — BASIN — A deep tin, earthenware, or enameled-iron pan in which pudding was baked or steamed.

Indian-Meal Pudding

One cup of yellow Indian meal, one quart and a cupful of milk, three eggs, half a cup of molasses, one generous tablespoonful of butter, one teaspoonful of salt, one pint of boiling water, half teaspoonful each of cinnamon and mace. Scald the salted meal with the water. Heat the milk in a farina-kettle; stir in the scalded meal, and boil, stirring often, for half an hour. Beat the eggs light; put in the butter and molasses, stirred together until they are several shades lighter than at first; add the spice; lastly, the batter from the farina-kettle, beaten in a little at a time, until all the ingredients are thoroughly incorporated. Grease a pudding-dish; pour in the mixture, and bake, covered, in a steady oven, three-quarters of an hour. Remove the lid, and brown. This is the genuine, old-fashioned New-England "Indian" pudding. Eat with sauce, or with cream and sugar. It is very nice. [Marion Harland, *The Post*, Washington, D.C., as it appeared in *Universal Cookery Book*, 1887]

Fig. 888. SPOUTED MOLD. 19th c. Earthenware. 9½" dia.; H: 3-1/8". American. Courtesy Keillor Collection.

Fig. 889. PUDDING MOULD. Tin. 7" to 9" dia. Lalance & Grosjean, 1890.

Fig. 890. PUDDING MOLD. Tin. F. A. Walker, c. 1870s.

Fig. 891. PUDDING MOLDS. Treasure House, 1891.

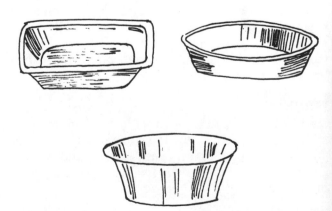

Fig. 893. PUDDING PANS & PUDDING DISH (bottom). Earthenware.

PUDDING PRICK — The 16th and 17th century term for a slender wooden skewer used to fasten the ends of a pudding gut.

PURÉE SIEVE — A large sieve, with a frame of wood or tin. The strainer, of strong wires or coarse netting, is strengthened and supported underneath by two cross-pieces of wire. The food was placed in the sieve and rubbed through with a wooden beetle or a heavy wooden spoon.

Pease porridge hot,
Pease porridge cold,
Pease porridge in the Pot
Nine days old.
Some like it hot,
Some like it cold,
Some like it in the pot
Nine days old.

[*First published ca. 1765 in London by John Newbery. He added this note: "The poor are seldomer sick for want of food, than the rich by the excess of it."*]

Purée of Peas

Wash a pint of green peas in cold water; then put them in a saucepan with boiling water and cook 20 minutes. Have them dry when done. Press them through a colander. Boil ½ pint milk, add a small onion, 3 or 4 cloves and a small sprig of parsley. Rub a tablespoon of flour and butter together. Strain the milk over the peas, put back in saucepan, stir in the flour and butter, let boil, stirring to prevent sticking. Season with salt and pepper & serve. [*Ladies Home Journal*, April, 1890]

QUEENSWARE — "The famous Queensware was developed after many trials not long after Wedgwood's establishment at Burslem (1759). It was of a rich cream color, and though often undecorated was molded in such attractive shapes that it secured immediate success. Wedgwood was all his life a very energetic, and astute business man, and this vogue of the new ware was accelerated by a stroke of business policy....when he presented Queen Charlotte with a number of his

most successful efforts. The Queen was at once greatly taken with the ware; and ordered a complete dinner set of it, also requesting him to name it for her, which was of course equivalent to a command, and gave rise to the name. One of the devices often used to achieve a decorative effect was the employment of open work patterns similar to those used in silver...." (Paul Stanhope, *The House Beautiful*, July 1897.)

Queensware was an earthenware pottery — a refinement of the long familiar *cream ware*. It was used for table services and for all kinds of dairy and culinary vessels. Many potteries copied Wedgwood's Queensware, from not long after he first made it in 1765 to well into the 19th century. Black or red transfer printing of tile designs first, and then ships, flowers and doggerel lines enclosed in floral frames, were the most common decorations aside from the bands of earth colors. This was an extremely popular export to America throughout the first third of the 19th century. *See also* **YELLOW or LIVERPOOL WARE**

QUERNE — A small, fairly primitive grinding mill for seeds, spices and grains. It consists of two round mill stones, about 9 or 10" in diameter, the upper one turned by a handle or knob.

Fig. 894. QUERNE. 18th or 19th century. Wood, stone. L: 13"; W: 7"; H: 17½". Swedish or Danish. Courtesy Keillor Collection.

QUIRL [*querl, quirler*] — A tool or cutting device for making decorative curls or twists of raw vegetables, such as potatoes, or butter.

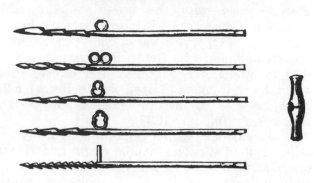

Fig. 895. QUIRLERS. Steel. F. A. Walker, c. 1870s.

RADISH GRATER — A large tin grater with a sturdy wire frame which also forms a handle. Used for making horse-radish. *See also* **GRATER**

RAISIN SEEDER — One of several types of gadgets or contivances for removing raisin seeds. The simplest has five parallel coarse wires set into a wooden block with a handle. This handle fits neatly into the palm, and the seeder is rocked over little piles of raisin — seeding "a pound in less then 10 minutes." Everett Raisin Seeder, Boston. (Advertisement in *Ladies Home Journal,* 1893.)

A more complicated seeder screw-clamps to a table edge, and has a hopper into which the *wet* raisins are fed. They are rolled through two rollers: one of hard rubber and one with tiny teeth. *"Enterprise;" "Everett;"* etc.

Fig. 896. COLUMBIAN RAISIN SEEDER. 1890s.

Fig. 897. RAISIN SEEDER. c. 1890. Wood, iron wire. L: 3¼"; W: 2". Everett Co., Boston. Courtesy Keillor Collection.

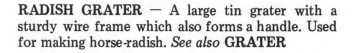

Fig. 899. RAISIN & GRAPE SEEDER. Tinned iron. Enterprise. The Enterprising Housekeeper, 1898.

Fig. 900. RAISIN SEEDER. Pat'd April 2, August 20, 1895. Nickel-plated cast iron, rubber. L: 11"; 2½" x 2-1/8" hopper. "Wet the Raisins," Enterprise Mfg. Co., Philadelphia. Courtesy Robert D. Franklin.

Fig. 901. RAISIN SEEDER. Pat'd Mar. 28, 1898. Cast iron, wire, rubber. H: 7¼". Lightning. American. Author's Collection.

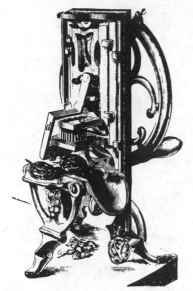

Fig. 902. RAISIN SEEDER. F. A. Walker, c. 1870s.

RANGE — A form of fire-grate, fireplace, or cooking apparatus. In the 18th century a range was a fire-place having at least one oven at the side, and a plate-iron top having openings for inserting pots and pans. *Range* means a row or series of things, hence the name. The fire was built inside one or several hearths at the bottom of the range. Count Rumford's range was built of brick, but by the beginning of the 20th century a range was a cast-iron, heavily ornamented cook stove. Each of the openings in the top had a *stove lid* which was put in place when the opening was not being used, or when the lesser indirect heat was needed. These were removed with a *stove lid lifter*.

Although *range* was the word first used for cooking fire-place, by the mid-19th century *cook-stove* or *stove* was used. These ranges or cook-stoves burned wood, coal or other combustibles, and later utilized kerosene or natural gas.

You may find it impossible to collect the huge cast-iron, steel, or nickel-plated ranges, but a collection can be made of the lovely, enameled oven door fronts, the porcelain drop handles, or perhaps the ornate, cast, stove ornaments — figures, scrolls, flowers and lyres — such as were produced by the Dover Stamping Company. *"Barstow;" "Acme;" "Marvin Smith;" "Gold Coin;" "Garland;" "Mason & Davis;" "Home Comfort Premium;" "Fearless Plain Top;" "Stewart;" "Sears;" "Bussey-McLeod;" "Paris Double Draft;" "Detroit;" "Kalamazoo;" "Sill;" "Roberts & Masters;" "Foster & Parry;"* etc. See *also* **HOB, STOVE**

"I think," said Barbara, boldly, "that a cooking-stove, all polished up, is just as handsome a thing as there is in the house!"

"It is clumsy, one must own," said Mrs. Holabird, "besides being suggestive."

"So is a piano," said the determined Barbara. [Adeline Whitney, *We Girls.* Boston: Houghton Mifflin, 1871]

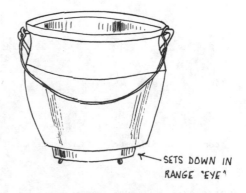

← SETS DOWN IN RANGE "EYE"

Fig. 903. RAISIN SEEDER. 1870s. Cast iron. H: 6½"; W: 4". As in F. A. Walker catalog. Courtesy Keillor Collection.

Fig. 904. STOVE POT. Cast iron.

Fig. 905, 906. STOVES & RANGES. Two cuts. The Great Industries of the United States. Hartford, Chicago, Cincinnati: J.B. Burr & Hyde, 1873.

Fig. 909. RANGE. Cast iron. 6 hole with reservoir [of water for heating] and closet. Grand Windsor Range. Montgomery Ward, 1895.

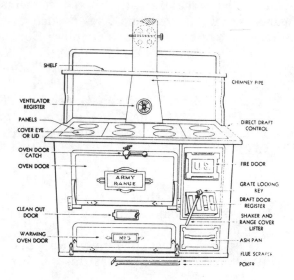

Fig. 907. ARMY FIELD RANGE showing parts of a basic coal-burning range. The Army Cook, War Department Technical Manual, United States Printing Office, 1946.

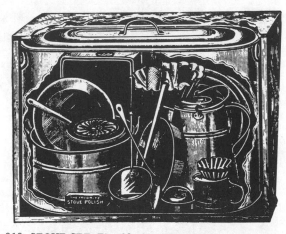

Fig. 910. STOVE SET. Tin. 38 pieces: wash boiler & cover, coffee boiler, steamer & cover, saucepan & cover, tin cup, 2 pie plates, kitchen spoon, cooking pan, pot cover, pepper box, nutmeg grater, tubed cake pan, meat fork, 3 sheet-iron bake pans, 4 cookie pans, biscuit cutter, coal shovel, ½ sheet grater, Surprise egg whip, 6 teaspoons, 6 tablespoons. Matthai-Ingram Company, c. 1890.

Fig. 908. RANGE. Malleable & charcoal iron. The People's Home Journal, Nov. 1914.

Fig. 911. COOK STOVE. Cast iron. 4 hole for wood or coal, with reservoir. The Modern Windsor Cooking Stove. Montgomery Ward, 1895.

Fig. 912. ELECTRIC RANGE. Universal Household Helps. Landers, Frary, Clark, c. 1920.

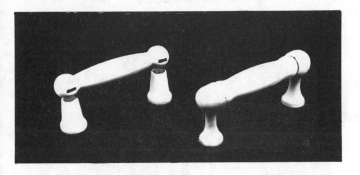

Fig. 913. STOVE HANDLES. c. 1920s Porcelain over iron. L: 6½" and 7". Author's Collection.

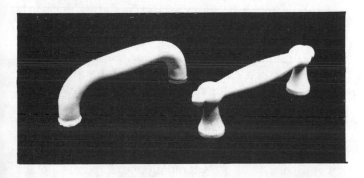

Fig. 914. STOVE HANDLES. c. 1920s. Porcelain iron. L: 5½". Author's Collection.

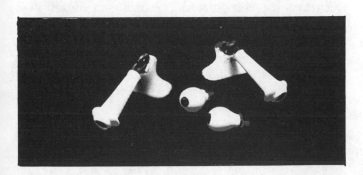

Fig. 915. STOVE KNOBS. c. 1920s. Enameled iron. L: 1¼" and 4". American. Author's Collection.

RANGE KETTLE — A kettle, usually of the type used for heating water, made to sit *in* the range or stove openings, and not to hang in the fireplace from a hook.

RANGE SIEVE or RANGE — A kind of sieve or strainer used for straining liquids but not for sifting dry meal. In cider-making, the apple juice is strained through a range; and so in cheese-making are the curds separated from the whey.

REAMER-JUICER — A reamer is a boring tool, grooved radially from the tip of a cone-shaped head, and used for boring out or enlarging holes. The shape of a reamer is ideal for getting the juice from halved citrus fruit. The grooves scrape out juice, pulp, and seeds and direct them to the dish beneath.

The simplest reamer-juicer is a lipped dish (often found now in the Depression glass green), the center of which is a reamer. More complex ones have moving parts by which means the fruit is pressed against the turning reamer.

Reamer-juicers were made in glass, aluminum, steel, nickel-plated steel, wood, pottery and early plastics. *See also* **JUICE EXTRACTOR, LEMON SQUEEZER**

Fig. 916. LEMON REAMER. c. 1870s. Lathe-turned wood. L: 6¼". American. Courtesy Emma Landau.

Fig. 917. LEMON SQUEEZER. Nickeled iron, aluminum. "Absolutely the only squeezer that will not splash juice all over the operator." Sears, Roebuck & Co., 1900.

Fig. 918. REAMER JUICERS. White glass, c. 1930. 5" dia.; H: 2½". Aluminum with funnel, c. 1910; 3-7/8" dia.; H: 3½". Small aluminum, c. 1910. 3-3/8" dia.; H: 2". American. Author's Collection.

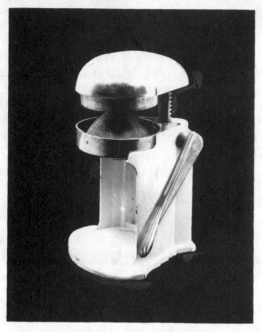

Fig. 919. JUICER. Pat'd 1937. Cast aluminum, chrome-plated & painted iron. H: 9¼"; W: 5-7/8". Juice-O-mat, Rival Mfg., Co., Kansas City, Mo. Courtesy Peter and Madeline Persoff.

Fig. 920. JUICER. 1920. Aluminum, painted tin. H: 10½"; W: 6-7/8". American. Author's Collection.

REFLECTING OVEN — *see* **APPLE ROASTER, BIRD ROASTER, BISCUIT OVEN, CHEESE TOASTER, MEAT SCREEN, SALISBURY PORTABLE KITCHEN, TIN KITCHEN** *"Universal;" "The Highland Hearth;"* etc.

Fig. 921. DUTCH OVEN. Tin. F. A. Walker, c. 1870s.

REFRIGERATOR — An apparatus, vessel, or chamber for producing and/or maintaining a low temperature. Ice was the source of cold from the early days of the colonies, when it was cut in blocks from frozen-over lakes or ponds, and stored in deep, straw or leaf-lined pits in the ground for use throughout the summer. Later, a good urban business built up around the warehouse storage of ice, and its delivery by wagon to the private home for use in the *ice box.* "A large wooden box, zinc or tin-lined, with the space between the tin and wood filled with powdered charcoal, having a place at bottom for ice, a drain, and moveable shelves and partitions." (*Beecher and Stowe,* 1869.) A form of mechanical refrigeration was developed, similar to modern air-conditioning, in the mid-19th century for refrigerated railroad cars, but it was many years before the method was applied to home refrigerators.

Early electric refrigerators had tiny freezing compartments and were not much of an improvement over the old ice-box except that ice no longer had to be bought, and drip pans no longer had to be emptied. The most familiar old electric refrigerator is perhaps the General Electric "monitor top," which lasted into the 1930s. Industrial designers did their best to get refrigerators out of the kitchen and into the air with all kinds of stream-lining motifs.

180

Fig. 922. REFRIGERATOR. Zinc-lined wood. F. A. Walker, c. 1870s.

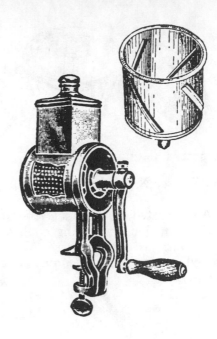

Fig. 925. CLIMAX FOOD GRATER & SLICER. Tin, iron, glass block. The Berdan Company, 1931.

Fig. 923. REFRIGERATOR. Ash, bronze trim, galvanized steel-lined ice chambers & shelves. H: 67"; W: 36"; D: 24". North Star Refrigerator. The G. M. Shirk Mfg. Co., 1893.

RETINNED WARE — *see* **BLOCK TIN**

REVOLVING GRATER — "This is as great an improvement in its way as the modern egg-beater is over a spoon. The 'world moves,' and even in the kitchen labor is lightened by the ingenuity of modern invention." (*Practical Housekeeping,* 1884.) *See also* **GRATER**

REYING SIEVE [*reeing, ree an*] — *Ree* means to winnow or clean in a sieve; a reying sieve is a coarse sieve for cleaning dried peas or corn. It is wood, with brass or iron-wire cloth.

RICE BALL — A wire-mesh hinged ball, about 5" or 6" in diameter, which was filled with cooked rice, and cooked again in deep fat.

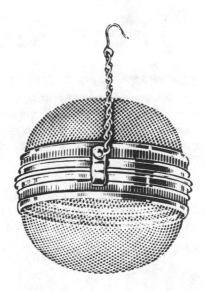

Fig. 926. RICE BALL. Wire, tin. 5½" dia. Holds 1 cup rice. Androck, 1936.

Fig. 924. REVOLVING GRATER, table-mounted. Universal Household Helps, Landers, Frary, Clark, c. 1920.

RICE BOILER — Either a covered mold for boiling rice in a form like a pudding; or a double boiler.

Fig. 927. RICE BOILER. Tin. F. A. Walker, c. 1870s.

RICE NAPPY — *see* **NAPPY**

RICER — A perforated cup with a levered press for "ricing" potatoes; that is, making cooked potato into rice-sized bits instead of a mash. Also used for other cooked vegetables. *"Genuine Kreamer;" "Henis;"* etc.

Fig. 928. FOOD PRESS or RICER. c. 1930. Tin, zinc-plated iron. L: 11"; 3-3/8" dia.; H: 4". Genuine Kreamer Press. American. Author's Collection.

RIDDLE [*hriddel, ruddle, ridder*] — A coarse-meshed sieve, used for separating corn from chaff, or for mincing such cooked vegetables as potatoes. A riddle has a circular wooden rim with a bottom formed of a strong wire mesh. *See also* **GARLIC RIDDLE, POTATO RIDDLE**

ROASTER — A kind of reflecting oven or spitted rack on which meat, fowl, fish or fruit could be roasted before the fire. *See also* **REFLECTING OVEN**

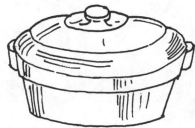

Fig. 929. ROASTER. Earthenware.

Fig. 930 REFLECTING OVEN. 19th century. Sheet iron. L: 12"; W: 7¾"; H: 10". Universal. American. Removeable shelf. Courtesy Keillor Collection.

ROASTING JACK — A contrivance for turning a spit on which meat is being roasted. *See also* **CLOCKWORK JACK, DOGS, SMOKE JACK**

ROASTING OVEN — *see* **TIN KITCHEN**

ROASTING PAN — A deep pan of iron or enameled ware, usually with a deep lid, for roasting fowl or meat. "The double pans sold in the market under the name of 'roasting pan' are really braising pans. Originally used for out of door cooking, the pan being placed on a bed of coals." (Mrs. Rorer, *Ladies Home Journal*, May 1900.) *See also* **BRAISING PAN, DUTCH OVEN**

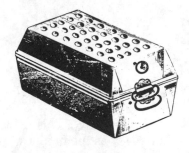

Fig. 931. ROASTING PAN or BAKER. Black tin. Self-basting, indented tip & bottom with ventilators. 14½" x 10" x 7"; 16½" x 11" x 7½". Matthai-Ingram Company, c. 1890.

ROAST-IRON — *see* **GRIDIRON**

ROCKINGHAM POTTERY — What is called *Rockingham pottery* was first made in America in 1845 in Jersey City. It resembled the ware from Rockingham, England. It is a dark brown, rather comely pottery with a high-fired glaze. It was later made in Bennington, Vermont; South Amboy, New Jersey; Philadelphia; Baltimore; Pottsville, Pennsylavania; and East Liverpool, Ohio. Pie plates, jugs, pitchers, table ware, baking dishes were all made of Rockingham pottery.

ROLLING PIN — A cylinder, either hollow or solid, of wood, tin, glass, metal, or ceramic, and usually fitted with knobs at each end. A rolling pin is used for rolling out pastry dough, making cracker crumbs, beating certain doughs, etc.

Glass rolling pins were originally made as salt containers, during the Napoleonic Wars in France. They were first produced of thick, pale green bottle glass about 1800. The open end was tightly corked, and both ends were in the form of small knobs. A cord could be knotted around the knob of one end and the salt bottle hung from a hook. The cold glass, heavy with its measure of salt, or whatever else came to be kept in it, made a wonderful rolling pin. Around the turn of the 20th century, glass rolling pins with screw-on metal caps were made — to be filled with ice water for rolling good pie-crusts.

The wooden pin with about 30 ribbed corrugations going around it was probably an oat crusher for making oatmeal, although it is often incorrectly identified as a cookie roller or noodle cutter.

"Some nice cooks think it very important, in making flaky pastry, to roll from you, and never towards you. Whether this is correct, I am unable to say from experience." (*Cornelius*, 1859.)

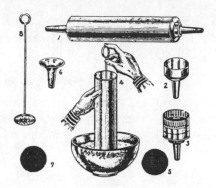

Fig. 934. COMBINATION ROLLING PIN, Egg Beater, Cream Whipper, Potato Masher, Butter Churner, Cake Cutter, Biscuit Cutter, Funnel, Strainer, Apple Corer. F. W. Seastrand, c. 1912.

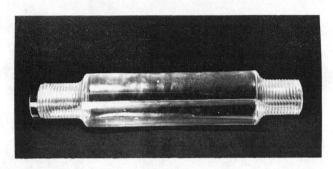

Fig. 935. ROLLING PIN. c. 1930s. Glass, metal screw cap. L: 14¼"; 2¾" dia. American. Author's Collection.

ROLL PAN — An iron pan for baking rolls in various forms. "Among iron goods used in kitchens are frying pans, waffle-irons, roll-pans, griddles for batter cakes, etc. Sometimes some of these things are so highly polished that they only require to be washed in soap and water and rubbed dry. ..." (*Parloa*, 1887.) "*Waterman's;*" etc.

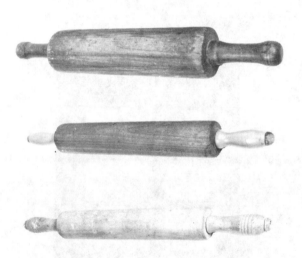

Fig. 932. ROLLING PINS. c. 1910 to 1940. Wood. Top one is one piece. L: 16¼" to 17". Dia. 1¾" to 2-5/8". American. Author's Collection.

Fig. 936. WATERMAN'S ROLL PANS. Cast iron. F. A. Walker, c. 1870s.

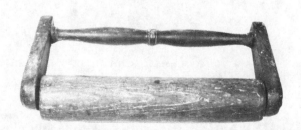

Fig. 933. ROLLING PIN. 19th century. Wood. L: 13"; W: 6½". American. Courtesy Keillor Collection.

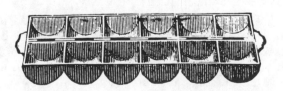

Fig. 937. FRENCH ROLL PAN. Cast iron. (Dover Stamping Co.). F. A. Walker, c. 1870s.

ROTARY BROILER — A gridiron with a long handle and three legs, the grid of which revolved. *See also* **GRIDIRON**

ROTARY SPIT and GRAVY BOAT — A long-handled iron utensil resembling a canoe, with a spit with small hooks suspended above it. The gravy boat caught the drippings of the small birds or game hooked on the spit.

ROTTENSTONE — Earth of ash-brown color, found only in England, and used for polishing metals. It is a decomposed, siliceous limestone. *Same as* **TRIPOLI**

RUNLET — A wooden measure holding approximately 18 gallons. *See also* **KILDERKIN**

RUSSIAN [*russia*] **IRON or PLANISHED IRON** — A special form of wrought iron used for roasting pans, baking pans, and dripping pans. "A special grade of sheet iron with a glossy black, slightly mottled appearance due to oxide adhering to the surface; it is produced by passing a pack of heated sheets back and forth under a steam hammer, the bit and anvil of which have indentations on their surfaces." (*Hutchinson*, 1918.) "Sheet-iron made in Russia, and having a smooth, glossy surface of a purplish color, sometimes mottled." (*Knight*, 1875.) "Russian Iron — The American product, or 'imitation Russian.' "(*Knight*, 1884.)

SAFE — A closet or cupboard, usually with perforated tin or zinc panels, or wire-mesh panels for air circulation. Used for the safe-keeping of pies, breads, milk, meat, and other foods. The safe, often called a *pie safe*, or a *meat safe*, was usually kept in a cool cellar. The panels, in the double doors and often the sides, were sometimes intricately punched designs of flowers, stars, eagles, pinwheels, and scrolls.

The cupboard was usually about 60" high. Sometimes the legs are long, and the body relatively small: this type is sometimes confused with a rabbit hutch or small chicken coop! Usually, however, the legs are about 6 to 8" long. Many of the safes you will see have partially rotted legs: "If ants are troublesome, set legs in cups of water." (*Beecher and Stowe*, 1869.) Larger bowls of water kept mice and other small vermin away.

Fig. 938. MEAT SAFE. L.H. Mace & Co. advertising flyer, c. 1880.

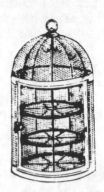

Fig. 939. MEAT SAFE. F. A. Walker, c. 1870s.

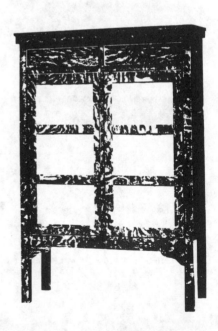

Fig. 940. SAFE. Oak, tin panels. H: 5'; W: 3'5". Acme Kitchen Furniture Co., 1910.

SALAD WASHER — A wire basket, nearly closed on top; either because it folds up that way, or was rigidly formed that way. Used for rinsing, then shaking or spinning dry salad greens.

Fig. 941. SALAD WASHER. Wire. F. A. Walker, c. 1870s.

Fig. 942. POTATO BOILER or SALAD WASHER. c. 1975. Iron wire. American. Courtesy Keillor Collection.

SALAERATUS — An impure bicarbonate of potash and much used as the main ingredient of baking powders, or alone as a rising agent.

SALAMANDER — A round flat disk of iron or other metal, with a long handle and at least two little legs near the neck. "It is made red hot and held over a dish which one wants to brown quickly without putting in the oven." (*Parloa*, 1887.) "A kitchen shovel is sometimes substituted...." (*Acton*, 1845.) [The mythical lizard-like salamander was supposed to live in fire.]

Chocolate Custard
Scald a qt. of milk; stir in 4 heaping tablespoonsful of grated chocolate and simmer two minutes to dissolve it; beat up the yolks of 6 eggs with 1 cup of sugar; add to the milk and chocolate; stir for 1 minute; then add vanila flavoring and pour into your custard cups, which should be waiting in pan ½ full of boiling water in the oven; cook until you see

that the custards are done; let them cool and then grate sweet almonds over the top; make a meringue of the whites of the six eggs and a little sugar; pile it on the top of each custard; grate more sweet almonds over that; set them in the oven to brown a little, or brown by holding a salamander or hot stove lid over them. [*Treasure House*, 1891]

Fig. 943. SALAMANDER. 18th century. Iron. L: 34"; 6½" dia. English. Courtesy Keillor Collection.

SALISBURY PORTABLE KITCHEN — A sort of enclosed brazier, invented by an Englishman, William Redman, in 1780. His description of it appeared in an abridged version in the 1873 *Abridgments of Specifications Relating to Cooking, Bread-Making, and the Preparation of Confectionery A.D. 1634-1866.*

"For roasting, boiling, or baking of any kind of provision. The body or furnace is made oval or round, of wrought or cast iron, tin or copper. Within it is placed a grate for the fire, and in the upper part a pot for boiling with water or steam, or a plate for baking. Underneath the fire is a vacuity open in the front, serving as a receptacle for the ashes as well as admitting a current of air to pass through the fire, thereby carrying off any smoke or dust through a tube or funnell affixed. A front is fixed to the furnace before the fire, which joins close to a reflector, purposely to confine the heat so as to roast and boil, or do either separately with a very small quantity of fire. The reflector is made of tin, brass, or copper. A spit goes through it, and at the bottom a dripping pan is so fixed as to draw off the gravy, that the meat may be easily basted at a door which is made on the top or any convenient part. A gridiron may be fixed occasionally in the place of the spit for broiling, with an additional reflector placed obliquely underneath it, or occasionally an iron plate may be placed in the reflector for the purpose of baking. They may also be made with two reflectors, to fix to the same body, for roasting two or more joints at once,..."

See also **BRAZIER, CONJURER, REFLECTING OVEN, TIN KITCHEN**

SALT BOX — A wooden, stoneware, or pottery box or other container with a lid. It was often hung on the wall, and was for keeping salt dry.

Fig. 944. SALT BOX. Greystone enameled ware. Matthai-Ingram Company, c. 1890.

Fig. 945. SALT JAR. Early 19th century. Brown pottery, white slip. H: 11 1/2"; W: 7 1/2". English. Courtesy Keillor Collection.

SALT GLAZE — A lead-free glaze for stoneware pottery made in the styles of the 17th and 18th century Dutch, German, and English pottery.

"Before the glorious Revolution ... here and there were scattered Potteries of Earthen-ware, imfamously bad and unwholesome, from their being partially glazed with a thin, cheap washing of Lead....It is wished the Legislature would consider of means for discountenancing the use of Lead in glazing, ... and encourage the application of the most perfect and wholesome glazing, produced only from Sand and Salts....

"What if public encouragement was to be given to homemade Stone-ware, rather than on Earthenware! In Stone-ware, Lead is never used; no other glazing need be used for stone than what is produced by a little common salt strewed over the ware, which operates as a flux to the particles of sand that stick on the sides of the ware, whilst it is in the furnace." (*Pennsylvania Mercury*, February 4, 1785.)

SARDINE SHEARS — A scissor-type can opener with very sharp curved blades and a spring-loaded handle. "Nothing made for opening cans is equal to sardine-shears which, with care, will last for a lifetime." (*Parloa*, 1887.)

Fig. 946. SARDINE SHEARS. F. A. Walker, c. 1870s.

SAUCEPAN — A cooking vessel of tin, earthenware, iron, aluminum, copper, or enameled ware, with a long handle and relatively straight sides and flat bottom. A *posnet* was an early saucepan, although the shape was quite different.

Saucepans were first cast, then pieced and soldered. Pans, at least tin pans, were not stamped in America until the last quarter of the 19th century, even though a patent for stamping copper saucepans was granted in England as early as 1834.

A divided saucepan has three or four wedge-shaped pans, making up the full circle, and was intended to save burner space on the range or stove. The divided saucepan was made from about 1870 on.

Fig. 947. SAUCEPAN LIDS & SAUCEPAN. Lids c. 1850s. Pan c. 1890s. Tin-lined copper, cast iron, brass rivets. Lids: 7" and 4½" dia. Pan: L: 13½"; H: 3". Probably American. Courtesy Mary Mac Franklin.

Fig. 948. SAUCE PAN. Stamped tin. From 4½" x 2" to 11½" x 4¾" — ½ qt. to 8 qts. Matthai-Ingram Company, c. 1890.

Fig. 949. CONVEX SAUCEPAN. Tin. From 4-1/8" to 10¼" dia. Lalance & Grosjean, 1890.

Fig. 950. SAUCE PAN. F. A. Walker, c. 1870s.

Fig. 951. SAUCEPAN COVERS. Tin, wood. 3½" to 14" dia. inside flange. Lalance & Grosjean, 1890.

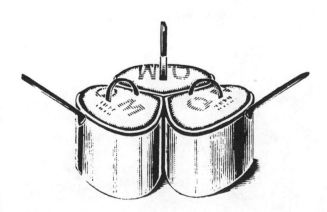

Fig. 952. DIVIDED SAUCE PANS, fuel-savers. Tin. This cut, like cuts of other utensils, appeared in many catalogues of the period. They were obtained from the manufacturer or from stock houses. This one, Montgomery Ward, 1893.

Fig. 953. TRIPLICATE SAUCE PAN. The People's Home Journal, Nov. 1914.

SAUCEPOT — A cooking vessel with ear handles.

Fig. 954. "WINDSOR" SAUCE POT. Tin. From ¾ to 10 qts. Lalance & Grosjean, 1890.

SAUSAGE STUFFER — A tin cylinder, or long rectangular box, of wood or tin, with a small tapered funnel-like outlet over which the sausage casing was fitted. A plunger, worked either by a crank or by pushing, pressed the sausage meat into the casing. *See also* **MEAT** and **FOOD CHOPPER, PUDDING**

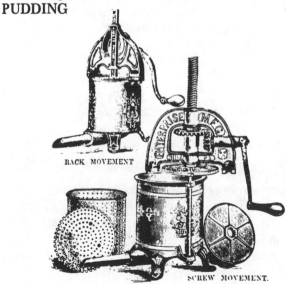

Fig. 955. SAUSAGE STUFFER, Fruit, Lard & Jelly Press. Pat'd July 11, 1876. Enterprise Manufacturing Co. of Pa., 1881.

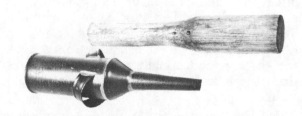

Fig. 956. SAUSAGE STUFFER. c. 1870s, 1880s. Tin, wood. L: 21"; 3½" dia. American. Courtesy Keillor Collection.

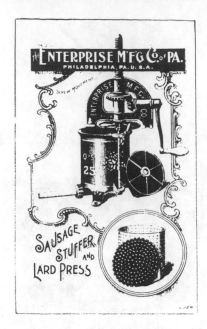

Fig. 957. ADVERTISING TRADE CARD. c. 1885. Blue, red, yellow lithographed card. 2-7/8" x 4¾". Enterprise Mfg. Co. of Pa., Philadelphia. Pictured is No. 25, the 4 quart size. This stuffer also came in 2 and 8 quart sizes. Author's Collection.

SAUTE PAN — A shallow pan with a long handle for quickly browning food in butter or other fat. *See also* **FRYING PAN**

SAVE-ALL — A container with a close lid for collecting and storing fat drippings and other "waste" fat to be used for making soap or candles, after it is clarified.

SCALES — The thrifty housewife had scales so that she could check the grocers' measures, and also because many recipes were measured in pounds or parts thereof. The four basic types of scales are: *platform* — with two platforms and a set of weights. On one platform, or pan, the food was placed. On the other, the cast-iron weights. The *dial scale*, often referred to as a "family scale," was more apt to go out of order. They were often highly decorated, japanned scales consisting of a box housing, a platform or pan on top, and a large dial reading in ounces and pounds. The *spring balance scale* — such as the pretty, brass-faced Chatillon scale — usually has a rectangular face marked in ounces and pounds, and a hook suspended from a spring. It was used with a weighing tray hung from it, or with the food hung directly on the hook. This type came in a number of sizes. The last type is the portable *lever*, or *steelyard scale* designed to be hung from a hook. At one end the food, usually meat, was hung, and the drop weight was moved along the scale until it balanced.

"No kitchen outfit is complete without scales. Two kinds come for use in the household. The old-fashioned is the better, as there is nothing to get out of order. These scales are more

cumbersome than the dial scales, but the latter are likely to require repairing." (*Parloa*, 1887.) "*Pelouze;*" "*American Family;*" "*U.S. Dial Co.;*" "*Acme;*" "*Chatillon;*" etc.

Apple Jam

Weigh equal quantities of brown sugar and good sour apples. Pare and core them, and chop them fine. Make a syrup of the sugar, and clarify it very thoroughly; then add the apples, the grated peel of 2 or 3 lemons, and a few pieces of white ginger. Boil it until the apple looks clear and yellow. This resembles foreign sweetmeats. The ginger is essential to its peculiar excellence. [*Cornelius*, 1859]

Fig. 958. PLATFORM SCALE. F. A. Walker, c. 1870s.

Fig. 959. PLATFORM SCALE. Iron. Weighs from ½ oz. to 25 lbs. Montgomery Ward, 1893.

Fig. 960. DIAL SCALES. F. A. Walker, c. 1870s.

Fig. 961. FAMILY SCALE. Steel & black enameled steel. Butler Brothers, 1899.

Fig. 962. DIAL SCALE. Pat'd 1898. Painted sheet metal. 6" square; H: 9¾". American Family Scale. Author's Collection.

Fig. 963. SPRING BALANCE SCALE. First pat'd Dec. 10, 1867; again Jan. 6, 1891, and Jan. 26, 1892. Brass, iron. L: 8"; W: 1-3/8". This one measures up to 25 lbs. Chatillon, New York. Author's Collection.

Fig. 964. SPRING BALANCE SCALE. Butler Brothers, 1899.

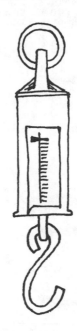

Fig. 965. SPRING BALANCE SCALE.

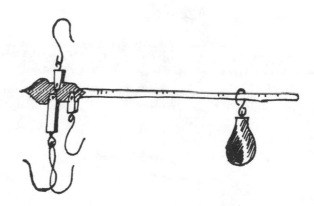

Fig. 966. STEELYARD SCALE.

SCOOP — An implement with a spoon— or gouged-shaped bowl, sometimes partially covered to form a receptacle, and used for cutting out portions of soft food or fruit, or as a serving-up, dipping-out or conveying utensil for mashed potatoes, flour, meal, and other food. *See also* **CHEESE-SCOOP, FLOUR-SCOOP, ICE CREAM-SCOOP, ICE SCOOP, MELON-SCOOP**

Fig. 967. SPICE SCOOPER. F. A. Walker, c. 1870s.

Fig. 968. SCOOPS. (Left) SPICE SCOOP. Stamped tin. 5" x 3½"; 5¾" x 3¾". (Right) TEA SCOOP. Stamped tin. Same measurements. Matthai-Ingram Company, c. 1890.

Fig. 969. GROCERS' SCOOPS. Tin, metal or wood handle. Lalance & Grosjean, 1890.

Fig. 970. (Top two) FAMILY SCOOPS. Tin, wood. 3½" x 5" to 4" x 6½". (Bottom) CANDY SCOOP. Tin, wood. 2¾" x 3¼". Lalance & Grosjean, 1890.

Fig. 971. (Top to bottom) CONFECTIONERS' SCOOP. Tin. 2½" x 4½" to 3" x 5¾". THUMB SCOOP. Tin. 2¾" x 5¼" to 4" x 7¾". SPICE SCOOP. Tin. 2½" x 3½" to 3¾" x 5½". TEA SCOOP. Tin. 2¾" x 5¼" to 4" x 7¾". Lalance & Grosjean, 1890.

SCOTCH BOWL — A lidless slope-sided kettle with a bail handle, of iron or fire-proof pottery, for the thick Scotch Broth barley soup, or for barley, oat, or cracked wheat porridge, or other cooked cereal. It was lidless because the soup or barley porridge had to be stirred constantly.

Cracked Wheat

1 pt. of the cracked grain; 2 qts. of water; boil in a smooth iron pot over a quick fire; stir in the wheat slowly; boil fast; stir constantly for the first ½ hour of cooking, or until it begins to thicken; lift from the quick fire, and place the pot where the wheat will cook slowly for an hour longer; keep it covered closely; stir now and then, and be careful not to let it burn at the bottom. When ready to dish out, it is a neat way to have molds moistened with cold water; cover lightly and set in a cool place; eat warm or cold with milk and sugar. [*Treasure House*, 1891]

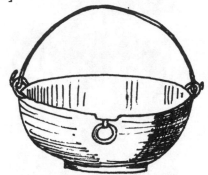

Fig. 972. SCOTCH BOWL. Cast iron.

SEARCER — A fine sieve, usually for flour.

SHORTS — Coarse flour. *See* MIDDLINGS

SIEVE — A broad, shallow, round utensil with a wire mesh, or woven horsehair bottom and a metal or bentwood rim. The meshes are available from coarse to fine. Sieves were also made with perforated tin bottoms. Sieves were used not only for flour or meal, but for straining wet food. A sieve differs from a sifter in that it has shallow sides, a flat bottom, and no moving parts. *See also* FLOUR SIFTER, GARLIC RIDDLE, HAIR SIEVE, JELLY SIEVE, RIDDLE, SEARCER

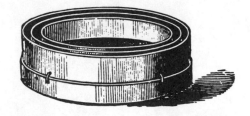

Fig. 973. SIEVES. F. A. Walker, c. 1870s.

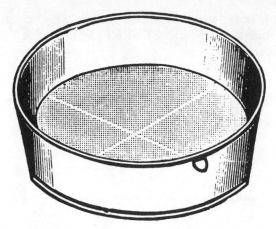

Fig. 974. SIEVE. Tin, wire mesh. 16 or 18 wires to the inch. Montgomery Ward, 1893.

Fig. 975. SIEVES. c. 1900. Perforated tin. Dia. 12-1/8"; H: 2¼". American. Author's Collection.

SIFTER — see FLOUR SIFTER

SINK — A basin or receptacle of metal, earthenware, vitreous pottery, stone, or wood, having a drain and a water supply. A *sink* can be large and stand on its own two or four legs; if two legs, it obviously must be fastened to the wall, usually with a splash-back . Or it can be small and meant to sit on some flat suface. It was used for washing dishes, pots, and food. "A galvanized iron sink is quite the best cheap sink obtainable, provided it has a galvanized back.... A drain board should be placed to the left of the sink. It is grooved and should be kept slightly lifted.... Upon this board a woven basket may be placed as a receptacle for dishes." (*Ladies Home Journal*, June 1899.) Catherine Beecher and Harriet Beecher Stowe presented a design for a kitchen in which the primary innovation was the built-in sink, with a molding and meat board, and a dish draining board which could be flipped over the sink to provide another work surface. Space for storing scouring materials, dish-towels, and save-alls, etc. was provided under the sink. This was in 1869.

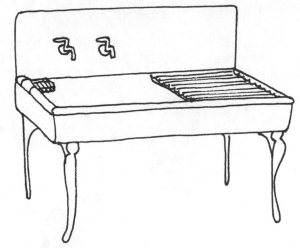

Fig. 976. SINK with splash-back & drain board.

Fig. 977. WALL-MOUNTED SINK with splash-back.

SINK BASKET — A wire basket for holding dishes in the sink, or a three-cornered basket placed in a corner of the sink. "Into this basket may be thrown all water containing kitchen refuse." (*Ladies Home Journal*, July 1899.)

Fig. 978. SINK STRAINER. Tolerton & Warfield Co., Sioux City, Iowa, c. 1900.

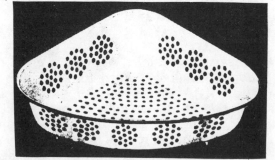

Fig. 979. SINK DRAINER. White enameled ware. Cream City. Geuder, Paeschke & Frey Co., 1925.

SINK BRUSH — see **BRUSHES**

SINK CLEANER — A squeegee-like implement, sometimes with a shovel at the other end, for scraping the sink.

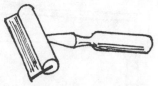

Fig. 980. SINK CLEANER. Wood, rubber. W: 5".

Fig. 981. SINK SHOVEL & SINK BRUSH. A. E. Rayment Supply Co., Rockford, Illinois, c. 1910.

SINK RACK — A wire, wood, or metal rack for holding dishes. *See* **DISH DRAINER**

SINK SHOVEL — A little shovel, like a child's sandbox shovel, for removing the bean strings, coffee grounds, or other kitchen refuse from the sink.

SIPPET — A small piece of toasted or fried bread used to eat with, and hence a sort of utensil, however temporary. A sippet was used through the 18th century for eating from trenchers, but as the trencher itself was sometimes bread, the sippet might have been a torn-off corner of the trencher. Sippets, used as a garnish, were specified in recipes into the 20th century.

> ### Stewed Green Peas
> Put your peas into a saucepan; toss them into a little butter; when hot add sufficient veal or chicken stock to moisten them with; simmer slowly; thicken slightly with flour and butter; place fried sippets round a dish, and serve the peas in the middle. [*Treasure House*, 1891]

SKEWER [*skuer*] — A long, wooden or metal pin with a looped end, graded in size for small birds up to large roasts. Skewers were used to attach the often-trussed meat to the spit for roasting. "Use only skewers enough to fasten the meat to the spit, as they furnish an outlet for the juices." (*Cornelius*, 1859.) Skewers were hung on racks or *skewer fraimes*: small, two-armed iron hooks which hung

from the mantle, lintel, or on the wall next to the fireplace. *See also* **BASKET SPIT, SPIT, BIRD ROASTER**

Fig. 982. SKEWERS. F. A. Walker, c. 1870s.

Fig. 983. SKEWER HOLDER & SKEWERS. Early-19th century. Wrought iron. Holder: l: 6"; skewers: L: 5¾" - 9". American. Courtesy Keillor Collection.

SKEWER-PULLER — A small, curved metal tool with a hole in one end which was used, rather like a claw hammer, for removing wooden skewers. "Housekeepers know from experience how difficult it is to remove the wooden skewers which provision dealers use in meats and poultry. There is, however, a little device which draws out the skewers with the greatest of ease. It is nickel-plated and costs 25 cents. It seems to me it should be sold at a lower price; still, one would probably last a lifetime." (Parloa, *Ladies Home Journal*, July 1899.) 25 cents *does* seem high, when one considers that something as complicated, for example, as the Dover egg beater was being sold for about 8 cents!

Fig. 984. SKEWER-PULLER. 1890s.

SKILLET [*skellet*] — A brass, copper, bell-metal, or cast-iron utensil more like a fat-bellied saucepan than a frying pan, although we use the words *skillet* and *frying pan* interchangeably today. The long-handled, deep skillet had either its own three little legs (like a posnet) or sat on a tripod or brandise. It rarely had a flat bottom.

Fig. 985. SKILLETS. Cast iron. 1½ qts., 2 qts., 2½ qts., 3½ qts. Country Hollow Ware. Matthai- Ingram Company, c. 1890.

Fig. 986. POLISHED BORDERED STOVE SKILLET. From 8" to 12" dia. Lalance & Grosjean, 1890.

SKIMMER — One of several types of utensils used for removing floating matter from the surface of a liquid; as cream from milk, or scum from boiled soup. The *milk skimmer* was a nearly flat, perforated or plain disk about 4" or 5" in diameter, which fit in the hand or had a long handle. Another, called a skimmer or a *pea-ladle* in old catalogs, was a wire basket with a long handle used for serving vegetables out of the water in which they were cooked. Skimmers were made in brass, tin, enameled ware, pottery, wood, and aluminum.

Always use cold water in making all soups; skim well, especially during the first hour. There is a great necessity for thorough skimming, and to help the scum rise, pour in a little cold water now and then, and as the soup reaches the boiling point, skim it off. [*Practical Housekeeping* 1884]

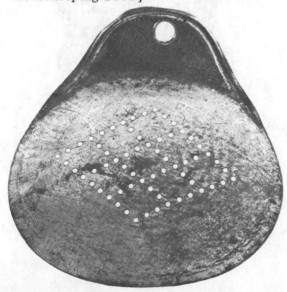

Fig. 987. MILK SKIMMER. c. 1890s. Perforated & stamped tin. 6" x 6". "Cream City Ware," Geuder, Paeschke & Frey Co., Milwaukee, Wisc. Courtesy Mary Mac Franklin.

Fig. 988. CREAM SEPARATOR, "which can be run by hand, steam, dog, sheep, or goat power." The cream separator took the place of the skimmers and strainers used to skim off the cream to be made into butter. *The Home Encyclopedia of Useful Information.* by D. Magner. L. G. Stahl, 1803.

Fig. 989. MILK SKIMMER. 1900-1920. White enameled metal. 5½" x 4". American. Author's Collection.

Fig. 990. SKIMMER. c. 1920s. Aluminum. L: 14"; 4-3/8" dia. WSuCL. Possibly German, as so many aluminum pieces of this type were. Author's Collection.

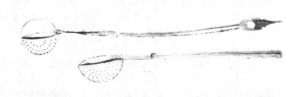

Fig. 991. SKIMMERS. 19th century. Wood, tin. (top) L: 24"; W: 3½". (bottom) L: 18"; W: 4". American. Courtesy Keillor Collection.

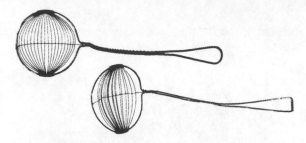

Fig. 992. VEGETABLE LADLES. c. 1880s-1900. Wire. L: 14"; W: 4½", 5". American. Author's Collection.

Fig. 993. PEA SKIMMER. Wire, wood. (Dover Stamping Co.). F. A. Walker, c. 1870s.

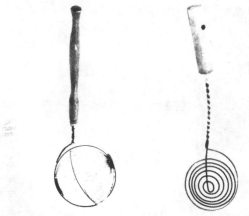

Fig. 994. VEGETABLE LADLES. (1) c. 1890. L: 13"; W: 4-3/8". (2) c. 1915. L: 13"; W: 3¾". Both wire with wood handles. American. Author's Collection.

SKIMMING DISH — An almost flat skimmer used in cheesemaking or for skimming milk. "A little broad flat Dish made of Wood, called by Dairy Women a Scimming Dish." (*Randle Holme*, 1688.) The Pennsylvania Dutch made wooden skimming dishes, often dated and with the initials of the "dairy woman." *See also* **CHEESE PRESS, FLIT**

SLAW CUTTER — *see* **CABBAGE CUTTER**

SLICE — One of several implements: a flat, long-handled implement for turning fried meat or eggs; a dough cutter; a fish server; a spatula for mixing batter; a sort of fire-shovel for clearing the oven before baking; and a peel used to place bread in , or remove it from, the oven, *See also* **EGG SLICE, FISH SLICE, PEEL**

SLICER — A sharp-edged implement for slicing bread, vegetables or meat. Vegetable and fruit slicers and parers came in many sizes and styles. They were primarily intended for making fancy or decorative slices for garnishes. *See also* **VEGETABLE CUTTER**

Fig. 995. COCOANUT CANDY TRADEMARK. Sourkrout. 1902.

SLOP PAIL,— BUCKET, or SWILL PAIL — Slop is, among other things, the refuse liquid or solid food of the kitchen, and a slop pail, or swill pail, is the bucket, basin, pail or other vessel used as a temporary container for the slops until they are thrown out or fed to the pigs. Refuse liquid included tea and coffee, and as some of the waste food was unsuitable for the pigs, probably two pails were kept. *Beecher and Stowe* recommended in 1869 a "slop bucket with tight cover, painted on the outside."

Fig. 996. SLOP JAR. Agate enameled ware. 11½" x 11½". Lalance & Grosjean, 1890.

Fig. 997. SLOP BUCKET. Greystone enameled ware, tin cover. 12 qts. Matthai-Ingram Company, c. 1890.

SMOKE JACK — A jack for operating a spit, by means of a pulley, with a large set of fan-like blades. It was set up in the mouth of the chimney and operated by the hot air and smoke rising in the chimney. *See also* **PORTABLE SPRING JACK**

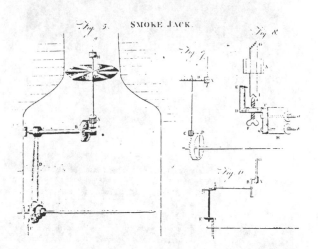

Fig. 998. SMOKE JACK. From an engraved plate in an 18th century book, unidentifiable. Notice the varieties of motion transfer—chain and pulley, bevel gear, etc. Author's Collection.

SOAP SAVER or SHAKER — A closed wire-mesh receptacle, or a square or oval perforated tin box, with a long handle. A soap saver held soap scraps or even whole bars of soap so that they might be swished around in dishwater to make suds.

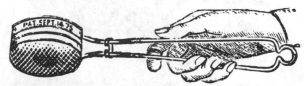

Fig. 999. SOAP SAVER. Pat'd Sept. 14, 1875. Wire. Matthai-Ingram Company, c. 1890.

SOAP SHAVER — A flat grater with large cutting holes for making soap shavings for suds.

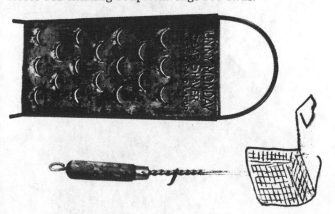

Fig. 1000. SOAP SAVER & SOAP SHAVER. Saver: c. 1925-1940. Wire mesh, wire, wood. L: 10"; W: 3". Shaver: c. 1900-1920. Tin. L: 10¾"; W: 4". "Sunny Monday - Saves Soap & Labor." American. Author's Collection.

SOAPSTONE — A smooth, greasy-feeling variety of the mineral *talc*. It was often used for griddles. *See also* **GRIDDLE**

SOUP DIGESTER — A vessel with a tight cover and a steam escape cock used for making soup and tenderizing meat. *See also* **DIGESTER**

SOUP-KETTLE — *see* **STOCK POT**

SOUP STRAINER — A large cone-shaped strainer with a handle. Also called a *gravy strainer. See also* **TAPERING STRAINER**

> Graham Soup
> 3 onions, 3 carrots, 3 turnips, 1 small cabbage; 1 bunch of celery; and a pint of stewed tomatoes; chop all the vegetables very finely; set over the fire in 4 or 5 quarts of water; when thoroughly boiled, strain and add to the soup about 2 teaspoons of Graham flour wet in cold water; a small piece of butter, pepper and salt; boil again about 20 minutes.
> [*Treasure House,* 1891]

Fig. 1001. SOUP STRAINER. Tin, tinned wire. Butler Brothers, 1899.

Fig. 1002. SOUP STRAINER. Pieced tin, wire mesh. 6", 10" dia. Matthai-Ingram Company, c. 1890.

SPATULA — "A limber knife, also called a pallet knife, used by housewives to clean bowls and utensils." (*Ladies Home Journal,* October 1901.) Some spatulas had narrow, one-inch blades, and others were much wider, and even perforated. *See also* **CAKE TURNER, SLICE**

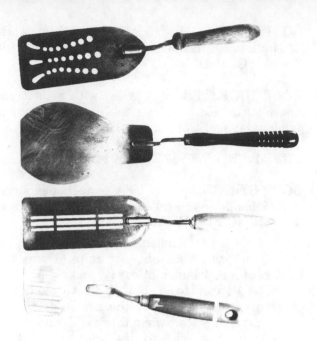

Fig. 1003. SPATULAS & CAKE TURNERS. Top to bottom. (1) Tinned steel, wood. L: 11"; W: 2½". Possibly A & J. (2) Tinned steel, wood. L: 12½"; W: 4". Cronk & Carrier Mfg. Co., Geneva, Ohio, before 1930. (3) Tinned steel, wood. L: 10¾"; W: 2½". Androck. (4) c. 1940. Stainless steel, wood. L: 10". A & J Ekco. All of these spatulas have the tiller handle. Author's Collection.

SPICE BAG — A cloth bag for dried spices, used when the loose spices were not wanted floating around in the food.

Spiced Vinegar

Put three pounds sugar in a three gallon jar with a small mouth; mix two ounces each of mace, cloves, pepper, allspice, turmeric, celery seed, white ginger in small bits, and ground mustard; put in six small bags made of thin but strong muslin, lay in jar, fill with best cider vinegar, and use it in making pickles and sauces. [*Practical Housekeeping*, 1884]

SPICE BOX — A box, usually having several compartments or drawers, to keep spices in "nests," one large box with a number of smaller boxes within. "For spice boxes, it is best to keep different sorts in small, separate painted tin boxes, each with tight lid and handle to hang it by, to nails driven along the edge of dresser shelf. Each box to have name painted on side. These are better than large boxes, in which, not withstanding the division, the spices are very apt to get mixed." (*Leslie*, 1840.) "Spice Boxes come in many forms. Little boxes labelled with various kinds of spice are fitted into one large box. If they were well-made they would be very desirable, but they are so poorly made, it is difficult to take the covers off or put them on.... A good one has three compartments on each side; the only objection being that the spices are not so well-protected as in case of little boxes within one large box. However, one does not keep much spice at a time in these

pantry boxes, and the saving of time and patience is a consideration." (*Parloa*, 1887.)

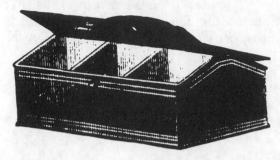

Fig. 1004. SPICE BOX. Japanned tin. (Dover Stamping Co.). F. A. Walker, c. 1870s.

Fig. 1005. SPICE BOX with cans. c. 1895. Gold, red & brown japanned tin. L: 9"; W: 6-1/8". Contains six small canisters for nutmegs, ginger, allspice, cloves, cinnamon, mace. Nutmeg grater attached inside lid. American. Author's Collection.

Fig. 1006. SPICE CAN TRAY & DREDGER. c. 1890. Japanned tin. (Tray) L: 5½"; W: 4¾"; H: 4¼". (Cans) 2-7/8" x 1¾". (Dredger) 3" x 1¾". Author's Collection.

Fig. 1007. SPICE BOX. 7 cans. Japanned tin. F. A. Walker, c. 1870s.

Fig. 1008. SPICE BOX. c. 1870s, 1880s. Varnished & stenciled wood and iron. 9" dia. American. Courtesy Keillor Collection.

Fig. 1011. DOUBLE SPICE MILL. 19th century. Wood, iron, sheet iron. H: 41"; W: 22". American. Courtesy Keillor Collection.

SPICE CABINET — A little wooden bureau with a number of labelled drawers for spices. They were designed and made to be hung on the wall.

In a 17th century inventory of a Captain George Corwin, was the note "Scriture or Spice Box...." (*Dow*, 1925.) The scriture, or escritoire, was usually a small cabinet with a number of drawers for keeping various writing instruments, inks and papers in.

Fig. 1009. SPICE CABINET. Ash wood. 12" x 18". Montgomery Ward, 1895.

SPICE MILL or GRINDER — A small hand mill for grinding spices. *See* HERB GRINDER, MILL, QUERNE

Fig. 1012. SPICE MILL. c. 1850s. Wood, leather. L: 10½"; W: 3¾" (boat); 10" x 4" (pestle). Norwegian. Courtesy Keillor Collection.

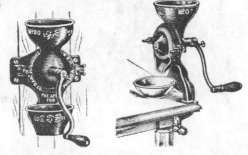

Fig. 1010. SPICE MILLS. Enterprise Mfg. Co. of Pa. The Enterprising Housewife, 1898.

Fig. 1013. COFFEE, SPICE & DRUG MILL. Enterprise Manufacturing Co. of Pa., 1881.

SPICE MORTAR — A mortar for pounding or braying spices.

SPICE RACK — A rack for holding cans or bottles of spices.

Fig. 1014. SPICE RACK. Japanned tin. "The Handle is convenient, and the rack can be set near when cakes are to be made, and when the work is done it may be set away on a shelf." Practical Housekeeping, 1881.

SPIDER [*speeder*] — A short-handled frying pan, originally with three legs to hold it above the coals in the fireplace.

Fig. 1015. SPIDER. Black steel. 13", 14", 15", 16", 18" dia. Matthai-Ingram Company, c. 1890.

SPILL — A slim piece of wood or twisted paper used to light a fire, and kept in a spill box or spill case. *See also* **MATCHES**

SPIT [*speet, spytt*] — A roasting implement consisting of a slender, sharp-ended rod of wrought iron fitted with a pulley or handle at one end. There were several ways by which the meat could be fastened to the spit. First, the spit was thrust through the meat, which was centered on it. Then, either a set of skewers were used to fasten the meat securely to the spit so that when it turned, the meat would turn; or a two-pronged fork, which was either welded to the center of the spit, or could be slid along and clamped with a thumb screw, was thrust through the meat to hold it in place. Slots or holes were made at short intervals the length of most spits, and it was through these that the skewers were stuck. *See also* **BASKET SPIT, CLOCKWORK JACK, DOGS, SKEWER, SMOKE JACK**

SPIT RACK — A simple wooden rack, usually above the fireplace, for holding roasting spits when not in use. Many households were equipped with several spits of different sizes and types.

SPONGE and BRUSH RACK — A fairly large wire basket, which hooked over the top or back of the sink, for holding washing sponges and brushes. "A sponge, especially when damp, is a nuisance. If hung up it moistens the wall, and if laid down it gets in every body's way and gathers dirt. The simple, neat and cheap wire basket which hangs on the wall is a good receptacle for it, or a 3-cornered piece of oil cloth, sustained by a string fastened at each corner, is a good make-shift for the same purpose." (*Practical Housekeeping*, 1884.)

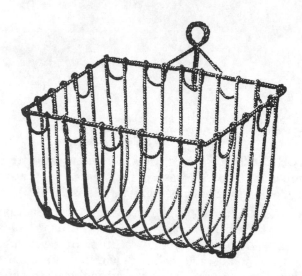

Fig. 1016. SPONGE RACK. Wire. F. A. Walker, c. 1870s.

SPRINGERLE MOLD — A carved wooden mold for making the small cookies long-favored by the Pennsylvania Dutch. The mold is divided into checkerboard squares — each with a sprightly or fancy patterns: hearts, flowers, riders on horses [*springerle* means *jumper*], even snakes — and is either a flat board or a wooden roller much like a rolling pin. The board or the roller is pressed to the dough.

Fig. 1017. SPRINGERLE MOLD. c. 1880s. Wood. 5" x 3¼". American. Courtesy Keillor Collection.

Fig. 1018. SPRINGERLE MOLD. 1860s. Wood. 6¾" x 9¼". Signed "F. G." American, Pennsylvania German. Courtesy Keillor Collection.

Fig. 1020. SPRINGERLE MOLD. c. 1880s. Wood. 4¼" x 3". American. Courtesy Keillor Collection.

Fig. 1021. SPRINGERLE ROLLER. c. 1880s. Carved wood. L: 14¾". Pennsylvania German. Courtesy Keillor Collection.

SQUASH STRAINER — A coarse strainer for removing the coarse fibers of squash or pumpkin when making pies. Sometimes the tapering strainer was called a squash strainer.

Fig. 1022. SQUASH STRAINER. Tin. F. A. Walker, c. 1870s.

Fig. 1019. SPRINGERLE MOLD, two sides. 19th century. Wood. 9" x 8½". Pennsylvania German. Courtesy Keillor Collection.

STAINLESS STEEL — A steel alloy, containing about 12% chromium, patented in 1911. It wasn't until about 1920, however, that it was used for kitchen utensils. "A steel which resists rust, does not corrode or scale, and is impervious to food acids (with the exception of mustard, plus vinegar and salt which equals muriatic acid...). The steel we now use is carbon steel.... Think of not having to scour or polish your knives. Think of the knife having an indefinite life and always looking highly polished. Soon, too, even the handle will be made of this steel, and the knife will look like a highly polished silver utensil. ...Its advent reminds one of the early days of aluminum utensils, doesn't it? The manufacturers are planning to make kettles, pots and pans of it, as they will wear well, and will not scale and wear as do iron ones." (*House and Garden*, March 1921.)

STEAK MAUL — *see* **MEAT FRET**

STEAMER, STEAM COOKER — A cooking vessel with a perforated tray for the food, in which the food is cooked by steam, not in boiling liquid. Some steamers were made so that several layers of food, each in a different container could be steamed over the same boiling water. This was a great space saver, and steamed food was, and is, considered healthful. One common type, the Toledo Cooker, was a metal utensil, nearly two feet tall and a foot square, with a copper pan at the bottom and a steam vent on top. The food was placed inside on shelves, and the cooker was placed on the stove or other heat source. It was patented in 1907, but steamers of the same sort were known from the middle of the 19th century. *"Toledo Cooker;" "Eureka;" "Peerless;" "Arnold;" "Sherman;" "Ohio;" "Beveridge Sanitary;" "Speir;"* etc.

Fig. 1023. BEVERIDGE STEAM COOKER. 4 or 5 vessels, from 8" to 12" dia. Matthai-Ingram Company, c. 1890.

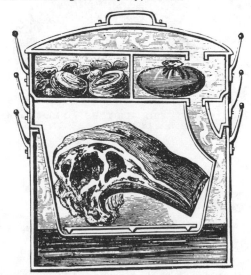

Fig. 1024. STEAM COOKER. F. A. Walker, c. 1870s.

STEEL — "Iron which has been greatly hardened by mixing with it a definite amount of carbon. It is thus malleable, weldable, fusible and temper-able." (Hutchinson, 1918.) In 1781 the process of reducing steel to a fluid was found, and thus cast steel became possible, but it was nearly 100 years before cast steel was produced in America. *See also* **CARBON STEEL, IRON, NICKEL STEEL, STAINLESS STEEL**

STEW PAN — A saucepan with one long handle, usually used with a close-fitting lid.

Fig. 1025. STEW PAN. (Probably Dover Stamping Co.). F. A. Walker, c. 1870s.

STEW POT — A kettle with ear handles.

STOCK POT — A large kettle kept on the back of the stove for the continuous low-heat cooking of meat and vegetable stock. "When soup is desired for a first course, daily, a soup-kettle (which has a double bottom) should be especially provided, with a faucet to draw off the clear soup to be seasoned for each day; and all the bones and bits of meat left after dinner can be thrown into the kettle, also bits of vegetables and bread, and the gravies that are left from roast meats and cutlets. In this way there will be nothing lost, and the soups can be varied by seasoning and thickenings of different kinds. Every 2 or 3 days, however, the contents of the kettle should be turned out, after all the liquid has been drawn off, and the kettle washed clean and scalded, for if this is not attended to, the soups will soon lose their piquant flavor and become stale." (*Practical Housekeeping*, 1884.) Between the save-all, the slop pail and the stock pot, surely *nothing* was wasted! *See also* **POT-AU-FEU**

Fig. 1026. SOUP STOCK POT. Copper, tinned inside, brass faucet. 10½" x 10¼", 13" x 11¾", 15" x 14". Lalance & Grosjean, 1890.

STONEWARE — A high-fired pottery used for jars, butter crocks and some pots. *See also* **SALT GLAZE**

Fig. 1027, 1028. . THROWING & FINISHING STONEWARE BOTTLE. Two cuts. Cyclopedia of Useful Arts & Manufacturers. Edited by Charles Tomlinson. New York, London: George Virtue, 1852, 1854. 2 Vol.

Fig. 1029. Typical STONEWARE JAR & JUG.

STOVE — *see* **RANGE**

STOVE LIDS — The flat plates covering the holes in the range top, where pots were set in. *See also* **SALAMANDER**

STOVE LID LIFTER — An iron device, often nickel-plated, with a hook at one end for lifting out the iron stove plates from stove or range top. Some provision was made for cooling the handle: it was either made of wood; or was a spirally-twisted heavy wire, or wrought or cast iron; or it was cast with a number of holes. *"Alaska;" "Zero;" and see the stove names under* **RANGE**

Fig. 1030. STOVE LID LIFTER. 18th or early-19th century. Wrought iron. L: 14". American. Courtesy Keillor Collection.

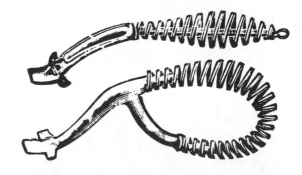

Fig. 1031. STOVE LID LIFTERS. Nickel-plated iron. Matthai-Ingram Company, c. 1890.

Fig. 1032. LID LIFTER or PIE PLATE LIFTER. c. 1880s. Hinged cast iron. L: 8". American. Courtesy Keillor Collection.

Fig. 1033. COVER LIFTER. Iron. F. A. Walker, c. 1870s.

Fig. 1034. STOVE LID LIFTER. Coppered iron. The Zero Lid Lifter. Montgomery Ward, 1893.

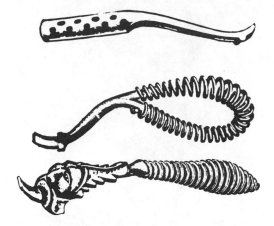

Fig. 1035. STOVE LID LIFTERS. Nickeled iron. Alaska Stove Lid Lifters. Montgomery Ward, 1890.

STOVE MAT or BOARD — An asbestos sheet, large or small, used to protect certain vessels from direct heat which would crack them. *See also* **ASBESTOS**

Fig. 1036. STOVE BOARD. Crystalized or embossed tin, paper lined. Round: 24, 26, 28, 30, 32, 34, 36". Square: same. Matthai-Ingram Company, c. 1890.

STOVE PIPE SHELF — A small rack which attached to, and around, the stovepipe — making a place for the salt and pepper dredgers, or for cups to warm, or for putting bread or roll dough to rise.

Salt-Rising Bread
Put half a teaspoonful of salt in half a teacupful of flour; pour on boiling water; work it well very stiff; put this where it will keep warm all night; next morning take a pint of milk, warm water, and as much salt as before; mix in flour till you make a good muffin-batter, and set it in warm water till it rises; then add flour to form a stiff dough, and

bake. This is the favorite bread all through the Valley of Virginia and Maryland. Some dyspeptics think it much more digestible than bread made up with other kinds of yeast. [Mary Stuart Smith, in *Virginia Cookery-Book*, as in *Strohm,* 1888]

Fig. 1037. STOVE PIPE SHELF. Japanned cast iron. 18" x 18", fits 6" stovepipe. Montgomery Ward, 1893.

STOVE SHOVEL — A small shovel for cleaning ashes, cinders, clinkers, and coals from the stove.

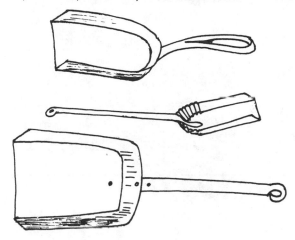

Fig. 1038. STOVE SHOVELS. Sheet iron, wrought or cast iron handles.

STRAINER — Usually a wire-mesh basket with a handle, and a knob or hook which rests on one side of a bowl while the handle supports the other side. Used for straining liquids, gravies, blancmange, and for sifting sugar upon cakes or salt into butter, etc. Some strainers were cloth bags, or perforated metal cones. An *extension strainer* had an extendible wire frame made to rest on the top of any sized pan, jar, or pail. A *free-rim strainer* clipped on the edge of the pot or pan and did not have to be held. A *spout strainer* clipped to the spout of a tea or coffee pot. *See also* **CHINESE STRAINER, COFFEE POT, COLANDER, JELLY STRAINER, SOUP STRAINER, TAPERING STRAINER, TEA STRAINER**

Fig. 1039. STRAINERS. Wire. (Dover Stamping Co.). F. A. Walker, c. 1870s.

Fig. 1040. BOWL STRAINERS. Wire. 4¼" dia. Matthai-Ingram Company, c. 1890.

Fig. 1041. SUGAR SIFTER. Tin. 3¾" x ¾". Lalance & Grosjean, 1890.

Fig. 1042. STRAINER. 1920 to 1930s. Screen, tin, wood. 8½" x 2½". American. Author's Collection.

Fig. 1043. TODDY STRAINER. Planished tin. F. A. Walker, c. 1870s.

Fig. 1044. CUP STRAINER. Planished tin. F. A. Walker, c. 1870s.

Fig. 1045. WINE STRAINER. Planished tin. F. A. Walker, c. 1870s.

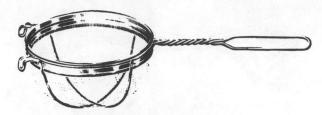

Fig. 1046. STRAINER. 6", 8" dia. Androck, 1936.

Fig. 1047. MILK STRAINERS. Pieced tin. (Top) Wire bottom. 8" to 11" dia. (Bottom) Hoop to be used with cloth. 8", 9-5/8" dia. Matthai-Ingram Company, c. 1890.

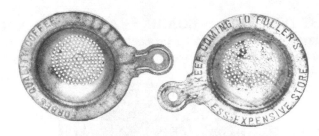

Fig. 1048. MILK STRAINERS. 1900-1915. Tin. L: 4-3/8" x 3¼". Forbes Quality Coffee; Keep Coming to Fuller's Less-Expensive Store. American. Author's Collection.

Fig. 1049. MILK STRAINER PAIL. Tin. F. A. Walker, c. 1870s.

Fig. 1050. EXTENSION STRAINER. 5", 6", 8" dia. Androck, 1936.

Fig. 1051. FRUIT JUICE STRAINER. Nickel plated steel, chromium plated with hand hammered finish. 4-1/8" dia. A & J. Edward Katzinger Company, 1940.

Fig. 1052. SPOUT STRAINER. (Probably Dover Stamping Co.). F. A. Walker, c. 1870s.

STRAINER SPOON — A large spoon, the bowl of which is partly a fine, wire-mesh sieve. *See also* **VEGETABLE LADLE, MIXING SPOON**

Fig. 1053. STRAINING SPOON. c. 1900. Tin, wood. L: 10". American. Author's Collection.

STRAINER STAND — A wooden frame for supporting a cloth bag strainer. *See also* **JELLY STRAINER**

SUGAR AUGER — *see* **FRUIT LIFTER**

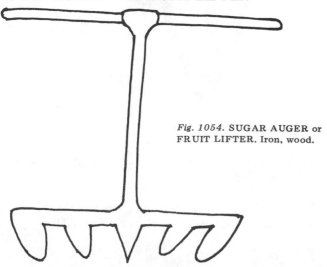

Fig. 1054. SUGAR AUGER or FRUIT LIFTER. Iron, wood.

SUGAR MOLD — A cone-shaped pottery or wooden mold, sometimes with a design but more often plain, which was used by pouring the hot sugar syrup into it to harden.

Fig. 1055. FILLING CONICAL SUGAR MOLDS. Cyclopedia of Useful Arts & Manufacturers. Edited by Charles Tomlinson. New York, London: George Virtue, 1852, 1854. 2 Vol.

SUGAR NIPPERS — A cast-iron or steel cutter, with small and leaf-like blades, which looks very much like the mouthparts of some strange exotic beetle. It was used to nip off sugar from the hard, cone-shaped loaf. Some nippers were mounted on a board, and all were made with a little knob, projecting from one of the handles, to protect the knuckles.

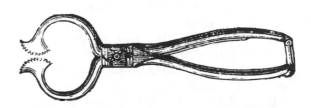

Fig. 1056. SUGAR CUTTER. F. A. Walker, c. 1870s.

Fig. 1057. SUGAR CONE wrapped in paper, SUGAR NIPPERS, SUGAR HAMMER. (1) H: 10"; 4¾" dia. (2) Iron, wood. With wooden base. L: 10"; W: 3¾"; H: 6". Probably English. (3) Iron. With knuckle guard. 10" x 3¼". (4) Steel. 8" x 3". Courtesy Keillor Collection.

SWAB — "Made of strips of linen tied to a stick, is useful to wash dishes, especially small, deep articles.... Some persons keep a deep and narrow vessel in which to wash knives with a swab, so that the careless servent cannot lay them in water." (*Beecher and Stowe, 1869.*) *See also* **CUP SWAB**

SWIZZLE STICK — A small branch of a pine tree with a number of shoots thrown out all around it. It was peeled of bark, the shoots trimmed to an inch or so, and the swizzle was used for mixing drinks and beating eggs by being rolled between the palms of the hands. *See also* **EGG BEATER**

Fig. 1058. PINE SHOOT SWIZZLE STICK.

SYENITE — One of the enameled wares — this one pink. Named from a pinkish, granite-like rock.

SYLABUB [*syllabub, syllibub*] **CHURN** — *see* **CREAM WHIP**

To Make very fine Syllabubs

Take a quart and half a pint of cream, a pint of rhenish, half a pint of sack, three lemons, and near a pound of double refined sugar; beat and sift the sugar, and put it to your cream; grate off the yellow of your three lemons, and put that in; squeeze the juice of the three lemons into your wine, and put that to your cream, then beat all together with a whisk just half an hour; then take it up all together with a spoon, and fill your glasses; it will keep good nine or ten days, and is best three or four days old; these are call'd *the everlasting Syllabubs.* [*E. Smith, 1753*]

Fig. 1059. SYLLABUB CHURN. Tin. F. A. Walker, c. 1870s.

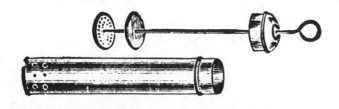

Fig. 1060. SYLLABUB CHURN. Pieced tin. 8" x 1¾"; 10" x 2". Matthai-Ingram Company, c. 1890.

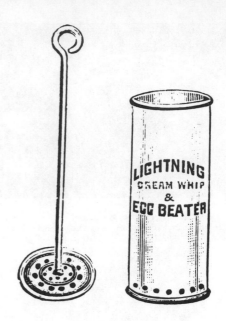

Fig. 1061. LIGHTNING EGG BEATER. Pieced tin. "The white of an egg can be beaten in one minute to a froth stiff enough to cut with a knife. It will enable one to make Mayonnaise dressing successfully. It is a success as a cream whip. The 'Lightning' is a simple contrivance — durable and easy to clean, but surprisingly in its results." Matthai-Ingram Company, c. 1890.

TAMIS [*tammy, tamis-bolter*] — A fine strainer or sieve of cloth, for straining soups or sauces. The name comes from the material *tammy* — a fine woolen cloth.

TAPERING STRAINER — A cone-shaped, perforated tin or wire-mesh strainer which could strain much more than a flat-bottomed strainer. Some were meant to be used with a long, tapering wooden pestle, the tip of which was put in the bottom of the strainer and which was rolled around the inside, pushing the food through.

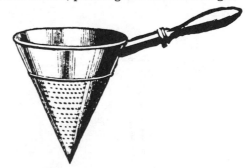

Fig. 1062. STRAINER. F. A. Walker, c. 1870s.

TEA BALL — *see* **RICE BALL**, but also a smaller ball, used for steeping tea.

TEA CADDY — A container for tea leaves, often just a japanned tin canister. *See also* **CADDY**

Tea

After the use of tea the mind is clear, the

206

imagination active, the senses alert, and the disposition to exert oneself increased.... [*Treasure House*, 1891]

Fig. 1063. TEA CADDY. Japanned tin. F. A. Walker, c. 1870s.

TEA KETTLE — A lidded kettle, copper with the inside heavily tinned; or tin with a copper bottom; or tin, copper and brass; or iron; or aluminum; or enameled ware. It was for boiling water for tea. Usually broad bottomed, with a short pouring spout, and either a simple bail handle or a very handsome handle with some sort of insulated grip. "If you use a copper tea-kettle, keep an old dish with sour milk and a cloth in it, wash the kettle with this every morning, afterward washing it off with clear water, and it will always look bright and new." (*Practical Housekeeping*, 1884.)

Fig. 1064. OIL STOVE TEA KETTLE. Stamped tin. 8½" dia. 3 quarts. Matthai-Ingram Company, c. 1890.

Fig. 1065. TEA KETTLE, with pit bottom. Galvanized cast iron. Alaska handle. For stoves Nos. 6, 7, 8, 9. Matthai-Ingram Company, c. 1890.

Fig. 1066. TEA KETTLE. Pat'd Sept. 9, 1913. Cast aluminum, wood. Dia. 8½". 4 quart size. Griswold, "Colonial Design, Safety Fill," Erie, Pa.

Fig. 1067. TEA KETTLE. c. 1910. Cast aluminum, wood. Dia. 10". Wagner Mfg. Co., Sidney, Ohio.

Fig. 1068. TEA KETTLE. c. 1903 to 1920. Cast aluminum, iron wire. Dia. 9". Wear-Ever, T.A.C.U. Co., All Courtesy of Paul Persoff.

Fig. 1069. TEA KETTLE. 1903 to 1915. Cast aluminum, wire. Dia. 8¼". No. 330, Wear-Ever, T.A.C.U. Co., (The Aluminum Cooking Utensil Co., was the selling organization created by the Pittsburg Reduction Company. The tradename "Wear-Ever" came in in 1903). Courtesy Paul Persoff.

TEA KETTLE BOILER or STEAMER — "A long tapering tin dish, with a long handle, large enough to fill the opening and long enough to reach down within half an inch of the bottom. It may have a cover of its own, or the cover of the tea-kettle may be used. It can be made by any tinner at a small cost, and is just the thing for cooking gruels, custards, etc., and serves as a steamer for puddings, brown bread, etc., for a small family." (*Practical Housekeeping*, 1884.)

TEA MAKER — A covered perforated spoon, or a tea ball, to be filled with tea leaves and suspended in the tea pot or cup to steep.

TEA POT — A spouted, lidded vessel, of tin, brass, silver, earthenware, china, pottery, etc., for brewing and serving tea. *Not* a kettle; and easily distinguishable as the spout is long and gracefully curved, and the base is small and often footed.

Fig. 1070. "BELLE" TEA POT. Agate enameled ware. 1, 2, 3, 4, 5 qts. Lalance & Grosjean, 1890.

Fig. 1071. TEA POT with tea ball. c. 1920. Aluminum, wood. H: 7¼"; W: 8½". Merit. American. Courtesy Melvin Adelglass.

TEA STEEPER — A tin or enameled ware cup with a lid, a handle and a spout. Also called a baby's food cup.

TEA STRAINER — A small, fine-meshed spoon, cup, or bowl — some of which had a handle and hooks for resting on the edge of the tea cup. Some were much smaller and had a spring clip which fit securely into the spout of the tea pot, straining the leaves out as the tea was poured. *"New Plunk;"* etc.

Fig. 1072. TEA STRAINER & DRIP. Aluminum. L: 6½". Goldberg, Bowen & Lebenbaum's Monthly Price Current, June 1895.

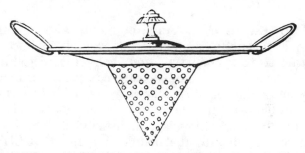

Fig. 1073. TEA EXTRACTOR. Planished tin. F. A. Walker, c. 1870s.

TELLAR [*teller, tiller*] KNIFE — A tellar or tiller knife is so-called from its handle which was shaped like the tiller of a boat; that is, it bent upwards and then parallel to the blade. As it allowed the fingers to fit between it and the table, while the blade remained against the surface, it was ideal for scraping dough or other sticky matter from the wooden table or dough board. It was also used as a *crumb knife* to remove crumbs from the tablecloth. "Don't use good knives for scraping the table. A teller knife costs 10 cents and will answer the purpose." (*Ladies Home Journal*, January 1902.)

TERNE-PLATE — Iron coated with a mixture of tin and lead; in point of fact — pewter-plated iron. *Terne* is French for *dull*. Terne-plate was used for lining packing cases. *See also* TIN

THIBBLE — *see* PEEL

TIDY RACK — A little wire or embossed metal rack used to hold a comb, a hand towel, and matches. It usually had a small mirror — diamond-shaped or round — set in it. It was nice for the cook to see if she looked tidy, but not nice for her hair to be combed into the stock pot.

Fig. 1074. TIDY RACK. c. 1895. Stamped tin with oriental motifs, mirror. L: 7"; W: 6¾". American. Author's Collection.

TIMBALE IRON — An iron mold, with a long crooked handle, dipped (while very hot) into a batter to form a coating, and then returned to hot fat to brown. It formed a pastry cup for timbales — creamed chicken, fish, cheese — or for fruit tarts. The mold came in a variety of forms — stars, flutes, round — and they could usually be screwed interchangeably to the handle. *See also* **BOUCHE IRON, DARIOLE MOLD, FRITTER BAKER, PATTY IRON**

TIN — The lightest and most fusible of metals, and employed as a coating for iron, brass, or copper cooking utensils as a protection against the poison verdigris, or the rust or scaling of iron. When used to plate iron, it was simply referred to as *tin*. Tin plating was done before 1620 in Europe, and the secret was taken to England and Wales in the late 17th century, and was employed in the manufacture of household utensils.

In America, Shem Drowne was the first tinsmith, although he had worked in sheet copper — making weathervanes — long before doing his first tin work in about 1720. Edward and William Pattison (sometimes *Patterson*) of Berlin, Connecticut, were the first tinware manufacturers in America. They worked from about 1740 to 1830, and Edward taught the art to so many that by the beginning of the 19th century, most of the households in Berlin had at least one practicing tinsmith! Edward would make up as large a quantity of tin goods as he could carry on his horse, in two huge baskets, and set off to peddle it around the New England countryside. After 1800 there was so much tinware being made that the market was, and had to be, expanded by a complicated system of salesmen and temporary smithies north into Canada, and down South. Tinsmiths and tinkers were finally replaced by the large manufacturers and wholesale and mail order houses.

Timothy Dwight wrote in 1823, after travelling around New England,

> For many years after tinned plates were manufactured in this place [Berlin] into culinary vessels, the only method used by the pedlars for conveying them to distant towns for sale, was by means of a horse, and two baskets balanced on his back. After the war, carts and waggons were used for this purpose, and have, from that time to present, been the only means of conveyance....
>
> The manner in which this ware is disposed of puts to flight all calculation. A young man is furnished by the proprietor with a horse, and a cart covered with a box, containing as many tin vessels as the horse can conveniently draw. This vehicle has been frequently exchanged for a waggon, and then the load is doubled. This prepared, he sets out on an expedition for the winter. A multitude of these young men direct themselves to the Southern states,... until he reaches Richmond, Newbern, Charleston or Savannah. ...Here he finds workmen sent forward to make as many pieces as he could sell during the season. At the end of spring, the pedlar sells cart and horse and heads back to New York and thence to New Haven. [*Dwight,* 1823]

The art of the tinsmith was one of pattern-making, edge-rolling, and soldering. His wares were used by everyone, and even when imperfect they were often more highly prized than heavy cast iron, which was not very portable. "The Dutch or Irish emigrant far away in his tent on the boundless prairies of the West, the boatman barging down his cotton over the bosom of the Mississippi, the Father of Waters, the rough miners of Nevada fighting with nature to extract the virgin silver from the heart of the Rocky Mountains, all require tin-ware in its rudest form, a tea-pot, a kettle, a pannikin, a wash-bowl, and requiring them are well aware that they will find them ready when desired at the nearest country store.... There is no doubt that the immense modern increase in the manufacturing and consumption of tin plates has resulted from the rapid increase in population." (*Flower,* 1880.) [In 1880, the population of the United States was 50,155,783 people, including over 62,000 Nevadans — some of them no doubt miners!]

The pieced-together tin ware from the early 19th century has an entirely different look from the later stamped work. Again, Flower writes: "We must not fail to call attention to the stamping factories and 'stamped ware' of [the United States].... Formerly the conversion of tin plates for domestic purposes might be almost called the 'gipsie's' trade — pots and kettles, made of the worst material, put together by idle worthless men, were hawked about, ... from village to village, and from door to door; and to call an honest man a 'tinker' was to use a term of reproach. Now, in all the large cities of the U.S., may be seen handsomely constructed factories of 3 or 4 stories, fitted with steam and hydraulic power, where by means of stamps which fall, or of presses which work by upward pressure, they convert circles varying from 14" to 26" into pans and wash bowls of every conceivable size and shape, made without seam from top to bottom and which are far superior to the old-fashioned, soldered up article as an express train is to the old stage coach...." (*ibid.*)

That is the view from the steaming heights of Industrialization. Even now, however, you will find that those "soldered up" wares have more charm than the stamped goods from the 1880s, and that the stamped wares have more appeal than the ones which came later.

"There are some householders who have tin ware left over from the past. To those we say, don't let it worry you; as they die out replace them with better, if you care to, but be loyal to what you have used if they have served." (*Peyser*, 1922.)
See also CAN, FRACTURES, JAPANNED WARE, WHITE METAL, X

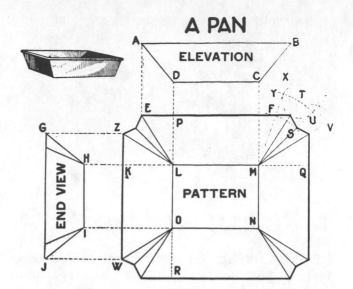

Fig. 1076. SHEET METAL PATTERN for a baking pan. Audels Plumbers & Steam Fitters Guide No. 4; Frank D. Graham. New York: Theo. Audel & Co., 1926.

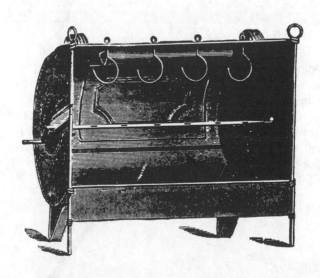

Fig. 1077. SOLDERING SET. A. E. Rayment Supply Co., Rockford, Illinois, c. 1910.

TIN KITCHEN — A tin reflecting oven, the open front of which faced the fire. The back was provided with a large hinged door for reaching and tending the food while it roasted. The oven was most usually a large cylinder set sideways, with four little legs. It varied in size from about 24" wide and high, up to 36" or 40" wide and high. *See also* REFLECTING OVEN, SALISBURY PORTABLE KITCHEN

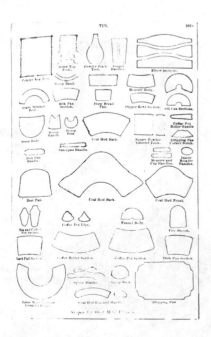

Fig. 1075. TINSMITHS' PATTERNS. Treasure House, 1891.

Fig. 1078. TIN KITCHEN. F. A. Walker, c. 1870s.

Fig. 1079. TIN KITCHEN. 19th century. Tin, iron. L: 23½"; W: 11½"; H: 17". American. Courtesy Keillor Collection.

TIPPING COPPER — A soldering iron, with a large, wedge-shaped copper head, and a heavy wire handle, used to melt and place a small bead of solder to the hole in the lid of a can after the lid was soldered on. *See also* **CAN**

Fig. 1080. TIPPING COPPER or soldering iron.

TOASTER — A hinged wire frame for holding slices of bread for toasting over the fire. Or a rack for holding bread for toasting over a range or stove. Or an appliance with electrically heated elements.

Older toasters, from the 18th century, were either a long-handled, two-pronged fork, or a wrought-iron rack with a long handle and two little legs for sitting on the hearth. Some of these latter had pivoting handles so that the toast could be turned without removing it from the toaster. Similar toasters, from the late 19th century, were either long-handled forks, or hinged, long-handled heavy wire implements which held the bread in a sort of Maltese cross or three-leaf clover frame. When the bread was toasted, the marks of the toaster left a pretty, light design.

Another sort of toaster was a metal and wire rack which held the toast upright over the burners of a gas stove. These are still sold by camp-stove manufacturers.

Finally, "a sheet of fine wire placed over the flames of a wood fire, a spirit lamp, or an oil stove will enable one to toast bread or crackers." (*Ladies Home Journal*, May 1899.) *See also* **BROILER, GAS TOASTER**

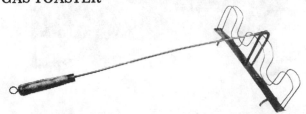

Fig. 1081. PIVOTING TOASTER. c. 1830. Wrought iron, iron wire, wood. L: 31"; W: 13¾". American. Courtesy Keillor Collection.

Fig. 1082. ROTARY TOASTER. 18th century. Wrought iron. L: 19"; W: 15½"; H: 6". American. Courtesy Keillor Collection.

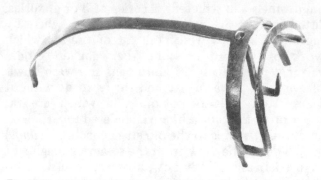

Fig. 1083. TOASTER. 18th century. Wrought iron. L: 12½"; W: 5"; H: 4". English. Courtesy Keillor Collection.

Fig. 1084. TOASTER. Late-19th century. Wire, wood. L: 16½"; W: 4¾". American. Courtesy Keillor Collection.

Fig. 1085. TOASTER. c. 1910. Wire, wood. L: 19"; W: 5-1/8". American. Courtesy Carmile S. Zaino.

Fig. 1086. TOASTER. Treasure House, 1891.

Fig. 1087. KRISPY BREAD TOASTER. Polished steel, coppered wire bread rest. 10½" dia. Androck, 1936.

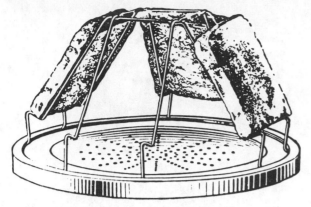

Fig. 1088. WORCESTER TOASTER. Tin, wire. 8-7/8" dia. Androck, 1936.

Fig. 1089. ELECTRIC TOASTER. Chromium plate. 11½" reflector. The Berdan Company, 1931.

Fig. 1090. TOAST RACK. Wire. "In a large family two will be required, as the delicious quality of the toast prepared in this way creates a demand for it." Practical Housekeeping, 1881.

TOAST FORK — A long-handled fork for toasting a single bread slice before the fire. Some were telescoping, and extended from about 12" to nearly 20". These are often brass and steel. A toast fork is very much like a flesh fork, except that it tends to be longer and the tines shorter.

Fig. 1091. TOAST FORK. F. A. Walker, c. 1870s.

Fig. 1092. TOAST FORK. F. A. Walker, c. 1870s.

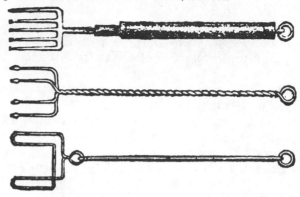

Fig. 1093. TOASTING FORKS. Treasure House, 1891.

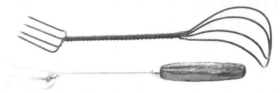

Fig. 1094. TOASTING FORKS. c. 1940. (Bottom) Stainless steel, wood. L: 12". A & J. (Top) Iron wire. L: 12½". One end is a potato scoop. Author's Collection.

TOOL STEEL — A high-carbon alloy steel, very hard, and capable of being tempered. Tool steel was used for many kitchen implements including can openers, choppers, and knives.

TRAMMEL [*tramel*] — A pawl and rachet, or saw-toothed iron bar with a adjustable hook which could be secured around any one of the teeth, or a tooth which could be placed in any one of the holes, in order to suspend a cooking vessel at the desired distance from the fire. The trammel itself was suspended from the pot crane.

Trammels are usually found in wrought iron, but there are some in steel, or brass. *See also* CRANE, LUG POLE EXTENSION, POT HANGER

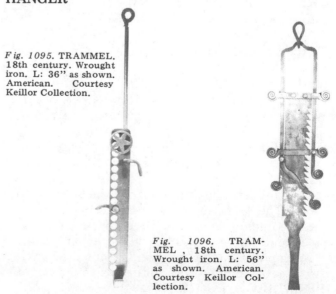

Fig. 1095. TRAMMEL. 18th century. Wrought iron. L: 36" as shown. American. Courtesy Keillor Collection.

Fig. 1096. TRAMMEL, 18th century. Wrought iron. L: 56" as shown. American. Courtesy Keillor Collection.

TRAMMEL CHAIN — A heavy iron chain, hung from lug pole or crane, which — with a pot hook — served for raising or lowering the pot hanging from it.

TREEN — Articles made of wood. *Treenware* is used to refer to such things as trenchers, beetles, wooden mortars, etc. *See also* **WOODENWARE**

TRENCHER — Originally a wooden vessel for serving or eating from, depending on its size. It was rectangular, round, or square, and at its most primitive was simply a plank slightly hollowed or dished out. A trencher could also be made of metal or earthenware. In the 14th and 15th centuries, or even later, it could be nothing but a thick slab of bread upon which food was ladled. *See also* **SIPPET**

Fig. 1098. TRIVETS. 19th century. (1, 2, 4) Wrought iron. (3) Brass, wood. (1) 5" x 4½". (2) 9½" x 4½". (3) 10¾" x 4¼". (4) 5" x 5" x 5". American. Courtesy Keillor Collection.

Fig. 1097. TRENCHER. Wood. 6¼" x 15½". JUG. Salt glaze. H: 3½". Albany (?). TWO-TINED FORKS. Steel, bone. L: 7½". SPOON. Horn. L: 9". DRINKING CUP. Horn. H: 3½". All 18th century. American. Courtesy Keillor Collection.

TRENCHER KNIFE — A knife for cutting bread into trenchers.

TRIPOLI — A fine earth, usually red-brown, used as a polishing powder. It is decomposed siliceous matter and was also called *rottenstone* and *goldsmith's earth*. Tripoli is from Africa. *See also* **WHITING**

TRIVET [*trevit*] — A three or four-legged metal stand of wire, wrought or cast iron, brass, steel or other metal, in any number of sizes and shapes for supporting hot cooking vessels on the hearth or the table. The larger ones were for the hearth. The most common small and large trivets are iron or steel and have a handle: either a long, usually wooden, straight handle sticking out the back; or two ear handles on either side. *See also* **BRANDIRON, FOOTMAN**

Fig. 1099. TRIVET. Dated 1821. Wrought iron. 15" sides; H: 13". English. Courtesy Keillor Collection.

Fig. 1100. TRIVET, with booted feet. Early-19th century. Wrought iron. L: 13", H: 2". American or French. Courtesy Keillor Collection.

Fig. 1101. TRIVET. 18th century. Wrought iron. 26½" x 16¾". English. Courtesy Keillor Collection.

Fig. 1102. TRIVET. 18th century. Wrought iron. L: 11"; W: 4½"; H: 1½". American. Courtesy Rita Keillor Collection.

TRUSSING NEEDLE — A large steel needle used for sewing up stuffed poultry.

TULANIA — A metal mentioned in several sources: an advertisement of 1797 reads "for sale....tin, iron and tulania table and tea spoons,..." and refers to the alloy of silver copper and lead called *tula* or *tula metal* — from Tula in Russia. Knight defined it as "the Russian mello- silver" in 1884. But he probably meant *niello* silver — a black alloy used to decorate other metals with an incised design. The incisions were filled with tula.

TUMBLER DRAINER — A shallow, rectangular tin or enameled ware pan with a perforated draining tray.

Fig. 1103. TUMBLER DRAINER. Oak grain & white painted tin. L: 14¼", 18½", 20½"; W: 10½", 13¼", 14¼". C. B. Porter Company, c. 1915.

TUMBLER TRAY — A wooden, tin, papier mache, or japanned tray with handles. It was used for carrying glass tumblers to and from the table. Some were divided by wires — rather like an old milk bottle carrier — which kept the tumblers from jostling and cracking each other. The tumbler tray is quite similar, although larger, to the knife and fork tray.

A tumbler is a drinking glass, without a foot. Originally it had a pointed or convex bottom which meant it could not be set down till empty!

TUNNEL — *see* FUNNEL

TUREEN — A deep, footed vessel with a lid, used for serving soups or sauces at the table, and made of tin, pottery, britannia, or pewter. "A very useful cooking utensil... a terrine... a finely glazed, fireproof dish, round or oval, always has a cover. May be used for slow cooking of meats or vegetables. May be put in the oven or on top of the range." (Parloa, *Ladies Home Journal*, May 1900.) The terrine was also used for serving on the table,

and was called a *tureen* or *terrine*. See also BRAISING PAN

Fig. 1104. TUREEN. c. 1870s. Tin, cast iron. L: 15½"; W: 9½"; H: 10". American. Courtesy Keillor Collection.[

Fig. 1105. SOUP TUREEN. Agate enameled ware. 6 qts. Lalance & Grosjean, 1890.

Fig. 1106. SOUP TUREEN, oval. Agate enameled ware, wood handle. 4 qts. Lalance & Grosjean, 1890.

TURNERIE [*turnery*] WARE — A woodenware utensil or part of a utensil made by a turner on a lathe. Many trenchers, bread boards, cups, bowls, chopping bowls, crock lids, and wooden handles are turnerie.

TWIRLER — A mixing implement with some sort of stationary agitator with a long handle. It was placed in a bowl or glass and the handle was twirled between the palms. *See also* **SWIZZLE STICK**

VEGETABLE BASKET — A wire basket used for draining vegetables after washing; or a larger basket meant for storing and gathering eggs or such vegetables as potatoes. *See also* **SALAD WASHER**

Fig. 1107. VEGETABLE BASKET. Wire. (Probably Dover Stamping Co.). F. A. Walker, c. 1870s.

VEGETABLE BIN — A tin stand or rack or cabinet, open to the air, for keeping vegetables which did not require refrigeration, such as potatoes, onions and carrots.

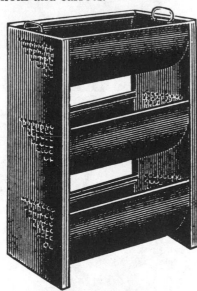

Fig. 1108. "FAVORITE" VEGETABLE BIN. Green, blue, ivory painted tin. H: 20-1/8"; W: 15"; D: 8". C. B. Porter Company, c. 1915.

Fig. 1109. VEGETABLE & FRUIT BIN. Green-painted tin, wire. H: 22"; L: 17"; W: 10". Androck, 1936.

VEGETABLE CHOPPER — One type was very like the nut chopper and had its own glass container, wooden disk in the bottom, and chopping blades. *See also* **CHOPPING KNIFE, MEAT CHOPPER, NUT CHOPPER**

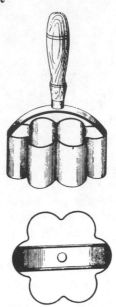

Fig. 1110. VEGETABLE CHOPPER. Pat'd 1901, Design No. 33,983. Laura Bavry, Chicago, Ill. Official Gazette, Jan. 29, 1901.

VEGETABLE CUTTER — A cutting blade or knife for making fancy slices or shapes from raw vegetables. Some were for cutting corrugated slices or julien strips; others resembled fancy paste cutters, and cut intricate shapes from thin slices of raw vegetable — stars, flowers, cloverleaves.

Garnishing

The art of garnishing dishes is the art of ornamenting them, and making them look elegant, and thus satisfying the eye as well as the palate. Various materials are used for this purpose. Among the most popular are cocks' combs, plovers, and hens' eggs boiled hard, prawns and small crayfish, button mushrooms glazed, stamped pieces of vegetables, such as carrot, turnip, parsnip, beet root, and truffles, stoned olives, gherkins, fried croutons of bread, aspic jelly, horse radish, cut lemon and parsley. Everything depends on the artistic arrangement of the ornamentation, determined by the taste of the garnisher. Where the taste has been cultivated, or where there is a natural faculty for decoration, the task of garnishing effectively is an easy one. ...Whipped cream is a delicate garnish for all Bavarian creams, blanc manges, frozen puddings and ice creams. [*Treasure House*, 1891]

Fig. 1111. VEGETABLE CUTTER. c. 1880. Wood, tin. L: 9"; W: 4¼". American. Courtesy Keillor Collection.

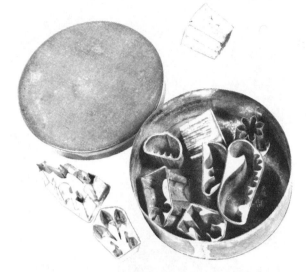

Fig. 1112. VEGETABLE CUTTERS, for garnishes. 10 pieces in can. c. 1870s. Tin. CAN: 4½" dia. J. Y. Watkins, New York. Courtesy Keillor Collection.

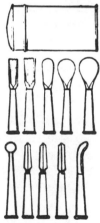

Fig. 1113. VEGETABLE CUTTERS. Tin. F. A. Walker, c. 1870s.

Fig. 1114. VEGETABLE CUTTER. Tin. F. A. Walker, c. 1870s.

Fig. 1115. BOX OF VEGETABLE CUTTERS, CORERS. Tin. F. A. Walker, c. 1870s.

Fig. 1116. VEGETABLE SLICER, table-mounted. Universal Household Helps, Landers, Frary, Clark, c. 1920.

Fig. 1117. PARIS ROTARY SLICER. 1913. Steel. L: 4-7/8". Castello's. American. Author's Collection.

VEGETABLE DIVIDER — "Two pieces of upright steel crossed. Placed on a platter, each of the four sections may be filled with a different vegetable, and then the divider removed." (*Woman's Home Companion*, April 1900.) It is quite probable that the cross-bladed fruit or *apple sectioner* might also be called a vegetable divider.

VEGETABLE LADLE — A wirework, long-handled ladle for serving vegetables from the pot, or for taking fritters or other frying food from the hot fat. *See also* MIXING SPOON, SKIMMER

VEGETABLE SLICER — *see* CABBAGE CUTTER, POTATO SLICER, VEGETABLE CUTTER

VEGETABLE SPOON — *see* MIXING SPOON, SKIMMER

VEGETABLE TONGS — Long-handled, curved-tined tongs for taking vegetables out of oven or kettle, or turning meats in the oven or steaks on the grill. *See also* **ASPARAGUS TONGS**

VERDIGRIS — The poisonous natural acetate of copper which occurs when copper is affected by certain acids. When highly acid foods or liquids come into contact with a copper cooking utensil either improperly or poorly coated with tin, and if the copper is not highly and recently polished if untinned, verdigris is formed. Copper kettles or utensils should be frequently and regularly retinned.

VIENNA CAKE or WAFFLE MOLD — A spiral coiled metal implement with a handle, used similarly to a timbale or bouche iron for making vienna cakes in hot lard.

Fig. 1118. VIENNA CAKE MOLD. F. A. Walker, C. 1875.

VIENNA CAKES — The batter is made from flour and milk, and of the ordinary thickness for making pan-cakes. To each quart of batter add four eggs, one TBS of sugar and a little salt.

The Mold is placed in the lard or butter, and remains until the lard is hot enough to commence frying the cakes . . . much higher temperature than for frying doughnuts. . . . Take hold of the handle and dip the coiled part halfway or more into the batter; lift from the batter, a sufficient amount of batter remains in the coiled part to make the cake, then place in the hot lard. . . . In a few seconds, remove the mold and hold over a proper receptacle. A slight rap on top of the coiled part will cause the cake to drop from the coil. Repeat until the frying has been completed. The cakes may be frosted if preferred. A little sugar and cinnamon sifted or sprinkled over the cakes will be found to improve and render them more palatable.

WAFER IRON — A cast or wrought-iron utensil with long handles called *reins*, and a hinged head with a design cast in it. The wafer iron is smaller than the waffle iron. It is usually round, but there are square, rectangular, and heart-shaped irons. The head, or mold, has a variety of motifs including religious, geometric, floral and patriotic. The rarest are the patriotic eagles and mottoes.

Wafers are eccliastical in origin, and the earliest irons are small and round.

Sweet Wafers

One pint flour, one tea-cup sugar, three eggs, one tablespoon butter, flavor with lemon, mix into a batter same as for cake, and bake in wafer-irons. [*Practical Housekeeping*, 1884]

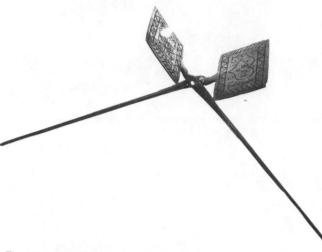

Fig. 1119. WAFER IRON. Dated 1787. Iron. L: 31½"; 5" x 8" wafer. "S. M. / ID ED." American. Courtesy Keillor Collection.

Fig. 1120. WAFER IRON, eagles & 13 stars. c. 1800. Iron. L: 27½", 5¼" dia. American. Courtesy Keillor Collection.

WAFFLE IRON — A cast-iron implement for baking waffles. The older ones, from the 17th and 18th centuries, had reins and a hinged waffle-mold head which was round, square, oblong, or heart-shaped. The waffle iron was cast with a grid, usually formed of small squares, but sometimes with small hearts, rounds or diamonds. The waffle iron, like the wafer iron, was rested on the grate or gridiron over hot coals in the fireplace.

Later irons, made for the range or stove top, had two parts: a heavy rim with a handle, and the hinged waffle iron itself, usually about 8" in diameter, which set into the rim. The iron was turned over for baking both sides of the waffle.

Even later, by the late 19th century, many waffle irons were oblong and were designed to make four, slightly rectangular waffles. The design of the grid has remained unchanged from the beginning, and maybe because there's nothing like the little indentations for holding melted butter and syrup.

218

Electric waffle irons from the early 1920s and 1930s are usually nickel-plated or chromium-plated and have elaborate filagree pedestals.

Rice Waffles

Boil half a pint of rice and let it get cold, mix with it one-fourth pound butter and a little salt. Sift in it one and a half pints flour, beat five eggs separately, stir the yolks together with one quart milk, add whites beaten to a stiff froth, beat hard, and bake at once in waffle-irons. [Mrs. S.C. Lee, Baltimore, in *Practical Housekeeping*, 1884.]

"The waffle iron is a very peculiar machine. The waffle is put in, locked up, baked on one side to a lovely brown, turned over, prison and all, until the other side is a still lovelier brown, and then released steaming hot ready for the table." (*ibid.*) "*Griswold;*" "*Orr Painter & Co.;*" "*John Savery & Sons, NYC;*" "*Landers, Frary & Clark;*" etc.

Fig. 1124. WAFFLE IRON. Early-19th century. Cast & wrought iron. L: 21½"; W: 5¼". Heart-shaped waffles. American. Courtesy Keillor Collection.

Fig. 1125. RANGE WAFFLE IRON. c. 1870s to 1890s. Cast iron. 8" dia. waffle; L: 18½". American. Courtesy Keillor Collection.

Fig. 1121. WAFFLE IRON. c. 1870. Cast iron. 11" dia. American. "Kartoffel waffeln" recipe on top: Potato waffles. ½ lb. cooked grated potatoes, ¼ lb. meal, ½ litre warm milk, 3 eggs, 50 grams butter, 20 grams yeast. Courtesy Keillor Collection.

Fig. 1126. WAFFLE IRON. c. 1870s. Cast iron. L: 15"; 6½" dia. waffle; 9½" dia. frame. American. Courtesy Keillor Collection.

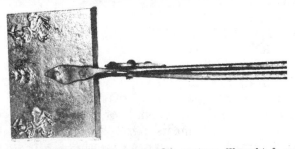

Fig. 1122. WAFFLE IRON detail. 18th century. Wrought & cast iron. L: 26"; 4¼" x 6" head. Depicts two Hessian soldiers on horseback, and a pine tree. American. Courtesy Keillor Collection.

Fig. 1123. WAFFLE IRON. 19th or late-18th century. Iron. L: 31"; W: 7". American. Courtesy Keillor Collection.

Fig. 1127. WAFFLE IRON. 19th century. Cast iron. L: 15"; W: 8" waffle. John Savery & Sons, N.Y. Courtesy Keillor Collection.

Fig. 1128. WAFFLE IRON. 19th century. Cast iron. L: 13"; 6¾" dia. waffle. Orr Painter & Co., 7 & 8, Reading, Pa. Courtesy Keillor Collection.

Fig. 1129. WAFFLE IRON. 8/9/1910? Cast iron. 8" dia.; L: 14". American. Courtesy Keillor Collection.

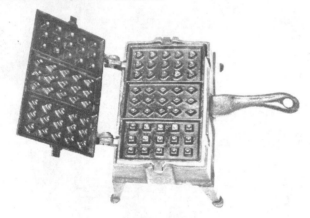

Fig. 1130. WAFFLE IRON. c. 1870s. Cast iron. L: 8"; W: 5"; H: 5". American. Courtesy Keillor Collection.

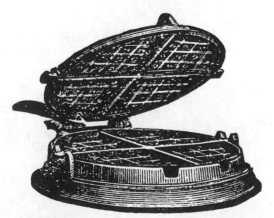

Fig. 1131. WAFFLE IRON. (Dover Stamping Co.). Practical Housekeeping, 1881.

Fig. 1132. WAFFLE IRON. Cast iron. 6" x 7", 7" x 8", 8" x 9", 9" x 10". Matthai-Ingram Company, c. 1890.

Fig. 1133. ELECTRIC WAFFLE IRON. Universal Household Helps, Landers, Frary, Clark, c. 1920.

Fig. 1134. ELECTRIC WAFFLE IRON. 1922-1923. General Electric Company.

WAITER — A tray for carrying.

WHETSTONE — A stone, natural or artificial, for sharpening and honing edge tools. *See also* **GRINDER**

WHIP CHURN — *see* **CREAM WHIP, SYLABUB CHURN**

WHISK — Several types of whisks have been used to beat eggs, and not all of them wire. A dried turkey wing; the stiff splints or twigs of the broom plant; even the fingers were used as a whisk. The most common type *was* wire — either a wire spoon, or the wood or metal-handled instrument with several bent wires. *See also* **EGG BEATER, WIRE WHISK**

Fig. 1135. EGG BEATER. F. A. Walker, c. 1870s.

Fig. 1136. WHISK. Wire, wood. F. A. Walker, c. 1870s.

WHITE METAL — A large family of alloys, composed chiefly of tin, antimony or lead. The family includes pewter, Babbitt metal, and britannia. It is a class entirely separate from yellow metals, or alloys in which copper is the primary constituent.

WIRE — Heavy iron wire has been used since Colonial times by the makers of kitchen utensils and implements. It was imported from England at first, and in America, wire was pulled for clockmakers before tinsmiths. Wire was used for handles, for supporting the rolled edges of tinware, for hooks, and for toasting implements.

WIRE DISH COVER — see **DISH COVER**

WIRE WHISK — A wire implement, made of a number of long wires bent like hairpins and set in a wooden or wrapped-wire handle. "The American has wooden handle, is light and not durable. The French has wire handle, is heavy, and wears well." (*Parloa*, 1887.) See also **EGG BEATER, WHISK**

WOODENWARE — Wooden utensils and implements such as sieve hoops, rolling pins, mashers and beetles, stir sticks, bread boards, butter and springerle molds, chopping bowls and trays, ladles, churns, pails, boxes, etc. The most commonly used wood was maple, as it was hard, dense, durable, and plentiful. Cedar, pine, hickory, ash, and oak were frequently used for cooper's ware. *Lignum vitae* was the hardest wood used, and was especially desirable for mortars and pestles. Burls, found on a number of trees, were hollowed and turned into beautiful bowls. The burl is a hard, woody growth, like a wart, and it occurs on walnuts, redwoods, myrtles, cherry, ash, birch, and maple trees, and the *arbor vitae*. As one walks around Colonial Williamsburg one can see many old, burled trees, and there are a number of burl bowls and ladles inside the restorations. *See also* **LIGNUM VITAE, TREEN**

X — Used, alone or in combination with other X-es, to designate quality in such things as tin, flour, and sugar. The more X-es, the more refined, and the higher the quality.

"Best tin has a smooth and rather dull-looking surface, and will stand great heat without becoming rough. Poor quality has a brighter surface. Most utensils should be made of XX tin; at least XXX, if not XXXX should be used for bread and cake pans when they are not made of sheet iron. Tin boxes need not be of this quality." (*Parloa*, 1887.)

YELLOW or LIVERPOOL WARE — A pottery which fires to a yellow color; a cream-ware; or with a yellow glaze. Used for mixing bowls, pitchers, nappies, etc., and for table ware. The first pottery imported to America was the cream-colored Liverpool ware. It was often transfer printed in black, red, brown or blue.

Yellow ware, as well as red ware, was also made in America — at first by hand, and then by machine — and was popular for dairy and culinary vessels, most familiarly mixing bowls. *See also* **QUEENSWARE**.

Fig. 1137. YELLOW & ROCKINGHAM WARE. Butler Brothers, 1899.

Fig. 1138. TOY RANGE. c. 1890. Pressed tin, brass, porcelain. L: 13"; W: 3"; H: 15". American. Courtesy Keillor Collection.

Fig. 1141. TOY STOVE. Tin, assorted colors. H: 7½"; W: 6½"; D: 4½". Imported. 2 ovens, 4 covered stew pans, covered tea kettle, 5 assorted dishes, long handled stew pan, 5 hangers [grater, dust pan, pie plate, bread pan, oval pan.] Butler Brothers, 1899.

Fig. 1139. TOY STOVE. Tin, assorted colors. H: 6½"; W: 5½"; D: 3¾". Imported. With 9 kitchen utensils - 3 covered stew pans, 3 miscellaneous dishes, handled stew pan, 3 hangers [grater, dust pan, pie plate] . BUTLER BROTHERS, 1899.

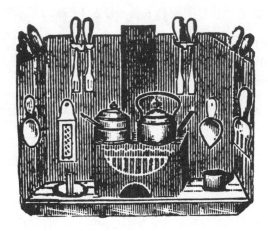

Fig. 1142. TOY KITCHEN. Embossed tin. L: 11"; H: 6½"; D: 2¼". Montgomery Ward, 1893.

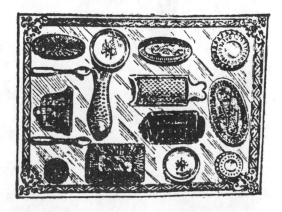

Fig. 1140. TOY KITCHEN SET. Painted & plain tin, on card. Card: 13¼" x 11". 15 articles. Imported. Butler Brothers, 1899.

Fig. 1143. TOY TIN KITCHEN SET. 19 tin utensils. Montgomery Ward, 1893.

Fig. 1144. TOY KITCHEN. c. 1880. Painted wood, metals. L: 30";
W: 17"; H: 15½". Quaker. Courtesy Keillor Collection.

Fig. 1147. MINIATURE FOOTMAN. c. 1830s, 1840s. Brass. L:
3½"; W: 2¾"; H: 3½". English (?). Courtesy Keillor Collection.

Fig. 1145. Detail TOY KITCHEN. Shows kettles, pie board, fry
pans, range, range kettles, cupboard, coal hod, knife & fork in
cupboard. c. 1880. Courtesy Keillor Collection.

Fig. 1148. MINIATURE CLOCK JACK. Early-19th century. Brass,
wood base. L: 3½"; W: 2¼"; H: 2½". Probably English. Courtesy
Keillor Collection.

Fig. 1146. TOY UTENSILS from kitchen. Figure   . Coffee grinder
(1" x 1" x 2½") slaw cutter (2½" x 1"), chopping knife, ramekin,
covered dish.

Fig. 1149. TOY EGG BEATERS. (Left) c. 1925. Tin, wood. L:
5½". Betty Taplin Beater. (Right) Pat'd Oct 9, 1923. Tin, wood.
Glass bowl missing. L: 5½". No. 68, A & J. Author's Collection.

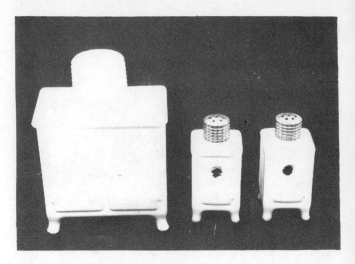

Fig. 1153. CONDIMENT & SUGAR SET. Late 1920s. White glass, white metal. H: 5"; H: 3-1/8". Made in the form of the General Electric "Monitor Top" refrigerators. Courtesy Melvin Adelglass. Even a kitchen clock was made in this form.

Fig. 1150. PAINT SALEMAN'S SAMPLE or DISPLAY PIECE. Early 1920s. Painted tin, painted cast iron. Galvanized tin repair. L: 12½"; W: 5"; H: 9½". Gas stove with opened door. Sapolin Paints, N.Y.C. Author's Collection.

Fig. 1154. HARD TIMES TOKEN. 1880s. Cast brass or bronze. 1" dia. Foster & Parry, Grand Rapids, Michigan. Converse reads: "Dealers in Stoves, Iron & Hardware. Wholesale & Retail." Author's Collection.

Fig. 1151.   TOY DISH DRAINER. C. 1910. Tinned wire. 6-1/8" x 3-5/8". (Fork for scale.) Loop Weld, Marlboro Wire Goods Co. Author's Collection.

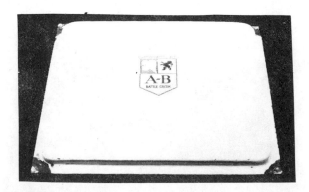

Fig. 1152. OVEN DOOR PANEL. c. 1920s. Enameled iron, white & colored. 10½" x 9½". Battle Creek Stove Co. Author's Collection.

Fig. 1155. ADVERTISING MIRROR. Early-20th century. Stamped tin. 1¾" dia. Garland Stoves and Ranges. Author's Collection.

Seek it Out: Where to Buy

For 't is a truth well known to most,
That whatsoever thing is lost,
We seek it, ere it come to light,
In every cranny but the right.

The Retired Cat.   William Cowper, 1731-1800

Now you have a good idea what there is to be collected. And this book covers only those things either manufactured or used in the United States. You may want to develop your collection along typical lines: that is, collecting all the stirrers, whisks and beaters you can find, no matter from what country or period. Or you may want to stay in a particular period, and even section of the country. For example, 18th century Virginia, or 19th century Pennsylvania, or West of the Rockies after 1849. You have other options. Collect just what you like. Collect just what you can afford, with a few extravagent treasures because you like them so much. Collect haphazardly and generally and not too selectively — and later you can weed out, and trade. Nothing that is collectible gets more plentiful. Instead it gets scarcer and more expensive.

You may be lucky enough to live in a section of the country, or able to visit, where there are lots of house auctions, garage sales, thrift stores, antique shops and shows, and flea markets. Some of these sources are available to us all. I started my collection with things purchased for five and ten cents at the Toledo St. Vincent de Paul's used goods stores, at the Goodwill, and the Salvation Army stores. These are still excellent sources, for not a day passes that someone doesn't hand over a box of junk to be sold for a charitable cause. You may have a hard time finding what you want. Often those boxes are a scramble of everything from butcher knives to battered aluminum saucepans. Take the time and the care to look through the whole box. Don't trust a top-layer riffle. You will find early-20th century kitchen gadgets in these stores; very few older things will end up there. While the gadgets were usually fairly well-made, they were also well-used, and moving parts are easily broken. The turn-of-the-century owner of a Dover egg beater might break it, and throw it away because she could replace it easily and inexpensively. You may not find her 1890 Dover, but the one she ordered from Montgomery Ward in 1905 might turn up in a box of kitchen junk.

Thrift stores are similar but smaller outlets for other people's throwaways. They may be private enterprises or charitable organizations. If you live in a fairly large town there may be several for you to visit. In New York there are well over a hundred thrift shops: paradise for the collector.

The secret to finding what you want is going regularly. Learn the technique each store has for storing and displaying its wares. One shop may always be good for a box in the corner; another may arrange their kitchen things on a shelf, just slightly and not very conveniently above eye level. Don't wear your best clothes. There is often a thick, black, gooey crust on old utensils.

One thrift shop here in New York recently featured a window display of old kitchen things. Their policy is to keep the window intact — the items unsold — until the Saturday which ends the week of display. Then it's first come, first served. A friend of mine and I were determined that I should get a particularly fine aluminum cake turner for this book. He arrived in blustery weather two and a quarter hours before the shop opened. I came second, an hour later. At ten after ten we walked out with our pick of the lot — a line of fifteen people behind us. Two of those fifteen had come to get the cake turner for their collections.

House auctions and auction houses are also good sources. These too should be attended regularly. Arrive early enough to inspect the lots. If there are lot numbers, write them down in a notebook, with a short description of the contents. All corrugated boxes look pretty much alike when you see them held up on the auctioneer's block. Try to co-operate with the man who wants to bid on the silver plate epergne which is in the same box as the cast-iron popover pan you want.

In 1884, the following advice appeared in *Appleton's Home Books*, Volume I:

> At auctions kitchen furniture is popularly supposed to go for a song.... These things are usually sold in lots and a person needing a waffle iron and muffin rings may find himself in possession of coal skuttles and dish pans.

Garage and basement sales are more good places to look. Watch the newspaper advertisements on Friday and Saturday. You may want to try the older neighborhoods first.

Church bazaars and rummage sales, and neighborhood street fairs will give you more opportunities to look for kitchen gadgets. You will find few, if any, 18th or early 19th century pieces. But the variety of the mass-produced wares is so great that you could never exhaust the possibilities.

Flea markets, particularly if they are well-established and large, will be the best and least expensive sources for most of the things you want to collect. It may take, as it has taken me, years to put together the kind of collection you want. It is a lot of fun to rummage along from stall to stall, picking up old kitchen utensils one after another. Often, thrown in among tools (which are collector's items themselves) are heavy cast-iron tools which turn out to be kitchen utensils. Talk to the people manning the tables: if they are old they may know something about the utensils from personal experience.

Last, but not the last resort (you may prefer to go first), are the antique shops and antique shows. Ten years ago it was an unusual antique shop that had any selection at all of 19th century kitchen gadgets. What was to be found was often not displayed at all, but pushed in bushel baskets under tables. Now attractive displays are made on pegboard or pine siding. The prices are higher than elsewhere, and it may suit you to buy only the very old or the very unusual in antique shops. Unfortunately, it is often in antique shops where old iron utensils have been painted black, and where steel has been wire-brushed and lacquered, and where wood handles have all been uniformly stained a rich reddish brown. The worst of all are the intentionally and artificially distressed surfaces — such as tin from the 1930s rusted and battered and sold as late 19th century. Buyer beware. Black paint and brown varnish can be laboriously removed, but the marks of the wire brush cannot. Tin, which was never meant to be scoured or left to rust, can hardly be saved from either. Good old tin has a rich glow like pewter. Newer tin often has patches of shiny plate. Some tin has been recently painted or decaled and is sometimes labeled "very old tole." It is not.

The antique show usually provides a selection of the best or most saleable from a large number of antique shops — often from several nearby states. Sometimes, much to your disappointment, you will hear from the dealer that she did not bring what you have asked for because it was too heavy to carry or it wouldn't sell.

Think of yourself as an archaeologist of sorts. You are collecting for your own pleasure or profit, but you are helping to preserve a large part of America's domestic history.

Keep It Up:
Use, Display and Care

"A little neglect may breed mischief." *Poor Richard's Almanac*, Benjamin Franklin 1706-1790

You may begin to wonder, as the collection piles up on table tops, in boxes, on shelves — what to do with everything? It isn't much satisfaction to know you've got a box full of egg beaters if they can't be displayed. As your collection grows, you will probably have to think in terms of rotating exhibitions, as museums do. Anything which hangs on a wall for a long time eventually becomes virtually invisible, and if you change from cake turners to egg beaters to graters every few months, you will be able to look at each thing with the same pleasure you had when you first found it.

Anything displayed in the kitchen will accumulate a layer of dusty grease. Every time you cook something in the frying pan, tiny particles of grease are propelled through the air and settle, inexorably, on the intricate blades and gears, and the polished surfaces of your collection.

Some things should never be displayed in the kitchen for this reason. Grease and dirt are hard on old japanned surfaces, for example — not much in themselves, but in their sudsy remedies. So put canisters and spice boxes on shelves in the living room. Anything which can be swished around in a pan of soapy water, or even water and ammonia, can be left to accumulate its layer of grease. This will happen very quickly. And unlike a layer of lubricating or protective oil — rubbed on the surface to protect it from rust — the grease is fairly hard and unpleasant. Nothing is quite so embarrassing as having an admiring friend reach for an attractive cake turner and find his hand covered with sticky goop. The situation is better for those who do not fry or broil. If you cook everything in a pressure cooker on a front burner, and you have an exhaust hood over the stove, you can put anything on display in your kitchen.

Some of the pieces in your collection will be very useful, and you may feel best about those things which can be kept in service after a hundred or more years. Most cooking utensils (seasoned if iron; tinned if copper; polished if brass; and scoured if aluminum) can be used with confidence. An old and well-cared-for cast-iron spider can't be replaced by anything, even, or especially, Teflon. Many of the old muffin and cake pans can be used. Do not try to scour them clean. Soak off any dried, crusty dough, but leave the browned surface. You will get better muffins and cakes, cooked more evenly because of the dark surface. Most of the old egg beaters are not suitable for use, but the *Aluminum Beauty* from 1920 is an excellent beater and easy to clean. Apple parers, chopping knives, meat grinders, coffee mills, toasting forks, parers and peelers, and many other gadgets and utensils are useful. But always consider that they must be washed and *dried* before they are put away.

Most of the things in your collection will not replace the more modern implements. But that does not mean they deserve to be lacquered, painted, varnished, or wired for electricity. It is not clever or "Early American" to make a floor lamp from a churn; to fill a copper kettle with stuffing, upholster the top in plastic leather, and make it an ottoman; to varnish a rolling pin, screw brass hooks into it, and make a key rack of it; or to fill the drawer of the coffee mill with a plastic flower arrangement. I do not want to labor the point, but I cannot think of a more lamentable homage to the fine design and appeal of old kitchen utensils.

As bad, or worse, is the practise of altering the surface finishes. This includes treating wood surfaces by staining, waxing with a stain wax, orange shellacking, heavily varnishing, heavily sanding, or painting — particularly in non-traditional colors; excessive sanding or wire-brushing of metal; painting with flat black enamel, or applying decals to any surface. I make exception for polishing and carefully lacquering brass pieces. But remember that you should re-lacquer every year or so. Painting a badly rusted piece of cast iron, after you have removed as much of the scale and rust as you can, is sometimes the only thing to do. But don't dip a rusted piece into a can of polyeurethane varnish to stop the rusting process. And don't spray-paint something with purple enamel because you like purple.

I will even advise that if you care about these old pieces, and have a curatorial respect for them, tell the dealers who stain, varnish and wirebrush everything into a glazed uniformity that you will not buy something which has been so treated, and that you do not like it.

Cleaning: Old and New Ways

ALUMINUM — An aluminum piece will usually need no more than rubbing with fine steel wool, or steel wool soap pads. If badly discolored, try boiling a solution of cream of tartar (two teaspoons to a quart of water) in the utensil, or cooking tomatoes or rhubarb in it. If it is a gadget, boil the gadget in such a solution. Scrape aluminum with a wooden spoon, flat stick, or rubber spatula to remove burned on food. Do not use strong alkaline, ammoniacal, or lye soaps or scouring powders on aluminum, as they will discolor it.

BRASS — Rub brass with powdered pumice and water on a cloth; or with a paste of rottenstone and sweet oil; or a solution of oxalic acid. The acid must be washed off, and the brass polished with whiting and a soft chamois. "A brass, bell-metal, or copper kettle should be cleaned immediately after it is used. Even when it is not used it will require occasional cleaning, otherwise it will collect tarnish or verdigris, which is a strong poison. After washing the kettle with warm water, put into it a teacupful of vinegar and a tablespoonful of salt; place it over the fire; when hot, rub the kettle thoroughly with a cloth, taking care that the salt and vinegar shall touch every part; then wash with warm water; next take some wood ashes or fine sand, and scour well; afterward wash with hot soap-suds, and finish by rinsing in cold water and wiping dry." (*Treasure House*, 1891.)

The new way, of course, is to use one of the commercially prepared liquid or cream brass cleaners. Use as directed on the container, but try it out on something small first. It may not give you the warm finish you want.

BRITANNIA — "To clean Brittania metal, use finely powdered whiting, sweet oil and yellow soap; mix with spirits of wine to a cream; rub on with a sponge; wipe off with a soft cloth and polish with a chamois skin." (*Treasure House*, 1891.)

Try using silver polish, put on heavily with a soft brush (use a face brush, not a fingernail brush or toothbrush), and while still wet, put on a thick lather of soft soap and rub the whole surface. Rinse in hot water, with water softener added, dry, and polish with a chamois.

COPPER — Clean the same way as you clean brass. Copper will be a bright pink after first being cleaned; don't worry, you haven't ruined it. Several old books recommend rubbing the copper kettle with room-temperature buttermilk, whey, or sour milk every day to keep it bright.

ENAMELED WARE — Boil peeled potatoes in it to remove stains. Soak off encrusted food and remove with a rubber scraper because heavy scouring will destroy the surface glaze.

IRON — Wrought iron resists rusting, but rust can be rubbed off with kerosene and scoured with steel wool. If necessary, let the kerosene soak on the rust stain until it is softened. "Stalks of *asphodel* [daffodil], dipped in *Colcothar* or *Crocus Martis* [red oxide of iron], reduced to a paste with sweet oil and properly applied to iron and brass utensils, proves a better preventative to rust than sandpaper or other rough materials." (*Willich*, 1821.)

Use scouring powder and steel wool to remove rust from cast iron, and if food is badly stuck on, soak or boil the utensil in a hot water and washing soda solution. If the utensil is to be stored or not used, for even a short time, coat it with unsalted fat or oil, or use a thin coating of paraffin.

To season a cast-iron utensil, so that it may be used, scour it clean, wash and dry thoroughly. Then apply a thick coating of salad oil to the inside, and set over a very low heat on the stove for two or three hours. Rub more oil or unsalted fat around every twenty minutes or so. Wipe the grease out, and wash in hot soapsuds; rinse and dry thoroughly. As the seasoning is a cumulative process, it must be repeated each time the utensil is used, for the first few weeks. *See also* **IRON** in the encyclopedic section.

JAPANNED WARE — "Wash it with a sponge dipped in clean cold water, wipe it dry and polish it with dry flour well rubbed on with a soft cloth." (*Treasure House*, 1891.)

Unfortunately, so much of the japanned ware from the turn of the century, which you will find, was of poor quality to begin with, and after fifty or seventy years of kicking around in kitchens and cupboards and boxes of "junk," it is not likely to be in good condition. If kitchen grease has been allowed to accumulate over a long period of time, it practically guarantees that you will lose some of the japanning when you try to clean it. Work carefully and slowly, and, of course, under no circumstances use any kind of scouring powder or action, nor any kind of solvent which will remove the grease and the japanning too.

PEWTER — Use the same technique as for britannia. Also: "The fashionable pewter, old and new, can be cleaned and kept bright by rubbing with a paste made of finely powdered wood ashes, salt and vinegar. If very black, apply oxalic acid with a woolen rag tied to a stick (do not let it touch the hands), then rub with whiting, first wet and then dry, to polish." (*Pictorial Review*, N.Y.C., May 1904.)

SPICE and COFFEE MILLS — Grind white rice through the mill. The *spiced* rice can be used as a thickener in cooking.

STEEL — Soften rust with petroleum, sweet oil, or one of the chemical brush-on rust removers, then rub with sandpaper, steel wool, or fine scouring powder depending on how badly rusted the metal is. Crocus cloth, or wet and dry paper works well too, for a next-to final polishing.

TIN — If badly rusted, there is nothing to do but scour or rub with steel wool. The rust is on the iron *under* the tin plating, and that is what you will be cleaning. Try to work as gently as you can: go slowly, and be careful.

"1. If tinware is well rubbed with lard and then with common unslacked lime, before being put away, it will never rust. This is also the best plan to remove rust. 2. Rub fresh lard over every part; then put it in an oven and heat it thoroughly; thus treated, any tinware may be used in water constantly, and remain bright and free from rust indefinitely." (*Treasure House*, 1891.)

"All kinds of tins, molds, measures, etc., may be cleaned by being well rubbed with a paste made of whiting and water; they should then be rubbed with a leather, and any dust remaining on them should be removed by means of a soft brush; finally, they must be polished with another leather. Always let the inside of any vessel be cleaned first, since in cleaning the inside the outside always becomes soiled.... Kerosene will make tin tea-kettles as bright as new. Saturate a woolen rag and rub with it.... Common soda is excellent for scouring tin, as it does not scratch the tin, and will make it look like new. Apply with a piece of moistened newspaper and polish with a dry piece." (*ibid.*)

WOOD — "For removing spots of grease,... take equal parts of fuller's earth and pearlash, ½ pound each, and boil in 1 quart of soft water; while hot, lay it on the wood," and leave it for twelve hours. (*Treasure House*, 1891.)

You can make your own supply of pearl-ash by burning some dried weeds and vegetable matter in a clean grate. The ashes are leached with water.

Some stains, if very light, and rough surfaces can be removed or smoothed with fine sandpaper.

ZINC — To remove tarnish, apply a solution of one part vinegar and twelve parts water, let stand a few minutes, and rinse. Dry thoroughly.

An Added Dimension: Related Collectibles

As an adjunct to your collection, you may find the appeal of related collectibles and antiques quite strong. The largest of these related fields is toys and miniatures. As long as children have played with toys, and played "house," they have used somthing to represent the gadgets and utensils, the stoves and work surfaces of the kitchen. Sometimes they had to use old worn out utensils, or sticks and cans, or boxes and boards. But miniature and toy kitchens, with all the furnishings, have been made for at least 150 years in this country. The early ones were handmade, by a father or uncle perhaps; the later ones were mass-produced. Sometimes salesman's samples fell into the hands of children, although it is unlikely that more than a few lucky children had them to play with. The sample stoves were well-made, working miniatures made on a scale of three inches to the foot. They could even be fed bits of wood or other fuel and demonstrated. Most miniatures, made for the delight of parlor-bound ladies, not the sometimes destructive play of children, were often finely made of brass and wood and other materials. They were table-top and mantle ornaments.

You may decide to collect pictures, prints and paintings of kitchens and kitchen utensils. This may include fine oils of interiors or still-lifes; engravings and woodcuts of the last two hundred years; or colorful and naive lithographed trade cards, advertising all sorts of merchandise, and given away by merchants to their customers in the 1880s and 1890s. Most of these are for enameled ware, and stoves or stove polishes. Related to these advertising cards are the advertising mirrors, receipt books, and medals with lithographed pictures of pots and pans, stoves, and groceries. Brass, copper, or aluminum tokens (sometimes called *hard times* tokens) and medals were struck to be given away by the retailers. Stove tokens are the most common among kitchen subjects, although you will find them for other implements and for groceries. Stamped tin mirrors were giveaways, as were stick pins and pin papers.

You may want to collect only the old trade catalogs, with their beautiful line-cuts and engraved pictures. A few of these are now available in reproduction, but there are many being cleared out of old desks and closets every week. It's a lucky thing that so many people, for so many years, have had the same trouble throwing things out that you and I have had! What is unfortunate is that there has been little systematic salvaging and collecting of these catalogs. Siegfried Giedion wrote in his Forword to *Mechanization Takes Command* (Oxford University Press, 1948), "an amazing historical blindness has prevented the preservation of important historical documents, of models, manufacturer's records, catalogues, advertising leaflets, and so on. Public opinion in general judges inventions and production exclusively from the point of view of their commercial success."

If you are interested in the huge, heavy ranges and cookstoves, but do not have room for them, there are limited possibilities for collecting stove parts — particularly the porcelain handles and drop-knobs, and the enameled plates set in the frames of oven doors. I have removed them from my only sources — stoves thrown out on the streets of New York. I would hesitate to recommend this archaeological travesty if it weren't true that these city discards would end up, within a few days, crushed and floating out on a garbage barge to a landfill site. I do not say buy beautiful stoves and ranges, mutilate them, and throw them away. Try to find a home for a stove today!

Other small collectibles, having little to do with actual cooking, can doubtless be found. All these things will give an historic dimension to a collection of gadgets and implements.

Appendix I
A Guide To Prices
"Revised 1978"

"For what is worth in anything,
But so much money as 't will bring?
    Hudibras, Samuel Butler 1600-1680

I am not, by any means, going to attempt to price each of the over 650 different things discussed in this book. A few of them are probably not available in any market or at any price. Some of the things lend themselves to group pricing: for example, most of the pots, pans, kettles and frying pans will fall into a certain price range according to age and material.

Any prices given here, in 1978, are naturally subject to argument. Prices change from month to month, year to year, and city to city. Demand may be very high for enamelled ware now, and will probably remain so. Other general categories such as brass and wrought iron utensils will probably go up in price unless a brisk reproduction business, which has got a good start now, destroys the market. The prices of some pieces may start to go down as it becomes apparent to dealer and collector that there is little charm or quality. Right now, kitchen gadgets and utensils hold a fascination for the collector because they have only recently come to be recognized as worthy of collecting.

Fads are involved in prices, and often are the trigger for reproduction. Don't buy too indiscriminantly. Look soberly at the prices and if a price seems too high to you, it probably is. Don't hand over three times the money you feel you should be paying.

Don't take my general price guides as Bible truth. You will soon learn to make your own mental price guide, or, if you feel more secure with it written down, write down the prices you see and pay and analyze them. It is a good idea to study the classifieds in such nationally distributed publications as *Antique Trader, Collector's Weekly,* and *Antique News.* Read *Antiques* and *Hobbies.*

Don't take every dealer's word for it that what he's selling is "real old," or "a genuine antique." Look at it, pick it up if you may, and study it.

I am not setting down the range of prices that you should have to pay, but rather what you may be asked to pay. It is up to you to decide how much you will pay. If you really like something, if your gut feeling is, "This is it!," you probably should buy it.

You know, of course, that prices will generally go up and you won't lose. Nothing which just keeps getting older gets less scarce and less dear at the same time. If you wait long enough, even an old shoe becomes an antique! Almost all of the pieces I include here are from the late 19th century and early 20th century. Generally it is true that the 18th and early-19th century utensils and implements are hand-wrought rarities which have been seriously collected for over seventy years, and are therefore expensive.

ADVERTISING TRADE CARDS & OTHER ITEMS — The cards will vary according to condition, ct, age, and particularly dealer. From 5 cents to $5.00. Other advertising items vary considerably in price, but tend to be more expensive than plain things. An egg separator with the name of a hardware store stamped in it will be twice as much as a plain one. Specific advertising items are especially expensive. Stove tokens go for between $3 and $15. Advertising mirrors bring $2 to $20.

ALUMINUM — Old aluminum should bring up to about $13 for a good cast pot or kettle. Other smaller gadgets and utensils will bring from 10 cents to $5. A month before this book was finished, I bought a very unusual aluminum spatula for 75 cents.

ANDIRONS — Depending on age and metal, andirons will bring between $25 and several hundreds of dollars. Brass andirons, rarely used in the kitchen, and desired now for living room fireplaces, will be more than $85 a pair, and closer to $350. Wrought-iron andirons from the 18th century will be difficult to find and very expensive. Most of what was available just a few years ago has been bought by collectors, museums or restoration projects.

APPLE PARERS — It is still possible to find old wooden apple parers for $10 to $15, but only with a great deal of luck. They have been recently advertised for as little as $35 and as much as $250. The fine, well-painted parers, and especially the bench types, will bring the most. The cast-iron parers are about $6 to $25, and several are still being manufactured.

APPLE ROASTERS — Like all the 18th century pieces, an apple roaster, or bird roaster, or any reflecting oven, will be expensive. It will bring upwards of $35 and more like $150 to $175.

APRONS — Lovely old aprons from the 1880s on can still be found in boxes at country auctions and in city thrift shops. Anything from 10 cents to $10.

ASBESTOS — Stove boards and mats are relatively unattractive to the collector seeking glamor, and you will find interesting pieces for under a dollar.

BAIN MARIES — A complete set, with what appear to be the original *bain marie* pans, would bring between $35 and $100. You would be lucky to spot a *bain marie*.

BAKING PANS — These are relatively undistinguished, and you will find most shallow pans, square or rectangular, for under a dollar.

BASKET SPITS — Spits, of the 18th and early 19th centuries, are very rare and hard to authenticate. But you could find one in a pile of old iron for a dollar, or hanging on a spit rack in an elegant shop for $35 to $100, or more.

BEATEN BISCUIT MACHINES — I have never seen one for sale — not to recognize it. But because of its mechanical intricacy, and its status as kitchen furniture, I would expect the prices to range from $25 to $75. Without the marble-top table, it is possible that you could find one at a flea market for as little as a dollar, especially if the dealer thinks it is part of a defunct washing machine.

BEETLES — An endless variety of all ages and woods and sizes. Expect real bargains for 5 cents up to $6 and others up to $15.

BISCUIT CUTTERS — Old biscuit cutters and doughnut cutters will bring up to $7 or $8 if handsome. A simple construction will be about $3. It is up to you to decide if it is truly old and if it is worth more than the 50 cents to $1.50 for the later cutters. Advertising will add $1 or so.

BOTTLE JACKS — Because of their rarity and attractiveness, these will bring between $20 and $250.

BOX GRATERS — Depending on patina and size, expect to pay between $3 and $18.

BRASS — Anything of brass is potentially attractive. It is usually easily polished, and the shop owner or dealer will take advantage of brass' innate beauty and elegance and charge you for it. "It's real brass," is heard a hundred times a day at flea markets and antique shows. Expect to pay for shininess, size, age, and intricacy. Anything from $1 to several hundred. Brass and copper are being imported from overseas and sold by the pound. If you look at it, you will see that most of it is obviously exotic stuff never used in the United States. Old brass is usually solid, and some newer things are plated. Take a magnet with you.

BREAD BOXES — Expect to pay from $1 to $25 if well-japanned and in good condition. Old advertising bread or cake boxes will bring a lot. The *Schepp's Cocoanut* box can bring as much as $50, although I bought one a few years ago for $3.50.

BREAD GRATERS — Large graters, such as bread graters, are sometimes expensive — $10 or $15 — and this is partly because of their size and their austere handsomeness. The material and age will also determine price.

BREAD KNIVES — There's quite a variety available, and as they were made very much alike in 1920, you can look forward to finding a lot of knives for very little money. Expect to pay from 10 cents to $5.

BREAD MIXERS — Often the mechanical devices bring more money just because they look so efficient. But a bread mixer, like other tin pieces, was often shoved to the back of the pantry, and thence to the barn or cellar where it rusted and was arrayed in cobwebs. You may find one for $3.50 to $20.

BREAD RAISERS — These are very pretty and graceful, and if lovingly polished and shining, you may pay up to $12 or $15. I found one recently for $2, dented and dull.

BREAD RASPS — You may find one in a tool chest with carpenter's rasps, and it will be priced according to the dealer's policy on old tools and *primitives*. Expect to pay from 50 cents to $10. Some of these are very old, and as a camoflage of rust and dust is often successful, there may be quite a number of bread rasps hiding across the country.

BROILERS — Depending on age and type, you can expect to pay from 50 cents and up for the self-basting broiler of the turn of the century, to $350 for a good wrought iron 18th century broiler that revolves.

BRUSHES — These are fun and attractive, but because of their nature they were discarded when they became worn down or dirty. Look for wire sink brushes, and these will be from 50 cents to $3.

BUTTER HANDS — In good condition, from $1 to $5 a pair.

CADDIES — Because these are still useful and often very ornamental, they may bring as much as $20 for japanning with an unusual design. The usual range is $2 to $15. Fine ones are very dear.

CAKE BOXES — $2.50 to $50, depending on decoration and condition. Even the rusty ones can be cleaned up, and you might not want to pass up a 50 cent cake box with a nice shape. *See also* **BREAD BOXES**

CAKE CUTTERS — The old ones are often as much as $12 or $15 if intricate or very unusual. Any patriotic design will bring even more. Very simple ones from the early 1900s are usually about $1.50. The rolling cake or biscuit or doughnut cutters may bring as much as $10, especially with any kind of advertising message. *See also* **BISCUIT CUTTERS**

CAKE PANS or **MOLDS** — These are quite decorative and sometimes the prices are too high. The same designs were made over a long period of time, and there are few apparent differences. Don't pay the $10 due an 1870 pan for a 1920 pan of similar design. Look at details of construction and manufacturers' names. You can expect to pay from 10 cents to $15, and much more for old earthenware cake pans and for molds such as the familiar lamb or chicken. Tubed or spouted cake pans will be about $3 or $4 more than the plain.

CAKE TURNERS — Here's one of the best collecting specialties. There is infinite variety, and cake turners and similar items are available from the 18th century to the present. Expect to pay $5 to $25 for the very old; and from 5 cents to $5 for the newer.

CANS — This is a separate collector's field. The most commonly found cans are those of baking powders, coffee, and tobacco. Expect to pay a lot for cans in good condition with colorful paper labels. Baking powder times, without labels, can still be found — dulled and spotted with rust — for under $1. Others between $2.50 and $35 and more.

CANDLEBOXES — These are usually sold as decorative accessories by dealers, and a fairly old one in good condition with its original paint might bring $35 or up. A recent ad for a candlebox from the 18th century asked for $195. They were made much the same for a hundred years.

CANDLESTICKS — Candlesticks are beloved by collectors and dealers alike. Nothing looks quite so nice as a table lit by candles. You will find that candlesticks are often priced too high. I have found a number under $25 and think that is a fair price for an ordinary seventy to one-hundred year old single stick. Hogscrapers bring about $8 to $50. Expect prices up to $250 for a single stick, almost solely depending on age, workmanship, material.

CANISTERS — Canisters are essentially what they've always been, and the prices are usually reasonable. If the japanning is quite unusual , or a nesting set is complete, old, and in fine condition, you may pay between $12 and $65. Otherwise, expect to pay between $1 and $7.

CAN OPENERS — Virtually thousands of brands and types to look for. Common prices between 5 cents and others up to $10.

CATALOGS — Old trade catalogs picturing kitchen utensils and gadgets are hard to find and expensive. Paper deteriorates, and many catalogs have literally been reduced to dust. Also, when the new catalogs were sent out, the note "Please discard all previous catalogues" was often prominent inside. Shudder to think of it! Expect to pay from $5 for a couple of pages or a flyer to $100 or more.

CHERRY STONERS — These bring between $5 and $25 and are usually in pretty good condition because of their original black enamel finish.

CHOPPING or MINCING KNIVES — These are available dating from the 1700s to the present. The early ones of wrought iron are quite expensive, and like all profitable antiques which can be reproduced, there is some danger of being fooled by skillful reproductions. Wrought iron and wood can be distressed well enough to fool the unwary. You will pay about $30 or more for old chopping knives; $5 to $15 for knives from the 1860s to 1880s; and up to $5 for newer ones.

CHOPPING BOWLS and TRAYS — Don't pay a lot for antique wooden primitives, unless you know exactly where the piece came from and who you are buying from. Chopping bowls have been made for 275 years in this country and you may find yourself paying an enormous price for a ten year old chopping bowl. Take a tour of a good housewares department in a department store. It will show you how many wooden items — bowl, boards, spoons, forks, spades, frets, pestles, etc. — are still being made and imported.

CHURNS — $5 to $50, although the small ones (for example the *Dazey* churn with its own glass jar) will bring pretty generally $7 to $18. An old wooden churn painted with buttermilk paint might bring from $35 to $75. A huge collection of churns would be just that: *huge*. And hard to house. If you have an empty barn, you may be able to get together a fabulous collection for little of nothing.

CLEAVERS — Old ones from $7 to $18 or $25. Newer ones, like the chopping knives, from $1 to $7.

CLOCKS — Clocks are sought by many collectors, and a lot of information is available. You should know something about the works if you are planning to pay more than $10. Under $10 you can afford to take the chance that the clock can be put in working order. Expect to pay between $25 and $350 for simple clocks appropriate for the kitchen.

CLOCK JACKS — Rare and expensive. Expect from $100 to $1000.

COAL HODS — This is one of the most popular import items of those wholesale firms specializing in importing "container loads" of antiques every week. The hods may be English, Dutch or German, and they will be found in shops all across the country. They may be old, but they weren't in America until the month before they appear in the shops. It would be a better idea to look for coal hods and scuttles at flea markets and junk stores. They may be dirty and encrusted with old ashes, and there may even be a clinker or two banging around inside. But you will more likely be getting a coal hod that was in this country during the 19th or early 20th century. Expect to pay from $2.50 to $25.

COFFEE MILLS — You may be shocked at the prices of these. After you look at quite a number you can spot unusual mills and expect to pay more for them. But common, wooden box mills with undistinguished metal parts, and an ugly coat of varnish should not be more than $8. Coffee mills, from Germany and France, are another popular import item. Expect to pay from $5 to $15 for a side mill, and from $5 to $65 for a box mill.

COFFEE POTS — These will range from 50 cents to $100, depending on the material. Certain graniteware pots bring high prices if perfect. Fine metals or interesting designs and handles bring higher prices. You will find many under $5 however.

COFFEE ROASTERS — Very hard to find and expensive. $15 to $65.

COLANDERS — These are sometimes irresistible. There's something about those holes...! Depending on age and material and condition, colanders will bring between 50 cents and $10. Look for old tin at $4 to $10; fine graniteware for $4 to $20; and aluminum for under $4.

COOKBOOKS — Books always seem to be priced arbitrarily — at least to the inexpert. And some book dealers think that any book printed before 1900 is rare and should therefore be expensive. You may find old cookbooks from the 19th century at a church bazaar for 10 cents, and at bookstores for $50 or more if really fine and unusual. Typical prices are between $4.50 and $12.

COPPER — Copper was often the base metal for all kinds of plating. Because polished copper is attractive and quite saleable, old pieces have often been stripped. *See also* **BRASS**

CORERS — You will find them from 5 cents to $5; but few, if any, corers are old enough, or unusual enough, to fairly bring more than $3.50. The exception is the mechanical corer, which would be priced higher than the mechanical parers because of their relative rarity. *See also* **APPLE PARERS**

CORK PRESSES — These are unusual and handsome, and will bring between $15 and $35 if the original paint is in good condition; or between $10 and $20 for the wooden ones if complete and old.

CORKSCREWS — Like the can openers, a collector's Elysian Field. Hundreds and hundreds of corkscrews are available, and are priced between 5 cents and $25 or more. Hope to find one of the old turned-wood-handled corkscrew with the brush intact.

CORN POPPERS — From $1 to $10; and a homemade one with charm could bring more.

CORRUGATED SPOONS — Like all the unusual cooking spoons, this one could be priced as high as $5. But try passing up the $5 one and look for something between 25 cents and $2.

CRANES — Hard to find if you are looking for anything distinguished. Also there are a number around that are not more than thirty years old. Don't pay a lot unless you know the provenance and the dealer.

CREAM WHIPS or SYLABUB CHURNS — These can be quite old, and in that case would be from $9 to $25. The complete range would be from $2.50 to $50.

CUCUMBER SLICERS — These will bring between $3 and $10, depending on age and patina.

CURFEWS — This is one of the very desirable fireplace accessories, made usually of brass, and sold now in fine shops. Expect to pay up to two or three hundred for a good old one. Hope to find one all dented and banged up for 50 cents in a pile of tire irons and kerosene cans.

CUTLET BATS — I would distrust any dealer who said unequivocally, "This is an antique cutlet bat." (Or *apple butter stick*, or *mush paddle*). Particularly if the price were more than $7. Buy wooden sticks if you like them, if the design is nice, if it looks genuinely used — not artfully distressed.

DANGLE SPITS — Like other very old fireplace equipment, these are hard to find and expensive. Be careful of recent imports — even if the piece itself is old. Of course you may not care whether a piece *was* used here in America, as long as it *could* have been.

DIPPERS — 5 cents to $15 or more: if handcarved and very unusual, or a quality metal.

DIGESTERS — I've never seen one for sale, and it is possible that they all blew up one by one. But if you can find an early patent date on one, or if you like the design, pay anything you want. You may have the first collection of digesters anywhere.

DINNER HORNS — If nicely japanned, and in good condition, expect to pay about $6 to $8. But 25 cents may get you one with dents or a loose flange.

DISH CLOTH HOLDERS — 15 cents to $3.

DISH COVERS — *Wire* ones are fun, because when they are stacked they make an interesting moire pattern. Pay from $1 to $6 for the round, or more if very large. The oval covers are more expensive. *Block tin* dish covers will vary from 25 cents to $2.50 depending on condition. If large or very old, with an interesting handle, expect up to $15.

DISH DRAINERS — I was delighted and surprised to find a beautiful, soap-bleached, wooden dish drainer for $1 at a recent flea market. I've also paid $7.50 for a perforated tin one. Expect from $1 to $10.

DOUBLE BOILERS — The older the more expensive. Look for complete ones with the two pans and one or two lids (depending on age and type), and expect to pay from $1 to $12. Enameled ware is more expensive than aluminum.

DOUGHNUT CUTTERS — *see* **BISCUIT CUTTERS**

DOUGH SCRAPERS — $3 to $15 depending on age and decoration — if any.

DREDGERS — 50 cents for simple tin to $15 for a good old japanned one. Much more if you find an early 19th century dredger in brass and/or pewter. Average price about $2.

DUTCH CROWNS — Another import item, and a popular decorator's piece. If old and unusual, expect to pay at least $100. If not old, don't buy it as an antique. Do get one for display.

DUTCH OVENS — If complete, and not rusted, from $3 to $20. You may find a cover here, a body there, and pay much less.

EGG BEATERS — This is one of the best kitchen utensils to collect. There is variety, infinite charm and personality. Look for prices between 50 cents and $20. The large *Dover* is about $10; the *Aluminum Beauty* is about $6 to $8; and the *A & J* with glass cup is about $3 to $10.

EGG CANDLERS — $1 to $10.

EGG CODDLERS — 50 cents to $15 depending on completeness and attractiveness.

EGG OPENERS — From $1 to $18. Some of the chicken scissors in a gold finish with black enameling are still made and sold in Europe, and in gift shops here. Don't buy a new one at antique prices.

EGG POACHERS — From $1.50 to $12.50 depending on condition, and the number of eggs it is possible to cook at one time.

EGG SEPARATORS — 5 cents to $5 depending on design and especially on the absence or presence of advertising mottoes.

EGG STANDS — 50 cents to $15 or more. If you are lucky enough to find one of the fabulous tree-like wire stands such as the *F. A. Walker* one, pay whatever you can — they are rare.

ELECTRICAL APPLIANCES — As a rule, old electric appliances are still very cheap. Because most people think of them as nothing but old and broken-down versions of newer, better gadgets which do work, they are available from 10 cents to $15. Look for waffle irons, toasters and coffee percolators. Don't try to use them unless you know what you are doing, or have them checked by a licensed electrician. Remember that one of the complaints about electric gadgets way back when was that they were not easily, if at all repairable.

ENAMELED WARE — This is a specialized collector's field, and there are numerous price guides and collecting guides. Expect to pay more than you thought you'd have to — if you aren't an experienced enameled ware collector. There are still bargains, but prices generally run from $3 to $60 or more, usually depending on age and color.

FENDERS — Part of the inventory of expensive fireplace equipment.

FIBRE WARE — Hard or next to impossible to find, and cheap to expensive when you do find it.

FIREBACKS — Extremely rare and expensive. Try to content yourself with the one at the local historic restoration, or with a copy of the excellent book *The Bible in Iron* by Henry Mercer, which covers stove plates and firebacks.

FIRE IRONS — Expensive fireplace equipment, and hard to find in original complete sets. Separate pieces may range in price from $2 to $35 or more.

FIRELESS COOKERS — Because of their size, and relative plainness, these are under $20 even if complete.

FISH KETTLES — With kettle, tray and lid, this would bring between $10 and $50 depending on the metal and condition.

FISH SCALERS — 25 cents to $5. Some people have a real thing for sculptural-looking tools. Fish scalers and meat frets are two such tools. Most will be about $1.50.

FISH SLICES — Depending on age and condition, from 50 cents to $5. If you find an early 19th century fish slice, perhaps with a fish design in the handle, expect to pay more than $45.

FLOUR BINS and SIFTERS — The likely price will be between $8 and $18. The best one I've found came from a pile of throwaways outside a thrift shop. It was complete and had a price tag of $3 left on it. Evidently no-one was willing to pay even that low price.

FLOUR SCOOPS — Depending on age and heft, these will be between 25 cents and $7. After you pick up a few, and get acquainted with the design and feel, you will be able to decide how much you want to pay for different types.

FLOUR SIFTERS — These are fun to look for, and there are a number of different styles. Prices range from $2 to $9. The *Hunter* sifter might bring $8; and the miniature *Hunter* which sold for 2 cents in 1889 would bring more than $10.

FLUE STOPPERS — As far as I know, no-one collects these, so the prices and the preferred selection should be enticing. I would say 10 cents to $5 if the lithograph is nice, and the brass plate in good condition.

FLY FANS — These are rare, and you should expect to pay between $25 and $100 if complete, even if the scrim is ragged.

FOOTMEN — Decorative and expensive. From $35 to $250 or more.

FORKS — Interesting table forks are still around in rusty-tined piles for 10 cents to $1. Cooking forks will be 10 cents to $50, depending on age and design. The average price will be about $3 to $8.

FRUIT JAR FILLERS and FUNNELS — 10 cents to $10, depending on condition and material. Enameled ware funnels will be more than tin or aluminum ones. Some wooden funnels were not handmade, but machine made. Average price about $2 to $3.

FRUIT JAR HOLDERS and WRENCHES — These are sought by the collectors of fruit jars, and you may expect to pay for the attention they get from those avid collectors. The jars themselves bring anywhere from 50 cents to $80 or more, and the holders and wrenches are found from 50 cents to $6. The average price would correspond to unusual can openers: about $3.

FRUIT LIFTERS and SUGAR AUGERS — $5 to $50 depending on size and condition.

FRUIT PARERS — The rotary type will be from $6 to $30; simple paring knives will be under a dollar.

FRUIT PRESSES — The ricer type will be between $2 and $8. The more intricate, and the older, will be up to $20.

FRY PANS — Old wrought and welded pans, with long handles, and of good size, will be between $25 and $100. Others, from the middle of the 19th century on, will range in price from 50 cents to $15 with an average of about $4.

GEM PANS — $1 to $8.

GRATES — From $5 in a junk yard to several hundred dollars if the grate is very old and has a fire back attached. Expect to pay an average of between $40 and $65.

GRATERS — The variety, the relatively small size and lightness, the attractiveness, and the fairly low prices make this an excellent specialty. Expect to pay from $5 to $15 for the mechanically interesting nutmeg graters, such as the *Edgar*; about $8 to $16 for the revolving graters; and $8 to $20 for the old hand-made graters with wooden backs. The full range is from 50 cents to $20.

GRIDDLES — Depending on age and material, and whether they are plain or hinged, these are between $3 and $25.

GRIDIRONS — The price depends on type and age. Old wrought-iron gridirons will bring upwards of $35. Tin ones, with little legs, will be from $15 to $25.

GRINDSTONES — Anywhere from $3 to $20 depending on type and attractiveness. A tabletop grinder, with the cast-iron parts in good condition, and the stone uncracked, should be about $12.

HAM BOILERS — Because anything of copper is generally more expensive than tin, copper ham boilers (which are tin-lined) and other boilers will be between $15 and $65. Tin boilers if complete will be between $10 and $20.

HERB GRINDERS or MILLS — $5 to $50 depending on age and type.

HOURGLASSES and EGG-GLASSES — Depending on the age, and where you find these, you can expect to pay between $5 and $65 or more. Shops that specialize in scientific tools and antiques will be a more expensive place to buy and hourglass than a regular antique shop. Decorative brass or cast-iron framed hourglasses will be more expensive than simple ones.

HULLERS, PINEAPPLE EYE SNIPS — About 25 cents to 50 cents.

ICE CHIPPERS etc. — Depending on age and appearance, from $1.50 to $7.

ICE CREAM FREEZERS — You will find them priced anywhere from $5 to $50. It is not likely you will be collecting many of these: like churns and kitchen tables they take up a lot of room. Average $10 to $15.

ICE CREAM MOLDS — These, like all molds, are almost a separate collecting category. They were made in so many appealing shapes, and hardly a person lives who doesn't like an occasional ice cream. The molds will be priced according to age and design subject and material. Pewter is more than tin. The range if $5 to more than $35.

ICE CREAM SCOOPS etc. — 25 cents to $12 or even $15 for such classics as the *Gilchrist No. 31*.

ICE PICKS — 10 cents to $5. If there is any advertising on the handle, and there is likely to be, the price will be closer to $5.

ICE TONGS — Priced according to age and size. Prices range from a low $3.50 to $35 or a little more.

INDIVIDUAL MOLDS — Sometimes a thirty year old *Jello* mold will bring more, because of the name, than a sixty year old individual patty or jelly mold. Look for 10 cents to $6 depending on age and design. A boxed complete set will be much higher.

IRON — Wrought iron is much older and more expensive than cast. It is so revered by the people who collect old tools, and by restorers, and is so relatively rare, that it is no wonder the prices are high. Know your dealer.

JAGGERS etc. — Jaggers will bring everything from 10 cents to $150. I saw a ten cent aluminum one at a local flea market, and a brass one for $10.

I have looked longingly at the lovely and rare scrimshaw jaggers that command such high prices. Reproductions and fakes have been put on the market, so be certain of the provenance of a scrimshaw piece before buying it. The average price for the average jagger is about $4 to $8.

JAPANNED WARE — Very old japanned ware is extremely rare and is to be considered a fine and elegant antique. Newer japanned pieces from the late 19th century, such as the brown spice box sets and canisters, bring about $12 to $15. The range for all japanned kitchen ware would be extreme: 50 cents to $65 or more. The early 19th century pieces might bring as much as $250.

JUICE EXTRACTORS — 25 cents to $15 or more. Ones with moving parts are the most expensive. A reamer type will be priced by age and material: wooden ones from 50 cents to $10; green Depression glass reamers in perfect condition from $4 to $10; aluminum reamers from 15 cents to $1.

KETTLES — Depending on the metal and the age and size, a kettle will bring between $1 and $100. Remember that copper, bell-metal, and brass utensils are higher than iron.

KITCHEN CABINETS — Hard to find in good condition, but available at country auctions and flea markets. Priced from $10 to over $125.

KITCHEN SAWS — Like bread and cake knives, these are often attractive. Prices from 50 cents to $4.

KITCHEN TABLES — $5, if you're lucky, to $100. You may find a great kitchen table, with turned legs and a broad, single-board top, in somebody's garage being used as a paint can table.

KNIVES — Knives are of such fascinating and infinite variety that it is impossible to price them all. When I went to Europe with my mother in 1966 I stunned myself and the customs authorities by returning with thirteen knives. You will pay between 10 cents and $10 for knives, a little more for unusual handmade or home-repaired ones. Average is $2.

KNIFE and FORK BOXES — 50 cents to $25 depending on material and finish. Very crude boxes may, because of their primitive character, bring more than something quite slim and elegant. Average price about $3 to $7.

KNIFE SHARPENERS — 10 cents to $12 depending on type and size.

LARD PAILS — Like all tin containers, the price will depend on style and condition. A lard pail, with original label and in clean shiny condition, might bring $20.

LARDING NEEDLES — Hard to find just one, and harder still to find a case with a set of needles inside. Between $8 and $18 with the case.

LEMON and **LIME SQUEEZERS** — Priced according to material and age, $2 to $22. *See also* **JUICE EXTRACTORS**

MATCH SAFES — Match safes were made in hundreds of styles, for over 200 years. The two most commonly called to mind are the brass double shell, and the painted tin box which holds a big match box. These will be between $1 and $6. Others, with moving parts, or of more intricate design or materials, will bring up to $20. Average about $8.

MEASURES — They come in sets, which are rare, and singles. Pewter is the most expensive. Copper, tin and glass measures are less. Prices range from 50 cents to $8 each, and from about $15 to $100 each. Recently advertised was a set of pewter, bulbous measures — from a gallon down to ½ pint, with eleven pieces. It was priced $1850.

MEASURING SPOONS — Very old ones just don't exist, but nice sets from the turn of the century and into the 20th century are between 5 cents and $1.50.

MELON SCOOPS — Undistinguished and from 5 cents to $1.

MILLS — From $5 to $35 or more. *See* **COFFEE MILLS, HERB MILLS**

MIXING SPOONS — From 10 cents to $5 depending on material and design. The handles are an indication of age. The average price will be about $2.

MOLDS — They were used frequently and every cookbook had many recipes for molded dishes. Perhaps this is why there aren't many of the delicate or easily-crushed gothic designs around. Expect to pay from $1 to $5 for the simple ones from the late 19th century; to $5 to $50 for complex ice cream and blancmange molds of the late 1870s and 1880s.

MORTARS and PESTLES — Priced according to material, age and size. A fine lignum vitae set might be $50 or more. A well-used burl set might bring more than $100. The *Wedgewood*, because it is common, would range from $15 to $50 depending on size.

MUFFIN PANS — Between $1 and $10, with an average of $3.50 to $5. It all depends on two things: the design of cups and the number of them. You might pay more for an unusual four-cup frame than an eight-cup frame. Turk's heads and fluted designs will be more than the plain. The cast-iron pans will be a bit more than the tin.

NUTCRACKERS — These will range in price from 25 cents to $20, or more. They are found in the simplest designs and in various humorous figural designs. The latter are, of course, more expensive. The average price for a lever nutcracker, which screwed to a table or counter top is from $7.50 to $15. Handheld metal crackers are about $3.50. Carved wooden crackers will bring from $5 to $18. Handmade nutcrackers, and very old ones, will be the most expensive.

NUTMEG GRATERS — *see* **GRATERS**

ONION PEELERS — Priceless.

PARING KNIVES — From 5 cents to $2. You can often find a stubby, homely, little carbon steel knife for a nickle. The people who price them seem to have an unaccountable affection for stainless steel, and think the carbon steel is worthless. Buy them and use them.

PASTRY FORKS — Depending on age and attractiveness, these will be between 25 cents and $4.

PASTRY SHEETS and BOARDS — Tin sheets, particularly if they have the curl at the end which holds the rolling pin, will be from $7 to $15. More if the rolling pin is there. The wooden boards will be about $5.

PATTY IRONS — $3 to $8 for sets.

PATTY PANS — Singly, about $1 or less. In sets, about $3.

PEA SHELLERS — If you can find one, you should expect to pay about $12 to $15 or more, depending on condition.

PEACH PARERS — A little higher than apple parers, because not so common. Between $12 and $25.

PEWTER — More expensive than brass, and not anywhere near so common. Pewter pieces were melted down during the Revolutionary War to be used for bullets, and 18th century things are next to impossible to find.

PIE RACKS — Depending on size and attractiveness, these will be between $4 and $15.

PITCHERS — 25 cents to $25 depending on material, age and original use. From 1870 to 1910 there was virtually no change in design, so know what you like if you don't know what you're looking at. Average price range is $2 to $6 for aluminum or tin; more for enameled ware; and a lot more for early 19th century pitchers of pieced tin.

POPOVER PANS — Pretty much alike, regardless of age. From $2 to $10.

POPPY SEED GRINDERS — Usually not in very good condition; the brass is soft and usually banged up. They can be repaired. The price is between $7 and $18.

PORRINGERS — There are many new reproductions which are not calculated to deceive the buyer, but are rather an acknowlegement of the good design of old porringers. The most common material is pewter or silver. Earthenware ones are also found. Prices from $5 to over $500. Know your hallmarks, dealer and pocketbook.

POTATO MASHERS — The wire and wood type will be between 25 cents and $5. Hard to determine age. *See also* **BEETLES**

POT CLEANERS — From 10 cents to $6. Chain cloths about $1.50.

POT HOOKS — $5 to $35 depending on age and intricacy.

POT STANDS — Wireware stands from five to one hundred years old, and from $1 to $10.

PUREE SIEVES — If complete with masher, priced between $4 and $12.

RAISIN SEEDERS — Like all the interesting mechanical devices, this is priced according to its gears and handles. Expect to pay from $6 to $15. The simple handheld *Everett* seeders will be from 50 cents to $2.

RANGES and STOVES — These will be priced according to present usefulness to the owner; ornateness, condition, and cleanliness and age. You could pay anything from $5 to several hundred dollars. A restored and re-nickeled 1906 *Garland* gas range was recently advertised for $700.

REFRIGERATORS — Turn of the century oak or zinc ice-boxes, which brought just $5 a few years ago, may bring more than $85 now. But a lot of the pricing depends on condition, attractiveness of the hardware, and the possible usefulness as a bar or cabinet.

ROLLING PINS — 25 cents to $100 depending on material and age. Old blown glass, particularly in colors, and pottery pins are rare and quite expensive. A tin one in good condition would be rare and probably between $5 and $15. Most wooden ones are $1 to $5.

ROLL PANS — These came in about fifteen different styles, and they are quite attractive. Like popover pans they will be between $2 and $10 depending on condition.

SAFES — Bought "as is" you will pay from $20 to $50. Refinished, these useful cabinets bring more than $85. The price also depends on the design and condition of the pierced tin panels, the design of the legs, and the molding.

SALESMEN'S SAMPLES — A wide range from $10 to $300. They are easily confused with toys, but unlike toys they often were constructed to work and had maker's names. Sample stoves can be bought for upwards of $50, but most bring from $150 to $200.

SAUCEPANS — 25 cents to $20 depending on age and material. Lidded saucepans will be more. Copper pans are between $5 and $15. Complete, and old divided-saucepans will be between $5 and $10.

SAUSAGE STUFFERS — $8 to $35 or more, depending on age and size and material. Handmade stuffers could bring up to $50. Small tin and wood ones will be an average of $10 to $15.

SCALES — $1 to $80 or more. The *family scales* are between $4 and $10, depending on decoration and condition. The *platform scales* are popular decorative pieces, and will be as high as $50 or $60. A lot depends on the quantity of brass decoration. The *spring balance scales*, not uncommon, are a good bargain: from $3.50 to $12.50 depending on size. The very large ones are not household scales and will be more.

SCOOPS — 50 cents to $10 depending on age and material. *See also* **FLOUR SCOOPS**

SIEVES — Common flour sieves, with simple wood or tin hoops, will be $1 to $3. A Shaker sieve, of plaided horsehair, will be upwards of $15, and closer to $35 if in good condition.

SINKS — You may want your collection to include

everything, so look for a good old cast-iron sink. Prices from $5 to $25.

SKEWERS — 10 cents to $100 or more if the skewer rack or *fraime* is there. If the set is complete and if it is fairly old, the price will start at about $20. One recently advertised set was $350.

SKILLETS — The really old skillets will come along once in a blue moon — like posnets. If you find one, expect to pay more than $65.

SKIMMERS — Milk skimmers, without advertising, will range from 25 cents to $4; with, they will bring a few dollars more. Other types of skimmers, depending on age or material will bring between $5 and $28. Enameled ware skimmers are about $8 if in good condition.

SMOKE JACKS — Forget it! Extremely rare and you will probably have to peer up some old chimneys to even see one.

SOAP SAVERS and SHAVERS — The savers go from $1 to $10 depending on whether they are wirework or perforated metal. The shavers are about $1 to $2.

SPATULAS — 10 cents to $4. *See* **CAKE TURNERS**

SPICE BOXES — $5 to $25 depending on shape and condition, and cases or racks. *See also* **JAPANNED WARE**

SPONGE RACKS — $8 to $15 depending on how much of the nickel-plate has worn off the brass wire, and on size and gracefulness.

STOVE LID LIFTERS — 50 cents to $10, but most likely about $1.50. Depends on interest and design of handle.

STRAINERS — 25 cents to $10 depending on type and age. Some have a lot more appeal than others. Average price from $2 to $3.

STRAINER SPOONS — $1 to $5 depending on condition of the mesh and how many other spoons it's jammed in with. The ratio works like this: the more objects in the box, the lower the price. The fewer objects on the table top, the higher the price. Some dealers use double psychology.

SUGAR NIPPERS — $8 to $30, with the average price for unmounted nippers about $15 to $18, and mounted from $20 to $50.

TEA KETTLES — $2 to $60 depending on material. Brass kettles start at about $30. Tin, or tin with brass trim, will be between $17 and $25. Plain old ordinary kettles, not to be scorned, will be between $6 and $8.

TIDY RACKS — $5 to $12.

TIN KITCHENS — $25 to $75 depending on size and condition. An 18th century tin kitchen would be more than $200.

TOASTERS — 25 cents to $10 or more. Because of the similarity between the simple wire toasters of the 1890s to the ones of the 1930s and 1940s, dealers don't make much of the age. Wrought iron ones from the 18th century will be between $35 and $150. Electric toasters from before 1940 will be between 50 cents and $15, depending on appearance, and association with other collecting fields such as Art Deco.

TOASTING FORKS — 50 cents to $20 depending on age and material. The telescoping forks from the 19th century will bring between $18 and $35. A number of them are now being imported from England.

TOYS and MINIATURES — A very expensive specialty. Stoves will be more than $25 and closer to $125 particularly if the set of pots and pans is complete. Single utensils will be between $2 and $15 depending on material and complexity.

TRAMMELS — $65 to $500 or more, depending on age and quality. You may find some cheaper, but they will probably be very recent imports and their provenance is not American.

TREEN — Anything made of wood acquires after a time a lovely patina which is impossible to duplicate with shoe polish, wax, or overnight weathering. You will learn to recognize old wooden pieces, but beware. Prices seem awfully high on some pieces, and unless you are quite sure of age or quality, don't pay the price.

TRIVETS — $6 to $60 or more. The average price will vary for the cast-iron because of age. The older wrought-iron trivets bring prices more than $18. Large trivets, which stand on the floor and are 12" to 14" high, start very close to $75. *See also* **FOOTMEN**

VEGETABLE BASKETS — Depending on size and where you buy them, the prices range from $1 to $20. If a dealer is selling you a nice potato basket to use as a magazine holder in your living room you may pay $12. If you buy one at a farmer's market, you may pay $1.50.

VEGETABLE BINS — Average price about $7 to $12. At garage sales and church bazaars you may find nice old ones for $1 or $2.

VEGETABLE LADLES — $1 to $7. Average about $2.50.

WAFER IRONS — These are treasures, and are priced accordingly. Expect to pay between $50 and $200 or more for a rare design. Early dated irons will be more than $150.

WAFFLE IRONS — The 18th century ones, with reins like the wafer irons, will be as expensive as wafer irons. But there are other types: the kind made for the range, for example, will bring between $12 and $25. The later ones, particularly the cruddy electric irons will be found for as little as 50 cents with an average of $5.

WIRE WHISKS and other WHISKS — 10 cents to $6. Even though these are still a standard piece of kitchen equipment, some dealers will put a next-to-brand-new whisk on sale for $5 as an antique. Beware.

YELLOW WARE — You can find excellent yellow ware bowls of the 1880s and 1890s, and often pay as little as $1 for a perfectly sound bowl. Always thwunk them with your fingernail. A dull thud indicates a crack somewhere — you may not even be able to see it. Prices for some yellow pottery go quite high. The range will be 50 cents to $50, with the average price for a 10" mixing bowl about $10. The early 19th century Liverpool ware is not considered here.

Appendix 2.
Table of Equivalent Measures for Cooking

A pound of flour is equal to one quart, or four cups.

A pound and two ounces of meal is equal to one quart.

A pound of butter is equal to a pint of butter, or two cups.

A goose-egg piece of butter is equal to about 3/4 stick or 3/8 cup.

A walnut-size piece of butter is equal to two heaping tablespoons.

A common tumbler equals a half pint or one cup.

A half-gill, or a wineglass equals four large tablespoons or a quarter of a cup.

A gill equals a teacup which is a half-cup or four ounces.

A gill equals eight tablespoons.

A pint equals sixteen fluid ounces or two cups.

A half-pint equals sixteen tablespoons or a cup.

A pound of sugar is equal to a pint of sugar, or two cups.

Appendix 3.

Table Showing the First Patent,
Design Patent, Reissue and Trademark Numbers
Issued in Each Year from 1836 to 1945, inclusive.

DATE	PATENT	DESIGN	REISSUE
1836	1		
1837	110		
1838	546		1
1839	1,061		7
1840	1,465		20
1841	1,923		30
1842	2,413		36
1843	2,901	1	49
1844	3,395	15	60
1845	3,873	27	67
1846	4,348	44	78
1847	4,914	103	91
1848	5,409	163	105
1849	5,993	209	128
1850	6,981	258	158
1851	7,865	341	184
1852	8,622	431	209
1853	9,512	540	229
1854	10,358	626	258
1855	12,117	683	286
1856	14,009	753	337
1857	16,324	860	420
1858	19,010	973	517
1859	22,477	1,075	643
1860	26,642	1,183	674
1861	31,005	1,366	1,106
1862	34,045	1,508	1,253
1863	37,266	1,703	1,369
1864	41,047	1,879	1,596
1865	45,685	2,018	1,844
1866	51,784	2,239	2,140

DATE	PATENT	DESIGN	REISSUE	TRADEMARK
1867	60,658	2,533	2,430	
1868	72,959	2,858	2,830	
1869	85,503	3,304	3,250	
1870	98,460	3,810	3,784	1
1871	110,617	4,547	4,223	122
1872	122,304	5,452	4,687	608
1873	134,504	6,336	5,216	1,099
1874	146,120	7,083	5,717	1,591
1875	158,350	7,969	6,200	2,150
1876	171,641	8,884	6,831	3,288
1877	185,813	9,686	7,452	4,247
1878	198,733	10,385	8,020	5,463
1879	211,078	10,975	8,529	6,918
1880	223,211	11,567	9,017	7,790
1881	236,137	12,082	9,523	8,139
1882	251,685	12,647	9,994	8,973
1883	269,820	13,508	10,265	9,920
1884	291,016	14,528	10,432	10,822
1885	310,163	15,678	10,548	11,843
1886	333,494	16,451	10,677	12,910
1887	355,291	17,046	10,793	13,939
1888	375,720	17,995	10,892	15,072
1889	395,305	18,830	10,978	16,131
1890	418,665	19,553	11,053	17,360
1891	443,987	20,439	11,137	18,775
1892	466,315	21,275	11,217	20,537
1893	486,976	22,092	11,298	22,274
1894	511,744	22,994	11,397	23,951
1895	531,619	23,922	11,461	25,757
1896	552,502	25,037	11,520	27,586
1897	574,369	26,482	11,581	29,399
1898	596,467	28,113	11,646	31,070
1899	616,871	29,916	11,706	32,308
1900	640,167	32,055	11,798	33,957
1901	664,827	33,813	11,879	35,678
1902	690,385	35,547	11,960	37,606
1903	717,521	36,187	12,070	39,612
1904	748,567	36,723	12,189	41,798
1905	778,834	37,280	12,299	43,956
1906	808,618	37,766	12,428	48,446
1907	839,799	38,391	12,587	59,014
1908	875,679	38,980	12,738	66,892
1909	908,436	39,737	12,906	72,083
1910	945,010	40,424	13,066	76,267
1911	980,178	41,063	13,189	80,506
1912	1,013,095	42,073	13,346	84,711
1913	1,049,326	43,415	13,504	89,731
1914	1,083,267	45,098	13,668	94,796
1915	1,123,212	46,813	13,858	101,613
1916	1,166,419	48,358	14,040	107,875
1917	1,210,389	50,177	14,238	114,666
1918	1,251,458	51,629	14,417	120,005
1919	1,290,027	52,836	14,582	124,066
1920	1,326,899	54,359	14,785	128,274
1921	1,364,063	56,844	15,018	138,556

DATE	PATENT	DESIGN	REISSUE	TRADEMARK
1922	1,401,948	60,121	15,257	150,210
1923	1,440,362	61,478	15,513	163,003
1924	1,478,996	63,675	15,739	177,848
1925	1,521,590	66,346	15,974	193,596
1926	1,568,040	69,170	16,240	207,437
1927	1,612,790	71,772	16,515	222,401
1928	1,654,521	74,159	16,841	236,987
1929	1,696,897	77,347	17,176	251,129
1930	1,742,181	80,254	17,550	265,655
1931	1,787,424	82,966	17,917	278,906
1932	1,839,190	85,903	18,312	290,313
1933	1,892,663	88,847	18,705	299,926
1934	1,941,449	91,258	19,038	309,066
1935	1,985,878	94,179	19,409	320,441
1936	2,026,516	98,045	19,804	331,338
1937	2,066,309	102,601	20,226	342,070
1938	2,104,004	107,738	20,610	353,324
1939	2,142,080	112,765	20,959	363,536
1940	2,185,170	118,358	21,311	374,062
1941	2,227,418	124,503	21,683	384,047
1942	2,268,510	130,989	21,992	392,581
1943	2,307,007	134,717	22,242	399,378
1944	2,338,081	136,916	22,415	404,974
1945	2,366,154	139,862	22,585	411,001
	(to 2,391,855)	(to 143,385)	(to 22,795)	(to 418,493)

Guide to Historic Restorations, Collections, and Museums
With Kitchen Utensils, Period Kitchens or
Displays of Articles Covered in this Book

*(rip) denotes *restoration in progress.*
Inter means Interstate Highway
US means U.S. Highway

ALABAMA

Arlington Ante Bellum Home & Gardens
331 Cotton Ave., S.W.,
Birmingham, Alabama, 35211

W.C. Handy Home & Museum
West College & Marengo Sts.,
Florence, Alabama, 35630

Oakleigh
350 Oakleigh Place,
Mobile, Alabama, 36604

Sturdivant Hall Museum
713 Mabry St.,
Selma, Alabama, 36701

Ivy Green, Helen Keller's Birthplace
Tuscumbia, Alabama, 35674

ALASKA

Anchorage Historical & Fine Arts Museum
121 W. 7th Ave.,
Anchorage, Alaska 99501

Tongass Historical Society Museum
Ketchikan Centennial Bldg.,
629 Dock St.,
Ketchikan, Alaska 99901

Trail of '98 Museum
7th & Spring Sts.,
Skagway, Alaska 99840

ARIZONA

Fort Verde State Historical Park, Commanding Officer's Quarters
State 79,
Campe Verde, Arizona, 86322

Pioneers Historical Museum
US 180,
north of Flagstaff, Arizona, 86001

*(rip) *Douglas Mansion, Jerome State Historical Park*
off US 89-A,
Jerome, Arizona, 86331

Arizona History Room
1st Nat'l Bank,
411 N. Central,
Phoenix, Arizona, 85004

Bayless Cracker Barrel Museum
118 W. Indian School Rd.,
Phoenix, Arizona, 85013

Old Governors Mansion
400 W. Gurley St.,
Prescott, Arizona, 86301

Collection of American Art, Arizona State University
(Suburb of Phoenix)
Tempe, Arizona, 85218

Tombstone Courthouse State Historical Park
State 80 off US 10,
Tombstone, Arizona, 85638

Tubac Presidio State Historical Park
US 19,
(South of Tucson)
Tubac, Arizona, 85640

Arizona Historical Society
949 E. 2nd St.,
Tucson, Arizona, 85719

Yuma Territorial Prison State Historic Park
US 80 Bus.,
Yuma, Arizona, 85364

ARKANSAS

Dryden Pottery Works
341 Whittington Ave.,
Hot Springs Nat'l Park, Arkansas, 71901

Wildwood 1884
808 Park Ave.,
Hot Springs Nat'l Park, Arkansas, 71901

CALIFORNIA

Kern County Museum & Pioneer Village
3851 Chester Ave.,
Bakersfield, California, 93301

Calico Ghost Town
Inter-15
11 miles NE of Barstow, Calif., 92311

The Leonis Adobe
23537 Calabasas Rd.
Calabasas, California, 91302

Farm Equipment Museum
Lake County Fairgrounds,
410 Martin St.,
Lakeport, California, 95453

Ranchos Los Alamitos
6400 E. Bixby Hill Rd.,
Long Beach, California, 90815

Old Town
50 University Place,
Los Gatos, California, 95030

Casa De Estudillo
2656 San Diego Ave.,
San Diego, California, 92102

*(rip) *Villa Montezuma*
1925 K. St.,
San Diego, California, 92101

Lighthouse, Cabrillo Nat'l Monument
End of Point Loma,
San Diego, California, 92106

San Jose Historical Museum
Kelley Park, Senter Rd. & Phelan Ave.,
San Jose, California, 95112

Far Far West Museum
358 S. Main St.,
Willits, California, 95490

Siskiyou County Museum
910 S. Main,
Yreka, California, 96097

COLORADO

McAllister House
423 N. Cascade Ave.,
Colorado Springs, Colorado, 80902

Commandant's Quarters, Fort Garland
US 160,
Fort Garland, Colorado, 81133

Dexter Cabin
Harrison Ave.,
Leadville, Colorado, 80461

(rip) Bloom House & Baca House
Main St.,
Trinidad, Colorado, 81082

(Write: State Historical Society 200 14th Ave., Denver,
Colorado, 80203.)

CONNECTICUT

John A. Stanton Memorial
63 E. Main St.,
Clinton, Connecticut, 06413

Stanley-Whitman House, Farmington Museum
37 High St.
Farmington, Connecticut, 06032

Henry Whitfield State Historical Museum
Whitfield St.,
Guilford, Connecticut, 06437

Connecticut Historical Society
1 Elizabeth St.,
Hartford, Connecticut, 06105

Sloane-Stanley Museum
US 7,
north of Kent, Connecticut, 06757

Denison Homestead
Pequit-Sepos Rd.,
Mystic, Connecticut, 06355

Marine Historical Society
Mystic, Connecticut, 06355

Leffingwell Inn
348 Washington St.,
New Milford, Connecticut, 06776

Captain David Judson House & Museum
967 Academy Hill,
(Near Bridgeport)
Stratford, Connecticut, 06607

Isaac Stevens House
215 Main,
Wethersfield, Connecticut, 06109

Silas Deane House
209 Main,
Wethersfield, Connecticut, 06109

Webb House
211 Main,
Wethersfield, Connecticut, 06109

Buttolph-Williams House
Broad & Marsh Sts.,
Wethersfield, Connecticut, 06109

DELAWARE

Amstel House
4th & Delaware Sts.,
New Castle, Delaware, 19720

Corbit-Sharp House & Wilson-Warner House
US 13,
Main St. at 2nd St.,
(Odessa, Delaware, 19730
(Administered by Winterthur)

Delaware State Museum
316 S. Governor's Ave.,
Dover, Delaware, 19901

Eleutherian Mills, The Hagley Museum
State 141,
(North of Wilmington)
Greenville, Delaware, 19807

Winterthur, Henry Francis DuPont Museum
State 52, Winterthur,
Wilmington, Delaware, 19735

DISTRICT OF COLUMBIA - *Smithsonian Institution:*

(1) Nat'l Museum of History & Technology
Constitution Ave.,
Between 12th & 14th Sts. N.W.,
District of Columbia, 20002

(2) Arts & Industries Bldg.
9th & Jefferson Drive, S.W.
District of Columbia, 20024

(3) Renwich Gallery
17th St. & Pennsylvania Ave. N.W.,
District of Columbia, 20006

Frederick Douglass Home
14th & W. Sts., S.E.,
District of Columbia, 20020

Old Stone House
3051 M. St., N.W.,
District of Columbia, 20007

FLORIDA

USA of Yesterday Museum
US 27,
Dundee, Florida, 33838

Jacksonville Children's Museum
1025 Gulf Life Dr.,
Jacksonville, Florida, 32207

Oldest House
322 Duval St.,
Key West, Florida, 33040

Properties of *Historic St. Augustine Preservation Board,*
Department of State,
P.O. Box 1987,
St. Augustine, 32084

Arrives House; Ribera House,
22 St. George St.
Gallegos House; Spanish Inn,
43 St. George St.
Salcedo Bakery.

Others in St. Augustine:

Oldest House,
14 St. Francis St.
Dr. Peck House,
St. George & Treasurey Sts.,
Ximenez-Fatio House; Casa de Hildago;
Lightner Museum.

Big Bend Farm, Tallahassee Junior Museum
6½ miles SW of Tallahassee,
at Lake Bradford

GEORGIA

Ante-Bellum Plantation, Industries of the Old South Area
Stone Mountain Park,
Inter-285, (east of Atlanta), 30083

Walker-Peters-Langdon House
716 Broadway,
Columbus, Georgia, 31901

Bedingfield Inn, Stewart County Historical Commission
Town Square,
Lumpkin, Georgia, 31815

Westville Village
Off Inter-75 on State 280
P.O. Box 1850,
Lumpkin, Georgia, 31835

Owens-Thomas House
124 Abercorn St., Oglethorpe Square
Savannah, Georgia, 31401

Telfair Academy of Arts & Sciences
121 Barnard St., at W. State St.,
Savannah, Georgia, 31401

HAWAII

Lyman House Memorial Museum
276 Haili St.,
Hilo, Hawaii, 96720

IDAHO

Try writing: *Idaho State Historical Society*
610 N. Julia Davis Dr.
Boise, Idaho, 83706

ILLINOIS

Bryant Cottage
State 105,
Bement, Illinois, 61813

Bishop Hill
North of US 34,
Bishop Hill, Illinois, 61419

Clover Lawn, David Davis Mansion
Davis & Monroe Sts.,
Bloomington, Illinois, 61701

Pierre Menard Home
adjoining Kaskaskia State Park
Near Chester, Illinois, 62233

Chicago Historical Society
Clark St. at North Ave.,
Chicago, Illinois, 61614

Dowling House
Main & Diagonal Sts.,
Galena, Illinois, 61036

Old General Store
223 S. Main St.,
Galena, Illinois, 61036

U.S. Grant House
Bouthillier & 4th Sts.,
Galena, Illinois, 61036

Carl Sandburg Birthplace
331 E. 3rd St.,
Galesburg, Illinois, 61401

Lincoln's New Salem
State 97,
south of Petersburg, Illinois, 62675

Lincoln Log Cabin
State 16 & 121,
south of Petersburg, Illinois, 62675

INDIANA

Hillforest Historical Foundation, Inc.
213 5th St.,
Aurora, Indiana, 47001

Wells County Historical Museum
211 W. Washington St.,
P.O. Box 143,
Bluffton, Indiana, 46714

Old Homestead
227 S. Court St.,
Crown Point, Indiana, 46307

Johnson County Historical Museum
150 W. Madison St.,
Franklin, Indiana, 46131

Children's Museum of Indianapolis
3010 N. Meridian St.,
Indianapolis, Indiana, 46208

Indiana State Museum
202 N. Alabama St.,
Indianapolis, Indiana, 46204

Tippecanoe County Historical Museum
10th and South Sts.,
Lafayette, Indiana, 47901

Jeremiah Sullivan House
304 W. 2nd St.,
Madison, Indiana, 47205

Octogenarian Museum
Matter Park,
Marion, Indiana, 46925

Spring Mill State Park
RR-2, State 60,
Mitchell, Indiana, 47446

Conner Prairie Pioneer Settlement
30 Connor Lane,
4 miles east of Noblesville, Indiana, 46046

Wayne County Historical Museum
1150 North A. St.,
Richmond, Indiana, 47374

Northern Indiana Historical Society
112 S. Lafayette Blvd.,
South Bend, Indiana, 46601

IOWA

Community Kitchen & Hearth Oven Bakery
Amana Colonies, State 220
(Near Cedar Rapids)
Middle Amana Village, Iowa, 52203

Museum of Amana History
State 220 to Junction US 6 & State 149,
Amana Colonies, Iowa, 52203

Historic General Dodge House
605 3rd St. at Story St.,
Council Bluffs, Iowa, 51501

Kinney Pioneer Museum
US 18,
west of Mason Cty., Iowa, 50401

Old Settlers & Threshers Association Heritage Museum
RR 4, Box 46 Walnut St.,
Mt. Pleasant, Iowa, 52641

(OS & TA has a slide presentation called "Country
Kitchen," 25 minutes, color, sound. Available from OS & T
Area 16 Media Center. 1200 E. Washington St., Mt.
Pleasant, 52641.)

Pella Historical Restoration Site
507 Franklin St.,
Pella, Iowa, 50219

Museum of History & Science
Park Ave. at South St.,
Waterloo, Iowa, 50701

KANSAS

Pioneer Museum
US 160, west of Main St.,
Ashland, Kansas, 67831

Fort Bissell
US 36,
west of Phillipsburg, Kansas, 67661

Kansas State Historical Society Museum
10th & Jackson Sts.,
Topeka, Kansas, 66612

Chisholm Trail Museum
502 N. Washington St.,
Wellington, Kansas, 67152

Wichita Historical Museum
3751 E. Douglas Ave.,
Wichita, Kansas, 67218

KENTUCKY

Old Fort Harrod State Park
State 150
Harrodsburg, Kentucky, 40330

Shakertown at Pleasant Hill, Inc.
RR 4, US 68,
(45 miles SW of Lexington)
Harrodsburg, Kentucky, 40330

*Mountain Life Museum, Levi Jackson Wilderness Road
State Park*
US 25,
2 miles South of London, Kentucky, 40741

Shakertown at South Union
US 68
(Near Bowling Green)
South Union, Kentucky, 42283

LOUISIANA

Fort Jesup State Historical Park
State 6,
(Between Alexandria & Shreveport)
6 miles NE of Many, Louisiana, 71449

Gallier House
1118-32 Royal St.,
New Orleans, Louisiana, 70116

1850 House, Pontalba Buildings
St. Peter & St. Ann Sts.,
at Jackson Square
New Orleans, Louisiana, 70116

*Acadian House Museum, Longfellow-Evangeline Memorial
State Park*
State 31,
north of St. Martinville, Louisiana, 70582

MAINE

Fort Western Museum
Bowman & Cony Sts.,
Augusta, Maine, 04330

Maine State Museum
State House,
Augusta, Maine, 04330

Old Conway House
US 1,
south of Camden, Maine, 04843

Dear Isle - Stonington Historical Society
Deer Isle, Maine, 04627

The Nordica Homestead Museum
Holly Rd. off State 4,
Farmington, Maine, 04938

The Norlands
Livermore Falls, Maine, 04254

Willowbrook Museum
State 11,
Newfield, Maine, 04056

Shaker Museum, Sabbathday Lake Shaker Community
State 26 (Near Portland)
Poland Spring, Maine, 04274

Hamilton House
Vaughan's Lane,
Near State 236 & 91,
South Berwick, Maine, 03908

York Gaol Museum
Off US 1-A,
York, Maine, 03909

Jefferds' Tavern
Off US 1-A
York, Maine, 03909

MARYLAND

Home of Roger Brooke Taney
121 S. Bentz St.,
Frederick, Maryland, 21701

Carroll County Farm Museum
Bishop St.,
Westminster, Maryland, 21157

Union Mills Homestead & Mill Museum
US 140, 7 miles N. of
Westminster, Maryland, 21157

MASSACHUSETTS

Colonel Ashely House
US 7 & State 7A
(south of Sheffield)
Ashley Falls Center, Massachusetts, 01222

General Sylvanus Thayer Birthplace
786 Washington St.,
Braintree, Massachusetts, 01484

Nurse House
149 Pine St.,
Exit 24 on State 128,
Danvers, Massachusetts, 01923

Historic Deerfield
(Near Greenfield)
Deerfield, Massachusetts, 01342;

Memorial Hall; Ashely House; Dwight-Barnard House;
Sheldon Hawks; Hall Tavern; Frary House; Wells-Thorne
House; etc.

White-Ellery House
274 Washington St.,
State 127, north of State 128,
Gloucester, Massachusetts, 01930

Beauport
Eastern Pount Blvd.,
State 128,
Gloucester, Massachusetts, 01930

Hadley Farm Museum
State 9,
Hadley, Massachusetts, 01035

Porter-Phelps-Huntington House, Inc.
State 47,
north of Hadley, Massachusetts, 01035

Fruitlands Museums
Prospect Hill Rd.
off State 110
Harvard, Massachusetts, 01451

The Old Ordinary
Lincoln St.,
Hingham, Massachusetts, 02043

Jeremiah Lee Mansion
161 Washington St.,
Marblehead, Massachusetts, 01945

Mattapoisett Historical Society Museum
5 Church St.,
Mattapoisett, Massachusetts, 02739

Nantucket Historical Assn.
Old Town Bldg., Union St.,
Nantucket Island, Massachusetts, 02554

New Bedford Whaling Museum
18 Johnny Cake Hill,
New Bedford, Massachusetts, 02740

Coffin House
16 High Rd.,
State 1-A,
Newbury, Massachusetts, 01950

Swett-Ilsley House
4 & 6 High Rd.,
Newbury, Massachusetts, 01950

Jackson Homestead
527 Washington St.,
Newton, Massachusetts, 02158

Jacobs Farm
Main St., State 3 to State 123
Norwell, Massachusetts, 02061

Hancock Shaker Community, Inc.
US 20,
near Pittsfield, Massachusetts, 01201

> *The Mary Earle Gould Collection is here, and*
> *may be seen by appointment.*

Plimoth Plantation
P.O. Box 1620, State 2-A
south of Plymouth, Massachusetts, 02360

Harlow Old-Fort House
119 Sandwich St.,
Plymouth, Massachusetts, 02360

Historic Salem
Salem, Massachusetts, 01970

Saugus Iron Works
244 Central St.,
Saugus, Massachusetts, 01906

Old Sturbridge Village
US 20 & State 131 Turnpike Inter-86
Sturbridge, Massachusetts, 01566

Browne House
562 Main St., State 20
Watertown, Massachusetts, 02172

Claflen-Richards House
State 1-A
Wenham, Massachusetts, 01984

Winslow Crocker House
King's Highway, State 6-A
Yarmouthport, Massachusetts, 02675

MICHIGAN

Henry Ford Museum & Greenfield Village
Village Rd. & Oakwood Blvd.,
Dearborn, Michigan, 48121

Dearborn Historical Museum, Commandant's Quarters
21950 Michigan Ave.;
McFadden-Ross House
915 Brady St.,
Dearborn, Michigan, 48124

Netherlands Museum
12th St. & Central Ave.,
Holland, Michigan, 49423

Indian Dormitory, Old Fort Mackinac
Mackinac Island,
Upper Peninsula, Michigan, 49757

Old Water Works Building Museum
W. First St.,
Manistee, Michigan, 49660

Marquette County Historical Society Historical Museum
Waterloo-Munith Rd.,
Waterloo, Michigan, 49259

MINNESOTA

Lumbertown, USA
US 371 to County 7
Brainerd, Minnesota, 56401

Cook County Historical Society
3rd St. & 1st Ave. W.,
Grand Marais, Minnesota, 55604

Fort Belmont
Junct. US 16 & 71,
Jackson, Minnesota, 56143

Blue Earth County Historical Society Museum
606 S. Broad St.,
Mankato, Minnesota, 56001

Hennepin County Historical Society
2303 3rd Ave. S.,
Minneapolis, Minnesota, 55404

Gibbs Farm Museum
2097 Larpenteur Ave. W.,
St. Paul, Minnesota, 55113

MISSISSIPPI

Gautier's Plantation Home
Hwy 90
Gautier, Mississippi 39553

MISSOURI

Arrow Rock State Park
State 41 near Inter-70
Arrow Rock, Missouri, 65320:

> The Tavern; Dr. Matthew W. Hall House; George Caleb
> Bingham House.

Mark Twain's Boyhood Home & Museum
208 Hill St.,
Hannibal, Missouri, 63401

Plaster House
200 block of Hill St.,
Hannibal, Missouri, 63401

Bottermuller House
205 E. 8th St.,
at Schiller St., off State 19,
Hermann, Missouri, 65041

Harry S. Truman Birthplace
US 160 & 71
Lamar, Missouri, 64759

(rip) Watkins Mill Historic Site
US 69,
Lawson, Missouri, 64062

Museum of the Yesturyears
State 13, south of US 24,
Lexington, Missouri, 64067

Bushnell County Museum
Inter-70,
west of St. Charles, Missouri, 63301

First Missouri State Capitol
208-214 S. Main St.,
St. Charles, Missouri, 63301

Amoureaux House
St. Mary's Rd.,
east of US 61,
Ste. Genevieve, Missouri, 63670

Doll Museum
1501 Penn St.,
St. Joseph, Missouri, 64503

Tower Grove House, Missouri Botanical Gardens
Tower Grove & Shaw Ave.,
South St. Louis, Missouri, 63110

Benton County Museum
Van Buren St.,
Warsaw, Missouri, 65355

Gateway to the West Museum
Weston, Missouri, 64098

MONTANA

Montana Historical Society Museum
225 N. Roberts,
Helena, Montana, 59601

Virginia City Restoration
State 15,
(South of Butte)
Virginia City, Montana, 59755

NEBRASKA

Knight Museum
908 Yellowstone Ave.,
Alliance, Nebraska, 69301

Arthur County Hostprical Society
Arthur, Nebraska, 69121

Homestead National Monument
State 4,
Near Beatrice, Nebraska, 68310

Brownville Museum
Main St.
Brownville, Nebraska, 68321

Officers' Quarters at Fort Robinson
US 20,
west of Crawford, Nebraska, 69339

Washington County Historical Museum
14th & Monroe Sts.,
State 73,
Ft. Calhoun, Nebraska, 68023

Stuhr Museum
US 34 & 281,
Grand Island, Nebraska, 68801

Hastings Museum
State 281 & 14th St.,
Hastings, Nebraska, 68901

Fairview. William Jennings Bryan House
Bryan Memorial Hospital Grounds,
Lincoln, Nebraska, 68506

Nebraska State Historical Society Museum
1500 R. St.,
Lincoln, Nebraska, 68508

Nebraska Statehood Memorial, Thomas P. Kennard House
1627 H. Street,
Lincoln, Nebraska, 68508

Harold Warp Pioneer Village
US 6 & 34, State 10,
south of Inter-80,
near Minden, Nebraska, 68959

Arbor Lodge State Historical Park
US 75,
Nebraska City, Nebraska, 68410

Antelope County Historical Collection
Neligh, Nebraska, 68756

NEVADA

Churchill County Museum
1050 S. Main,
Fallon, Nevada, 89406

Nevada Historical Society
1650 N. Virginia St.,
Reno, Nevada, 89503

NEW HAMPSHIRE

Canterbury Shaker Museum
Off State 106, (Near Concord)
East Canterbury, New Hampshire, 03224

New Hampshire Historical Society
30 Park St.,
Concord, New Hampshire, 03301

Barrett House
Main St.,
off State 124
New Ipswich, New Hampshire 03071

Strawbery Banke
P.O. Box 300
Portsmouth, New Hampshire, 03801:

> Clark House; Chase House; Keryan Walsh House; Governor
> Goodwin Mansion.

NEW JERSEY

Campbell Museum
375 Memorial Ave.,
off US 50,
Camden, New Jersey, 08101

Museum of Early Trades & Crafts
Main St. & Green Village Rd.,
Madison, New Jersey, 07940

McKonkey Ferry Museum
Adjacent to *Washington State Park*
US 29,
NW of Trenton, New Jersey, 07782

NEW MEXICO

Kit Carson House & Museum
US 64,
Taos, New Mexico, 87571

Old Cienega Village
Rte 2, Box 214
Sante Fe, New Mexico 87501

NEW YORK

Albany Institute of History & Art
125 Washington St.,
Albany, New York, 12224

Cherry Valley Museum
Main St.,
Cherry Valley, New York, 13320

The Farmers Museum
St. 80,
1 mi. N   of Cooperstown, New York, 13326

Bronck House
State 9-W,
South of Coxsackie, New York, 12051

Fort Ticonderoga
State 73,
1 mi. NE of Fort Ticonderoga, New York, 12883

Prouty-Chew House
543 S. Main St.,
Geneva, New York, 14456

Johnson Hall
Hall Ave.,
West of Johnson, New York, 10933

Rock Hall
Broadway,
Lawrence, New York, 11559

Museum Village of Smith's Clove
Exit 129, State 6 & 17M,
Monroe, New York, 10950

*(rip) *Genesee County Museum*
Flint Hill,
Mumford, New York, 14511

New York City:

Brooklyn Museum
178 Eastern Pkwy & Wash. Ave.,
Brooklyn, N.Y., 11238

Jumel Mansion
Jumel Terrace
W. 161st St. off St. Nicholas Avenue,
Manhattan, N.Y.C. 10032

Metropolitan Museum of Art
5th Ave. & 82nd St.,
Manhattan, N.Y.C., 10028

Museum of the City of New York
5th Ave. & 103rd St.,
Manhattan, N.Y.C., 10025

New York Historical Society
170 Central Park West.,
Manhattan, N.Y.C., 10024

> The excellent Bella C. Landauer Catalog collection is housed here.

*(rip) *The Old Merchant's House*
29 E. 4th St.,
Manhattan, N.Y.C., 10003

Richmondtown Restoration & Staten Island Historical Society Museum
302 Center St., Richmondtown,
Staten Island, N.Y.C., 10306

Carborundum Museum of Ceramics
3rd & Falls St.,
Niagara Falls, N.Y., 14303

Old Bethpage Village Restoration
So. of Long Island Expwy.
Round Swamp Rd.,
Old Bethpage, Long Island, New York, 11804

Shaker Museum
State 66
(Near Albany)
Old Chatham, New York, 12136

Campbell-Whittlesey House
130 Spring St.,
Rochester, New York, 14608

Rochester Museum & Science Center
657 East Ave.,
Rochester, New York, 14607

*(rip) *Van Nostrand Starkins House*
Roslyn Landmark Society
Roslyn, New York, 11576

New York Historical Museum
Southampton, New York, 11968

Sleepy Hollow Restorations
Tarrytown, New York, 10591:

Philipsburg Manor
US 9,
Upper Mills,
North Tarrytown, 10591
Van Cortlandt Manor
off US 9,
Croton-on-Hudson, 10521
Sunnyside, Washington Irving's Home
Tarrytown, New York, 10591

Century House Restoration
Watkins Glen, New York, 14891

The Old McClurg Mansion
US 20 & State 17,
Westfield, New York, 14787

NORTH CAROLINA

Historic Bath
State 92,
Bath, North Carolina, 27808

Bennett Place
Off US 70 & Inter-85,
near Duke Univ.
Durham, North Carolina, 27706

James Iredell House
107 E. Church St.
Edenton, North Carolina, 27932

Charles Aycock Birthplace
off US 117,
Fremont, North Carolina, 27830

Tryon Palace
George St. between Eden & Metcalf Sts.,
New Bern, North Carolina, 27932

James K. Polk Birthplace
(Near Charlotte)
Pineville, North Carolina, 28134

Mordecai House & Mordecai Historic Park
1 Mimosa St.,
Raleigh, North Carolina, 27611

Potter's Museum
US 220,
north of Seagrove, North Carolina, 27341

Zebulon B. Vance Birthplace
Off Blue Ridge Pkwy., east of US 19, US 23
(Near Ashville)
Weaverville, North Carolina, 28787

Old Salem, Inc.
Inter-40, US 52,
Winston-Salem, North Carolina, 27108

NORTH DAKOTA

Lewis & Clark Trail Museum
Alexander, North Dakota, 58831

State Historical Society
Liberty Memorial Bldg.
Bismarck, North Dakota, 58501

Buffalo Trails Museum
(Near Williston)
Epping, North Dakota, 58843

The Forsberg House
815 3rd Ave. S
Fargo, North Dakota, 58102

Fort Totten
Beside Devils Lake,
Fort Totten Indian Reservation, North Dakota, 58335

Stutsman County Memorial Museum
321 3rd Ave. SE,
Jamestown, North Dakota, 58401

Chateau de Mores
US 10 & Inter-94
(Near the Badlands)
Medora, North Dakota, 58645

Foley Museum Complex, Hoffman Home
Medora, North Dakota, 58645

Northwest Historical Society
State Fairgrounds
Minot, North Dakota, 58701

Geographical Center Historical Society Pioneer Village
Rugby, North Dakota, 58368

Richland County Historical Museum
7th Ave. & 2nd St.,
Wahpeton, North Dakota, 58075

Bonanzaville Pioneer Village
West Fargo, North Dakota, 58078

OHIO

Hale Farm & Western Reserve Village
SE of Inter-77,
Bath, Ohio, 44210

Century Village Museum
State 87 & 700,
Burton, Ohio, 44021

Adena
Allen Ave. off State 104
Chillicothe, Ohio, 45601

Durell Farm Museum, Center of Science & Industry
280 E. Broad St.,
Columbus, Ohio, 43215

> This very fine collection was assembled over a period of many years by Edward Durrell

Ohio Historical Center
Inter-71 & 17th Ave.
Columbus, Ohio, 43210

Warren County Museum
US 42, south of State 63,
Lebanon, Ohio, 45036

Allen County Historical Society Museum
600 block of W. Market St.,
Lima, Ohio, 45801

The Country Store
State 39
(SE of Mansfield)
Lucas, Ohio, 44843

Campus Martius Museum
Washington & 2nd St.,
Marietta, Ohio, 45750

Spring Hill, Massillon Museum Foundation
Massillon, Ohio, 44646

Wolcott House Museum
1031 River Rd.,
(Near Toledo)
Maumee, Ohio, 43537

Milan Historical Mus.,
10 Edison Dr.,
Milan, Ohio, 44846

Schoenbrunn Village State Memorial
Off US 250 Bus. & State 259,
New Philadelphia, Ohio, 44663

Pioneer Farm & House Museum
Brown Rd., Hueston Woods State Park,
Oxford, Ohio, 45056

Piqua Historic Area, Johnson House & Farm
State 66,
Piqua, Ohio, 45356

Toledo Museum of Art
Monroe St.,
Toledo, Ohio, 43602

Number One House, Zoar Village State Memorial
State 212 off Inter-77,
Zoar, Ohio, 44697

OKLAHOMA

Museum of Western Prairie
Altus, Oklahoma, 73521

Black Kettle Museum
State 283,
Cheyenne, Oklahoma, 73628

Sod House Museum
State 8,
between Cleo Springs & Aline, Oklahoma, 73729

Western Trails Museum
2229 Gary Freeway, US 66
SW of Clinton, Oklahoma, 73601

Old Town Museum
US 66,
SW of Elk City, Oklahoma, 73644

No Man's Land Historical Museum
Sewell St.,
Goodwell, Oklahoma, 73939

Chisholm Trail Museum & Seay Mansion
11th & Overstreet St.,
Kingfisher, Oklahoma, 73750

Murray-Lindsay Mansion
Lindsay, Oklahoma, 73052

Oklahoma Historical Society Museum
NE 19th St. & 2100 Lincoln Blvd.,
Oklahoma City, Oklahoma, 73105

Cherokee Strip Historical Museum & Henry S. Johnston Library
east of Junct. US 64 & Inter-35,
W. of Perry, Oklahoma, 73077

Pioneer Woman Museum
701 Monument Rd.,
Ponca City, Oklahoma, 74601

OREGON

Coos-Curry Pioneer & Historical Assoc. Museum
Simpson Park,
North Bend, Oregon, 97459

Beekman House
Jacksonville, Oregon, 97530

Pioneer Village
State 238,
Jacksonville, Oregon, 97530

Oregon Historical Society
1230 SW Park Ave.,
Portland, Oregon, 97205

Bybee-Howell House
US 30, Howell Park Rd.,
Sauvie's Island, Portland, Oregon, 97236

PENNSYLVANIA

Old Economy Village
Ambridge, Pennsylvania, 15003

Hopewell Village National Historic Site
State 345,
south of Birdsboro, Pennsylvania, 19508

Mercer Museum, Bucks County Historical Society
Pine & Ashland St.,
Doylestown, Pennsylvania, 18901

Fort Hunter Museum
US 22 & 322,
north of Harrisburg, Pennsylvania 17110

Hershey Estates Museum
Hershey, Pennsylvania, 17033

Pennsylvania Farm Museum of Landis Valley
2451 Kissel Hill Rd., Old Reading Rd.,
near Lancaster, Pennsylvania, 17601

Pennsylvania Dutch Folk Culture Society, Inc.
Lenhartsville, Pennsylvania, 19534

Fort Ligonier
US 30 & State 711
Ligonier, Pennsylvania, 15658

Buten Museum of Wedgwood
146 N. Bowman Ave.,
Merion Pennsylvania, 19066

Pennsbury Manor
so. of Morrisville, Pennsylvania, 19067

Perelman Antique Toy Museum, Abercrombie House
2nd & Spruce Sts.,
Philadelphia, Pennsylvania, 19106

Woodford Mansion-The Fairmount Park Houses
33rd & Dauphin St.,
Philadelphia, Pennsylvania, 19132

Daniel Boone Homestead
off US 422,
9 mi. SE of Reading, Pennsylvania, 18603

Mill-Bridge Craft Village
off State 30 on Fairview, Rd., Box 73,
Soudersburg, Pennsylvania, 17577

The Amish Village
State 896, off US 30,
Strasburg, Pennsylvania, 17579

Eagle Americana Shop & Gun Museum
State 741,
west of Strasburg, Pennsylvania, 17579

Colonial Valley
State 116 off US 30,
York, Pennsylvania, 18705

RHODE ISLAND

The Breakers
Ochre Pt. Ave. & Ruggles Ave.,
Newport, Rhode Island, 02840

South Country Museum
Scrabbletown Road, Box 182
North Kingstown, Rhode Island, 02855

SOUTH CAROLINA

Charleston Museum
121-125 Rutledge Ave.
Charleston, South Carolina, 29401

Historic Walnut Grove Plantation
near intersect. of Inter-26 & State 221
8 mi. SE of Spartanburg, South Carolina, 29301

SOUTH DAKOTA

Ducotah Prarie Museum
Aberdeen, South Dakota, 57401

Verendrye Museum
Fort Pierre, South Dakota, 57532

Lake County Historical Museum, Dakota State College
Madison, South Dakota, 57042

Museum of Pioneer Life
1311 S. Duff St.,
Mitchell, South Dakota, 57301

Robinson Museum
Memorial Bldg.,
Pierre, South Dakota, 57501

Pettigrew Museum
131 N. Duluth Ave.,
Sioux Falls, South Dakota, 57104

W.H. Over Museum, University of S.D.
Vermillion, South Dakota, 57069

TENNESSEE

Cravens House off State 148
on Look out Mountain,
Chattanooga, Tennessee, 37409

Colonel Francis Ramsey House
Thorngrove Pike,
Knoxville, Tennessee 37914

Governor William Blount Mansion
200 W. Hill Ave., at State St.,
Knoxville, Tennessee 37902

Museum of Appalachia
Norris, Tennessee, 37828

TEXAS

Fort Worth Museum of Science & History
1501 Montgomery St.,
Ft. Worth, Texas, 76107

Pioneer Museum
311 W. Main St.,
Fredericksburg, Texas, 78624

Harris County Heritage Society
1100 Bagby St.,
Houston, Texas, 77002

Ranch Headquarters Museum, Texas Tech University
Box 4499,
Lubbock, Texas, 79409

Henkel Square, Texas Pioneer Arts Foundation
Round Top, Texas, 78954

Winedale Inn
Box 11, Round Top, Texas, 78954

Institute of Texan Cultures, University of Texas
San Antonio, Texas, 78294

San Jose Mission
6539 San Jose Dr.,
San Antonio, Texas 78214

UTAH

Fairview Museum
Fairview, Utah, 84629

Pioneer Village Museum
2998 S. 2150 East (Connor St.),
Salt Lake City, Utah, 84109

Daughters of Utah Pioneers Museum
200 N. Main,
Salt Lake City, Utah, 84103; and
    Parowan, Utah, 84761

VERMONT

The Bennington Museum
State 9, W. Main St.,
Bennington, Vermont, 05201; and their
Topping Tavern Museum
East Rd.,
Shaftsbury, Vermont, 05262 (near Bennington)

Sheldon Museum
Park St.,
Middlebury, Vermont, 05753

Shelburne Museum
US 7,
Shelburne, Vermont, 05482
(South of Burlington)

Farrar-Mansur House
Weston, Vermont, 05161

Vermont Country Store
State 100,
Weston, Vermont, 05161

VIRGINIA

Scotchtown
Rt   685, Scotchtown,
Beaverdam, Virginia, 23015;
    Under *Association for the Preservation of Virginia
    Antiquities*, 2705 Park Ave., Richmond, 23220.

Southwest Virginia Museum
W. First St. & Wood Ave.
Big Stone Gap, Virginia, 24219

Smithfield Plantation
Rt   314 off Rt   460 Bypass
Blacksburg, Virginia, 24060
(Under APVA. See Scotchtown)

Red Hill Shrine
State 600,
SE of Brookneal, Virginia, 24528

Shirley Plantation
State 5, near James River
Charles City, Virginia, 23030

Ash Lawn
State 53, 3 mi. SE of
Charlottesville, Virginia, 22901

Michie Tavern Museum
State 53, Bx. 7A, 3 mi. SE of
Charlottesville, Virginia, 22901

Monticello
State 53,
Charlottesville, Virginia, 22901

George Washington's Birthplace
State 3, 38 Mi. E. of
Fredericksburg, Virginia, 22575

Kenmore
Lewis St. & Washington Ave.,
Fredericksburg, Virginia, 22401

Mary Washington House
1200 Charles St.,
Fredericksburg, Virginia, 22401
(Under APVA. See Scotchtown)

Stoner's Store
1202 Prince Edward St.,
Fredericksburg, Virginia, 22401

Jamestown (APVA)
State 30 near Williamsburg
Jamestown, Va. 23081

Mount Vernon
Mt. Vernon, Virginia, 22121

Wachovia Museum, Old Salem, Inc.
Old Salem, Virginia, 24153

Birthplace of Woodrow Wilson
Coulter & Frederic Sts.,
Staunton, Virginia, 24401

Strasburg Museum
Off Inter-81, King St.,
Strasburg, Virginia, 22657

Stratford Hall Plantation
County 214
Stratford, Virginia, 22558

The Rolfe-Warren House
State 31,
north of Surry, Virginia, 23883

Smith Fort Plantation
Rt   31
Surry County, Virginia, 23883
(under APVA. See Scotchtown)

Colonial Williamsburg
U.S. 60
Williamsburg, Va. 23185

WASHINGTON

Pioneer Village & Willis Carey Historical Museum
Cashmere, Washington, 98815

Lincoln County Historical Museum
Park & 7th Sts.,
Davenport, Washington, 99122

Cowlitz County Museum
Courthouse Annex,
Kelso, Washington, 98626

Museum of History & Industry
2161 E. Hamlin St., McGurdy Park,
Seattle, Washington, 98112

Historical Museum
Tieton Dr. at S. 21st St.,
Yakima, Washington, 98902

WEST VIRGINIA

Fayette County Historical Society
Ansted, West Virginia, 25812

West Virginia State Government Archives . . . Museum
400 E. State Capitol
Charleston, West Virginia, 25305

Harpers Ferry National Historical Park
Shenandoah St.
Harpers Ferry, West Virginia 25425

Jackson's Mill Museum
Weston, West Virginina, 26452

WISCONSIN

Old Wade House
Center St.,
Greenbush, Wisconsin, 53026

Tallman Restorations
440 N. Jackson St.,
Janesville, Wisconsin, 53545

Tallman House; Stone House; Milton House Museum
State 59 & 26,
Milton, Wisconsin, 53563

The Bartlett Museum,
2149 Lawrence St.,
Beloit, Wisconsin, 53511

Museum of State Historical Society of Wisconsin
816 State St.,
Madison, Wisconsin, 53706

Pendarvis
114 Shake Rag St., US 151
Mineral Point, Wisconsin, 53565

Little Norway
US 151 & County Rd. JG,
west of Mt. Horeb, Wisconsin, 53572

Villa Louis
Villa Louis Rd.,
Prairie du Chien, Wisconsin, 53821

Barron County Historical Society Museum
Old Hwy 8
Barron, Wisconsin, 54812

Langlade County Historical Society Museum
404 Superior Street
Antigo, Wisconsin, 54409

WYOMING

Fort Bridger
Inter-80
Bridger, Wyoming, 82933
(Betw. Evanston & Cheyenne)

Fort Laramie National Historic Site
Fort Laramie, Wyoming, 82212

CANADA

Heritage Park
off Hwy. 2 to Glenmore Reservoir
Calgary, Alberta

Homestead Antiquities Museum
Dinosaur Trail,
Drumheller, Alberta

St. Albert Museum
Hwy 2,
(Near Edmonton)
St. Albert, Alberta

Reynolds Museum
Wetaskiwin, Alberta

King's County Museum
Centennial Bldg.,
Hampton, New Brunswick

Ross Farm Museum
Hwy 12,
north of Chester, Nova Scotia

Gananoque Museum
10 King St., W.,
Ganonoque, Ontario

Historic Fort York
Garrison Rd. & Fleet St.,
Toronto, Ontario

National Heritage Ltd.,
322 King St. W.,
Toronto, Ontario

   *(rip) Fort William

Muskoka Pioneer Village
Huntsville, Ontario

Fanshawe Pioneer Village
Hwy 22 & Fanshawe Rd.,
London, Ontario

Canadian Cabin Museum
Hwy 401 E. & Courtice Rd.,
Oshawa, Ontario

Note: Every effort has been made to make this listing as complete as possible — within reasonable bounds. Most of the entries have period kitchens or collections of utensils and kitchen tools. Others have displays and demonstrations related to such general subjects covered in this book as iron, tin or pottery.

Most are permanent displays; however, a few store most of their collection out of sight because of limited space.

The periods covered are from the middle-17th century to the early-20th. The kitchens and utensils seen will be as they might have been in log cabins, lean-tos, adobes, plantations, frame houses, shacks, brick and stone houses, and sod houses.

The list was compiled over a period of many months — using advice and information from museums, historical socities, and helpful individuals. Several letters were sent to each state. Any state not represented here, and there are only a few, did not respond to the letters. This doesn't mean that collections are not on view somewhere in the state.

If you plan to visit, write first for information on hours, seasons, rates, tours, and publications. Some are not open year round and a very few have not completed their restorations.

BIBLIOGRAPHY

"Knowledge is of two kinds: we know a subject ourselves, or we know where we can find information upon it."

Life of Johnson James Boswell, 1740-1795

Abell, Mrs. L. G. *The Skillful Housewive's Book*. New York: 1846.

———. *Abridgements of Specifications Relating to Cooking, Bread-Making, and the Preparation of Confectionery, A.D. 1634-1866*. London: Office of the Commissioner of Patents, 1873.

Acton, Eliza. *Modern Cookery. in All Its Branches*. London: 1845.

Alcott, William Alexander. *The Young House-Keeper, or Thoughts on Food and Cookery*. Boston: G. W. Light, 1838, 1842.

American Artisan and Patent Record. New York: American Artisan, 1864-1875. Volumes 1-17 weekly; volumes 18, 19 monthly.

Americana. New York: American Heritage Publishing Co., Bimonthly.

(The) American Heritage Cookbook and Illustrated History of American Eating and Drinking. New York: American Heritage Publishing Co., 1964. Incomparable illustrations, tasty recipes and invaluable biographies.

Andrews, Edward Deming. *The Community Industries of the Shakers*. New York: New York State Museum, 1932. Handbook No. 15.

Antiques. New York: Straight Enterprises, Monthly. This valuable magazine has long published (1922-date), and undoubtedly will continue to publish excellent articles on the early homes of America. Consult their advertising page "Historic Houses, Landmarks, and Museums."

Antiques Journal. Dubuque, Iowa: Babka Publishing Co., Monthly.

Antique Trader. Dubuque, Iowa: Babka Publishing Co., Weekly.

Appleton's Home Books. 3 volumes, New York: Appleton, 1881-1884.

Atwater, Helen. *Selection of Household Equipment*. Washington, D.C.: United States Government Printing Office, 1915.

Babcock, Emma Whitcomb. *Household Hints*. Volume II, Appleton's Home Books. New York: Appleton, 1881.

Beecher, Catherine E. *A Treatise on Domestic Economy for Young Ladies*. New York: Harper & Bros., 1845. Revised edition, 1855.

———, and Harriet Beecher Stowe. *American Woman's Home, or Principles of Domestic Science, Being a Guide to the Formation and Maintenance of Economical, Healthful, Beautiful and Christian Homes*. New York: J. B. Ford & Co., 1869.

Beeton, Mrs. S. C. (Isabella M.). *Beeton's Every-day Cookery and Housekeeping Book*. New York: D. Appleton & Co., 1872. Recently reprinted in facsimile.

———. *Book of Household Management*. London: Ward, Lock & Tyler, 1868.

Beitz, Les. *Treasury of Frontier Relics*. New York: Edwin House, 1966.

Bishop, John Leander. *A History of American Manufacturers from 1608-1860*. Philadelphia: E. Young & Co., 1861.

Breazeale, James F. *Economy in the Kitchen*. New York: Frye Publishing Co., 1918.

Bullock, Helen. *A National Treasury of Cookery. Recipes of: Ante Bellum America; Early America; Victorian America; The Young Republic; The Westward Empire*. 5 volumes. New York: Heirloom Publishing Company, 1967.

Burgess, F. W. *Chats on Household Curios*. New York: F. A. Stokes Co., 1914.

———. *Chats on Old Copper & Brass*. New York: F. A. Stokes Co., 1914.

Butler Brothers Christmas Catalogue. New York & Chicago: Butler Brothers, ca. 1900.

Calder, Ritchie. *The Evolution of the Machine*. New York: American Heritage Publishing Co., and The Smithsonian Institution, 1968.

Carson, Jane. *Colonial Virginia Cookery*. Williamsburg, Virginia: Williamsburg Research Studies, Colonial Williamsburg, 1968. One of the few books to present colonial recipes in their original form, with information on early kitchens and cooking methods. Carson's introductory material on cookbooks is fascinating.

Chase, Stuart. *Men and Machines*. New York: The Macmillan Co., 1929.

Child, Lydia Maria. *The Frugal Housewife. Dedicated to Those Who are Not Ashamed of Economy*. London: T. F. & J. Tegg, 1832.

———. *The American Frugal Housewife*. Boston: Carter, Hendee & Co., 1835. "A fat kitchen maketh a lean will." Franklin.

Christensen, E. O. *The Index of American Design*. New York: The Macmillan Co., 1950.

(The) Chronicle Ambridge, Pennsylvania: Early American Industries Association, 1933-date, Quarterly. This very small, but always interesting publication is available to members of the Association. The stated purpose of the E.A.I.A. is "to encourage the study and better understanding of early American industries in the home, in the shop, on the farm and on the sea; also, to discover, identify, classify, preserve and exhibit obsolete tools, implements, and mechanical devices, which were used in early America."

Coffin, Margaret. *The History and Folklore of American Country Tinware, 1700-1900*. Camden, New Jersey: Thomas Nelson & Sons, 1968.

Collector's Weekly. Kermit, Texas: Collector's Media, Inc.

Cooley, Anna Maria and Wilhelmina H. Spohr. *Household Arts for Home and School*. 2 volumes. New York: The Macmillan Co., 1920.

Cornelius, Mrs. (Mary Hooker). *The Young Housekeeper's Friend*. Boston: Charles Tappan, 1846; Thompson, Bigelow and Brown, 1859.

Cutbush, James. *The American Artists Manual, or Dictionary of Practical Knowledge in the Application of Philosophy to the Arts and Manufacturers. Selected from the Most Complete European Systems, with Original Improvements and Appropriate Engravings. Adapted to the Use of Manufacturers of the United States*. 2 volumes. Philadelphia: Johnson & Warner, and R. Fisher, W. Brown, 1814.

D'Allemagne, Henry Rene. *Decorative Antique Ironwork, A Pictorial Treasury*. Paris: 1924. Reprint. New York: Dover Publications, Inc., 1968.

Devoe, Shirley Spaulding. *The Tinsmiths of Connecticut*. Middletown, Connecticut: Connecticut Historical Society, Wesleyan University, 1968.

Dossie, Robert. *The Handmaid of the Arts*. London: Printed for J. Nourse, 1764.

Dover Stamping Company 1869. Facsimile. Princeton, New Jersey: American Historical Catalog Collection, The Pyne Press, 1971.

Dow, George Francis. *The Arts and Crafts in New England 1704-1775, Gleanings from Boston Newspapers*. Topsfield, Massachusetts: Wayside Press, 1927.

——. *Domestic Life in New England in the 17th Century – A Discourse Delivered in the Metropolitan Museum of New York to Open the American Wing*. Topsfield, Massachusetts: Perkins Press, 1925.

Dwight, Timothy. Travels in New England and New York — 1796-1815. 4 volumes. London: W. Baynes & Son, 1823. Dwight was President of Yale College.

Earle, Alice Morse. *Home Life in Colonial Days*. New York: The Macmillan Co., 1899.

Eaton, Allen Hendershott. *Handicrafts of New England*. New York: Harper, 1949.

——. *Handicrafts of the Southern Highlands*. New York: Russell Sage Foundation, 1937.

Enterprise Mfg. Co. of Pa. Patented Hardware Manufacturers and Iron Founders. Catalog. Philadelphia: Enterprise Manufacturing Co., 1881.

Fairbairn, Sir William. *Iron; Its History, Properties and Process of Manufacture*. Edinburgh: A. & C. Black, 1865.

Flower, Philip William. *History of the Trade in Tin*. London: G. Bell & Sons, 1880.
> Lively historical account not equalled anywhere.

Fuller, Edmund. *Tinkers and Geniuses, The Story of the Yankee Inventors*. New York: Hastings House, 1955.

George, Henry. *Progress and Poverty*. New York: D. Appleton, 1880.
> Especially Book IV, Chapter 2, on the development of a typical early settlement.

Giedion, Siegfried. *Mechanization Takes Command, A Contribution to Anonymous History*. New York: Oxford University Press. 1948.
> A nimble-witted serious investigation of how human lives have been and are affected by mechanization. One section is entitled *Mechanization Encounters the Household*. Very readable and extremely well-illustrated.

Glasse, Mrs. Hannah. *The Art of Cookery Made Plain and Easy*. London: 1747. Alexandria, Virginia: 1805, 1812.

Gobright, John Christopher. *The New York Sketchbook and Merchants Guide, A Directory*. New York: J. C. Gobright, 1859.

Goodholme, Todd S. *Domestic Cyclopedia of Practical Information*. New York: Henry Holt & Co., 1877.

(The) Good Housekeeping Discovery Book No. 1, Compiled from the Pages of Good Housekeeping Magazine. New York: Good Housekeeping, 1905.

Gould, Mary Earle. *Antique Tin and Tole Ware: Its History and Romance*. Rutland, Vermont: Charles E. Tuttle Co., 1958.

——. *The Early American House*. Rutland, Vermont: Charles E. Tuttle Co., 1965.

——. *Early American Wooden Ware*. Rutland, Vermont: Charles E. Tuttle Co., 1962.

Hamilton, Alexander. *Report of the Secretary of the Treasury of the United States on the Subject of Manufacturers, Presented to the House of Representatives*. Washington, D.C.: December 5, 1791.

Hankenson, Dick. *Trivets*. Maple Plain, Minnesota: 1963.

Harland, Marion [*pseud.*] Mary Virginia Hawes Terhune. *House and Home, A Complete Housewife's Guide*. Philadelphia: The Franklin News Co., 1889.

Harrison, Molly. *The Kitchen in History*. New York: Charles Scribner's Sons, 1972.

Haywood, Eliza F. *A Present for a Servant-Maid. Necessary Cautions and Precepts to Servant-Maids for Gaining Good-will and Esteem*. Dublin: G. Faulkner, 1755, 1771.

Hazen, Edward. *The Panorama of Professions and Trades, or Every Man's Book*. Philadelphia: Hunt, 1836.

Herman, Judith, and Marguerite Shallett Herman. *The Cornucopia*. New York: Harper & Row, 1973.
> A salmagundy of recipes, folklore, and tidbits.

Hobbies. Chicago: Lightner Publishing Corp., Monthly.

Hodgson, A. (Mrs. Willoughby Hodgson). *The Quest of the Antique*. London: H. Jenkins, Ltd., 1924.

Holloway, Laura C. *The Hearthstone, or, Life at Home, a Household Manual*. 1883.

Holme, Randle. *The Academy of Armory*. London: Printed for the Roxburghe Club, 1905. First published in 1688.

(The) Home Cook Book, Tried and True Recipes Compiled from Recipes Contributed by Ladies of Toledo and Other Cities; Published for the Joint Benefit of the Home for Friendless Women and the Orphan's Home. Toledo, Ohio: T. J. Brown, Eager & Co., 1876.

House and Garden. New York: Conde Nast Publications, 1901-1921, Monthly.
> Book Reviews of *The Furniture of Our Forefathers* by Esther Singleton & Russel Sturgis, New York: 1900. September 1901. "The Earliest Decorative Pottery of the White Settlers in America," by Edwin Atlee Barber. June 1902. "The Use of Electricity in the House," by C. D. Wood. January 1907. "The Knife-Life of the Kitchen," March 1921. "Brushing Up on Brushes," by Ethel Peyser. April 1921. "Early American Household Pottery," by M. Holden. April 1921.

The Housewife. New York: A. D. Porter Co., 1899-1904, Periodical.

Hutchinson, Elsie Lillian. *The Housefurnishings Department – Department Store Merchandise Manual*. New York University, The Ronald Press Co., 1918, 1922.

Jenkins, J. Geraint. *Traditional Country Craftsmen*. London: Routledge & Kegan Paul, 1965. British crafts but excellent.

Kane, Joseph Nathan. *Famous First Facts*. New York: H. W. Wilson, 1950.
> An abridged paperback version is in print, published by Pocket Book Editions, a division of Simon & Schuster.

(Edward) Katzinger Company Price List 53: Katzinger Tinware and Ovenex, A & J Kitchen Tools & Bath Fixtures, Geneva Forge Cutlery. Chicago: Edward Katzinger Co., 1940.

Kauffman, Henry J. *American Copper and Brass*. New York: Thomas Nelson & Sons, 1968.

——. *Early American Copper, Tin, and Brass*. New York: Medill McBride, 1950.

——. *Early American Ironware, Cast and Wrought*. Rutland, Vermont: Charles E. Tuttle Co., 1966.

Keller, A. G. *A Theatre of Machines*, New York: The Macmillan Co., 1965.

Kellogg, Ella Ervilla Eaton. *Science in the Kitchen*. Battle Creek, Michigan: Good Health Publishing Co., 1910. First published in 1893.

Kitchen Ware. New York: National Retail Dry Goods Association, ca. 1922.

Knight, Edward H. *American Mechanical Dictionary*. 2 vol. New York: J. B. Ford & Co., 1874. New York: Hurd & Houghton, and Cambridge: The Riverside Press, 1876.

——. *The Practical Dictionary of Mechanics 1874-1877*. Supplement. Boston: Houghton, Mifflin & Co., 1884.

Ladies Delight Cook Book, No. 1. Boston: A. P. Ordway & Co., Proprietors of Sulphur Bitters, 1886.

Ladies Home Journal. Philadelphia: Curtis Publishing Co., 1887-1920, Monthly.

Lalance & Grosjean Manufacturing Co. Catalog. New York: Lelance & Grosjean, February 15, 1890.

Lantz, Louise K. *Old American Kitchenware, 1725-1925*. Camden, New Jersey and Hanover, Pensylvania: Nelson and Everybody's Press. 1970.

——. *Price Guide to Old Kitchenware*. Hydes, Maryland: Louise K. Lantz, 1965.

Lea, Elizabeth E. *Domestic Cookery, Useful Receipts, and Hints to Young Housekeepers*. Baltimore: Cushings and Bailey, 1859. This was the 10th edition. The first was in 1851.

Leslie, Miss Eliza. *The Housebook; or, a Manual of Domestic Economy*. Philadelphia: Carey & Hart, 1840.

Lifshey, Earl. *The Housewares Story*. Chicago: National Housewares Manufacturers Association, 1973.

> This is a copiously illustrated, information-packed book by an expert of many years. It proves that the *Housewares Magazine* (formerly *House Furnishing Review*) which dates back to 1894 and is published by Harcourt Brace Jovanovich, has an enviable record for printing interesting information.

Lindsay, Seymour. *Iron and Brass Implements of the English House*. London and Boston: The Medici Society, 1927. New edition, *Iron and Brass Implements of the Eng. and American House*. Bass River, Massachusetts: C. Jacobs, 1964.

> This book, illustrated with skillful drawings, is considered a bible by serious collectors of old iron.

List of Patents for Inventions and Designs Issued by U.S. from 1790-1847. Washington, D.C.: Gideon, 1847.

Lord, Priscilla Sawyer, and Daniel J. Foley. *The Folk Arts and Crafts of New England*. New York: Chilton Book Co., 1965.

L. H. Mace & Co. 1883. Facsimile. Princeton, New Jersey: The American Historical Catalog Collection, Pyne Press, 1971.

Made of Iron. Exhibition catalog. Houston, Texas: University of St. Thomas Art Department, 1966.

> This 288-page catalog, beautifully designed and illustrated, contains two valuable essays: the *Introduction* by Stephen Grancsay, Curator Emeritus, Arms and Armor, The Metropolitan Museum of Art, New York; and *On the Nature of Iron* by Cyril Stanley Smith, Institute Professor, Massachusetts Institute of Technology, Cambridge. Smith's chapter contains *A Technical View of Iron Art* and a bibliography.

Marot, Helen. *The Creative Impulse In Industry*. New York: E. P. Dutton & Co., 1918.

Mason, Charlotte. *The Ladies' Assistant for Regulating and Supplying the Table*. London: Printed for J. Walter, 1787.

Masters, Thomas. *A Short Treatise Concerning Some Patent Inventions for the Production of Ice, Artificial Cold etc., Also the Newly Improved Culinary Utensils*. London: 1850.

Materials for the Household, Circular No. 70. Washington, D.C.: U.S. Government Printing Office, 1917.

Matthau-Ingram Co. Illustrated Catalogue of Sheet Metal Goods. Baltimore, Maryland: ca. 1890.

Matthews, Mary Lou. *American Kitchen Collectibles, Identification and Price Guide*. Gas City, Indiana: L-W Promotions, 1973. Some good catalog reprint pictures, negligible text.

Mercer, Henry C. *The Bible in Iron*. Doylestown, Pennsylvania: Bucks County Historical Society, 1914.

> The title page for the third edition, 1961, reads: *The Bible In Iron; Pictured Stoves and Stoveplates of the Pennsylvania Germans. Notes on Colonial Firebacks in the U.S., the Tenplate Stove, Franklin's Fireplace and the Tile Stoves of the Moravians in Pennsylvania and North Carolina, Together With a List of Colonial Furnaces in the U.S. and Canada by Dr. Henry C. Mercer. Revised, Corrected and Enlarged by Horace M. Mann. With Further Amendments and Additions by Joseph E. Sandford, Editor of This Third Edition.* [The second edition was in 1941.] An extremely valuable and readable book.

Milham, Willis H. *Time & Timekeepers Including the History, Construction, Care and Accuracy of Clocks and Watches*. New York: The Macmillan Co., 1947.

> This book, first printed in 1923 and written by a professor of astronomy, is interesting in relation to the clockwork jacks — weight and spring-driven.

Minchinton, W. E. *The British Tinplate Industry, A History*. Oxford, England: Clarendon Press, 1957.

Montgomery Ward Catalogue, Chicago: Montgomery Ward Co., 1893, 1895, 1900.

> A facsimile of the 1895, No. 57, catalog has been printed by Dover Publications, New York.

Morley, Christopher. *The Haunted Bookshop*. Garden City, New York: Doubleday, Page & Co., Inc., 1923. First published by Doubleday in 1918. J. B. Lippincott Company, New York, now has it in print.

Morse, Sidney. *Household Discoveries: An Encyclopedia of Practical Recipes and Processes*. Petersburg, New York: The Success Co., ca. 1909.

Mumford, Lewis. *The Myth of the Machine, Technics and Human Development*. New York: Harcourt Brace Jovanovich, Inc., 1966.

> Another book, by a prolific and always thoughtful and developing writer and thinker, which is a philosophical excavation of the ever-more acceptable belief that mechanical progress can mean social regress. This book should not be the only Mumford book you read.

——. *Technics and Civilization*. New York: Harcourt, Brace & Co., 1934.

——. *The Transformations of Man*. New York: Author, 1956.

Mundey, Alfred Holley. *Tin and the Tin Industry*. London: Sir I. Pitman & Sons, Ltd., 1926.

Nevins, Allan. *The Emergence of Modern America*. New York: The Macmillan Co., 1927.

New York Times. Newspaper. New York: 1890-1910, Daily.

Nutting, Wallace. *Furniture Treasury (Mostly of American Origin); All Periods of American Furniture With Some Foreign Examples in America; Also American Hardware and Household Utensils*. New York: The Macmillan Co., 1928. Fifth Printing, 1965, is two volumes in one.

> A "humbly presented" huge book showing 5000 examples of furniture and utensils.

Nystrom, Paul H. *Bibliography of Retailing*. New York: Columbia University Press, 1928.

Objects for Preparing Food. Exhibition catalog, Washington, D.C. and New York: The Renwick Gallery of the National Collection of Fine Arts, Smithsonian Institution, and the Museum of Contemporary Crafts of the American Crafts Council, 1972.

> This well-researched, typological exhibition was held in New York from September 1972 to January 1973, and from February 1973 to April 1973 in Washington.

Oxford English Dictionary. The Compact Edition in 2 volumes. New York: Oxford University Press, 1971.

> This amazing, pre-computer achievement, published in parts between 1888 and 1928, was first conceived by the Philological Society in England in 1858. It is an unimaginably rich source of information on every subject, including kitchen utensils and cookery.

Parloa, Miss Maria. *Kitchen Companion. A Guide For All Who Would be Good Housekeepers*. Boston: Estes and Lauriat, 1887.

> Miss Parloa was the founder of the Original Cooking School in Boston.

Pearse, John Barnard. *A Concise History of the Iron Manufacture of the American Colonists up to the Revolution*. Philadelphia: Allen, Lane & Scott, 1976.

Peet, Louise Jenison, and Lenore E. Sater. *Household Equipment*. New York: John Wiley & Sons, Inc., 1934, 1940.

Pegge, Samuel, Editor. *The Forme of Cury, A Roll of Ancient English Cookery; Compiled, about A.D. 1390, by the Master-Cooks of King Richard II*. London: J. Nichols, 1780.

Peyser, Ethel R. *Cheating the Junk-Pile*. New York: Dutton, 1922.

Phipps, Frances. *Colonial Kitchens, Their Furnishings, and Their Gardens*. New York: Hawthorne Books, Inc., 1972.

> A well-written, clear, and honest book. Imperative to read if you are furnishing or restoring an old kitchen, and want it to be authentic.

C. B. Porter Co. Catalogue Illustrating and Describing Paint Enameled Tinware, Nursery Refrigeration, Water Coolers, Extra Heavy Paint Enameled Tinware, Plain Pieced Tinware, Etc. Philadelphia: C. B. Porter Co., ca. 1920.

Powers, Beatrice F., and Olive Floyd. *Early American Decorated Tinware*. New York: Hastings House, 1957.

Practical Housekeeping. A Careful Compilation of Tried and Approved Recipes. Minneapolis, Minnesota: Buckeye Publishing Co., 1884. First published in 1881 as *Buckeye Cookery*.

Prime, Alfred Coxe. *The Arts and Crafts in Philadelphia, Maryland, and South Carolina, 1720-1785*. Topsfield, Massachusetts: Walpole Society, 1929.

——. *. . . 1786-1800*. Topsfield, Massachusetts: Walpole Society, 1932.

Randolph, Mary. *The Virginia Housewife: or, Methodical Cook*. Baltimore, Maryland: Plaskitt & Cugle, 1831. Philadelphia: 1855.

Rawson, Marion Nicholl. *Country Auction*. New York: E. P Dutton & Co., 1929.

——. *Handwrought Ancestors*. New York: E. P. Dutton & Co., 1936.

Robacker, Earl F. *Pennsylvania Dutch Stuff, A Guide to Country Antiques*. New York: A. S. Barnes & Co., 1944.

Roe, James Wickham. *Connecticut Inventors*. Pamphlet, New Haven, Connecticut: Committee on Historical Publications, Yale University Press, 1934.

Romaine, Lawrence B. *Guide To American Trade Catalogs 1744-1900*. New York: R. R. Bowker Co., 1960.

Rorer, Mrs. Sarah Tyson. *Good Cooking*. Philadelphia: Curtis Publishing Co., Ladies Home Journal House Library, 1898.

Sandford, Joseph. see Henry Mercer.

Scientific American. The Advocate of Industry and Enterprise, and Journal of Mechanical and Other Improvements. New York: Scientific American Publishing Co., 1845-1859, Monthly.

Scientific Artisan, A Journal of Patents, Science, Art, Discovery, Inventions, Etc. Cincinnati: American Patent Co., November 1858-April 1860, Weekly.

Sears, Roebuck & Co., Catalog. Chicago: Sears, Roebuck & Co., 1902, 1920-1920.

> A facsimile edition of the 1902 catalog was printed by Crown Publishers, Inc., Bounty Books, in 1969. It is interesting, but incomplete and badly printed. The 1895 Montgomery Ward facsimile, published by Dover, is much better and contains nearly the same merchandise.

Shaker Handicrafts. Exhibition catalog. New York: Whitney Museum of American Art, 1935.

Silcock, Arnold, and Maxwell Ayrton. *Wrought-iron: Its Decorative Use*. New York: Charles Scribners, 1929.

Smith, Mrs. E[lizabeth]. *The Compleat Housewife: Or, Accomplished Gentlewoman's Companion Being a Collection of Upwards of 700 of the Most Approved Receipts in Cookery, Etc. . . . To which is added a Collection of Above 300 Receipts of Medicines, With Directions for Marketing*. Williamsburg, Virginia: 1742. London: 1773.

> The 1742 edition was the first American edition, but the book was published in England before then. The 1773 edition was the 18th. A facsimile edition, taken from copies in the British Museum of the 15th (1753) and the 18th editions was published in 1968 by Literary Services and Productions, Ltd., 26 Old Brompton Road, London, SW7. It contains an excellent glossary.

Sonn, Albert H. *Early American Wrought Iron; Volume 3, Andirons, Broilers, Trammels, Etc.* 3 volumes. New York: Charles Scribners, 1928.

> A good companion to Lindsay, and also with drawings by the author.

Spinning Wheel. Hanover, Pennsylvania: Everybodys Press, Monthly.

Splint, Sarah Field. *The Art of Cooking and Serving.* Cincinnati: Proctor and Gamble, 1929.

Sprackling, Helen. *Customs on the Table Top. How New England Housewives Set Out Their Tables.* Sturbridge, Massachusetts: Old Sturbridge Village, 1958, 1966.

Stark, Lewis M. *The Whitney Cookery Collection.* New York: New York Public Library, 1959. Bibliographical catalog.

Stoudt, John Joseph. *Early Pennsylvania Arts and Crafts.* New York: A. S. Barnes, 1964.

Strohm, Gertrude. *The Universal Cookery Book, Practical Recipes for Household Use. Selected from the Most Eminent Authorities Including Marion Harland, The Boston Cook-Book, Miss Parloa, American Home Cook-Book, Mrs. Washington, Virginia Cookery-Book, Thomas J. Murrey, Presbyterian Cook-Book, Miss Corson, Every-Day Cook-Book, and Many Others, Together with Original Recipes.* New York: Frederick A. Stokes & Brother, 1888.

Swank, James Moore. *History of the Manufacture of Iron in All Ages, and Particularly in the United States for Three Hundred Years. From 1585-1885.* Philadelphia: Author, 1884.

Thompson, Sir Benjamin (Count Rumbord). *Complete Works.* 4 volumes. Boston: American Academy of Arts & Sciences, 1870-1875.

> An edited, collected works in four volumes has been printed by Belknap Press in Cambridge, Massachusetts, 1968-1970.

Toulouse, Julian Harrison. *Fruit Jars, A Collector's Manual.* Camden, New Jersey, and Hanover, Pennsylvania: Everybodys-Nelson Press, 1969.

Treasure House of Useful Knowledge, An Encyclopedia of Valuable Receipts in the Principal Arts of Life, ... Compiled and Edited by Henry B. Scammel. St. Louis, Missouri (?): Buckland Publishing Co., 1885, 1891.

> "— a maximum of book with a minimum of preface...." This book has truly been a treasure house to me in my trips back to the 19th century. Mr. Scammel, in the compilation of over 1,600 pages, drew on many authorities and sources, as he said, "Whose name is legion." He admits to giving no credits, but rather to using all the space for cold facts: a list, if given, would have been headed by *"The Scientific American,* Spon's reference works, Cassell's publications," and others.

Ure, Andrew. *A Dictionary of Arts, Manufacturers and Mines.* England (?): 1839.

U.S. Patent Office, *Official Gazette.* Washington, D.C.: U.S. Government Printing Office, 1873-1930, Weekly.

> The *Gazette* was and is published weekly, and is usually bound monthly. It contains indexes of inventions and inventors; pictures and short patent descriptions, in chronological order, of each patent; and notices concerning changes in classification and legal matters. Thoroughly enjoyable for all, including serendipitous, journeys into the past.

Vosburgh, H. K. *Tinsmith's Helper and Pattern Book.* Unionville, Connecticut: Union Printing Co., 1879.

(F. A.) Walker & Co. Illustrated Catalogue of Useful and Ornamental Goods Suitable for the Parlor, Dining-Room, Kitchen and Laundry. Boston. F. A. Walker & Co., ca. 1870-1875.

Wallance, Don. *Shaping America's Products.* New York: Reinhold Publishing Corp., 1956.

(The) Washburn Company Illustrated Price List No. The Androck Line. Massachusetts and Illinois: The Washburn Co., 1936.

Willich, Anthony Florian Madinzer. *The Domestic Encyclopedia, Or a Dictionary of Facts and Useful Knowledge, Comprehending a Concise View of the Latest Discoveries, Inventions, and Improvements Chiefly Applicable to Rural and Domestic Economy.* 5 volumes. Philadelphia: W. Y Birch and A. Small, 1803-04. 3 volumes, with additions by Dr. Thomas Cooper. Philadelphia: A. Small, 1821.

> The 1803-04 edition was the first American edition. This book with Knight's *Mechanical Dictionary* and Scammel's *Treasure House,* form a down-home triumvirate which might have made a Renaissance man out of any late-19th century man or woman.

Wills, Geoffrey. *Collecting Copper and Brass.* New York: Bell Publishing Co., 1962.

Wilson, Mrs. W. H. *Mrs. Wilson's Cook Book.* Nashville: 1914.

Woman's Home Companion. New York and Springfield, Ohio: Crowell & Collier Co., 1897-1902, Monthly. Formerly *Ladies' Home Companion.*

Wright, Richardson. *Hawkers & Walkers in Early America, Strolling Peddlers, Preachers, Lawyers, Doctors, Players and Others, From the Beginning to the Civil War.* Philadelphia: J. B. Lippincott, 1927.

——. *Wrinkles & Recipes, Compiled from Scientific American* New York: Scientific American Publishing Co., 1875.

or

Wrinkles & Recipes, Compiled from Scientific American New York: Scientific American Publishing Co., 1875.

INDEX

The letter-by-letter alphabetical mode used in this index, and in the main body of the encyclopedia, is based on running all the letters together regardless of how many words are involved. For example, all entries beginning with potato come after pot but before pot chain, pot cleaner, etc.

Recipes are included in the body of the index itself, as well as being listed separately. In the index they are prefaced with an asterisk*.